The Graph Music of Morton :

Morton Feldman is widely regarded as one of America's greatest composers. His music is famously idiosyncratic, but, in many cases, the way he presented it is also unusual: in the 1950s and 1960s, he often composed in non-standard musical notations, including a groundbreaking variety on graph paper that facilitated deliberately imprecise specifications of pitch and, at times, other musical parameters. Feldman used this notation, intermittently, over seventeen years, producing numerous graph works that invite analysis as an evolving series. Taking this approach, David Cline marshals a wide range of source materials – many previously unpublished – in clarifying the ideology, organisation and generative history of these graphs and their formative role in the chronicle of post-war music. This assists in pinpointing connections with Feldman's compositions in other formats, with works by other composers, notably John Cage, and with contemporary currents in painting. Performance practice is examined through analysis of Feldman's non-notated preferences and David Tudor's celebrated interpretations.

DAVID CLINE completed his PhD in Music at Goldsmiths, University of London, in 2011 and was a fellow of the Institute of Musical Research at the School of Advanced Study, University of London in 2013–15. His research has appeared in *Perspectives of New Music* and *Twentieth-Century Music*.

Music Since 1900

GENERAL EDITOR Arnold Whittall

This series – formerly *Music in the Twentieth Century* – offers a wide perspective on music and musical life since the end of the nineteenth century. Books included range from historical and biographical studies, concentrating particularly on the context and circumstances in which composers were writing, to analytical and critical studies concerned with the nature of musical language and questions of compositional process. The importance given to context will also be reflected in studies dealing with, for example, the patronage, publishing, and promotion of new music, and in accounts of the musical life of particular countries.

Titles in the series

The Graph Music of Morton Feldman

David Cline

CAMBRIDGE
UNIVERSITY PRESS

CAMBRIDGE
UNIVERSITY PRESS

University Printing House, Cambridge CB2 8BS, United Kingdom

One Liberty Plaza, 20th Floor, New York, NY 10006, USA

477 Williamstown Road, Port Melbourne, VIC 3207, Australia

314-321, 3rd Floor, Plot 3, Splendor Forum, Jasola District Centre, New Delhi - 110025, India

79 Anson Road, #06-04/06, Singapore 079906

Cambridge University Press is part of the University of Cambridge.

It furthers the University's mission by disseminating knowledge in the pursuit of education, learning and research at the highest international levels of excellence.

www.cambridge.org
Information on this title: www.cambridge.org/9781107521414

First published 2016
First paperback edition 2018

A catalogue record for this publication is available from the British Library

ISBN 978-1-107-10923-0 Hardback
ISBN 978-1-107-52141-4 Paperback

For Helen, Ben, Hannah and Grace

You left us and you wrote this piece on graph, giving us this freedom of playing in those three ranges – high, middle, and low – and then we went in and played the piece, and it was then that the musical world changed.

John Cage in conversation with Morton Feldman, 9 July 1966

Contents

Figures

Acknowledgements

I would like to thank those who helped in compiling the source materials that underpin this analysis, especially Amy Beal, John Bewley, Jason Cady, Gene Caprioglio, Jeanette Casey, Ryan Dohoney, D. J. Hoek, John Holzaepfel, Patricia Lent, Felix Meyer, Raoul Mörchen, Keith Potter, David Vaughan and Chris Villars. I would also like to thank Robert Morris, for sharing unpublished research with me, and Frank Denyer, Jorge Mester, John Tilbury, Jan Williams, Christian Wolff and the late Gerd Zacher, for sharing their memories of Feldman and his music. I owe a special debt of gratitude to Keith Potter, not only for the reason given above, but also for his advice and encouragement during my doctoral research at Goldsmiths, University of London, which formed the basis of what follows. I am also grateful to Arnold Whittall, Vicki Cooper, Fleur Jones and Sarah Starkey, who provided helpful advice on preparing this version of the text for publication by Cambridge University Press.

The Paul Sacher Foundation has proved an invaluable resource. Additionally, I am very grateful to the Foundation for the award of a research grant, which facilitated the longest of my several trips to Basel, and for its hospitality during all my visits. My thanks also go to the Institute for Musical Research at the School of Advanced Study, University of London for supporting my postdoctoral research on Feldman's graph music over several years.

I am very grateful to Barbara Monk Feldman for her permission to quote from Feldman's unpublished letters, interviews and writings, to Arthur Antheil McTighe and Judith Donoher for their permission to quote from unpublished letters of George Antheil and to the Paul Sacher Foundation, Northwestern University and the J. Paul Getty Trust for giving me permission to reproduce sketches and other materials from their collections. The photograph of Merce Cunningham's company with Robert Rauschenberg's costumes and backdrop for *Summerspace*, by Richard Rutledge, appears courtesy of the Merce Cunningham Trust. Copyright clearance for musical examples was obtained from the following sources:

Projection 1 © Copyright 1962 by C. F. Peters Corporation, New York. Reproduced by kind permission of Peters Edition Limited, London on behalf of C. F. Peters Corporation, New York.

Projection 2 © Copyright 1962 by C. F. Peters Corporation, New York. Reproduced by kind permission of Peters Edition Limited, London on behalf of C. F. Peters Corporation, New York.

Projection 3 © Copyright 1964 by C. F. Peters Corporation, New York. Reproduced by kind permission of Peters Edition Limited, London on behalf of C. F. Peters Corporation, New York.

Projection 4 © Copyright 1959 by C. F. Peters Corporation, New York. Reproduced by kind permission of Peters Edition Limited, London on behalf of C. F. Peters Corporation, New York.

Projection 5 © Copyright 1964 by C. F. Peters Corporation, New York. Reproduced by kind permission of Peters Edition Limited, London on behalf of C. F. Peters Corporation, New York.

Intersection 1 © Copyright 1962 by C. F. Peters Corporation, New York. Reproduced by kind permission of Peters Edition Limited, London on behalf of C. F. Peters Corporation, New York.

Marginal Intersection © Copyright 1962 by C. F. Peters Corporation, New York. Reproduced by kind permission of Peters Edition Limited, London on behalf of C. F. Peters Corporation, New York.

Intersection 2 © Copyright 1963 by C. F. Peters Corporation, New York. Reproduced by kind permission of Peters Edition Limited, London on behalf of C. F. Peters Corporation, New York.

Intersection 3 © Copyright 1962 by C. F. Peters Corporation, New York. Reproduced by kind permission of Peters Edition Limited, London on behalf of C. F. Peters Corporation, New York.

Intersection 4 © Copyright 1964 by C. F. Peters Corporation, New York. Reproduced by kind permission of Peters Edition Limited, London on behalf of C. F. Peters Corporation, New York.

Ixion © Copyright 1962 by C. F. Peters Corporation, New York. Reproduced by kind permission of Peters Edition Limited, London on behalf of C. F. Peters Corporation, New York.

Atlantis © Copyright 1962 by C. F. Peters Corporation, New York. Reproduced by kind permission of Peters Edition Limited, London on behalf of C. F. Peters Corporation, New York.

...Out of 'Last Pieces' © Copyright 1962 by C. F. Peters Corporation, New York. Reproduced by kind permission of Peters Edition Limited, London on behalf of C. F. Peters Corporation, New York.

The Straits of Magellan © Copyright 1962 by C. F. Peters Corporation, New York. Reproduced by kind permission of Peters Edition Limited, London on behalf of C. F. Peters Corporation, New York.

The King of Denmark © Copyright 1965 by C. F. Peters Corporation, New York. Reproduced by kind permission of Peters Edition Limited, London on behalf of C. F. Peters Corporation, New York.

In Search of an Orchestration © Copyright 1969 by Universal Edition (London) Ltd, London. Reproduced by kind permission of Universal Edition (London) Ltd.

Variations © Copyright 1999 by C. F. Peters Corporation, New York. Reproduced by kind permission of Peters Edition Limited, London on behalf of C. F. Peters Corporation, New York.

Earlier versions of parts of Chapters 4, 5 and 7 were published in 'Allover method and holism in Morton Feldman's graphs', *Perspectives of New Music*, vol.

51, no. 1 (Winter 2013), 56–98 © Copyright 2013 by *Perspectives of New Music*; and 'Straightening the record: Morton Feldman's return to graph music', *Twentieth-Century Music*, vol. 10, no. 1 (March 2013), 59–90 © Copyright 2013 by Cambridge University Press. Elements that have been reused are reprinted by kind permission of their publishers.

My wife Helen provided detailed feedback on several drafts and much other invaluable advice over many years. I would especially like to thank her and Ben, Hannah and Grace – who have grown up with this project – for supporting my efforts in so many ways.

Introduction

Morton Feldman's graphs merit attention because they altered the course of Western classical music, as John Cage observed in the epigraph to this volume. Early examples quickly gained notoriety in new music circles in the United States, becoming some of the very first musical works presented in a strikingly new notation to receive public attention. Moreover, they greatly affected Cage's own music, initially inspiring his recourse to chance operations and graph paper and subsequently encouraging his own experiments with indeterminacy and new notations. It is also likely that they affected the music of Earle Brown, who had already used similar ideas as tools in the compositional process without allowing them to take centre stage.[1] Cage and Brown would go on to become leading proponents of graphic notations and indeterminacy, the use of which would flourish in the United States and Europe in the late 1950s and throughout the 1960s.

There are other reasons for interest in these works within the narrower field of Feldman studies. In terms of sheer numbers, they represent approximately one-quarter of Feldman's published output from the 1950s and 1960s and one-eighth of his entire catalogue, meaning that an understanding of his music as a whole is impossible without recourse to them. Additionally, his tendency to switch between graph notation and other formats in the 1950s and 1960s is a singular aspect of his approach that invites scrutiny, as is the fact that the grids that underpin the presentation of his graphs eventually surfaced in modified form in his non-graph works.

Despite their historical pedigree, Feldman's graphs have been performed only infrequently and relatively few recordings have been issued.[2] First commercial releases of three, including *In Search of an Orchestration* (1967), which Feldman regarded as the culmination of this subset of his music, appeared as recently as 2005, and in four cases, there remains only one extant recording at this time.[3] Given that the graphs allow a

---

[1] According to Cage, Feldman's graph music 'opened the doors for both me, and for Christian Wolff, and later for Earle Brown' ('An interview with John Cage', by Anthony Brown, *Asterisk: A Journal of New Music*, vol. 1, no. 1 (December 1974), 29).

[2] *The King of Denmark* (1964) is an exception. For a discography, see www.cnvill.net/mfhome.htm.

[3] *Morton Feldman: Composing by Numbers – The Graphic Scores 1950–67*, Mode Records, mode 146, which was released in 2005, included the first recording of *Intersection 1* (1951) and the only

greater degree of legitimate variation between performances than more traditional works of Western classical music, the dearth of material to compare is disappointing.

A possible reason for the infrequency of performances is that these are relatively short works for instrumental combinations that are sometimes unusual, which may make them difficult to programme, unlike Feldman's late, long works, many of which can stand alone. Although there are five graphs for solo instruments, which should be easier to package in a concert setting, three of these are imposing works for virtuoso performers. In addition, Feldman's graphs occupy an awkward middle ground in the music of the second half of the twentieth century. On the one hand, being indeterminate, they require greater input from performers than more conventionally notated pieces, and this may lessen their appeal in some quarters. On the other hand, they are not nearly as permissive as many of the indeterminate works they helped inspire, and this may lessen their appeal to those attracted to indeterminacy. Feldman's own writings also reveal a more restrictive conception of how these works should be played than is evident from the scores, and these additional layers of control may have alienated otherwise-sympathetic performers.

To date, the graphs have generated surprisingly little musicological commentary. Even though Feldman composed his last graph almost fifty years ago, this monograph is the first comprehensive overview of the series and many individual graphs are discussed in detail for the first time in its pages. There can be no doubt that his use of indeterminate pitches and distaste for compositional systems are significant barriers to conventional methods of musical analysis. Additionally, some commentators may believe that Feldman regarded the graph series as a failed experiment and that this is the reason why he turned away from graph music in the late 1960s, but if so, they are mistaken. Others may take the view that Feldman's graphs are like the pieces with fixed pitches and indeterminate durations that dominated his output in the 1960s in being tangential to the overall thrust of his music, viewed in its entirety, and can therefore be safely ignored. True, it is difficult to see them as precursors of his long, late works, but this is a legitimate reason for ignoring them only if the long, late works represent the only truly significant music he composed. This monograph aims not only to fill the gap in the literature, but also to encourage a positive reappraisal of this currently under-appreciated series.

issued recordings of *Marginal Intersection* (1951) and *In Search of an Orchestration*. The only issued recordings of *Ixion* (1958) for chamber ensemble and *Atlantis* (1959) were released in 1997 (*Music for Merce*, BMG Music, 09026-68751-2) and 2000 (*Atlantis*, Hat Hut Records, hat [now]ART 116), respectively.

Scope

Feldman's use of the term 'graphs' in connection with these works reflects the fact that he composed them on printed graph paper.[4] It also reflects his mode of presentation, which is more graph-like than conventional staff notation,[5] with time notated proportionately along the horizontal axis in a manner comparable with the proportional specification of a variable on the abscissa of a line or scatter graph.[6] Feldman was not the first composer to use graphs, graph paper or proportional notation. For example, Joseph Schillinger taught a method of composing that utilised all three in the 1930s and early 1940s, but only as tools in the process of composing fully conventionally notated works; contrast Feldman's graphs, which were the finished products of his creative efforts and meant for use in performance.

It is more than the paper and treatment of time that connects Feldman's graphs with one another, making it natural to view them as a cohesive series, even though they were composed over a lengthy period between 1950 and 1967. To begin with, they are his most arresting scores, a consequence of their being presented in an original, and particularly distinctive, notation. Details vary, but all feature symbols set within a given or implicit grid of squares inherited from his graph paper. Another shared characteristic is that they are all indeterminate, in that they do not specify some musical parameters as precisely as fully conventionally notated works.[7] That said, they were not the first indeterminate works composed in the modern era, as has sometimes been claimed.[8] Precursors include *The Unanswered Question* (1908) of Charles Ives,

[4] Feldman highlighted his use of graph paper on several occasions. For a representative example, see 'Crippled symmetry' [1981], in B. H. Friedman (ed.), *Give My Regards to Eighth Street: Collected Writings of Morton Feldman* (Cambridge, MA: Exact Change, 2000), 147.

[5] Feldman alluded to the graph-like character of his presentation in Morton Feldman *et al.*, '4 musicians at work', *trans/formation*, vol. 1, no. 3 (1952), 168.

[6] Conventional notation is graph-like in its representation of pitch, but not in its treatment of time. Richard Rastall has claimed that it represents time 'graphically' because time is presented as 'moving from left to right horizontally' (*The Notation of Western Music: An Introduction* (London: Dent, 1983), 1). The weakness of this position is evident from the fact that the same could be said of written English.

[7] This monograph uses the term 'indeterminate' and its cognates only in this way unless otherwise indicated. It is true that the term 'indeterminacy' was not part of the vocabulary of classical music at the time that Feldman began composing graph music; its use was not established until Cage gave an influential course of lectures that highlighted the term at the Darmstadt International Summer Course for New Music in 1958. Nevertheless, as Cage was quick to point out ('Composition as process: II. Indeterminacy' [1961], in *Silence: Lectures and Writings*, 5th edn (London: Marion Boyars, 1999), 36), the concept of indeterminacy that he outlined is applicable to Feldman's graphs.

[8] Calvin Tomkins, *The Bride and the Bachelors: The Heretical Courtship in Modern Art* (New York: Viking Press, 1965), 108. On one occasion, Feldman went almost as far ('The avant-garde: progress or stalemate?', *New York Times*, 5 March 1967, D27). Philip Thomas made a closely related error in

which requires only a loose coordination between sections of the orchestra, *Random Round* (1914), a musical game designed by Percy Grainger in which individual performers enter at will and play from a choice of material, and a number of works composed by Henry Cowell. The latter include *Mosaic Quartet – String Quartet No. 3* (1935), the five movements of which may be played in any order, and his 'elastic' works for dance, composed in the late 1930s, which feature a range of adjustable elements. Even so, Feldman's earliest graphs do seem to have been the very first instrumental works in modern musical history in which pitches were specified imprecisely; given the central place traditionally accorded to pitch in Western classical music, this is their most radical feature.

Seventeen graphs, listed in Table I.1, have been published and these are the focus of the following discussion. All were published in Feldman's lifetime; consequently, it is safe to assume that they were works he was happy to publicise. Several unpublished graphs are also discussed. The decision to ring-fence examination of two of these within an appendix was driven by their use of *sui generis* notations, meaning that they require special treatment. Nonetheless, these atypical graphs are significant, not only because they are Feldman's most radical experiments in indeterminacy, but also because they were influential in shaping the course of the series and relaying its influence in Europe.

Aims and approach

The many connections between these works argue against discussing each of them individually in turn; doing so would involve considerable duplication or an uncomfortable amount of cross-referencing. In addition, some graphs invite more commentary than others; reviewing them individually would highlight this imbalance. The alternative course followed here is to view them en masse from several thematic perspectives. This avoids unnecessary repetition and facilitates giving them differing degrees of attention. The biggest challenge it creates is how to introduce a sizeable number of individual works, some of which may be unfamiliar. This is addressed through a preliminary chronological survey, distributed over two chapters, that highlights some of each graph's salient features. The first chapter addresses the *Projections* and *Intersections*, which are referred to collectively in this monograph as *early* graphs; the second addresses the *later* graphs – that is, all those that followed.

suggesting that the *Projections* were the first indeterminate works ('Determining the indeterminate', *Contemporary Music Review*, vol. 26, no. 2 (April 2007), 130).

Table I.1. *Feldman's published graph series, by completion date*

Graph	Instrumentation	Given completion date	Catalogue no.	Approx. duration[9]
Projection 1	Cello solo	1950	EP6945	2'50"
Projection 2	Flute, trumpet, violin, cello and piano	3 Jan 1951	EP6940	4'40"
Projection 3	Two pianos	5 Jan 1951	EP6961	1'30"
Projection 4	Violin and piano	16 Jan 1951	EP6913	4'40"
Projection 5	Three flutes, trumpet, three cellos and two pianos	1951	EP6962	2'10"
Intersection 1	Orchestra	Feb 1951	EP6907	12'30"
Marginal Intersection	Orchestra	7 Jul 1951	EP6909	5'50"
Intersection 2	Piano solo	Aug 1951	EP6922[10]	9'00"
Intersection 3	Piano solo	Apr 1953	EP6915[11]	2'20"
Intersection 4	Cello solo	22 Nov 1953	EP6960	3'00"
Ixion	Chamber ensemble	Aug 1958	EP6926	–
Atlantis	Chamber ensemble (two versions)	28 Sep 1959	EP6906	8'00"
Ixion	Two pianos	–	EP6926a	–
. . .Out of 'Last Pieces'	Orchestra	Mar 1961	EP6910	8'50"
The Straits of Magellan	Flute, horn, amplified guitar, harp, piano and double bass	Dec 1961	EP6919	4'50"
The King of Denmark	Percussion solo	Aug 1964	EP6963	5'10"
In Search of an Orchestration	Orchestra	–	UE15324	7'40"

[9] Based on indications of tempo in the published editions of the scores.
[10] Also included in EP67976.   [11] Also included in EP67976.

A main aim is to reconstruct Feldman's own ideas about these works. Understanding his perspective, which was highly idiosyncratic, helps to explain why certain graphs have the properties they do and why the series developed as it did. On a more practical level, it helps clarify a number of ambiguities in his presentation, attributable to his penchant for unduly brief explanations. It also facilitates a better appreciation of how Feldman conceived these works being performed. No doubt there are those who are uncomfortable placing too much weight on this particular aspect of a composer's thinking, believing instead that performers should be free to impose their own tastes provided that they replicate the essential properties of the given work. Even so, Feldman's views are surely of interest even to those attracted to such a position, not only because of the well-known difficulties involved in distinguishing between constitutive properties of musical works and the non-constitutive preferences of composers, but also because of their utility as benchmarks.

Feldman's own words – from published and unpublished sources – are therefore centre stage in what follows.[12] These often employ a highly personal language, involving parallels with painting, which can be difficult to interpret. Despite that, they merit scrutiny, because they often reveal more about his perspective and music than a cursory review might suggest. Like some of his sketch materials, they also raise interesting questions, which this monograph seeks to address, about the relationships that exist between Feldman's music on graph paper and his works presented in other notational formats.

Another aim is to assess the strengths and weaknesses of his ground-breaking graph notation. Feldman developed his own multifaceted rationale for its use while remaining sensitive to what he regarded as its chief weaknesses. As will become clear, his reservations were instrumental in driving changes to the notation that had a profound impact on the resulting music, and they also played a part in his eventual return to more conventional means of expression. The critical assessment of the notation developed in what follows diverges from Feldman's own in a number of places, and argues that his residual concerns could have been addressed.

Historical context is also a focus. For example, the graphs are located within Feldman's wider output from the 1950s and 1960s and relative to events in his professional and personal life that affected their development. Inevitably, this involves discussion of a remarkable period of intense

---

[12] Most of the published sources are to be found in the following texts: Walter Zimmermann (ed.), *Morton Feldman Essays* (Cologne: Beginner Press, 1985); Friedman (ed.), *Give My Regards*; Chris Villars (ed.), *Morton Feldman Says: Selected Interviews and Lectures 1964–1987* (London: Hyphen Press, 2006); and Raoul Mörchen (ed.), *Morton Feldman in Middelburg: Words on Music* (Cologne: MusikTexte, 2008).

mutual influence that operated between him and Cage during the early 1950s. It also highlights the equally remarkable influence exerted on him by contemporary currents in painting, which penetrated not only the way in which he spoke and wrote about his music, but also its ideological underpinnings and, indeed, its very essence. Feldman's close association with many leading painters of the time is well known, but the powerful impact of their art on his remains imperfectly understood. As will become clear, the works and working methods of Jackson Pollock and Robert Rauschenberg, in particular, deeply influenced the nature of his graph music. Sometimes, the discussion leans heavily on biographical data, but this is not a biography.[13] Such details are included either because they are useful in locating the graphs in context or because they are integral to appreciating an aspect of the series.

Feldman was notoriously coy on the subject of compositional method and generally preferred to portray himself as working intuitively, without premeditation or specifiable techniques, in a manner that he described as composing 'by ear'.[14] This volume aims to reveal more than Feldman may have been comfortable in disclosing. A detailed examination of his sketches and published graph scores points to his use of several compositional devices, including number strings, elastic form, collage, superimposition and, perhaps, proportional and rhythmic structures. It also suggests that his use of these devices was answerable to an over-arching holism that constrained global aspects of each graph. This is not to say that he composed systematically or even methodically; the techniques he employed affected only some elements of his graph music and many other aspects of it are not explicable in these terms. Others have tried to pinpoint elements of Feldman's compositional approach in these works. Rather than dealing with their views in the main text, I have opted instead to present my reservations in a second appendix.

The practice of performing the graphs is also addressed, not only through assessment of Feldman's non-notated preferences, but also via discussion of David Tudor's approach to playing this music. Tudor was a vitally important force in disseminating the burgeoning repercussions of Feldman's recourse to indeterminacy within the United States and internationally in the 1950s and 1960s, but analysis reveals facets of his

---

[13] For a summary biography, see Sebastian Claren, 'A Feldman chronology', in Villars (ed.), *Morton Feldman Says*, 255–75.

[14] 'Conversations with a young composer', unpublished typescript circa 1956, David Tudor Papers, Getty Research Institute, and Feldman's comments in Philip Guston, 'Conversation with Morton Feldman (1968)', in Clark Coolidge (ed.), *Philip Guston: Collected Writings, Lectures, and Conversations* (Berkeley: University of California Press, 2011), 92.

approach that appear incompatible with conclusions about Feldman's notation and his non-notated preferences reached elsewhere in this study.

Last, but not least, an attempt is made to describe this music from a listener's perspective. Much of it is justifiably termed 'pointillist', but this rather broad-brush description belittles important differences between individual graphs and, more importantly, between those from different periods. The discussion of this aspect of the series is not concentrated in a specific chapter, but is, instead, widely dispersed.

The overall aim of this monograph, therefore, is to provide a multi-faceted survey of this particular subset of Feldman's output, which highlights its inherent interest and credits it with a more pivotal role in the history of twentieth-century classical music than it is usually accorded. What emerges is not just an extended case study in musical indeterminacy – itself a desirable output, in my view – but also a picture of a groundbreaking series of musical works that deserves wider recognition.

1 Early graphs, 1950–1953

Beginnings

In an article published in 1967, Feldman described the genesis of his graph music:

> In the winter of 1950 I wrote what was probably the first piece of indeterminate music. John Cage, David Tudor and I were having dinner. I walked into the other room and wrote on graph paper some indeterminate music for cello – no notes, just indications of high, low, middle, short, long, loud, soft.[1]

Feldman had known Tudor since the mid-1940s, when he was studying composition with Stefan Wolpe and Tudor was studying with Wolpe and his wife Irma.[2] His friendship with Cage was forged later, after a chance encounter at Carnegie Hall, New York City, in January 1950,[3] shortly after Cage had returned from a stay in France. Christian Wolff, a high school student, arrived on the scene a few weeks later, initially as Cage's student. The four friends – Cage, Feldman, Tudor and Wolff – met frequently in the ensuing months, assisted by the fact that Feldman – by then twenty-four years of age and working, during the day, in his father's clothing manufacturing company – moved into the same New York City apartment block as Cage. As Wolff recalled, 'basically we just hung around together for a year or so'.[4]

In an interview conducted in 1983, Feldman gave a more picturesque account of the beginnings of his graph music:

> I was living in the same building as John Cage and he invited me to dinner. And it wasn't ready yet. John was making wild rice the way most people don't

---

[1] 'The avant-garde: progress or stalemate?', D27.

[2] For Feldman's early contacts with Tudor, see John Holzaepfel, David Tudor and the Performance of American Experimental Music, 1950–1959, unpublished PhD thesis, City University of New York (1994), 9.

[3] For Feldman's account of this meeting, see 'Liner notes' [1962], in Friedman (ed.), *Give My Regards*, 4. Elsewhere, Feldman remembered having seen Cage previously at a 'soirée' organised by the Wolpes ('Conversation about Stefan Wolpe, Austin Clarkson, 13 November 1980', in Villars (ed.), *Morton Feldman Says*, 98).

[4] 'Christian Wolff', interview, in Geoff Smith and Nicola Walker Smith (eds.), *American Originals* (London: Faber and Faber, 1994), 253.

know how it should be made. That is, just waiting for boiling water and then putting new boiling water into the rice and then having another pot boiling and then draining the rice, etc, etc, so we were waiting a long time for the wild rice to be ready. It was while waiting for the wild rice that I just sat down at his desk and picked up a piece of notepaper and started to doodle. And what I doodled was a freely drawn page of graph paper – and what emerged were high, middle, and low categories. It was just automatic – I never had any conversation about it heretofore, you know – never discussed it. [. . .] Actually I didn't have any kind of theory and I had no idea what was going to emerge, but if I wasn't waiting for that wild rice, I wouldn't have had those wild ideas.[5]

These accounts are broadly consistent with Cage's recollections. In a conversation with Feldman recorded in 1966, Cage recalled:

it was your music, really, that opened up everything, your piece, what was it called, I think the first one was for piano [. . .] David Tudor and I were in the other room. You left us and you wrote this piece on graph, giving us this freedom of playing in those three ranges – high, middle, and low – and then we went in and played the piece, and it was then that the musical world changed.[6]

In lectures delivered in 1988–9, Cage described the events in question as follows:

in the place where i lived [. . .] morton feldman went into the room with the piano and i stayed at my desk which was in the bedroom with david tudor shortly morton feldman came back with his first piece of graph music where on graph paper he simply put numbers and indicated high middle and low how many high notes how many middle notes how many low notes and nothing else there were squares of the graph that he left empty so there were no notes there at all after he showed it to me and to david tudor david tudor went to the piano and played it[.][7]

It is not entirely clear whether the sketch that Feldman produced in Cage's apartment was an early version of *Projection 1*, the first of the published graphs. In Feldman's earlier account quoted above, he remembered the sketch as for cello, suggesting that it may have been, but his later account portrays what he produced as more embryonic in character and possibly not conceived with a particular instrument in mind. Cage, unlike

[5] 'An interview with Morton Feldman, Jan Williams, 22 April 1983' [1983], in Villars (ed.), *Morton Feldman Says*, 153.
[6] John Cage and Morton Feldman, *Radio Happenings I–V: Recorded at WBAI New York City, July 1966–January 1967* (Cologne: MusikTexte, 1993), 17.
[7] *I–VI* (Cambridge, MA: Harvard University Press, 1990), 238–40, with Cage's punctuation.

Feldman, remembered Tudor, or perhaps those present, playing from the sketch at the piano, which fits with its being a piano work or something of a more preliminary kind. Indeed, Cage's earlier account tentatively suggests that it was, indeed, for piano.

All the accounts agree that Feldman's sketch did not specify the pitches of the indicated sounds, suggesting that this aspect was present from the very beginning. In addition, they all agree that it gave the register of each sound as high, middle or low. Feldman's earlier account suggests that he specified whether each sound should be played loud or soft, but this type of information was not given in any of the earliest surviving materials and, in the absence of additional evidence that this was the case, it seems reasonable to assume that here his memory was in error.

It is possible that Feldman's original sketch has survived. Around 1966, Cage solicited manuscripts for possible inclusion in a book to benefit the Foundation for Contemporary Performance Arts.[8] The resulting collection includes several sketches of Feldman's more conventionally notated works.[9] It also includes a one-page sketch of two systems of hand-drawn graph notation, in which a number of individual cells and horizontal groups of cells are shaded (Figure 1.1). The sketch also includes two incomplete systems, which are empty.

The intended instrumentation of the sketch is not clear. Certainly, the presentation fits with its being a work for cello, piano or, alternatively, something more provisional in character. Even so, the musical content appears unrelated to that of *Projection 1* and its layout is considerably simpler, and these points argue against classifying it as an early version of the published work.

A notable aspect of this item is the hand-drawn character of the grids, which fits with the suggestion in Feldman's testimony from 1983 that he 'doodled [. . .] a freely drawn page of graph paper'. Also, the presentation and organisation of the material strongly suggests that it is a very early example. One indication of this is the division of the uppermost system into units containing four columns – an aspect of Feldman's presentation found only in graphs from 1950 to 1951 – but a more involved reason for thinking it contemporary with *Projection 1* is outlined in Chapter 4. Although the grids are not populated by numbers, as suggested by Cage in his 1988–9 lectures, this is also true of *Projection 1*, and it is reasonable to suppose that here it was Cage's memory that was in error. If the sketch is,

---

[8] Selections were published in John Cage and Alison Knowles (eds.), *Notations* (New York: Something Else Press, 1969).
[9] John Cage Collection, Northwestern University Music Library.

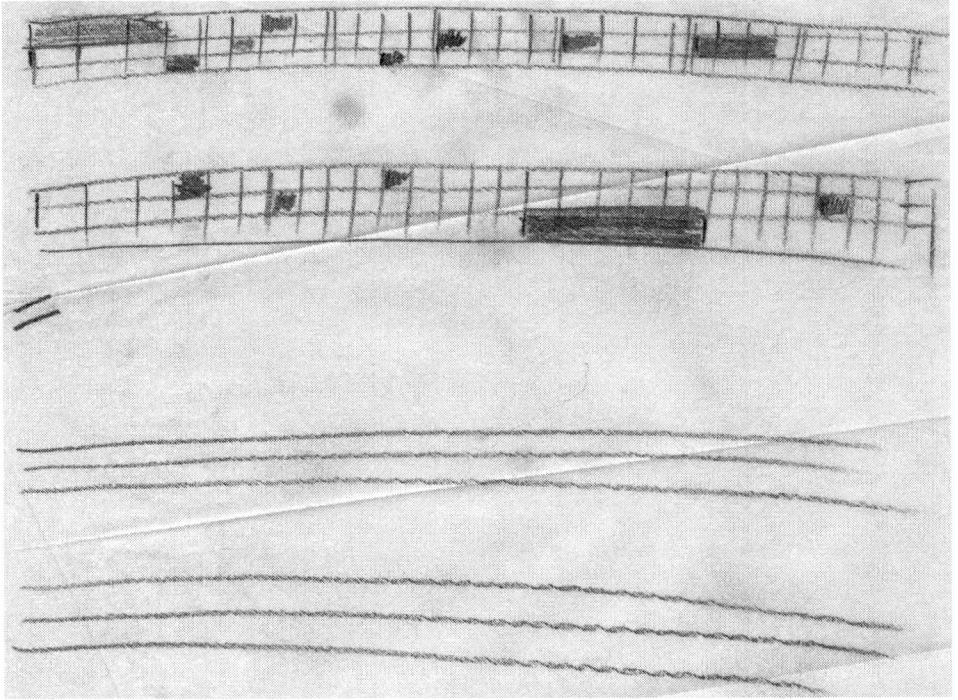

Figure 1.1 Untitled sketch

indeed, the one that Feldman 'doodled' in Cage's apartment, then this would explain why Feldman and Cage regarded it as worthy of preserving. Even so, it is difficult to see how this conjecture might be confirmed, unless they showed it to someone who could testify to its origin.

Feldman's later account of the genesis of his graph music portrayed the original creative act as wholly spontaneous rather than the culmination of a process of thought, but on other occasions he focused on alleged advantages of the format, suggesting a more calculated method of discovery. Be that as it may, there is no other evidence – in his surviving notebooks, for example – to suggest that he actively searched for a new notation before finding one. The assumption here, therefore, is that the original creative act was spontaneous, and that the claimed advantages of the graph format were conceived by him in its aftermath.

On one occasion, late in life, Feldman suggested that his method of combining specified and unspecified elements in his graphs and his subsequent works with fixed pitches and indeterminate durations, which he began composing in 1957, had been grounded in a Hegelian doctrine of 'unified opposites' that he had picked up from Wolpe.[10] Nevertheless, one wonders whether there were other, more direct influences on his innovation. One candidate is Schillinger's 'System of Musical Composition', which its creator taught in the United States in the 1930s and early 1940s, as already noted. In *The Schillinger System of Musical Composition*, published posthumously in 1946, Schillinger wrote:

> The adoption of the *graph* method for the recording of musical composition and performance has obvious advantages over the present system of musical notation. In the first place, it offers as much precision as is desired; in the second, it stimulates direct associations with the pattern of a given component [...] Graph notation records individual components through individual curves. The special components of sound are frequency, intensity, and quality – and they may be recorded through the corresponding individual graphs. By means of such notation the composer can define his intentions with the utmost precision; the performer can then decipher the desires of the composer to the latter's full satisfaction. [...] The horizontal direction [...] expresses time in all graphs; the vertical direction [...] expresses variation of some special component: pitch, intensity, quality. [...] The best graph paper to use is that ruled 12 x 12 per square inch; the reason for this is the versatility of the number 12 with respect to divisibility and the definition of an octave of the equal temperament of twelve for the pitch.[11]

There are some similarities between the ideas expressed in this passage and Feldman's, most notably in Schillinger's recourse to graph paper and the suggested use of the horizontal axis as a proportional indication of time. It has been suggested, on these grounds, that Feldman's graph music may have stemmed from Schillinger's graph method.[12] Feldman's contacts with Schillinger's ideas are not documented, but even if he remained unaware of them during his music studies in the 1940s, it is distinctly possible that he heard of them during the early months of his acquaintance with Cage, for it is known that Cage had visited Schillinger in 1943.[13]

That said, Feldman's ideas diverged from Schillinger's in ways that make it difficult to see a clear chain of influence. For example, Schillinger recommended the use of several graphs in connection with a single work, one for each of several musical parameters. By implication, his graphs were

---

[10] 'To have known Stefan Wolpe', www.cnvill.net/mfwolpe.htm (accessed 24 June 2015).

[11] *The Schillinger System of Musical Composition* (New York: Carl Fischer, 1946), 244–5.

[12] David Kershaw, Tape Music with Absolute Animated Film: Prehistory and Development, unpublished PhD thesis, University of York (1982), 206.

[13] Cage discussed his visit in Arnold Jay Smith, 'Reaching for the cosmos: a composers' colloquium', *Down Beat*, 20 October 1977, 19.

not intended for use in conventional performances, although he sometimes suggested that they might eventually be used as inputs to music-producing machines. Instead, he and his pupils used graphs as intermediate stages in the production of more conventionally notated works.[14] Chapter 10 argues that Feldman himself worked from graph-like intermediaries to more conventionally notated scores on a number of occasions. Nevertheless, it is clear, for reasons given in Chapters 4 and 8, that he did not originally envisage his published graphs being used in this fashion. Although others would go on to use them in this way, they were, for him, performable works that were the finished products of his creative enterprise, not merely intermediate stages. Also, Schillinger hoped to use his graphs as a method of specifying his intentions 'with the upmost precision', as he explained in the passage quoted above, and his advocacy of graph paper that is ruled 12 x 12 per square inch was evidently grounded in the presupposition that pitch is to be specified at least as precisely as in more conventionally notated music.[15] Contrast Feldman's diametrically opposed idea of using graphs as a method of controlling pitch less precisely.[16]

Cage's own work is another possible influence. In terms of presentation, for example, Feldman's use of a grid may owe something to the grid-like charts of possible outcomes that Cage was using at this time in composing his *Concerto for Prepared Piano and Chamber Orchestra* and *Sixteen Dances*.[17] Moreover, Cage had made use of a grid-like structure, which is similar to those used subsequently by Feldman, in organising his *Quartet* (*c*. 1937).[18] This particular work, for unspecified percussion instruments,

---

[14] Earle Brown, 'The notation and performance of new music', *The Musical Quarterly*, vol. 72, no. 2 (1964), 189.

[15] For Schillinger's desire for 'total control of every aspect of all musical situations', see *ibid*.

[16] In the late 1930s, Grainger used graphs in three works for theremins – *Free Music 1*, *Free Music 2* and *Beatless Music* – to specify 'tonal glides and curves' with greater precision than is possible with conventional notation ('Free Music' [1972], in Teresa Balough (ed.), *A Musical Genius from Australia: Selected Writings by and about Percy Grainger* (Nedlands, WA: University of Western Australia, Dept of Music, 1982), 143). These were not performed until after Feldman's death, and it seems less likely that he would have known of them. The scores, which consist of line graphs of pitch and intensity on graph paper, were for use in performance (*ibid.*, 144).

[17] Neither was finished until 1951. However, the first movement of the *Concerto* was completed in the summer of 1950 whereas the second movement and the first of the sixteen dances were completed in the autumn. This suggests that Cage's use of charts may have pre-dated Feldman's graph notation, *pace* Kenneth Silverman, *Begin Again: A Biography of John Cage* (New York: Alfred A. Knopf, 2010), 100. Cage described his use of charts in Jean-Jacques Nattiez (ed.), *The Boulez-Cage Correspondence* (Cambridge University Press, 1993), 92–7.

[18] Cage's manuscript is reproduced in Richard H. Brown, 'The spirit inside each object: John Cage, Oskar Fischinger, and "the future of music"', *Journal of the Society for American Music*, vol. 6, no. 1 (2012), 98–100. This article suggests incorrectly that Cage's notation is proportional (*ibid.*, 98).

is thought to have been composed after a short apprenticeship with the experimental filmmaker Oscar Fischinger.[19] At that time, Fischinger's animation method involved sketching the planned movement of individual figures across the cinema screen in an invented notation on graph paper, and it seems to have been this that led Cage to use similar paper in composing the final movement of *Quartet*.[20] If Feldman was aware of this when he sketched his graph notation for the first time, then this would imply an indirect causal link, via Cage, between his graph format and Fischinger.

Wolff's *Madrigals* – a long-forgotten indeterminate work, dated 20 October–2 November 1950, but first published and performed more than fifty years later – is yet another candidate as an influence. This work, originally conceived for three voices,[21] does not specify absolute pitches. Instead, relative pitches of specified vowel sounds within individual phrases are indicated for each vocalist by the placement of note heads versus a one-line stave. Its possible role in the origins of Feldman's graph music hangs on the question of when, precisely, Cage hosted his wild rice dinner party. For reasons about to become clear, this is uncertain.

Projections

The precise date on which Feldman completed *Projection 1*, the first of his published graphs (Example 1.1), is not documented: the surviving sketches are undated, the published edition is simply dated 1950 and nothing else points unequivocally to a narrower date range.

Various factors suggest that he may have finished it in the month of December. For example, in Feldman's 1967 account of the genesis of his graph music, quoted above, he mentioned inventing the format in 'the winter of 1950'. Moreover, years later, he recalled his *Piece for Violin and Piano*, a conventionally notated work completed on 17 November 1950, the same day on which Tudor first performed Boulez's *Deuxième Sonate* (1948), as a crucial turning point in his music,[22] which strongly suggests that he

---

[19] The manuscript is dated 1935, but there is reason to think it was composed somewhat later (*ibid.*, 97–8).

[20] *Ibid.*, 95, 98.

[21] Wolff revised *Madrigals* in 2001 for subsequent publication. The explanatory notes with the revised version, 'for 3 voices or a combination of 3 of voice(s) and instrument(s)', specify that instruments can perform one or more of the voice parts. They also mention another early work for voice and percussion that is indeterminate with regard to pitch that has not been published. Wolff remembers composing this before *Madrigals*. Christian Wolff to David Cline, 29 February 2012 (email).

[22] 'Johannesburg lecture 2: Feldman on Feldman, August 1983', in Villars (ed.), *Morton Feldman Says*, 177.

Example 1.1 *Projection 1*, page 1

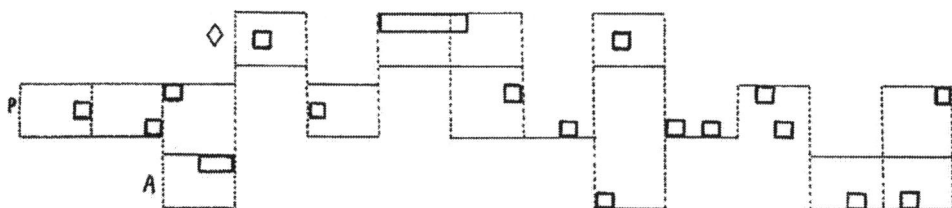

remembered it pre-dating his first graph. In addition, it is known that he would complete the next three *Projections* within a period of only two weeks, beginning with *Projection 2* on 3 January 1951, and this is consistent with the assumption of a period of frenetic activity, following Cage's wild rice dinner party, resulting in a string of new works, the first being *Projection 1*. Other factors point to an earlier date and a longer interval between *Projection 1* and *Projection 2*, however. To begin with, it is hard to imagine why Wolff's *Madrigals* was so completely overlooked – not only by Feldman and Cage, but seemingly also by Wolff himself – if it had been an indeterminate precursor of Feldman's graph music.[23] Moreover, on 18 November 1950, the day after Feldman completed *Piece for Violin and Piano*, Cage wrote that 'Feldman's music [. . .] changes with each piece',[24] which seems to indicate that the stylistic metamorphosis marked by *Piece for Violin and Piano* was not the only one that Feldman's music had, by then, sustained.[25]

Although the two surviving sketches of *Projection 1* do not help in pinpointing its completion date, they are instructive for other reasons. One, which is among Tudor's surviving papers, is arranged on a single, untitled page of graph paper on which Feldman sketched an alternative presentation of the opening of the work, and the unusual layout of this page suggests that he experimented with alternative presentations of the grid after inventing the graph format.[26] In the published edition of *Projection 1*,

---

[23] In the notes with the published edition, Wolff described *Madrigals* as 'a piece written long ago, not then performed, and pretty much forgotten'.

[24] Nattiez (ed.), *The Boulez-Cage Correspondence*, 78.

[25] In an interview published in 1973, Feldman stated untruthfully that he composed his first graphs before meeting Cage ('I met Heine on the Rue Fürstemberg' [1973], in Friedman (ed.), *Give My Regards*, 114). For an assessment of his motives, see Brett Boutwell, 'Morton Feldman's graphic notation: *Projections* and trajectories', *Journal of the Society for American Music*, vol. 6, no. 4 (2012), 472–3.

[26] Although the musical content specified by the sketch is clearly related to the opening of *Projection 1* in its published form, there are significant differences and these suggest that the former pre-dates the latter.

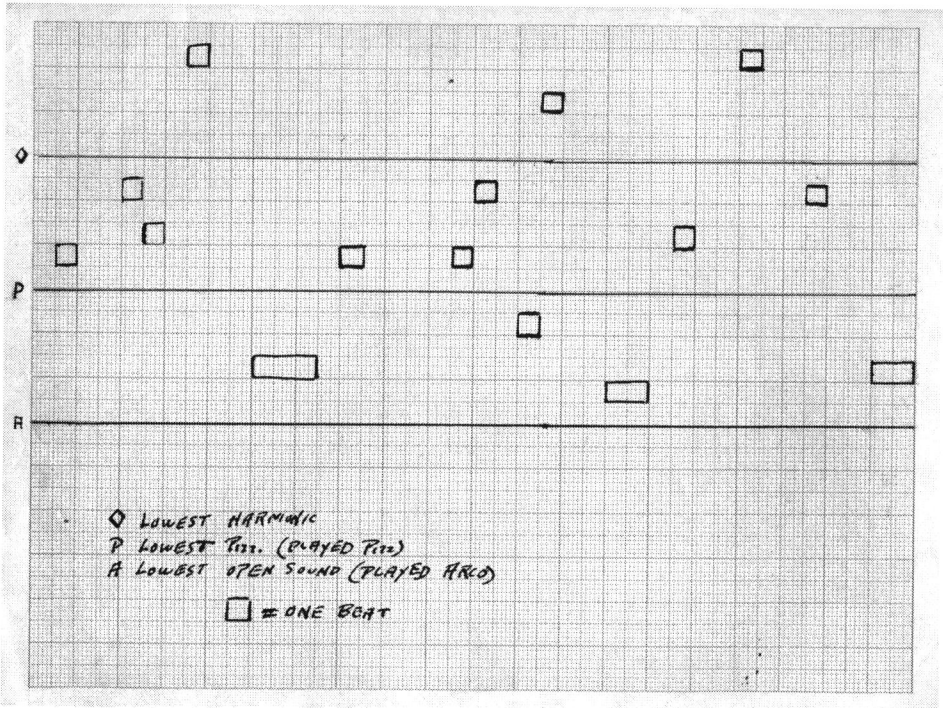

Figure 1.2 *Projection 1*, sketch, alternative presentation of the grid

he allocated three grid rows (high, middle and low) to each of three timbres (harmonic, pizzicato and arco), but in the alternative presentation he allocated each timbre six rows (Figure 1.2).[27] There is no evidence that Feldman made any further use of the six-row format.[28]

The only other surviving sketch, titled 'Composition for Cello (Projection 1)', includes a dedication to Seymour Barab, which does not

---

[27] 'Sheet of graphic notation, n.d.', David Tudor Papers, 1884–1998 bulk 1940–66, Getty Research Institute, Los Angeles (980039).

[28] One commentator has speculated that this was the page sketched in Cage's apartment (Boutwell, 'Morton Feldman's graphic notation', 458–9), but this is unlikely. The grid is printed, not, as Feldman remembered, 'freely drawn'. Also, the page is obviously scored for a stringed instrument. Legend has it that Tudor could play anything – even the raisins in a slice of fruitcake ([Unsigned: C], 'Composing by knucklebone', *Time*, 13 April 1962, 56). Even so, one would have expected an attempt, by him, to play this particular sketch – using extended piano techniques, for example – to have elicited more than the bland comments about his performance at Cage's wild rice dinner party in the passages quoted above.

appear in the published edition.[29] In all likelihood, Feldman's choice of instrument was influenced by the pool of performers available to him; it is known that he was on good terms with several cellists, including Barab and his high school friend Daniel Stern at this time. Sadly, details of the first performance of *Projection 1* have not survived, although Wolff has a 'faint memory' of hearing it played, possibly by Barab, at an 'informal gathering' in Cage's studio apartment in 1950–1.[30]

Notable aspects of this relatively short work include frequent changes in timbre, which add colour, and the slow tempo specified in the explanatory notes provided with the score of 72 beats or, in Feldman's terminology, *ictuses* per minute 'or thereabouts'. This tempo guidance is shared by the first six graphs in the series and would come to be regarded within Feldman's circle as one of his trademarks at this time.[31] It coincides with the typical resting heart rate of an adult human being,[32] which some evidence suggests exerts a comforting influence, attributable to its 'super-familiarity achieved from constant repetition'.[33]

Given that the average density of activity per ictus is low, the music is sparse and the frequent intrusion of lengthy pauses generates a highly fragmentary listening experience. Occasional sustained sounds seem to hang in mid-air and add to the general feeling of stasis. Perhaps the work's most striking aspect is the longest silence, nine seconds in length at the given tempo, which dominates the closing moments and serves as a false ending. This is followed by two short sounds – both pizzicato – and a final silence, which marks the true ending of the work.

Feldman's decision to score his second graph – *Projection 2* – for flute, trumpet, violin, cello and piano was also a practical one, connected in this case with Cage's concurrent projects. Cage, who had been collaborating with Merce Cunningham since 1943, completed the first of his *Sixteen Dances* for flute, trumpet, four percussionists, piano, violin and cello, for Cunningham's *Sixteen Dances for Soloist and Company of Three*, on 25 October 1950 and he worked on the remaining movements into 1951. A piano reduction was premiered with Cunningham's dance at Bennett Junior College in Millbrook, New York on 17 January 1951,[34] but the

[29] 'Sketchbook 1', Morton Feldman Collection, Paul Sacher Foundation. See Figure 3.1 (Chapter 3).

[30] Christian Wolff to David Cline, 29 November 2010 and 8 December 2010 (emails).

[31] Martin Iddon, *John Cage and David Tudor: Correspondence on Interpretation and Performance* (Cambridge University Press, 2013), 11.

[32] Walter Zimmermann, 'Morton Feldman – der ikonolast', in Zimmermann (ed.), *Morton Feldman Essays*, 11.

[33] Desmond Morris, *The Naked Ape: A Zoologist's Study of the Human Animal* (London: Jonathan Cape, 1967), 143.

[34] Programme, Bennett Junior College, 17 January 1951.

ensemble version was played for the first time a few days later, with the
second performance of Cunningham's dance, at Hunter College
Playhouse, New York City on 21 January.[35] This subsequent programme
included the premiere of Wolff's recently composed *Trio (I)* and what was
almost certainly the first performance of *Projection 2*, and there can be little
doubt that Feldman consciously selected an instrumentation for this graph
that was sufficiently similar to the one that Cage was already working with
to facilitate its inclusion on the programme that evening.[36]

Cage reported that Feldman's work received a mixed response, being
'hissed and bravoed'.[37] *Dance Magazine* complained that the music by
Feldman and Wolff 'consisted of lonesome tootles and squeeks [*sic*] separated by stretches of bleak silence',[38] but the *New York Herald Tribune*
singled out Feldman's work for special criticism:

> [*Projection 2*] seems to have started the whole childish trend with his gimmick
> of indicating merely the note-lengths and ranges (high, low, medium) and
> allowing the players otherwise to choose any notes, within these broad limits,
> according to the caprice of the moment. The result was not even amusing.
> Perhaps the players had fun, for it is like a game of Ghost, and the dreary
> pauses between the sounds were like those tiresome moments when you wait
> for someone to fish for the right letter.[39]

In fact, the lengthy pauses highlighted by the reviewer are rather less
frequent in *Projection 2* than in *Projection 1*, although the longest example,
which occurs just after the midpoint, lasts a full ten seconds. This and the
polyphonic character of some passages mean that the density of activity per
ictus, although low, is somewhat higher here. Longer sounds are also more
common, and these sometimes overlap in staggered sequences, especially
in the second half, producing longer chords that evolve over time and
which also serve to lessen the apparent discontinuity. The most impressive
of these, which lasts twenty-three seconds at the given tempo, is located at
the very end of the work and involves elements contributed by every

---

[35] The tenth dance is dated 26 December 1950, the twelfth is dated 22 December 1950 and the title page is dated 19 January 1951 (i.e. two days after the first performance).
[36] The performances of *Trio (I)* and *Projection 2* are not marked as premieres in the programme (Programme, Hunter College Playhouse, 21 January 1951), but no previous performances are documented. Feldman described the event in 'Captain Cook's first voyage: an interview with Morton Feldman, Richard Wood Massi, 3 March 1987' [1989], in Villars (ed.), *Morton Feldman Says*, 225. David Nicholls noted the similarity in the instrumentations of *Sixteen Dances* and *Projection 2* (*John Cage* (Urbana: University of Illinois Press, 2007), 51).
[37] Iddon, *John Cage and David Tudor*, 9.
[38] Doris Hering, 'The season in review', *Dance Magazine*, vol. 25, no. 3 (March 1951), 16.
[39] Arthur Berger, 'Music news: Jeritza back, "Dybbuk" off; chance games', *New York Herald Tribune*, 28 January 1951, Section 4, 8. Berger summed up his views on the evening's music thus: '[t]he intellectual content is at its lowest' (*ibid.*).

instrument. In the last few seconds, all the instruments play simultaneously for only the third time.

The explanatory notes provided with *Projection 1* do not mention dynamics, but those with *Projection 2* specify that they should be kept 'very low'. In fact, several of Feldman's subsequent comments indicate that absence of guidance in *Projection 1* was an oversight and that 'very low' dynamics were also intended in its case.[40] As will become clear, such oversights are not uncommon in Feldman's graph scores. Having said that, his intentions are usually discernible through lateral comparison with neighbouring graphs or by studying his surviving statements or sketch materials. One effect of the constraint on dynamics is to lessen perceived differences in timbre: lower dynamics generally result in a lower intensity of higher harmonics in a sound relative to its fundamental tone.

Projection 3 and *Projection 4* are dated 5 January 1951 and 16 January 1951, respectively – that is, shortly before the first performance of *Projection 2*. Once again, the instrumental combinations that Feldman chose reflect a practical bias. He could count on the services of Tudor and at least two less capable pianists – Cage and himself – hence his decision to score *Projection 3* for two pianos. The only surviving sketch of *Projection 4* is dedicated to the violinist Frances Magnes,[41] who Feldman seems to have met through Ralph Shapey,[42] another of Wolpe's students, and it is likely that she and Tudor gave the first performance on 25 May 1951 at the Eighth Street Artists' Club – often referred to more simply as *the Club* – in New York City.[43] Tudor's subsequent history of engagement

[40]   Feldman stated that all the *Projections* have very low dynamics in 'Liner notes', 6, and Feldman *et al.*, '4 musicians at work', 168. He stated that *Projection 1*, in particular, has very low dynamics in ' . . .Out of "Last Pieces"', in Edward Downes (ed.), *New York Philharmonic, One Hundred Twenty-Second Season 1963–64, The Avant-Garde – Program V, 6–9 February 1964* (programme booklet, Philharmonic Hall, Lincoln Center, New York, 6–9 February 1964), G. *Pace* Frank Denyer, 'Feldman's search for the ecstasy of the moment', liner notes with *Morton Feldman: The Ecstasy of the Moment*, Etcetera Record Company, KTC 3003, 5–6, and Ryan Vigil, 'Compositional parameters: *Projection 4* and an analytical methodology for Morton Feldman's graphic works', *Perspectives of New Music*, vol. 47, no. 1 (Winter 2009), 233, 236.

[41]   'Sketchbook 1', Morton Feldman Collection, Paul Sacher Foundation. The dedication does not appear in the published edition.

[42]   Frances Magnes, Interview by John Holzaepfel, White Plains, New York, 22 July 1999, unpublished transcript.

[43]   A printed invitation to this event indicates that it included music by Boulez, Cage and Feldman (Invitation, 39 E. 8th St., 25 May [1951], Morton Feldman Collection, Paul Sacher Foundation). It also lists the order of play as follows: New Music Quartet; Intermission; Frances Magnes, violinist; Intermission; David Tudor, pianist. One attendee noted that Cage's *String Quartet in Four Parts* (1950) was performed (Judith Malina, *The Diaries of Judith Malina, 1947–1957* (New York: Grove Press, 1984), 167), and it is highly likely that Tudor played Boulez's *Deuxième Sonate*, a mainstay of his repertoire in 1951. Given that the featured composers had yet to compose a work for solo violin, it seems probable that Tudor accompanied Magnes in

with indeterminacy indicates that he relished the freedoms provided by this new type of music, but this was not true of many more conservative musicians. For example, Magnes, in an interview recorded in 1999, remembered being 'embarrassed' by not knowing exactly which notes she was supposed to be playing.[44]

Projection 3 is the shortest of Feldman's graphs, lasting only one and a half minutes in performance at the given tempo. It includes very few sounds – one pianist plays twenty sonorities, while the other plays just seventeen. In addition, Feldman specifies the silent depression of piano keys in many places, as he had in *Projection 2*, and these were surely meant to result in a wash of sympathetic resonances, which the evidence of the available recordings suggests are, in fact, often inaudible. Pauses become more frequent in the closing stages, which therefore possess a noticeably more discontinuous aspect. Even though the score indicates that dynamics are 'very low', the character of the work ensures that they are not entirely even. Chords grow in complexity as the music unfolds before becoming simpler in the closing stages, and this generates subtle gradations of dynamics, which grow during the first two-thirds of a performance before subsiding.

The sound world of *Projection 4*, in which dynamics are 'low', differs from those of the previous *Projections* in its emphasis on short sounds, one ictus in length. These dominate both parts and give the music a more pointillist aspect. Another difference stems from the presence of extended passages in which the placement of sounds highlights the regular pulse – still 72 ictuses per minute 'or thereabouts' – which is consequently more evident. The longest passage of this type occurs early on (ictuses 40–54) and lasts thirteen seconds at the given tempo. During this period, the piano plays short sounds, lasting a single ictus, on every other beat, and this very regular rhythm is replicated by the violin, which also plays short sounds, but in every intervening ictus. The net effect is an alternating sequence of entrances on consecutive beats.[45] Similar structures appear on four subsequent occasions and there are many shorter passages of this type. Comparable arrangements, which also highlight the pulse, had appeared

---

the middle section of the programme, and it is reasonable to assume they played *Projection 4*, which was originally dedicated to Magnes, as previously noted. No doubt Feldman would have been keen to present one of his graphs in this forum.

[44] Interview by John Holzaepfel.

[45] Brett Boutwell has highlighted this passage for similar reasons (A Static Sublime: Morton Feldman and the Visual, 1950–1970, unpublished PhD thesis, University of Illinois at Urbana-Champaign (2006), 140–1, and '"The breathing of sound itself": notation and temporality in Feldman's music to 1970', *Contemporary Music Review*, vol. 32, no. 6 (December 2013), 535).

in the previous *Projections*, but they are much shorter and considerably less frequent.

Projection 5 is dated 1951, and no more precise specification than this survives, but it was probably composed in the early part of the year, at around the same time as *Projections 2–4*. The earlier of the two surviving sketches has had its numbering changed from an initial figure of '5' to '3' and then back to '5', while the later sketch is titled 'Projection 3'.[46] This suggests that Feldman may have begun composing it before turning to the work now known as *Projection 3* (i.e. in the period from 3 to 5 January) but the assumption here is that the official numbering reflects the order in which the works were completed.

Projection 5 is a short work, scored for nine instruments with 'very low' dynamics, that is similar in character to *Projection 2*, most notably because longer sounds are more common and because many of these overlap in staggered sequences, resulting in a somewhat less fragmentary listening experience, as in the earlier work. The frequency with which lengthy pauses or extended silences occur is also similar, but in this case they are focused in the second half. That said, entrances are situated on consecutive beats more frequently here, particularly during the second quarter; thus, the last two *Projections* are marked by a pronounced heightening of apparent pulse.

There are also problems in dating several of Feldman's conventionally notated works from this time, but it is likely that he was working on at least some of them during the period in which he composed the *Projections*, the most likely candidate being *Four songs to e. e. cummings*, which is simply dated 1951, but which was performed, possibly for the first time, early in the year, on 11 February.[47] This interchanging between formats – graph and staff notation in this case – is an early example of his favoured way of working in the 1950s and 1960s. He once compared it with an artist alternating between producing paintings and sculptures,[48] and it was an approach that would characterise his music until 1970. The graphs dominated his output in early 1951, but there would be longer periods in which works in conventional notation or his notations for fixed pitches and indeterminate durations dominated his output subsequently.

Cage, who had helped Feldman in perfecting the presentation of the earliest graphs, in which 'only the utterly essential lines remain',[49] regarded them as an important breakthrough, which is why he began 'generally

---

[46] Morton Feldman Collection, Paul Sacher Foundation.

[47] Programme, Columbia University, 11 February 1951.

[48] '*Soundpieces* interview, Cole Gagne and Tracy Caras, 17 August 1980' [1982], in Villars (ed.), *Morton Feldman Says*, 91.

[49] Iddon, *John Cage and David Tudor*, 8.

broadcasting' his faith in Feldman 'to the point of fanaticism', as he put it, soon after the first graphs were completed.[50] Also, as Cage himself underlined, they had an immediate effect on his own music, one that would shape his output for the rest of his life. In composing the first two movements of *Concerto for Prepared Piano and Chamber Orchestra* and then *Sixteen Dances*, Cage had applied predefined sequences of moves on his grids of possible outcomes to guide his selections.[51] In the third movement of the *Concerto*, composed immediately after *Sixteen Dances*, probably in January–February 1951, he modified this method. Inspired by Feldman's example of relinquishing control of some musical parameters and by the Chinese *Book of Changes* (*I Ching*), he ceded elements of control to chance by tossing coins to determine his selections.[52] In *Music of Changes*, which Cage worked on during most of the rest of 1951, he extended the use of chance to decisions about many other aspects of the work – including tempos, durations, dynamics and the number of layers of activity to be superposed – by creating additional charts. This was a method that he would go on to use in composing several other works in 1951–2, including *Imaginary Landscape No. 4* (1951), a work that he had been contemplating since 1948 and which he would go on to dedicate to Feldman.[53] Here he relinquished control, not only through recourse to the *I Ching*, but also in another way, for the work is scored for twelve radios with unpredictable outputs that depend upon the time and location of performance.[54]

Feldman's use of the term 'projection' in the titles of his first five graphs is suggestive on several levels. To begin with, its abstract character telegraphs the fact that this is absolute music, but on another level his use of

---

[50] *Ibid.*, 9. Years later, Cage still regarded the graphs as having been an important breakthrough. See the epigraph to this volume (taken from Cage and Feldman, *Radio Happenings*, 17) and his comments in 'An interview with John Cage', 29.

[51] John Cage, 'Composition as process: I. Changes' [1961], in *Silence*, 25–6.

[52] See Cage's accounts in these sources: Cage, *I–VI*, 237–45; 'An autobiographical statement (1989)' [1991], in Richard Kostelanetz (ed.), *John Cage: Writer – Previously Uncollected Pieces* (New York: Limelight Editions, 1993), 243; and 'John Cage', in Bálint András Varga, *Three Questions for Sixty-Five Composers* (University of Rochester Press, 2011), 41. He also cited a lecture by Daisetz Suzuki as an inspiration ('Composition as process: I. Changes', 25–6, and 'Tokyo lecture and three mesostics', *Perspectives of New Music*, vol. 26, no. 1 (Winter 1988), 7). For other factors that may have affected him, see Kyle Gann, *No Such Thing as Silence: John Cage's 4'33"* (New Haven: Yale University Press, 2010), 85–102.

[53] Cage described his idea for *Imaginary Landscape No. 4* in 'A composer's confessions' [1992], in Kostelanetz (ed.), *John Cage: Writer*, 43, and his method of composing it in 'Composition: to describe the process of composition used in *Music of Changes* and *Imaginary Landscape No. 4*' [1952], in *Silence*, 57–9.

[54] Cage had used radios as ensemble instruments in previous works, but his decision to foreground them in *Imaginary Landscape No. 4* points to a heightened interest in their unpredictable outputs.

the term resonates with outside factors. For example, Feldman would have enjoyed the tacit reference to psychoanalytic theory – he was already devoted to being in analysis at this time.[55] More importantly, he must have meant to allude to the ideas of Edgard Varèse, who he first met through Wolpe in the 1940s.[56] Varèse, who Feldman came to revere,[57] used the expression 'sound projection' to refer to a kinetic property of sounds, which he described as the 'feeling that sound is leaving us with no hope of being reflected back, a feeling akin to that aroused by beams of light sent forth by a powerful searchlight – for the ear as for the eye, that sense of projection, of a journey into space'.[58] In the printed programme note for the Hunter College Playhouse performance of *Projection 2*, an uncredited author – probably Feldman himself – used an almost identical terminology, suggesting that '[t]he title of this work refers to the projection of sounds into space'.[59] Surely it was no coincidence that Feldman had attended a lecture given by Varèse at the Club on 10 November 1950.[60] This lecture contained an account of his discovery of 'sound projection', which he also referred to as 'spacial [*sic*] projection', while listening to Beethoven's Seventh Symphony in 'the Salle Pleyel in Paris [...] by reason of [its] miscalculated acoustical construction'.[61]

On another level, Feldman's use of a common term in the titles of his first five graphs demonstrates that he regarded them as closely related to one another. Decades later, he explained that he sometimes wrote 'sets of pieces' in which he explored an idea using different instrumentations,[62] and the five *Projections*, which feature similar dynamics, the

---

[55] Iddon, *John Cage and David Tudor*, 28, and Earle Brown, 'An interview with composer Earle Brown', by John Yaffé, *Contemporary Music Review*, vol. 26, nos. 3/4 (June/August 2007), 295.

[56] Feldman mentioned their first meeting in 'Conversation about Stefan Wolpe', 107. Sebastian Claren recognised the allusion to Varèse but also suggested an unlikely connection with cellist Pierre Fournier (*Neither: Die Musik Morton Feldmans* (Hofheim: Wolke Verlag, 2000), 45).

[57] See his comments in 'Sound, noise, Varèse, Boulez' [1958], in Friedman (ed.), *Give My Regards*, 2.

[58] 'The liberation of sound', in Elliott Schwartz and Barney Childs (eds.) with Jim Fox, *Contemporary Composers on Contemporary Music*, expanded edition (New York: Da Capo Press, 1998), 197.

[59] Programme, Hunter College Playhouse, 21 January 1951.

[60] Nothing points unequivocally to Feldman having attended. However, his admiration for Varèse and his growing attachment to the Club make it probable that he was there.

[61] Edgard Varèse, 'The Art-Science of music today', amended typescript, Edgard Varèse Collection, Paul Sacher Foundation, 4b, 6. For the origins of Varèse's lecture, see Heidy Zimmermann, 'Recycling, collage, work in progress: Varèse's thought in speech and writing', in Felix Meyer and Heidy Zimmermann (eds.), *Edgard Varèse: Composer, Sound Sculptor, Visionary* (Woodbridge: Boydell Press, 2006), 268, 270.

[62] 'Johannesburg lecture 2', 177–8.

same tempo and a broadly comparable sound, certainly fit this bill. As will become clear, the titles of the next group of graphs that he went on to compose also contain a common term – 'intersection' – signalling affinities between them and differences from the *Projections*.[63]

Intersections

The *Intersection* series marked a significant shift in Feldman's thinking. Typically, though not always, register is specified as high, middle or low, as in the *Projections*, but there are material differences, described by him as follows:

> In the *Projections* only register (high, middle or low), time values, and dynamics (soft throughout) were designated. Later in the same year (1951) I wrote *Intersection I* [*sic*] and *Marginal Intersection*, both for orchestra. Both these graph pieces designated only whether high, middle or low register of the instrument was to be used within a given time structure. Entrances within this structure, as well as actual pitches and dynamics, were freely chosen by the performer.[64]

In the *Projections*, Feldman had indicated the onset and duration of each sound, but these parameters are specified less precisely in the *Intersections*, in which performers enter anywhere within an indicated period, with Feldman adding the proviso that a performer, having entered, should hold the sound until the end of the period in which it occurs. It appears to have been for this reason that he named them *Intersections*: the title seems to allude to an alleged similarity between this new element of performer choice and the instructions given by traffic signals at a road intersection. As he put it, 'time was the distance, metaphorically, between a green light and a red light'.[65] This aspect gives the performer greater freedom to determine the durations of sounds and to alter their placement relative to the pulse. Another differentiating feature is that, in general, dynamics are freely chosen by each performer,[66] whereas in the *Projections* they are 'low' or, more commonly, 'very low', as previously noted. Once again, Feldman adds a proviso: that the dynamics of each sound must be

---

[63] Feldman also worked on six *Intermissions* (1950–3) and four *Extensions* (1951–3) during this period.

[64] 'Liner notes', 6.

[65] 'The future of local music' [1985], in Friedman (ed.), *Give My Regards*, 173. Elsewhere, Feldman attributed the link with traffic lights to Cage ('Traffic light music', interview by Charlotte Phelan, *Houston Post*, 26 February 1967, 24).

[66] *Intersection 1* specifies one loud sound. *Marginal Intersection* specifies loud and soft sounds in some places.

sustained at the same level until the end of the given duration, where feasible.[67] At least in part, these changes were Feldman's experiments in extending indeterminacy to new elements of his compositions. The introduction of imprecise indications of pitch was the most important innovation in the *Projections*, and it is only natural that he would have wished to try applying similar ideas to other parameters.

It is doubtful that Feldman saw the freedom given to performers in selecting dynamics as a notable success because he rarely returned to this idea subsequently.[68] One potential problem in ensemble works is that performers are free to choose markedly different levels, resulting in some instruments dominating the overall sound. Another is that louder dynamics emphasise the intensity of the higher harmonics in a sound relative to its fundamental tone, as previously noted, and this accentuates its timbral identity, something that, usually, he was keen to avoid – hence his comment '[t]oo much instrument, I can't hear the music' after a jazz concert at the Club in the early 1950s.[69] He certainly regarded his use of imprecise instructions about when to enter as more successful, however, because this idea reappeared in later graphs and was enlarged upon in his works with fixed pitches and indeterminate durations.

Feldman had reservations about tying the temporal evolution of his music too tightly to a steady beat from early on in his career, and there can be little doubt that this was another factor driving the transition from the *Projections* to the *Intersections*. In the *Projections*, he tied entrances and note durations to a steady pulse, meaning that the unfolding in time of these works was insensitive to unpredictable aspects of actual sounds in performance that he had come to regard as temporally suggestive. His response in the *Intersections* was to loosen up the imposed restriction by allowing the performer some latitude in choosing an appropriate moment at which to enter.

Intersection 1 is dedicated to Cage and dated February 1951. The score is marked 'for orchestra' but it contains only four distinct parts – labelled 'winds' (i.e. woodwinds), 'brass', 'violins and violas' and 'cellos and

---

[67] The feasibility constraint is not stated explicitly, but is evidently intended.

[68] In *Ixion* for chamber ensemble, he specified a more limited degree of freedom ('dynamics are low, with an occasional loud sound freely chosen by the performer'). Explanatory notes with pre-publication copies of the score of *Ixion* for two pianos state that '[d]ynamics are free', but these are not included with the published edition. In *Atlantis* and the graphs composed after *Ixion* for two pianos, Feldman reverted to giving general guidance about dynamics similar to that found in the *Projections*. In *Atlantis*, the performers play 'as softly as possible', whereas in the graphs from . . .*Out of 'Last Pieces'* onwards, dynamics are 'very low' or 'extremely low'.

[69] Reported in Natalie Edgar (ed.), *Club Without Walls: Selections from the Journals of Philip Pavia* (New York: Midmarch Arts Press, 2007), 61.

basses' – making it uncommonly sparse for an orchestral score. Evidently, many performers are to read from each part. What gives this idea interest is that Feldman's imprecise specifications of pitch, entrances and dynamics are likely to elicit a different response from each musician. This anticipates the better-known use of a similar device in his *Piece for Four Pianos* (1957), a work with fixed pitches and indeterminate durations in which the four pianists are likely to play at differing speeds from identical parts.

Dynamics are as described above but, in this case, all instruments except the woodwinds are to be fitted with mutes, and this mitigates the associated flexibility.[70] Even so, the large scale of the ensemble, a generally higher density of activity per instrument per ictus and the greater latitude given to the performers in choosing dynamics are bound to produce music that is more full-blooded than that of the *Projections*.

Feldman's insistence on sustained sounds being held until the end of the indicated time brackets is likely to have interesting repercussions provided that performers do not coordinate their entrances – a strategy not precluded by the wording of Feldman's explanatory notes. One is that lengthy time brackets will generally be associated with longer sounds, even though individual performers may enter at different times, because there will often be those who choose to enter near the earliest permitted time of entry. Another effect is the progressive accumulation of activity within longer time brackets, attributable to the probable staggering of entrances. This crescendo effect is likely to be most pronounced when the ensemble is large.

The work consists of a number of blocks of near-continuous sound of varying lengths that are separated by lengthy pauses, and it is the differences between the lengths of these blocks, their constantly changing internal make-up and the disruption caused by the intervening pauses that define the listening experience. Four loosely defined phases can be discerned, the first containing three long blocks of sound, each around a minute in length, which are made audibly distinct by the presence of substantial pauses between them. This extends throughout the first quarter. Activity within these blocks is constantly evolving, both because entrances within extended time brackets pile up – the crescendo effect described above – and because of overlapping time brackets in different parts. This is followed by a second phase, which spans the second quarter and contains numerous distinct blocks that are much shorter in length. Many of the longest pauses are heard here, and the listening experience is highly fragmentary. The third phase consists of a

---

[70] An additional constraint appears on page 8, where one square contains the letter 'L'. This symbol is not explained in the accompanying notes, but those with *Marginal Intersection* – the next graph in the series – indicate that the letters 'L' and 'S' stand for loud and soft, respectively. This is another early example of oversight in Feldman's presentation.

single block of sound lasting almost two minutes at the given tempo, and this is followed by a final phase that encompasses the last third of the work in which the blocks are of intermediate length. Whereas all four sections of the orchestra are similarly active until this point, the woodwind and brass sections dominate this closing section.

In the same month in which *Intersection 1* was completed, Feldman and Cage both delivered lectures at the Club, with Feldman's entitled 'The Unframed Frame: Modern Music'.[71] A week later, Cage delivered his 'Lecture on Something', which referred to Feldman's interest in 'no-continuity' between sounds and described his music, especially the graphs, in enthusiastic terms.[72] This must have boosted Feldman's reputation among the leading lights of the New York arts scene who attended, but it was also an early source of misunderstanding. Cage presented the graphs as if grounded in his own emerging ideas on aesthetic indifference and about mirroring life in art, which were not part of Feldman's thinking, then or subsequently.[73]

The Club was a hub of Abstract Expressionism and Feldman's rising profile within it was symptomatic of his growing involvement with that movement; the artists became enthusiastic attendees at concerts of his (and Cage's) music and he would count many of its luminaries as friends in due course. The text of his lecture is lost, but its title suggests that it drew parallels between painting and music. It tells more than this because it surely refers to an article about Pollock, titled 'Unframed space', published the previous August.[74] This reported Pollock's favourable response to the view that his paintings 'didn't have any beginning or any end',[75] and it may be that Feldman argued for a corresponding avoidance of narrative structure in music. In an interview recorded in the 1980s, he remembered his early desire for a music in which '[t]here was no narrative, no beginning, no end – a completely open and indefinable structure'.[76]

Phillip Pavia's brief notebook entry on Feldman's lecture, which reads '[j]azz is too instrumental, not human; music needs a plane as in painting',[77] is also revealing. The importance of the picture plane – and fidelity

[71] Edgar (ed.), *Club Without Walls*, 161.   [72] 'Lecture on something' [1959], in *Silence*, 132.

[73] Cage registered this mismatch in prefatory remarks with *ibid.*, 128. For a discussion, see Boutwell, 'Morton Feldman's graphic notation', 463–5.

[74] Berton Roueché, '"Unframed space," *The New Yorker*, August 1950' [1950], in Pepe Karmel (ed.), *Jackson Pollock: Interviews, Articles, and Reviews* (New York: Museum of Modern Art, 1999), 18–19.

[75] *Ibid.*, 19.

[76] 'Morton Feldman: touch', interview, 20 May 1985, in Michael Auping, *30 Years: Interviews and Outtakes* (Fort Worth, TX: Modern Art Museum of Fort Worth in association with Prestel, 2007), 143.

[77] Edgar (ed.), *Club Without Walls*, 161.

to it through the use of shallow pictorial space – was a key theme in art criticism at this time, most notably in Clement Greenberg's influential writings.[78] Feldman's own notebooks suggest that was seeking a correspondingly flattened conception of musical space in this period. A discussion of this and its impact on his music appears in Chapter 4.

It was around this time that Feldman received an invitation to write music to accompany a recently recorded film about Pollock by Hans Namuth and Paul Falkenberg – further proof of his rising profile among the painters.[79] He also met and befriended Philip Guston, a high school chum of Pollock's, after seeing his *Red Painting* at an exhibition at the Museum of Modern Art.[80] This canvas was the first abstract painting that Guston had exhibited and is now viewed as marking his shift away from an earlier figurative mode to Abstract Expressionism.[81] Feldman would come to regard Guston as his closest friend.[82]

It was also around this time that Feldman began working on *Intersection 2* and then *Marginal Intersection*.[83] The latter was finished first, in July 1951, the former shortly thereafter, in August. He also worked on several conventionally notated works, including *Structures* for string quartet, dated March 1951, *Variations* for solo piano, dated 21 March 1951, and his unpublished music for the film *Jackson Pollock*, mentioned above, which is dated May 1951 and scored for two cellos. *Variations* consists entirely of unattached grace notes, manifesting the same discomfort with pulse that had been partly responsible for the shift from the *Projections* to the *Intersections*.[84]

Although *Marginal Intersection* is scored for a 'large' orchestra,[85] there are only eleven instrumental parts ('[Wood]winds', 'Brass', 'Strings' etc.), most of which are to be read by several performers, as in *Intersection 1*. Feldman's description of the orchestra in notes supplied with the published edition leaves much to the discretion of the conductor and is worth quoting:

---

[78] See, for example, 'Towards a newer Laocoon' [1940], in David Shapiro and Cecile Shapiro (eds.), *Abstract Expressionism: A Critical Record* (Cambridge University Press, 1990), 61–74.

[79] The film – *Jackson Pollock* – was premiered on 14 June 1951.

[80] Feldman remembered meeting Guston '[a] few weeks' after attending the exhibition ('Philip Guston: 1980/the last works' [1981], in Friedman (ed.), *Give My Regards*, 128). The exhibition, titled 'Abstract Painting and Sculpture in America', ran from 24 January to 25 March 1951.

[81] Robert Storr, 'Guston's trace', in Harriet S. Bee (ed.), *Philip Guston in the Collection of the Museum of Modern Art* (New York: Museum of Modern Art, 1992), 10.

[82] 'Liner notes', 4, and 'Captain Cook's first voyage', 218.

[83] Iddon, *John Cage and David Tudor*, 13.

[84] *Intermission 5* (1952) for solo piano also exhibits the same discomfort.

[85] A surviving sketch includes the residue of a typed note that lists fifty-two woodwind and brass instruments (Morton Feldman Collection, Paul Sacher Foundation).

<u>Marginal Intersection</u> requires a large orchestra which also includes piano, xylophone, vibraphone, amplified guitar, 2 oscillators (one for high frequencies, the other for low), a sound-effects recording of riveting, at least 6 percussionists with a large selection of wood, glass, (or less breakable substitutes) and metal objects, (aluminium pots, etc. etc.)

This, then, is the most overtly 'far out' of the published graphs. Even so, it betrays clear signs of outside influence. Some of these were highlighted by Feldman in a 1983 interview, in which he explained that his 'models for percussion at that time were from the Gamelan Orchestra, John Cage's early '40s pieces, and Varèse's work, where the instruments were used en masse, not soloistically'.[86] Cage's influence is evident not only in the use of 'found' percussion instruments, but also in the pervasive presence of the oscillators, which Cage had used previously in *Imaginary Landscape No. 3* (1942).[87] The equally pervasive presence of a sound effects recording of riveting form a possible link with Varèse not mentioned by Feldman. The sound of riveting is redolent of the snare drum rolls, rapidly clicking mechanical ratchets and rattling castanets found in much of Varèse's percussion music.

Feldman's explanatory notes with the published edition of the score do not mention an important detail hinted at by the use of the term 'marginal' and highlighted in many other sources, which is that the oscillators should be set to produce inaudible frequencies.[88] Both of the surviving sketches and an early set of typed notes clearly indicate that the oscillator frequencies are to be set outside the audible range.[89] Moreover, Cage described the work as 'sounds heard between 2 limits: inaudible high + inaudible low! – which are notated but will not be heard', in an early letter to Tudor and in similar terms elsewhere.[90] In an article published in *Kulchur* in 1963, the year after the score was first published, Feldman stated that the oscillators 'cannot be heard, but are "felt"'.[91]

---

[86] 'An interview with Morton Feldman, Jan Williams', 151.

[87] Many of Cage's works from the 1940s involve 'found' percussion instruments. *Third Construction* (1941) and *Imaginary Landscape No. 2 (March No. 1)* (1942) are examples.

[88] The only available recording, included on *Morton Feldman: Composing by Numbers – The Graphic Scores 1950–67*, Mode Records, mode 146, features oscillators producing audible sounds.

[89] Morton Feldman Collection, Paul Sacher Foundation.

[90] Iddon, *John Cage and David Tudor*, 13, and 'Experimental music: doctrine' [1955], in *Silence*, 16.

[91] 'Marginal Intersection (1951), Intersection 2 (1951), Intermission 6 (for one or two pianos)', *Kulchur*, vol. 3, no. 11 (Autumn 1963), 33. This article includes an excerpt from the published edition of the score bearing the copyright date of 1962 (*ibid.*, 34). This excerpt is not reprinted in Friedman (ed.), *Give My Regards*.

One possibility is that Feldman's failure to mention this detail in the published edition was the result of vacillation, but this makes it unclear why he refrained from revising the published edition after regaining faith in his original concept, as evidenced by his comments in *Kulchur*. More probably, the omission from the published edition was another example of accidental oversight. This may appear far-fetched, given the unusual character of the missing details and their evident importance for the resulting sound, but it enables us to explain the absence of a revision, if we assume he remained unaware of his error.

The idea of invoking bodily experiences in the audience went far beyond Cage's previous experiments with oscillators. No doubt Feldman regarded it as a natural extension of his continuing interest in very soft sounds that are barely audible,[92] but it may also have been connected with Varèse's project of expanding the range of audible frequencies available to the composer.[93] As in *Ecuatorial* (1934), this typically focused on the use of high frequencies that lie just below the upper threshold of hearing.[94] Perhaps Feldman's idea was also connected with work recently undertaken by Harold Burris-Meyer, an acoustic engineer who had been experimenting, successfully, with the use of subsonics to stimulate bodily sensations in theatre audiences.[95] In 1951, Varèse and Burris-Meyer were collaborating with one another on the design of a device that would allow the playback of tape recordings at variable speeds.[96]

The opening of *Marginal Intersection* – which consists of several bursts of inaudible, but felt activity from the oscillators, followed by a long sequence of sounds of clinking glass – announces its ultramodern credentials. Thereafter the faster tempo of '128 or thereabouts' ensures a quicker succession of more fleeting sounds than in previous graphs. The ensemble texture varies from dense to thin. In some places its thinness is used to

---

[92] 'Morton Feldman: touch', 143.   [93] Varèse, 'The liberation of sound', 197–8.

[94] Malcolm MacDonald, *Varèse: Astronomer in Sound* (London: Kahn & Averill, 2003), 268–9.

[95] Harold Burris-Meyer, 'Theatrical uses of the remade voice, subsonics and reverberation control', *The Journal of the Acoustical Society of America*, vol. 13, no. 1 (July 1941), 17–18. Elsewhere, Burris-Meyer stated that '[it] has been shown that frequencies beyond the audible range at both ends of the spectrum stimulate measurable psycho-physical reactions that can be effectively employed in music' ('The place of acoustics in the future of music', *The Journal of the Acoustical Society of America*, vol. 19, no. 4, part 1 (July 1947), 534).

[96] Harold Burris-Meyer to John S. Boyers, Magnecord, Inc., 7 May 1951, Edgard Varèse Collection, Paul Sacher Foundation; and Wen-Chung Chou, 'A Varèse chronology', *Perspectives of New Music*, vol. 5, no. 1 (Autumn–Winter 1966), 9. Cage referred to Feldman's use of 'super- and sub-sonic' sounds that are '"felt"' and Burris-Meyer's theatre work in the same sentence in an untitled typescript, dated 1955 ([Untitled, typescript, headed 'Dartmouth Spring '55'], John Cage Papers, Special Collections and Archives, Wesleyan University, 8).

highlight a particular sonority that is placed within an otherwise silent passage and heard as an isolated event, such as a brief splash of sound from the brass (ictuses 208–9), a chord from the piano (ictus 496) or the amplified guitar and piano sounding together (ictuses 582–4). The overtly experimental aspect of the work is reaffirmed in the closing moments in which a blast of ultrasound is played as the sound effects recording is gradually faded out.

Intersection 2 was the first of three published graphs intended for virtuoso performers. It was written for Tudor and dedicated to him, and evidently intended to tax his keyboard skills; years later, Mauricio Kagel described the technical difficulty as 'sadistic'.[97] In its published form, the work is marked by yet another increase in tempo, to 158 ictuses per minute except in the closing stages in which the score specifies even brisker rates. Chords often involve very large numbers of notes – the pianist is sometimes required to depress more than ten keys, sometimes in all three registers, simultaneously – and they often appear in rapid successions.

The density of activity varies considerably, with long stretches of lively and sometimes frenetic activity placed alongside long, quiescent passages peppered with lengthy pauses. The livelier stretches usher in a new sound world in Feldman's graph music, not just because of their occasional ferocity, but also because of their lack of apparent fluidity: the music is almost entirely pointillist in the sense that it is heard as a disjointed series of small units that resist smooth sequential integration, whereas previous graphs include periods of greater fluidity interrupted by lengthy pauses and extended silences.

The more quiescent passages become more prevalent in the closing stages of the work, despite the fact that the tempo increases, initially to 198 ictuses per minute before falling back to 172 and then rising to 178. Consequently, the work as a whole is marked by a gradual – if not smooth – progress from greater to lesser activity.

In all the available recordings, the livelier passages are also marked by a very clear sense of pulse. No doubt this is attributable to the frequent presence of long sequences of sonorities in consecutive ictuses. It also reflects the technical difficulty of playing sonorities consisting of varying quantities of notes in rapid succession; this limits the pianist's ability to deliver a more irregular placement of entrances, meaning that the theoretical possibility afforded by the score of placing sounds anywhere within a time bracket is of limited practical value in these passages. Similar

---

[97] Mauricio Kagel to Morton Feldman, 23 June 1962, Morton Feldman Collection, Paul Sacher Foundation.

comments apply to dynamics, which are theoretically free but not usually low in these passages.

After completing *Intersection 2*, Feldman began working on a new graph – apparently lost – that Cage described in a letter to Tudor as 'an Intersection over an Arty [*sic*] Shaw record'.[98] Cage had first used excerpts from phonograph recordings of the music of other composers in the early 1940s in *Credo in US* (1942) and Feldman was following his friend's example, but Cage's letter reveals that he disliked Feldman's concept ('not "valable"') and indeed Feldman's whole approach at this time ('Poor Morty's life is all mixed up + I'm afraid his present music too [. . .] He always looks for an easy way out').[99] This show of ill humour coincided with the arrival of Earle Brown in New York City and may have been connected with it. Cage and Cunningham met Brown and his wife Carolyn, who would become the leading female dancer in Cunningham's troupe, in April 1951 in Denver, Colorado and the Browns met Feldman while visiting New York shortly before Cage sent his letter.[100] Although it would be another year before they relocated from Denver, this visit should probably be seen as concluding the formation of what is usually referred to as the 'New York School' of composers – Brown, Cage, Feldman and Wolff. His arrival seems to have created tension. Years later, Cage recalled that Feldman was intent on preserving the exclusivity of his relationships with Cage, Tudor and Wolff and 'infuriated' by Cage's attempts to integrate Brown into the group.[101] According to Cage, this disrupted the closeness of the relationships that he, Feldman, Tudor and Wolff had previously enjoyed.[102] Brown strenuously denied this,[103] but Cage's bad tempered comments in his letter to Tudor give his account weight. In all likelihood, Wolff's departure to Harvard University in September to study classics further destabilised the previous state of affairs by diminishing his output of new musical works and his contacts with other members of the group. These tensions seem to have been short-lived, however. In Cage's next letter to Tudor, he reported that 'Morty + I are fine',[104] and it seems to have

---

[98] Iddon, *John Cage and David Tudor*, 28.   [99] *Ibid.*

[100] Brown visited New York City in July or August (Carolyn Brown, *Chance and Circumstance: Twenty Years with Cage and Cunningham* (New York: Alfred A. Knopf, 2007), 9–12). Cage mentioned Brown's visit in the same letter in which he criticised Feldman's music (Iddon, *John Cage and David Tudor*, 28).

[101] 'Anything I say will be misunderstood: an interview with John Cage', by William Duckworth, *Bucknell Review*, vol. 33, no. 2 (1989), 23.

[102] *Ibid.*

[103] 'Earle Brown interview with John Holzaepfel', 23 March 1992, unpublished transcript, Earle Brown Music Foundation.

[104] Iddon, *John Cage and David Tudor*, 30.

been around this time that Cage recopied the scores of *Projection 4* and *Intersection 2*, which he regarded as 'too messy'.[105] Cage's renderings, in his unmistakable handwriting, were the ones chosen by Feldman for publication in the early 1960s.[106]

In December 1951, Cage received a long letter that laid the foundations for Feldman's lifelong hostility towards Boulez, who Cage had befriended in France.[107] Boulez, who had been sent the scores of one or more *Intersections* in the summer of 1951,[108] dismissed them cursorily as '[m]uch too <u>imprecise</u> and too <u>simple</u>' in a letter to Cage in August.[109] However, the December missive included a long and sustained attack that focused on the alleged impossibility of specifying irrational durations in the graph format and culminated in the claim that 'they let themselves go dangerously to the <u>seduction of graphism alone</u>'.[110]

Tudor gave the first performance of *Intersection 2* on 1 January 1952 at the Cherry Lane Theatre, New York City in a programme that also included the first complete performance of Cage's *Music of Changes*,[111] but 1952 was to be a musically unproductive year for Feldman, with only four short conventionally notated works for solo piano known to have been completed.[112] Two statements by him about his graphs were published early in the year, however. One appeared above an excerpt from Cage's rendering of *Projection 4* in an article in the journal *trans/formation*, which also included statements by Boulez, Cage and Wolff.[113] The other statement appeared in a review article by Cowell, which focused on the same four composers, in the 'Current chronicle' section of *The Musical Quarterly*.[114] As well as a short description of Feldman's approach and a compressed version of his *trans/formation* text, this also included an excerpt from the score of an otherwise lost graph, titled

---

[105] Feldman, 'I met Heine on the Rue Fürstemberg', 115

[106] See Examples 3.4 and 3.10 (Chapter 3), Example 4.4 (Chapter 4), Example 5.14 (Chapter 5), Examples 6.5–6.6 and 6.12 (Chapter 6) and Example 9.7 (Chapter 9).

[107] Nattiez (ed.), *The Boulez-Cage Correspondence*, 112–27. For an example of Feldman's hostility, see 'Sound, noise, Varèse, Boulez', 1.

[108] It is not clear if these are among those that survive.

[109] Nattiez (ed.), *The Boulez-Cage Correspondence*, 103, with Boulez's underlining.

[110] *Ibid.*, 116, with Boulez's underlining.

[111] Flyer/programme, Cherry Lane Theatre, 1 January and 10 February 1952.

[112] *Intermissions 4–5, Extensions 3* and *Piano Piece 1952*. A letter refers to unspecified 'troubles' and ill health (Morton Feldman to David Tudor, 15 June 1953, David Tudor Papers, Getty Research Institute).

[113] Feldman *et al.*, '4 musicians at work', 168. The inclusion of an excerpt from Cage's rendering in this article suggests that the recopying exercise took place the previous year, as indicated above. Given that Feldman completed *Intersection 2* in August 1951, it is therefore reasonable to assume that Cage recopied both scores during the period August–December.

[114] 'Current chronicle', *The Musical Quarterly*, vol. 38, no. 1 (January 1952), 123–36.

'Intersection #3', for violin, viola 'or both', woodwinds '(any kind and amount)' and cello, which he seems to have discarded subsequently.[115] These articles and Cage's advocacy must have helped to enhance Feldman's public profile, as did Aaron Copland's reference to the graphs in his Charles Eliot Norton lectures, delivered at Harvard in the academic year 1951–2.[116] Indeed, Feldman's graphs were almost certainly the first graphic scores composed after the Second World War to receive a degree of public exposure.

Marginal Intersection also received its first performance in 1952. This was conducted by David Broekman towards the end of the year, on 9 November, in one of a series of 'Music in the Making' concerts at the Cooper Union for the Advancement of Science and Art, New York City.[117] In an interview, recorded years later, Feldman recalled borrowing 'plastic dishes and those old heavy aluminium pots and pans' from his mother for the performance.[118] The entire series was reviewed in the *International Musician*,[119] which singled out *Marginal Intersection* for special criticism, ridiculing Feldman's use of graph paper, dismissing the work as a 'rather amusing experiment' and implying that it was merely a 'stunt'.[120] Even so, the reviewer did us a great service by quoting some of Feldman's remarks from the stage that night, which Chapter 8 uses in deciphering how, at that time, he envisaged his graphs being performed. The printed programme note lists Feldman's work as 'Marginal Intersection No. 1',[121] as does one of the two surviving sketches. This suggests that at the end of 1952 Feldman

[115] *Ibid.*, 131. Alistair Noble described this excerpt as from an early version of *Intersection 1* (*Composing Ambiguity: The Early Music of Morton Feldman* (Farnham: Ashgate, 2013), 11), but the numbering clearly indicates that it was a more recent work – probably the one that Feldman was composing when he compiled his submission. It seems unlikely that he would have included a discarded sketch of a work completed many months previously for inclusion in such a prestigious publication.

[116] 'Musical imagination in the Americas (1952)' [1952], in Richard Kostelanetz (ed.), *Aaron Copland: A Reader – Selected Writings 1923–1972* (New York: Routledge, 2004), 78.

[117] The date of the concert does not appear in the printed programme, but is given elsewhere ([Unsigned: E], 'Music here this week', *New York Herald Tribune*, 9 November 1952, Section 4, 8). The concert received a cursory review the following day ([Unsigned: F], '"Music in the Making"', *New York Herald Tribune*, 10 November 1952, 13). The 'Music in the Making Concerts' were intended to 'rehearse modern American music in public' so that the audience could 'actively participate in putting together a piece for performance' (David Broekman, 'Music in the making: may make jobs for musicians', *International Musician*, February 1953, 10).

[118] 'An interview with Morton Feldman, Jan Williams', 151.

[119] Peggy Glanville-Hicks, 'Music in the Making at Cooper Union', *International Musician*, March 1953, 13, 35.

[120] *Ibid.*, 35.

[121] Programme, Cooper Union for the Advancement of Science and Art, undated [9 November 1952].

was still expecting to compose another 'Marginal Intersection' for inaudible frequencies.

Meanwhile, Cage continued to work apace, and there are numerous links between his ongoing projects and Feldman's graph notation. For example, a few days after the concert on New Year's Day 1952, referred to above, he rattled off a work on graph paper of his own, adapting elements of Feldman's original idea for somewhat different purposes. This new work – *Imaginary Landscape No. 5*, dated 12 January 1952 – gives directions about playing phonograph records in making a recording on eight monaural tapes and is therefore unlike the graphs that Feldman is known to have completed at this stage in not being intended for live performance.[122] As in Feldman's graphs, the notation of time is proportional, with the horizontal axis in this case indicating the period in which each record plays, but here an eightfold division of the vertical axis is used to specify activity on each tape and dynamics are explicitly notated on a scale of 1–8. Another difference stems from Cage's use of the same chance-based method of selecting materials from charts that he had established in previous works.[123] There is no compelling reason to think that Feldman used similar processes, and although he tended to avoid criticising Cage's approach specifically, he openly opposed all such highly organised methods of composing in his subsequent writings.

Imaginary Landscape No. 5 was the first of two works that Cage composed for his 'Project for Music for Magnetic Tape',[124] which made tape recordings, typically, by cutting and splicing pre-recorded sounds. Cage's second work for the project, *Williams Mix* (1952), composed using a similar method, was also presented on graph paper. As in *Imaginary Landscape No. 5*, the eightfold division of the vertical axis is used in specifying the contents of eight monaural tapes. However, in this case, these are to be assembled by splicing sounds from a sound bank of field and prepared recordings, with a system of coded labels on the graph indicating the types of selections to be used. Once again, the horizontal axis is used in presenting a proportional indication of time, but here it is stretched to such an extent that the score functions as a template – 'like a dress-maker's pattern'[125] – in the cutting and splicing process. This had considerable utility in specifying and discharging a large variety of rather complex cuts, but it also resulted in an uncomfortable expansion in

---

[122] For the brevity of the compositional process, see Cage's comments in Nattiez (ed.), *The Boulez-Cage Correspondence*, 130.

[123] James Pritchett, The Development of Chance Techniques in the Music of John Cage, 1950–1956, unpublished PhD thesis, New York University (1988), 184–5.

[124] Nattiez (ed.), *The Boulez-Cage Correspondence*, 130.   [125] *Ibid.*, 131.

the overall length of the score, for the four minutes and fifteen seconds of this particular work are presented on no less than 192 graph pages.

Water Music, which Cage also composed around this time, is noteworthy for other reasons. The theatrical elements of this work, which is scored for a pianist equipped with a stopwatch, whistles, water, a radio, a wooden stick, a pack of playing cards and 'four objects' suitable for preparing a piano during the course of a performance, have no precedents in Feldman's music. However, Cage's use of a strikingly original notation, which combines conventional staff notation, words and phrases, numbers and graphics and is, in this case, to be made visible to the audience during the course of a performance, can also be seen as part of the causal chain that stretches back to his wild rice dinner party, even though his flamboyant calligraphy differs markedly from the more austere aspect of Feldman's graph notation.

Imaginary Landscape No. 5 and *Williams Mix* are closer in spirit to the *Projections* than those *Intersections* completed by this stage because they specify onsets and durations of the notated materials, but while cutting and splicing the tapes for *Williams Mix*, Cage followed up with another graph in which the treatment of time differentiates it from Feldman's previous efforts. *Music for Carillon (Graph) No. 1* (1952) was the first of Cage's *Music for Carillon* series and the first of many works that he would go on to compose using random methods of drawing points directly onto grids or staves, in this case using a template created by cutting holes in a folded sheet of paper. On this occasion, entrances and relative pitches are specified, but durations and absolute pitches are not. The horizontal axis is used in presenting a proportional indication of time, whereas the vertical axis represents relative pitch. Cage's idea was that this fitted it for use with a carillon of any range, as the performer could simply superpose the compass of his or her instrument and read off implied pitches.[126]

One important difference between this new idea and Feldman's is that Cage intended his score to be used in producing a transcription from which the performer would then play, whereas Feldman's graphs were originally intended for use in performance – an aspect of Feldman's thinking discussed in Chapters 4 and 8. Another is Cage's idea of specifying entrances but not durations, which contrasts with Feldman's alternative approach in the *Intersections* of giving the performer a degree of flexibility in deciding when to enter but specifying where the resulting sound should end. No doubt Cage's strategy was driven by the difficulty of predicting the

---

[126] For further details, see James Pritchett, *The Music of John Cage* (Cambridge University Press, 1993), 92.

duration of a given bell's decay, but it was not fit for Feldman's project in the *Intersections*, which was to diminish the audible sense of pulse that characterised some passages in the *Projections*. Freeing entrances is more effective in blurring the edges of the temporal frame underpinning these works than freeing exits would have been because the attack of a sound – its first, most distinctive and, in some cases, its loudest aspect – is usually its most noticeable feature.[127]

In the same year (i.e. 1952), Cage also completed *Music for Piano 1*, the first work in his *Music for Piano* series. Although these are not presented on graph paper, they deserve mention because they are among the very first works composed by Cage that have indeterminate elements, meaning that they too can be seen as casually related to Feldman's first graphs. Like *Music for Carillon (Graph) No. 1*, the works in this series were composed using random point-drawing methods, but in this case by simply marking any apparent imperfections on the music paper. Pitches are specified, but in each work there are other parameters – details vary – that are not given.

Meanwhile, during this period, Brown was emerging as an integral member of Feldman's circle. Tudor performed Brown's music for the first time, alongside works by Cage, Feldman, Wolff and others, in early 1952, while he was still living in Denver.[128] This was the first of countless occasions on which works by these four men would be presented together, most often by Tudor, and there can be little doubt that this underpinned the perception of them as a 'school'.[129] After relocating to New York City in August, Brown commenced working on Cage's magnetic tape project,[130] and soon after arriving he composed a series of compositions, published as *Folio*, which included several indeterminate works in unusual notations. The best known of these is *December 1952* (1952), which consists of a series of horizontal and vertical lines of various lengths

---

[127] On the importance of its being first, see John A. Sloboda, *The Musical Mind: The Cognitive Psychology of Music* (Oxford: Clarendon Press, 1985), 174. On the distinctiveness of a sound's attack, see Fritz Winckel, *Music, Sound and Sensation: A Modern Exposition* (New York: Dover, 1967), 34. The attacks of sounds from pianos and percussion instruments are their loudest feature, but the intensity of sounds from wind instruments builds up in the first few moments to a plateau level that the performer can choose to maintain.

[128] This performance took place on 10 February 1952 at the Cherry Lane Theatre.

[129] The use of the term 'New York School of composers' has been criticised, not only because it excludes Tudor, but also because it may imply a degree of homogeneity of output that most agree was not present. See, for example, Christian Wolff, 'Experimental music around 1950 and some consequences and causes (social-political and musical)', *American Music*, vol. 27, no. 4 (Winter 2009), 425, 439. Even so, the term captures the fact that their music was often presented at the same concerts and the fact that three of the four (Brown, Cage and Feldman) had personal and/or ideological links with New York School painting.

[130] C. Brown, *Chance and Circumstance*, 6.

and thicknesses on a single page, which the explanatory notes state should be read 'in any direction from any point in the defined space for any length of time and may be performed from any of the four rotational positions in any sequence' by any number of any instruments 'and/or sound-producing media'.[131] This extended the use of indeterminacy in music to such an extent that it is questionable whether it establishes a standard of correctness in performance.[132] As Brown explained subsequently, this was 'the most extreme point I went to. After this there's hardly anything else you can take away from the performer except the page itself'.[133]

The extent to which Feldman's graphs affected this evolution in Brown's music is difficult to establish with any certainty. Brown preferred to portray himself as having been a first mover, inspired primarily by the spontaneity and directness of Pollock's 'drip' paintings and the mutability of Alexander Calder's mobiles, acting independently of both Feldman and Cage,[134] but chronology suggests otherwise. For example, Brown's interests in incorporating elements of indeterminacy, proportionality and graphics in finished musical works seem to have emerged in late 1952, two years after Feldman began working with them and more than a year after his first contacts with Feldman. That said, Brown was an authorised instructor of Schillinger's system and would already have been familiar with the use of similar ideas as tools in the compositional process, and his own testimony suggests that he was applying them prior to his first encounter with Cage.[135] Perhaps what he picked up from Feldman was the idea that these tools could take on greater importance and even be set centre stage.

---

[131] The score is reproduced in many places. See, for example, Paul Griffiths, *Modern Music and After*, 3rd edn (Oxford University Press, 2010), 32.

[132] Brown was adamant that *December 1952* was 'the first truly "graphic" score' ('Notes on some works: 1952–1971', *Contemporary Music Newsletter*, vol. 6, no. 1 (January/February 1972), 1). This suggestion is hard to square with the ordinary use of the term 'graphic', which seems equally applicable to Feldman's graph notation. Brown's view is more credible if the use of the term is restricted to compositions that lack prescriptive content – that is, those that do not establish standards of correctness in performance.

[133] [Untitled, on notational problems], in Carlton Gamer and Barney Childs (eds.), *American Society of University Composers: Proceedings of the Fifth Annual Conference, April 1970* (New York: American Society of University Composers, 1972), 10.

[134] Brown mentioned these extra-musical influences in many of his extant writings. However, on one occasion he added that it was impossible to trace the origin of his inspiration for *December 1952* 'except within the experience of myself in relationship to composers that I met in New York, such as Cage and Feldman and Wolff' ('On December 1952', *American Music*, vol. 26, no. 1 (Spring 2008), 6).

[135] 'Some notes on composing', in Gilbert Chase (ed.), *The American Composer Speaks: A Historical Anthology, 1770–1965* (Baton Rouge: Louisiana State University Press, 1966), 302–3. Brown qualified as an authorised instructor of the Schillinger system in 1950 after studying at the Schillinger House School of Music (Boston) in 1946–50 ('An interview with composer Earle Brown', 292).

On one occasion, Brown explained that in Denver he 'didn't have nerve enough' to present the score of an early string quartet in the rapidly produced line drawing notation on which it is based,[136] and perhaps it was this nerve that he found through Feldman's example.

Feldman's musical productivity greatly improved in 1953, and among the works he completed were two *Intersections* that would prove to be his most technically demanding graphs to perform. The first of these was *Intersection 3* for solo piano, dated April 1953, and, like *Intersection 2*, dedicated to Tudor. This short, but sometimes ferocious work, could be seen as a radically compressed remodelling of its predecessor, in which the livelier passages of *Intersection 2* are stuffed with additional activity and the long, quiescent passages are reduced to brief interludes.[137] In fact, this new work specifies a larger number of notes for the pianist to play in total, despite the fact that the implied duration of a performance at the indicated tempo (a steady 176 ictuses per minute in this case) of 2'20" is only one-quarter of the implied duration of *Intersection 2*.[138] The result is a work characterised by volcanic activity requiring a pyrotechnic display of virtuosity and, as in the livelier passages in *Intersection 2*, an inevitable recourse to clusters. An indication of the degree of difficulty involved is given by the fact that the pianist is required to depress more than ten keys per ictus 141 times and more than twenty keys per ictus on twenty-five occasions. Arguably, however, it is the few moments of relative calm that occasionally appear between periods of furious activity that really stand out once one acclimatises to the listening experience. The most striking of these, which appears early in the second half, between ictuses 242 and 255, features a single middle register note set between the work's two longest pauses.

In June, Feldman wrote to Tudor that he wished to write 'a music like violently boiling water in some monstrous kettle', but, he added, 'I can't seem to get the water hot enough or the kettle large enough to do it. The last INTERSECTION, which I wrote for you [i.e. *Intersection 3*], is just an unrealized hint of what is to come'.[139] Despite Feldman's misgivings, his image of violently boiling water does capture something of the sound of *Intersection 3* in performance, with all the available recordings creating a general impression of furiously agitated activity. Nevertheless, this activity is not turbulent, like boiling water. As in the livelier passages of *Intersection 2*, the tempo is so fast and the density of notes so high that the

[136] [Untitled, on notational problems], 12–13.
[137] Having said that, there does not appear to be any formal link between the two works.
[138] A total of 3,254 notes are specified in *Intersection 3* versus 3,145 in *Intersection 2*.
[139] Morton Feldman to David Tudor, 15 June 1953.

performer's flexibility in placing sounds within consecutive time brackets is of limited practical value. This produces a rhythmically organised result, with much of the music marked by a clear sense of uniform pulse.

Intersection 4, dated 22 November 1953, is another work for a virtuoso performer; in this case a cellist. Tempo is given as 80 ictuses per minute, less than half that of the immediately preceding graph, but even so, there are many places in which this score also makes extreme demands. The principal difficulty stems from the fact that it regularly specifies large numbers of notes that are to be played 'simultaneously (if possible)'. The fact that the score specifies three or more sounds in a single ictus on thirty-five occasions indicates the enormity of the challenge, which is heightened by the fact that the playing method is always specified, and is most commonly pizzicato. In the most extreme case, at ictus 131, no less than thirteen pizzicato sounds – three in the high register and ten in the low register – are specified. The conditional form of Feldman's instruction about simultaneity mitigates the immediate difficulty, and when called upon is bound to diminish any perception of pulse. However, it also creates its own challenge, which is how to play the specified number of sounds in some other way within the indicated span, either consecutively or in consecutive groups.

Another notable aspect of this particular work in performance is the very frequent interpolation of lengthy pauses. These give it a 'stop–start' feel, with activity presented in discrete bursts, and the overall impression is of each burst being presented as an object for individual inspection. These bursts are typically short, but they are generally longer and more complex around the boundaries between the first and second quarters and between the third and fourth quarters.

During the course of 1953, Feldman also completed two atypical graphs that proved to be his most radical surviving explorations of indeterminacy, neither of which were published in his lifetime. The one-page score of *Intersection+*, dated spring 1953, is presented on graph paper, but the extremely unusual organisation of the musical material on the page differentiates it from every other work in Feldman's graph series. For example, it is immediately apparent that the horizontal axis is not being used to refer to units of regular pulse. Interpreting the notation is hindered by the fact that no explanatory notes survive, but Tudor recalled it allowing the performer to 'go from any box to any other'.[140] This was also a feature of *December 1952*, which seems to indicate that Brown's amplifications of Feldman's

[140] 'From piano to electronics', interview by Victor Schonfield, *Music and Musicians*, vol. 20, no. 12 (August 1972), 25.

original ideas were now exerting an influence on Feldman's own think-ing.[141] Brown's thoughts on mobility would crystallise at around this time in his *Twenty-Five Pages* (1953). The score consists of twenty-five unbound pages to be performed in any order or inversion by one to twenty-five pianos, but even so the composer's control of the resulting sound in performance is much more clearly in evidence here than in *December 1952*.

Intersection for Magnetic Tape, the second atypical graph that Feldman completed in 1953, was composed for Cage's magnetic tape project, and it seems to have superseded an abandoned 'Marginal Intersection #2', which had also been intended for magnetic tape. A skeletal outline of the opening of the latter includes an empty grid flanked above and below by frames labelled for inaudible high and inaudible low frequencies,[142] but *Intersection for Magnetic Tape* makes no use of these. The one-page score has many unusual aspects, and a set of explanatory notes has survived in this case, as has a recording of the master tapes subsequently spliced by Cage and Brown. Once again, the horizontal axis of the graph is not used in the standard manner; nor is it used as in *Intersection+*. Perhaps the most striking aspect of the work is the extreme demands it places on the splicer. This is because many columns in the score individually specify splicing hundreds or even thousands of tiny slithers of tape. One of these instructs the splicers to cut and paste 19,800 sounds into 43″ sections on five monaural tapes, for example, and the implied density of spliced sounds per inch is much higher than this in other places.

In a liner note with an LP record issued in 1962, Feldman summarised his debt to Cage as follows: '[q]uite frankly, I sometimes wonder how my music would have turned out if John had not given me those early permissions to have confidence in my instincts'.[143] The many points of contact between their works and ideas outlined in this chapter, and else-where in this volume, demonstrate that a much more direct and symbiotic influence operated between them during the early years of their friendship than this account would suggest. Probably, Feldman's version was meant to address lingering perceptions of him as Cage's 'pupil' or 'disciple'.[144] These

---

[141] Noble has argued that *Intermission 6* for one or two pianos, Feldman's only other mobile work, which is usually dated 6 December 1953, may have been sketched on 6 December 1952, in which case his first use of mobility was contemporary with Brown's (*Composing Ambiguity*, 111–13).

[142] Morton Feldman Collection, Paul Sacher Foundation.   [143] 'Liner notes', 5.

[144] For 'pupil', see Cornelius Cardew, 'The American School of John Cage', in Edwin Prévost (ed.), *Cornelius Cardew: A Reader* (Matching Tye: Copula, 2006), 39, and Virgil Thomson, 'Rockwell, John: a conversation with Virgil Thomson' [1977], in *A Virgil Thomson Reader* (Boston: Houghton Mifflin, 1981), 535. For 'disciple', see Fred Grunfeld, 'Cage without bars', *Saturday Review*, vol. 20, no. 3 (4 February 1960), 35, and Nicolas Slonimsky, 'Chamber music

were wide of the mark, but his alternative history was a convenient, but misleading oversimplification. No doubt their enthusiasm for each other's projects did play an important part in encouraging their individual efforts, but it should by now be clear they also affected one another more directly, not by formal prompting, as between teacher and student, or by slavish imitation, as between master and disciple, but by mutual inspiration through reciprocal example.

in America (1963)' [1963] in Electra Slonimsky Yourke (ed.), *Nicolas Slonimsky: Writings on Music, Volume 4* (New York: Routledge, 2005), 40.

2 Later graphs, 1958–1967

Temporary break with graph music

For almost five years after completing the *Intersections*, Feldman avoided graph notation, focusing his efforts initially on more conventionally notated works and then on indeterminate works in which pitches are precisely notated, but durations are not given. This hiatus was unlike the intervals between other graphs in the series, not only because it was longer, but also because Feldman attributed it to a temporary loss of faith in the format. In 1962, he explained that he 'abandoned' graph music in this period:

> After several years of writing graph music I began to discover its most important flaw. I was not only allowing the sounds to be free – I was also liberating the performer. I had never thought of the graph as an art of improvisation, but more as a totally abstract sonic adventure. This realization was important because I now understood that if the performers sounded bad it was less because of their lapses of taste than because I was still involved with passages and continuity that allowed their presence to be felt.[1]

Evidently, Feldman disliked the choices that some performers were making. He gave a colourful description of the kind of problem he had experienced in a lecture delivered in the winter of 1963–4:

> [U]nfortunately, one of the situations that happened [. . .] is that we began to hear the instrumentalists making my particular composition. The reason that was happening is because even though in my own mind I was hearing sound very abstractly, every time – for example, one particular piece where it's most obvious – every time the xylophone would have, say, four seconds for a solo situation in which, even though I would give him the amount of sounds to play in that particular situation, even though I would tell him how

---

[1] 'Liner notes', 6. For a similar statement, see '*Soundpieces* interview', 91. In a lecture delivered in 1972, Feldman stressed his concerns about the role of pulse in the *Intersections*, but it seems unlikely that this was the principal reason why he changed course in 1953–4 given that he initially refocused on producing conventionally notated works that – the same lecture makes clear – he tended to see as beset by a similar problem. See 'Morton Feldman Slee Lecture, November 20, 1972: Baird Hall, University at Buffalo, The State University of New York', http://library.buffalo.edu/music/special-materials/morton-feldman/mfslee315.html (accessed 24 June 2015).

to play it, what he actually played was of such a horrendous nature that I realized that there was something wrong.[2]

Feldman did not say which work was being performed, but it is clear from the context in which he spoke that his remarks concern an early graph, which means that it must have been *Marginal Intersection*.[3] Nor did he say what made the xylophone sound so 'horrendous', but his comments elsewhere indicate an intense dislike for what he regarded as formulaic choices, reflecting conditioned responses or remembered sequences, and it may have been an issue of this type – the playing of scales or familiar combinations, for example – that spoiled the performance for him.

It is not entirely clear, from Feldman's description, whether the xylophonist intended to sabotage the performance. However, in 1963, Feldman described a different case in which, plainly, sabotage was intended:

> I would designate a certain amount of notes to play in the graph things, and I would hear 'Yankee Doodle' coming out of the horn section. The players decide together, before the concert, actually to sabotage it – and they decided in this particular section they were going to play 'Yankee Doodle,' with the amount of notes called for and in the register in the score.[4]

Once again, Feldman did not identify the work being performed, but in this case it was probably *Intersection 1* or *Marginal Intersection*.[5]

Another problem emerged with *Intersection for Magnetic Tape*. Unfortunately, Feldman disliked the tapes that Cage and Brown produced with it in early 1954. Brown remembered that Feldman 'rejected' the 'piece',[6] but there can be little doubt that he rejected their efforts, not his own. Many years later, he explained that he withheld publication of the score because he believed others would 'make it sound more interesting

---

[2] 'Morton Feldman with Dore Ashton – place, date not given', unpublished transcript, Oral History of American Music, Yale University Library, 8.

[3] *Marginal Intersection, Atlantis* and *...Out of 'Last Pieces'* utilise xylophones and were all composed and performed before Feldman made these remarks. However, Feldman's comments in other parts of the same lecture indicate that he was speaking of one of his earlier graphs – that is, *Marginal Intersection*.

[4] 'Around Morton Feldman: interview by Robert Ashley, New York City, March 1963', unpublished transcript, Morton Feldman Collection, Paul Sacher Foundation, 14. Wolff's recollections are similar. See 'In a kind of no-man's land. Conversation with Cole Gagne' [1993], in Gisela Gronemeyer and Reinhard Oehlschlägel (eds.), *Christian Wolff: Cues: Writings and Conversations* (Colgne: MusikTexte, 1998), 254, and 'A chance encounter with Christian Wolff', interview by Frank J. Oteri, www.newmusicbox.org/articles/a-chance-encounter-with-christian-wolff/ (accessed 24 June 2015).

[5] Wolff has suggested that it was *Intersection 1*. Christian Wolff to David Cline, 29 November 2010 (email).

[6] 'An interview with composer Earle Brown', 295.

than the piece should sound',[7] which indicates that the perceived problem was in the act of realisation.

Feldman's attitude must have accentuated the impact of a quarrel between him and Brown over the use of mathematics in composing that also occurred around this time. Feldman, it seems, was so offended that he began to give Brown the cold shoulder, a situation that would persist for several years;[8] this also placed new stress on his relationship with Cage. Initially, Feldman's position was that he did not want the tapes played in public, and this must have upset his friends, who had certainly invested a great deal of time and effort in producing them.[9]

Tudor gave the first performance of *Intersection 3* on 28 April 1954 at Carl Fischer Concert Hall, New York City,[10] but a few months later, in August, he and Cage moved to Stony Point to join a nascent community of artists in the countryside north of New York, while Feldman and Brown stayed in town.[11] Wolff remained at Harvard until he graduated in the spring of 1955, before leaving for Florence on a Fulbright scholarship.[12] In the following year, Brown began working as an editor and recording engineer at Capitol Records, which, he later recalled, left him little time to compose,[13] although he would regularly decamp to Europe in order to immerse himself in its thriving new music scene. These changes further disrupted the chains of mutual inspiration, encouragement and support that had previously operated between members of the group, and it is doubtful whether it is useful to think of them as a group – let alone a 'school' – from this point onwards.

---

[7] *'Soundpieces* interview', 87.

[8] See, for example, Earle Brown, 'An interview with Earle Brown', by Amy C. Beal, *Contemporary Music Review*, vol. 26, nos. 3/4 (June/August 2007), 350, and Christian Wolff, 'Cage and beyond: an annotated interview with Christian Wolff', by David Patterson, *Perspectives of New Music*, vol. 32, no. 2 (Summer 1994), 72. Renée Levine Packer described this aspect of Feldman's character in *This Life of Sounds: Evenings for New Music in Buffalo* (New York: Oxford University Press, 2010), 142.

[9] Cage wrote: '[i]t has been a great source of sorrow to me to lose your friendship' (John Cage to Morton Feldman, 15 March 1954, Morton Feldman Collection, Paul Sacher Foundation). Feldman replied that the tapes should be played 'only at concerts made financially possible by Williams [who financed Project for Music for Magnetic Tape]' because '[t]here is definitely an obligation due to him in this matter' (Morton Feldman to John Cage, 18 March 1954, John Cage Collection, Northwestern University Music Library).

[10] Programme, Carl Fischer Concert Hall, 28 April 1954.

[11] C. Brown, *Chance and Circumstance*, 105–6.

[12] Michael Hicks and Christian Asplund, *Christian Wolff* (Urbana: University of Illinois Press, 2012), 21.

[13] '"Selbsportrait" for Donaueschingen, 1965', unpublished typescript circa 1965, Earle Brown Music Foundation, 6.

Return to graph music

By 1957, Feldman had been working exclusively in conventional notation for more than two years, producing works predominantly for solo piano or small ensembles.[14] However, it was then that he began developing methods of giving indeterminate guidance about the durations of sounds with precisely specified pitches, initially in *Piece for Four Pianos, Piano (Three Hands)* and then *Two Pianos*. In 1972, he explained that the 'problem' with precisely notated music was that:

> the rhythmic placement of my sounds never seemed just right. It was years later that I realised that it was [...] this aspect of trying to set something into a steady pulse which seemed so contradictory to the music I was writing. [...] Whatever ideas developed happened after a concert of the precisely written two-piano piece I wrote for David Tudor and John Cage. [...] The pianos were pretty bad. During the run-through before the concert, it was decided to ignore some of the strict rhythms and just cue in each other instead. When I got back to New York, I began to compose sounds independent of its [*sic*] rhythmic progression, remembering a distorted performance that in actuality did nothing to take away from the nature of the music.[15]

This was the second time that Feldman's dissatisfaction with the use of a regular pulse prompted a change in direction in his music. In 1951, it had been a factor driving the transition from the *Projections* to the *Intersections* and now, in 1957, it occasioned him to change his approach once again. In all likelihood, his reservations still centred on the insensitivity of a regular pulse to nuances of actual sounds in performance; he continued to see it as an imposed frame within which sounds were forced to fit. The *Intersections* addressed this concern only partially, by giving the performer some flexibility in choosing when to enter, but the works with fixed pitches and indeterminate durations went further by giving performers much greater control of rhythm.

These new works are notated in various modified forms of staff notation, usually without bar lines or time signatures, although later variants do include more conventionally notated passages in which these are present. Pitches are specified in the normal way, but note heads are typically presented without tails, except in more conventionally notated inserts where these are present. Dynamics are invariably low, and although indicative guidance about tempo is given, the performer is always accorded greater-than-normal latitude in deciding upon durations and sometimes

---

[14] These include *Piano Piece 1956 A* (1956), *Piano Piece 1956 B* (1956), *Three Pieces for String Quartet* (1956) and *Two Pieces for Six Instruments* (1956).

[15] 'Morton Feldman Slee Lecture'. The precisely notated work referred to is *Two Pieces for Two Pianos* (1954).

spacing.[16] In *Piece for Four Pianos* and *Two Pianos*, the performers read from identical parts, but, normally, this is not the case.

Despite his previous reservations, Feldman recommenced composing graph music in 1958, and it is distinctly possible that growing interest in indeterminacy and graphic notations within his circle and elsewhere played a part in his change of heart. In 1957, for example, Varèse acquired a 'sudden interest' in jazz,[17] composing an untitled graphic score that was performed by jazz musicians in jam sessions attended by Brown and Cage.[18] Meanwhile Wolff, who had experimented briefly with indeterminacy in 1950, returned to it decisively in 1957, the year after he returned to Harvard to commence postgraduate studies, with *Sonata for three pianos* and *Duo for Pianists (I)*; both require the performers to decide which selections from given material they play during specified time brackets. The former was premiered in New York City in April, and this was followed by the premiere of the latter at Harvard in December.[19] Soon after, Wolff composed *Duo for Pianists (II)*, a work constructed upon broadly similar lines, except that in this case, the form is open and the order in which the sections are to be played is determined for each performer by unpredictable elements of the other pianist's playing. This idea – of using cueing procedures to guide the course of a performance – would colour his music from then on.

Cage's interest in indeterminacy and graphic notations also intensified around this time. He had already experimented with novel presentations and indeterminate elements in *Water Music*, his *Music for Carillon* and *Music for Piano* series, and in an open-ended work that he began composing in 1953 that consists of self-contained compositions that are played independently or together with one another in any combination.[20] However, his experiments became more radical in 1957, when he composed *Winter Music* and started working on *Concert for Piano and Orchestra*, the solo piano part of which is a large compendium of graphic notations that includes a variant on Feldman's graph format.[21] This process of radicalisation would

---

[16] For detailed discussions of Feldman's various notations for fixed pitches and indeterminate durations, see Keith Potter, An Introduction to the Music of Morton Feldman, unpublished MA thesis, University of Wales (1973), 34–59, and Boutwell, '"The breathing of sound itself"', 537–44, 548–57.

[17] Olivia Mattis, 'From bebop to poo-wip: jazz influences in Varèse's *Poème électronique*', in Meyer and Zimmermann (eds.), *Edgard Varèse*, 309.

[18] *Ibid.*, 312. The score is reproduced as 'cat. 194' (*ibid.*, 316).

[19] Stephen Chase and Philip Thomas, *Changing the System: The Music of Christian Wolff* (Farnham: Ashgate, 2010), 220.

[20] The individual compositions are known as 'time-length' pieces because their titles (e.g. *59½" for a String Player*) refer to their approximate duration in performance.

[21] This is labelled 'AY' and described by Cage in the accompanying notes as 'graph music'.

culminate in a new model of composition that abstained from producing finished scores and which focused instead on delimiting processes that could be used in producing them in disciplined ways. The first work of this new type – *Fontana Mix* – was composed immediately after he gave his celebrated lectures, titled 'Composition as process', at the Darmstadt International Summer Course for New Music in September 1958. His second lecture, which highlighted the term 'indeterminacy' and applied it to several musical works, including *Intersection 3*,[22] cemented its presence in the vocabulary of Western classical music.[23]

International interest in indeterminacy and graphic notations was also emerging at this time, and it seems likely that Tudor's first visits to Europe in 1954 and 1956 played a decisive role in this phenomenon. Tudor toured Europe with Cage in the last three months of 1954, during which he played a number of indeterminate works, including Cage's *Music for Piano 4–19* (1953), Brown's *Four Systems* (1954), which had been hastily composed for him on a sheet of cardboard as a last-minute birthday gift, and *Intersection 3*. Tudor returned to Europe twice in 1956, attending the Darmstadt International Summer Course for New Music with Wolpe in July, where he performed, gave workshops and participated in a variety of other events, before returning to Germany to commence a month-long Europe-wide tour in November. Like its predecessor, this tour included works by all four New York School composers, but on this occasion alongside works by several Europeans. Once again, *Intersection 3* and *Four Systems* were among the works he played.

No doubt Brown's physical presence also had an impact; he made his first trip to Europe in late 1956 and early 1957, during which he renewed his acquaintance with Boulez and Luciano Berio, both of whom he had previously encountered in New York City. He also met with other leading figures in the European new music scene, including Bruno Maderna and Karlheinz Stockhausen.[24]

Boulez was, by this time, already familiar with Feldman's graph notation, which he had first encountered in 1951, and with some of Brown's *Folio* works, which he saw on paper (and apparently disliked) on his first visit to the United States in late 1952.[25] However, Stockhausen, another prime mover in new music circles during the 1950s and 1960s,

---

[22] 'Composition as process: II. Indeterminacy', 36.

[23] For the origins and effects of this lecture, see Rebecca Y. Kim, In No Uncertain Musical Terms: The Cultural Politics of John Cage's Indeterminacy, unpublished PhD thesis, Columbia University (2008), 128–207.

[24] C. Brown, *Chance and Circumstance*, 166.

[25] *Ibid.*, 42; Earle Brown to David Tudor, 9 February 1977, David Tudor Papers, Getty Research Institute; E. Brown, 'An interview with Earle Brown', 341; and Pierre Boulez, '…"ouvert", encore…', *Contemporary Music Review*, vol. 26, nos. 3/4 (June/August 2007), 339.

seems to have become aware of them through Tudor's visits. Tudor spent several days with him during his 1954 tour, playing him several works, among them *Intersection 3*,[26] and the pianist recalled that they discussed *Intersection+* during one of his 1956 visits.[27]

Later that year, European interest in indeterminacy began to surface in the concert hall. Boulez conducted a performance of a recently revised version of Stockhausen's *Zeitmasse*, which now included indications of tempo that sometimes depend on the playing abilities of the ensemble, in Paris in December 1956,[28] and premiere performances of other indeterminate works from Europe would soon follow. For example, Tudor played Stockhausen's *Klavierstück XI* (1956) at Carl Fischer Hall in New York City in April 1957 and Boulez performed his own *Troisième Sonate* (1957) at the Darmstadt International Summer Course for New Music a few months later, in September.[29]

Although Feldman had previously 'abandoned' graph music, working with it had given him considerable experience in a newly fashionable area and a distinctive notation of his own to work with, and it is easy to imagine that he would have seen returning to it at this time as a desirable career move.[30] However, for reasons about to become clear, there was, in addition, a more specific need for a change in his orientation at this juncture.

Ixion and *Atlantis*

A more pressing reason for Feldman's change of heart was a request from Cunningham for a composition to accompany a new dance, to be unveiled at the Eleventh American Dance Festival held at Connecticut College, New London, Connecticut in August 1958. This dance, which is now known as *Summerspace*, has come to be regarded as one of Cunningham's 'signature' works.[31]

---

[26] Amy Beal, *New Music, New Allies: American Experimental Music in West Germany from the Zero Hour to Reunification* (Berkeley: University of California Press, 2006), 72.

[27] 'From piano to electronics', 25; 'David Tudor: interview with Peter Dickinson, Ibis Hotel, London, July 26, 1987', in Peter Dickinson, *CageTalk: Dialogues with and about John Cage* (University of Rochester Press, 2006), 86; and his comments reported in Joan Peyser, *Boulez: Composer, Conductor, Enigma* (London: Cassell, 1977), 124.

[28] Michael Kurtz, *Stockhausen: A Biography*, trans. Richard Toop (London: Faber and Faber, 1992), 86.

[29] Tudor and Boulez promoted these works aggressively in the ensuing months. See Paul van Emmerik, 'A John Cage compendium', www.xs4all.nl/~cagecomp/1912-1971.htm (accessed 24 June 2015), and Peter O'Hagan, '"Trope" by Pierre Boulez', *Mitteilungen der Paul Sacher Stiftung*, no. 11 (April 1998), 29.

[30] Brown described this side of Feldman's character in 'An interview with Earle Brown', 354.

[31] For Cunningham's request, see the explanatory notes with the published edition of Feldman's score. For *Summerspace* as a 'signature' work, see David Vaughan, *Merce Cunningham: Fifty Years* (New York: Aperture, 1997), 112.

Cunningham mentioned his initial conception of the dance and Feldman's involvement in the project to Robert Rauschenberg, who Feldman first met in 1953 and who had been designing costumes and sets specifically for use with Cunningham's dances since 1954:

> I'm trying to get two pieces done for this-here Festival. [. . .] one [i.e. *Summerspace*] with new work, a new intersection for orchestra by Morty. about 15 minutes long, seems to be doing with people and velocities, at least a hell of a lot of it is on the fast side, four girls and remy and myself, i have the feeling it's like looking at part of an enormous landscape and you can only see the action in this particular portion of it. i hope it's dazzling rather than willy-nilly.[32]

Perhaps it was Cunningham's comment that 'it's like looking at part of an enormous landscape' in which 'you can only see the action in this particular portion of it' that gave Rauschenberg the idea of using an allover scheme that he hoped would camouflage the dancers when they stopped moving, and which eventually led him to select the same pointillist-like design, consisting of a dense array of luminous dots of various colours on a neutral background, for the costumes and set (Figure 2.1).[33] In Rauschenberg's words: 'I wanted to work with the dancers and the movement as camouflage [. . .] As they moved you could see them, but if they stopped you couldn't'.[34]

Feldman worked independently of Cunningham, consistent with the Cage/Cunningham aesthetic of combining music and dance that have the same duration, and, in some cases, but not here, the same time structure, but which are otherwise unrelated.[35] However, in an interview conducted in 1976, he explained that he learned of Rauschenberg's intended approach

---

[32] Merce Cunningham to Robert Rauschenberg, 12 July 1958, in Merce Cunningham, *Changes: Notes on Choreography*, ed. Frances Starr (New York: Something Else Press, 1968) [n.p.], with Cunningham's punctuation. The other dance mentioned by Cunningham is *Antic Meet*. 'remy' refers to Remy Charlip.

[33] For more photographs of Rauschenberg's costumes, see Vaughan, *Merce Cunningham*, 109–11.

[34] Reported in Robert Tracy, 'a Summerspace for Merce', *Dance Magazine*, July 1999, 56. According to David Vaughan, 'the dancers did not in fact quite "blend" with the backcloth' (*Merce Cunningham*, 110). Michelle Potter has suggested that Rauschenberg's choice of the same design for costumes and set also served to 'activate' the backdrop: 'whenever a dancer moved, the backcloth was set in motion; whenever he or she paused, its movement was arrested' ('"A license to do anything": Robert Rauschenberg and the Merce Cunningham Dance Company', *Dance Chronicle*, vol. 16, no. 1 (1993), 9).

[35] Cunningham's *Second Hand* was a notable exception to this general rule, being designed to follow the phraseology of Cage's *Cheap Imitation* (1969). For representative statements of the Cage/Cunningham aesthetic, see Merce Cunningham, 'Space, time and dance (1952)' [1952] in Richard Kostelanetz (ed.), *Merce Cunningham: Dancing in Space and Time* (London: Dance Books, 1992), 39, and John Cage, 'Four statements on the dance: in this day. . .' [1957], in *Silence*, 94–5.

Figure 2.1 Cunningham's company with Rauschenberg's costumes and backdrop for *Summerspace*, circa 1959–61. Dancers (left to right) are: Viola Farber, Judith Dunn, Remy Charlip, Carolyn Brown and Marilyn Wood.

and decided to 'melt into the decor'.[36] His idea was to mirror Rauschenberg's design by producing a 'score' that is 'pointillistic',[37] a term that he would also use, subsequently, to describe the intended

---

[36] '*Studio International* interview, Fred Orton and Gavin Bryars, 27 May 1976' [1976], in Villars (ed.), *Morton Feldman Says*, 65.
[37] *Ibid.*

acoustic effect.[38] The slowly unfolding lines of most of his works with fixed pitches and indeterminate durations, which overlap one another in unpredictable ways, were patently unsuited to producing this type of sound, which may have been a reason why he turned instead to graph music.

The work that Feldman went on to compose was *Ixion* for a chamber ensemble of 13–19 instruments,[39] dated August 1958, his first graph since the end of 1953. Cunningham's comment in his letter to Rauschenberg that the dance would be 'about 15 minutes long' suggests another reason why Feldman may have felt that music with fixed pitches and indeterminate durations would be poorly suited to this project. These works are inherently of variable length; consequently, they cannot be tailored to fit a defined time span, meaning that it would have been necessary to curtail a performance artificially to ensure it ended with the dance. This left him to choose between conventional notation, in which 'the rhythmic placement of my sounds never seemed just right',[40] and graph notation, which he seems to have regarded as rhythmically imperfect, but preferable, at this time.

Although Cunningham described it as an 'intersection', the graph that Feldman went on to compose differs markedly from its immediate predecessors, and not only in its renunciation of entirely free dynamics; in this case, they are 'low, with an occasional loud sound freely chosen by the performer'. For example, Feldman's method of achieving the desired 'pointillistic' effect was to alter the meaning previously ascribed to number symbols, a move that would have important repercussions on the sound of all his subsequent graphs. In the *Projections* and *Intersections*, numbers indicate the quantity of sounds to be produced simultaneously. However, in his new graph, Feldman used them to indicate the quantity of sounds to be produced consecutively, permitting him to specify more than one sound per instrument in a single ictus. This facilitated a proliferation of shorter sounds within individual units of pulse and the presentation of arrays of musical dots that had an evident affinity with Rauschenberg's arrays of luminous dabs of paint. This proliferation was instrumental in producing a noticeably different sound, which possesses a much stronger sense of forward flow than in the graphs that pre-dated the temporary break with graph music,[41] and this makes Feldman's description of it as

---

[38] 'Neither European nor American. Conversation with Konrad Boehmer, 2 July 1987', in Mörchen (ed.), *Morton Feldman in Middelburg*, 642.

[39] Three flutes, clarinet, horn, trumpet, trombone, piano, 3–7 cellos and 2–4 double basses.

[40] 'Morton Feldman Slee Lecture'.

[41] Ironically, it also reduced the performer's scope to adjust rhythmic aspects of a performance in response to nuances of the sounds emerging.

'pointillistic' – a term usually reserved for highly disjointed music that resists smooth sequential integration – idiosyncratic.

Another important innovation was Feldman's use of generic register guidance. Instead of specifying the register of each sound individually, as he had tended to previously, he specified that all sounds be played in high registers, except in a brief section close to the middle of the work, marked with labels, where only low registers are to be used. The resulting preponderance of high, bright sounds gives the forward flow a sparkling aspect that mirrors the bright, luminous colours of Rauschenberg's paint.

Perhaps it was this noticeably different sound that led Feldman to describe *Ixion* as 'not a characteristic score of mine'.[42] Be that as it may, numbers tended to be used in the same way in subsequent graphs. This means that the new sound colours much of his subsequent graph music, and although these works are not overtly linked with one another by sharing the same name, there are sufficient affinities between them to warrant regarding them as a single group – the *later* graphs – even though this chapter subdivides them into two consecutive subsets. This subdivision reflects a possible difference in ancestry outlined in Chapter 7.

Two aspects of *Ixion* merit highlighting at this stage. One is a puzzle about tempo, with the notes that accompany the published edition of the score stating that each box is 'equal to MM [*sic*] or thereabouts'. It seems likely that the apparently incomplete state of this remark was connected with the indeterminate duration of *Summerspace*, but the nature of the connection and the reason why Feldman would have expressed himself in this unusual way are initially unclear. The other aspect that merits attention is the abundance of large-scale structure; indeed, this is, arguably, the most overtly structured of any of his graph works.[43] Structural elements include: a low register intermission, situated close to the centre of the composition, which divides it into three sections; long repeated or near-repeated passages; three rectangular areas of the grid, of increasing length that all feature the number '1' in every cell; and a concluding climax in which the density of sounds rises steeply to a peak far above levels found elsewhere.

Ixion was premiered with *Summerspace* on 17 August 1958 during the Eleventh American Dance Festival by an ensemble conducted by Cage, with Tudor at the piano.[44] Music rehearsals had not proceeded smoothly. In interviews, Earle Brown remembered Feldman interrupting proceedings

---

[42] 'Studio International interview', 65.

[43] *Pace* Feldman's assessment in 'Neither European nor American', 642.

[44] Programme, Eleventh American Dance Festival, Frank Loomis Palmer Auditorium, Connecticut College, 17 August 1958.

and criticising a performer for playing pitches that he disliked, even though they were consistent with the notation,[45] and eventually Cage felt forced to prepare part-books in a quasi-conventional notation because the musicians 'didn't have the time or inclination' to learn to play from Feldman's graph.[46] As will become clear, this would have lasting repercussions on the way in which Feldman's late ensemble graph music would be presented to performers.

Dance, decor and music were brought together for the first time only in the final dress rehearsal, consistent with Cunningham's normal practice.[47] Inevitably, this resulted in occasional, unforeseen coincidences between music and dance that were a characteristic feature of his output.[48] Cunningham's enjoyment of these is evident in a letter to Feldman written soon after the premiere in which he observed that '[t]here was one incredible sound out of the trumpet that came just after a soft passage of David's that hit right at the peak of one of my movements and it was like being carried along by the wind'.[49] *Dance News* did not share his enthusiasm, however, with its reviewer noting the pointillist decor and costumes but describing the work as 'otherwise pointless'.[50] She also registered an apparent mismatch between the 'general air of sunniness' of the dance and the title of Feldman's score,[51] which appears to refer to the mythological king of Thessaly, whose rather sordid life story ends with his being bound to a perpetually revolving wheel in Hades. The episode that seems to have appealed to Feldman was connected in his mind with a growing distrust of classifying artistic achievements – of giving them a name – and was described by him as follows:

> Do you know that marvelous myth of Ixion? [. . .] Where this man has a very beautiful horse and he didn't want anybody to steal it [. . .] So he decided that he wasn't going to give it a name. Zeus saw the horse and stole it. So Ixion ran all over the place, looking for the horse, but he couldn't call it; you see, it had no name.[52]

---

[45] 'Earle Brown interview with Douglas Cohen', 24 May 1983, unpublished transcript, Earle Brown Music Foundation.

[46] Cage and Feldman, *Radio Happenings*, 181.

[47] Feldman, 'Neither European nor American', 644.

[48] For examples in other dances, see Stephanie Jordan, 'Freedom from the music: Cage, Cunningham and collaborators', *Contact*, no. 20 (Autumn 1979), 18; C. Brown, *Chance and Circumstance*, 99; and Christian Wolff, [Untitled, liner notes], *Music for Merce 1952–2009*, New World Records, 80712–2, 101.

[49] Merce Cunningham to Morton Feldman, postmarked 25 August 1958, Morton Feldman Papers, Music Library, State University of New York at Buffalo.

[50] P. W. Manchester, 'Dance in review', *Dance News*, vol. 33, no. 1 (September 1958), 16.

[51] *Ibid.*

[52] Cage and Feldman, *Radio Happenings*, 177. His mistrust of classification is evident in 'Neither/ nor' [1969], in Friedman (ed.), *Give My Regards*, 80–1. In a subsequent article, he suggested that

For Feldman, this was the start of a period of renewed interest in producing graph music, but graphs would never again dominate his output, as they had done in 1951. The majority of his published works from the next decade utilise his notations for fixed pitches with indeterminate durations, with graph music being the principal alternative notational format, except in 1959 in which he produced only one work of each of these types. That said, he remained unsatisfied with his ongoing efforts in conventional notation and would publish only one of several conventionally notated works that he completed in this period – namely, *Structures* (1962) for orchestra.[53] In this respect, the first LP release of his music in 1959 gives a somewhat distorted view of his published output from this period. Alongside recordings of two graphs (*Projection 4* and *Intersection 3*) and one work with fixed pitches and indeterminate durations (*Piece for Four Pianos*), it also included recordings of five of his conventionally notated works from 1951 to 1956.[54]

It was also a period in which relations between Feldman and Cage were strained, a circumstance observed by Carolyn Brown, who attributed it to Feldman's refusal 'to be pigeonholed as a mere member of "Cage and his school."'[55] These tensions are apparent in their published writings. In an article published in *It is* in 1958, Feldman complained that '[c]hance is the most academic procedure yet arrived at',[56] evidently a condemnation of Cage's methods and hardly 'friendly fire', as one commentator has suggested.[57] Two issues later, in 1959, Cage reciprocated, criticising Feldman's music, which 'seems more to continue than to change' and which is 'sometimes too beautiful'.[58] He also noted Feldman's recently interventionist stance in rehearsals of his graph music – presumably a reference to the confrontation in music rehearsals for *Summerspace*. According to Cage, the character of its beauty 'which formerly seemed to me to be heroic, strikes me now as erotic' for '[o]n paper [. . .] the graph pieces are as heroic as ever; but in rehearsal Feldman does not permit the freedoms he writes to become the

naming is often a precursor to summary dismissal ('Give my regards to Eighth Street' [1971], in Friedman (ed.), *Give My Regards*, 93).

[53] Completed scores in conventional notation from this period that remain unpublished include an untitled work for two pianos (1958), *Piece for Seven Instruments* (1960), *Score for Untitled Film* (1960), *Wind* (1960) and *Followe Thy Faire Sunne* (1962). Morton Feldman Collection, Paul Sacher Foundation.

[54] *New Directions in Music 2/Morton Feldman*, Columbia Masterworks, MS 6090.

[55] *Chance and Circumstance*, 198.   [56] 'Sound, noise, Varèse, Boulez', 1.

[57] Noble, *Composing Ambiguity*, 108.

[58] See the prefatory remarks with his 'Lecture on something', 128. The intended slight is clearer in a letter to Peter Yates from the following year: 'Feldman is still writing graph music disturbingly like what he did nearly 10 yrs. ago. Whereas I'm going on changing as usual' (John Cage to Peter Yates, 6 June 1960, Peter Yates Papers, Mandeville Special Collections Library, UC San Diego).

occasion for license'.[59] Cage had previously admired what he once saw as Feldman's heroism in relinquishing controls to the performer;[60] plainly, he did not approve of Feldman's new, more critical stance.

Having completed *Ixion*, Feldman considered adding parts for vibraphone, glockenspiel and harp. An amended sketch of the finished work has had parts for these instruments added in his handwriting along the bottom of its first eight pages.[61] This interest in a more diversified ensemble culminated in the composition of a new graph, *Atlantis*, dated 28 September 1959, which is scored for the same instrument types as *Ixion* plus vibraphone, harp and several other additions. This process of diversifying the instrumentation of the immediately preceding graph in producing a new one would become the norm in the graphs for large ensembles that he would go on to compose, which are scored for larger and larger configurations. As a result, there are clearer connections between the instrumentations of these works than in the *Projections* and *Intersections*, the instrumentations of which were largely unrelated and often reflected Feldman's resource of available performers.

The significance, for Feldman, of the title 'Atlantis', which may have been another allusion to Greek mythology, is not documented, but it is known that he had previously contemplated using it with the only other work that he completed in 1959, a composition for solo piano with fixed pitches and indeterminate durations now known as *Last Pieces*.[62] In the final movement of this particular work – marked '[v]ery fast' – the score specifies that '[d]urations are free for each hand', thereby replicating the effect of two performers playing independently of one another from unlike parts, as in *Piano Four Hands* (1958), within a work for a solo performer.

Atlantis is scored for seventeen instruments, but the explanatory notes with the published edition of the score indicate that an 'alternate' version for a smaller ensemble of ten instruments may also be played. It was this version that was performed first, at the Kaufmann Concert Hall, New York City on 6 February 1960 by an ensemble conducted by Cage, and again featuring Tudor on piano.[63] The music has many similarities with *Ixion*. Once again, the pronounced emphasis on the high register and the use of numbers to indicate the quantity of sounds to be produced consecutively – except in the piano part in this case – create a sparkling array of musical specks and a strong sense of forward flow, but here the occasional interjections of loud sounds are no longer required, with all sounds being played

[59] Prefatory remarks with Cage's 'Lecture on something', 128.
[60] 'Lecture on Something', 134.   [61] Morton Feldman Collection, Paul Sacher Foundation.
[62] Claren, *Neither*, 557.
[63] The printed programme lists ten performers, indicating that the 'alternate' version was played (Programme, Kaufmann Concert Hall, 6 February 1960).

'as softly as possible'. Other notable differences include the fact that a tempo – 92 ictuses per minute – is explicitly stated in the published edition and the fact that the piano is highlighted in several ways. For example, the explicitly tripartite division of register into high, middle and low ranges using three rows of the grid is reinstated in its case whereas generic guidance of the type found in *Ixion* – '[a]ll sounds chosen are to be played in the high register of the instrument, except for a brief section in which low sounds are indicated' – continues to apply elsewhere. This means that the piano is the only instrument that plays in all three registers, which is bound to make it stand out in the listening experience, and this effect is heightened by Feldman's orchestration. Although ensemble passages predominate, there are many places in which the piano plays unaccompanied or with only occasional interventions from other instruments. The longest of these appears in the closing stages and lasts around 30 seconds at the given tempo.

Yet another significant difference that warrants highlighting is the lesser degree of overt structure. *Atlantis* also includes a low register intermission, in its case placed almost one-third of the way through the work as a whole, but the other aspects of surface structure in *Ixion* highlighted above are noticeably absent. At least in part, this reflects the fact that the published editions of the two scores represent different stages in what might loosely be termed 'the compositional process', for reasons explained in Chapter 7.

The published edition of *Ixion* for two pianos is not dated, but an unpublished set of explanatory notes, reproduced in Chapter 9 (Figure 9.2), bears the date 15 January 1960. This new version of *Ixion*, like its namesake, from which it was transcribed, was designed to be performed with Cunningham's *Summerspace*, but in this case by Tudor and Cage, who were the two musicians that toured with Cunningham at this time. The transcription was premiered by them soon after being completed, with the second performance of *Summerspace* on 28 January 1960.[64]

A brief review of the publication history of the score of this particular work demonstrates the need for a lateral approach to interpreting Feldman's graph scores in at least some places, if one aims to avoid wilfully misconstruing his intentions, for it was issued initially without any explanatory notes.[65] It is true that the notation itself is highly suggestive, but

[64] Programme, Fine Arts Theatre, Western Illinois University, 28 January 1960.
[65] See copies in the British Library and the library of the Paul Sacher Foundation.

even so a multitude of unintended and unwanted interpretations become feasible if it is read in isolation.

This raises the question of how we can be sure that these readings were unwanted by him, and the answer is that everything else – the common title, the organised method of transcription from one to the other and the fact that the two works were both designed for use with the same choreography and costumes – points to a commonality of sound with *Ixion* for chamber ensemble. The somewhat later inclusion of the set of explanatory notes from the chamber ensemble work with the transcription appears to confirm this, although it is not documented whether this addition was Feldman's initiative, but even if it was not, a lateral reading that interprets it in the light of its predecessor is, in my view, the only legitimate course.

Last graphs

Shortly after transcribing *Ixion*, Feldman completed the first of five numbered *Durations* (1960–1). These are compositions with fixed pitches and indeterminate durations in which the performers, after a coordinated first entrance, play with a minimum of attack and dynamics that are 'very low' from different parts in unsynchronised fashion. He would work on this series and several other compositions of a similar type through 1961, during which he would also finish two new graphs.

It is very likely that he began work on another graph before turning to the latter, however. The two surviving sketches are titled 'The Straits of Magellan', but this particular work is not to be confused with a graph with the same name, yet to be discussed, for it is scored for a most unusual ensemble of sixteen instruments that includes a baritone saxophone, a euphonium, three trombones and three cellos. Neither of the sketches is dated and neither appears to be complete,[66] but internal evidence suggests that they pre-date . . .*Out of 'Last Pieces'* – the first of the two graphs that he finished in 1961.[67]

The instrumentation of . . .*Out of 'Last Pieces'*, which is dated March 1961, is an extended version of the one used in *Atlantis*. The principal changes were the expansion of the woodwind and brass sections plus the addition of an electric guitar, a celesta and several percussion instruments. The work is evidently intended for a symphony orchestra with extra percussion minus violins and violas, the absence of violins and violas

---

[66] Morton Feldman Collection, Paul Sacher Foundation.
[67] Both sketches are similar in appearance to *Atlantis*. Some elements in the later sketch have been modified in a manner first seen in . . .*Out of 'Last Pieces'*, however.

being part of a deliberate strategy of utilising what Feldman would later term 'inventive' orchestral configurations.[68] Once again, generic register guidance applies, except in the piano part, which is highlighted by the fact that the tripartite division of the grid is retained in its case. Five instruments are free to play in any register, but others are to play high, except in several passages located close to the centre of the score in which labels indicate that specific sections play low.

A notable aspect of the score is the re-emergence of extended time brackets, many of which overlap in staggered sequences, and it is clear that Feldman intended longer sounds to be played in these cases, even though entrances are officially at the discretion of individual performers. This turn of events marks an important shift away from the sound-world of the three previous graphs, in which there are almost no opportunities for performers to play sustained sounds, and in this regard ...*Out of 'Last Pieces'* marks a partial return to the earlier sound of the *Projections* and *Intersections*.[69] Having said that, the retreat is only partial, both because the density of sounded ictuses remains very high, as it was in *Ixion* and *Atlantis*, and because of the pervasive use of numerals higher than '1', which typically indicate larger numbers of consecutive sounds in individual ictuses, and which ensure a dot-like construction and flowing aspect. The indicated tempo is 80 ictuses per minute, and dynamics are 'very low' throughout.

The density of indicated activity varies markedly by ictus, but the average level measured over somewhat longer periods remains broadly unchanged until early in the second half, in which a period of heightened activity, corresponding to page 8 of the published edition of the score, is followed by three noticeably distinct passages. The level of activity indicated in the second of these is similar to that found in the first half of the work, but this is preceded by a short period of much thinner activity and followed by a longer passage, which closes the work, in which activity is similarly sparse.

The closing stages are also distinguished by being notated in an unusual manner, for the last page of the score is marked by a more conventionally notated insert in the piano part. This was the first time that Feldman had mixed different types of notation, but the practice of doing so would become common in his non-graph works composed in 1963–9. His use of grace notes, which appear in several places, most notably in a vertical

---

[68] 'Toronto lecture, 17 April 1982', in Villars (ed.), *Morton Feldman Says*, 143–4.
[69] There are no extended time brackets in either version of *Ixion* and only six in *Atlantis*.

line running down the exact centre of the last page, was also a first as this was the first occasion on which he used a conventional musical symbol – albeit in unorthodox fashion for, as in *Variations*, they appear unattached – in a graph score.

...*Out of 'Last Pieces'* received its premiere performance at Cooper Union on 17 March 1961, during a 'Music in the Making' concert conducted by Howard Shanet with Tudor at the piano. The *New York Times* noted its 'charming, delicate sound' and highlighted its flowing aspect, describing it as having 'burbled along like a wayward stream, now quietly, now bubbling up'.[70] This seems to have been one of the first occasions on which Feldman's graph music attracted favourable press comment. The previous year, the premiere performance of the 'alternate' version of *Atlantis* had received unfavourable notices.[71]

The title '...Out of "Last Pieces"', which is surely among the most unusual in Feldman's entire catalogue, is something of a puzzle. H. Wiley Hitchcock suggested the following explanation: 'Morton Feldman's four short *Last Pieces* [...] were the last he had written at that time; that's all the title signifies. (He went on to move "out of *Last Pieces*," and those four words are the title of his next opus.)'[72] The authoritative tone of this rather banal explanation suggests that it may have come from Feldman himself, but even so, it is not credible. This is because Feldman's dating of these works – the final movement of *Last Pieces* is marked 3 April 1959 – places them almost two years apart, and several other works, including *Atlantis*, appear to have been completed in the intervening period. Given that each of the four movements of *Last Pieces* bears a precise date, it seems unlikely that these are inaccurate. The dating of ...*Out of 'Last Pieces'* is potentially less secure, both because the given date is less precise and because it happens to coincide with that of the first performance, which means it is possible that Feldman used the latter as a guide. Still, it is highly unlikely that ...*Out of 'Last Pieces'* preceded *Atlantis*, given the notable similarity between the notations of *Ixion* and *Atlantis* and the significant differences between them both and the one used in ...*Out of 'Last Pieces'* (more of which below). This points to ...*Out of 'Last Pieces'* being a subsequent work, in which case the problem with Hitchcock's explanation still stands. Consequently, it is likely that the unusual title signals a different

---

[70] Raymond Ericson, 'Music-in-Making ends its season', *New York Times*, 18 March 1961, 17.

[71] Eric Salzman, 'Mittler recalls quartet's debut', *New York Times*, 8 February 1960, 36, and Lester Trimble, 'Music', *The Nation*, 20 February 1960, 175–6.

[72] 'Last Pieces for piano; A Joyous Procession and a Solemn Procession. For high and low voices, trombones, and percussion; Ittrospezione No. 2 per orchestra', *Notes*, 2nd Ser., vol. 21, no. 4 (Autumn 1964), 609.

and perhaps deeper connection with *Last Pieces*; this is an issue addressed briefly in Chapter 7.

The second graph that Feldman completed in 1961 was the work now known as *The Straits of Magellan*, which appears to be otherwise unrelated to the earlier abandoned graph with the same name, described above; once again, the significance of the title is not documented, but it was clearly one that he was keen to use.[73] In terms of presentation, this graph, which is dated December 1961, marks a turning point in the series. Numerals had been the predominant symbols utilised in the graph scores up until this point, resulting in a rather austere look. In . . .*Out of 'Last Pieces'*, he had expanded this resource somewhat by including grace notes, but in *The Straits of Magellan* he also included many other symbols, which create a significantly more complex visual aspect. The additions include letters, Roman numerals, shapes, arrows and pictograms, sometimes alone but also in combinations.

This new resource of symbols allowed him to specify new timbres and effects, such as col legno, tremolo, flutter and double tonguing, upwards and downwards slides, broken chords and even repetitions. This adds variety to the resulting sound, and creates a general impression of a somewhat larger ensemble. Nevertheless, it would be wrong to see this greater specificity as signalling an emerging discomfort with indeterminacy per se and as heralding his eventual rapprochement with conventional notation. In one important respect, *The Straits of Magellan* exhibits the highest degree of indeterminacy yet seen in the graph series. No register is given in connection with approximately two-thirds of the total number of notated events; this being left to each performer's own discretion.

Dynamics are 'very low throughout', but even so the notation implies different degrees of quietness in some places and therefore an element of notated depth not seen in previous graphs. For example, although most of the sounds from the trumpet and horn are to be produced with mutes, a significant proportion of them are notated as open. Short crescendos and diminuendos in the parts for horn and trumpet, and in one place in the part for contrabass, are probably intended to produce a similar effect.

Like . . .*Out of 'Last Pieces'*, this music combines aspects of the restless, flowing sound of *Ixion* and *Atlantis* with more static passages, which are reminiscent of *Projection 2*, *Projection 5* and the two orchestral *Intersections*. As a result, the perceptible flow is less sustained than in

---

[73] A surviving sketch of the opening of a work for an ensemble of thirty-three instruments, also titled 'The Straits of Magellan', appears otherwise unrelated to the published work or the earlier work with the same name described in the main text. 'Sketchbook 13', Morton Feldman Collection, Paul Sacher Foundation.

the former. In the available recordings, passages evoking a strong sense of movement are juxtaposed with more quiescent material with lower levels of overall activity and longer time brackets that has a more static aspect. The tempo is set at 88 ictuses per minute in this case.

Feldman and Brown were back on friendly terms by this time. An exchange of letters from the autumn of 1961 discusses a joint release on record of some of their more recent works and it also refers to an associated 'gala' performance of their music at a major venue in New York City,[74] which Cage remembered promoting.[75] Brown had recently completed *Available Forms I* (1961), possibly the first workable open form composition for orchestra, in which the conductor uses a large movable arrow on a placard displaying numbers to communicate his decisions to the orchestra during the course of the performance. He had also left Capitol Records to become the producer of the Contemporary Sound Series for Time Records and was, for that reason, ideally placed to bring the idea of a Brown–Feldman LP to fruition.

Early in 1962, Feldman followed Cage and Wolff in signing an exclusive publishing contract with the C. F. Peters Corporation.[76] He must have regarded his graphs favourably at this time, as there were seven on the first list of nineteen works for publication that he submitted to its president, Walter Hinrichsen.[77] Still, no new graphs were composed by Feldman in 1962 or in the very prolific year of 1963. The former was marked by the completion of *Structures* for orchestra, the first work in conventional notation since 1956 that he regarded as fit for publication, whereas the latter witnessed a whole host of new outputs, including *De Kooning* and the entire *Vertical Thoughts* series. These marked the start of a new phase in his production of works with fixed pitches and indeterminate durations.

This new phase is marked, initially at least, by the introduction of networks of vertical and diagonal lines between stemless note heads in

---

[74] Earle Brown to Morton Feldman, 4 October 1961, Morton Feldman Collection, Paul Sacher Foundation; and Morton Feldman to Earle Brown, 12 October 1961, Earle Brown Music Foundation.

[75] 'John Cage (b. Los Angeles, 1912; d. New York, 1992)', in William Duckworth, *Talking Music: Conversations with John Cage, Philip Glass, Laurie Anderson, and Five Generations of American Experimental Composers* (New York: Schirmer Books, 1995), 16.

[76] Cage signed in 1960 (Nicholls, *John Cage*, 64). Wolff signed later that year (Hicks and Asplund, *Christian Wolff*, 32). Cage recommended Feldman (Silverman, *Begin Again*, 173).

[77] The first nineteen titles submitted were numbered EP6901–19 for publication (Walter Hinrichsen to Morton Feldman, 7 June 1962, C. F. Peters Corporation). The seven graphs were *Atlantis* (EP6906), *Intersection 1* (EP6907), *Marginal Intersection* (EP6909), *. . . Out of 'Last Pieces'* (EP6910), *Projection 4* (EP6913), *Intersection 3* (EP6915) and *The Straits of Magellan* (EP6919).

some passages. These specify whether sounds in different parts should be played simultaneously and, if not, the order in which they should be played, with Feldman usually adding the proviso that 'each instrument enters when the preceding sound begins to fade'. This results in a largely sequential presentation of sonorities in which the decay of each one is given centre stage.[78] These works also include passages in staff notation, in which one or more sonorities or, more often, a pause is conventionally notated.[79]

The Straits of Magellan was first performed by the Contemporary Chamber Ensemble under Arthur Weisberg on 11 October 1963 at Town Hall, New York City, where it was played alongside other works by Feldman, including all five in the *Vertical Thoughts* series, and several by Brown as part of a two-man show – plainly the gala event mentioned in their 1961 exchange of letters.[80] Feldman's music received an enthusiastic review in the *New York Times* the following day and, subsequently, in *The Musical Quarterly*.[81]

Soon after signing with the C. F. Peters Corporation, Feldman spoke of growing recognition for his music,[82] and it is clear that, by the middle of 1963, he had been contacted by Leonard Bernstein's assistant about the possibility of one of his works being performed by the New York Philharmonic Orchestra.[83] Eventually, ...*Out of 'Last Pieces'* was chosen, and it was this work that was played, alongside compositions by Brown and Cage, on four consecutive evenings in February 1964 in the last of a series of programmes billed as 'The Avant-Garde'.[84] Also included in these 'Music of Chance' concerts were ten bars from a BBC

[78] Boutwell, '"The breathing of sound itself"', 548–9.

[79] This pattern is modified in *Vertical Thoughts 4* and *Vertical Thoughts 5*, in which the network of vertical and diagonal lines is not present. In the former, this is because the work is for solo piano. In the latter, it reflects the fact that the only performer who plays outside the conventionally notated passages is the percussionist. *Vertical Thoughts 4* is also marked out by an absence of conventionally notated passages.

[80] The other Feldman works played were *For Franz Kline* (1962) and *The Swallows of Salangan* (1960). Programme, Town Hall, 11 October 1963.

[81] Theodore Strongin, 'The music of Morton Feldman and Earle Brown is presented: works that leave decisions to performers are heard in Town Hall concert', *New York Times*, 12 October 1963, 21, and H. Wiley Hitchcock, 'Current chronicle: United States, New York', *The Musical Quarterly*, vol. 50, no. 1 (January 1964), 93–6.

[82] [Unsigned: A], 'Brushed off for years, avant garde music finally gaining recognition', *Variety*, 21 February 1962, 53.

[83] Walter Hinrichsen to Morton Feldman, 17 June 1963, C. F. Peters Corporation.

[84] The concerts were held at Philharmonic Hall, Lincoln Center, New York City on 6–9 February. The works by Brown and Cage were *Available Forms II* (1962) and *Atlas Eclipticalis* (1962) with *Winter Music*.

computer-generated work, a free improvisation by the orchestra in which Bernstein's role was to serve 'only as a kind of general guide, or policeman',[85] and two more conventional works, which were presumably added in an attempt to mollify Philharmonic subscribers. Feldman had high hopes of these performances, one of which was broadcast on radio, believing that Bernstein would make the public 'catch on'.[86] However, they do not seem to have been a great success. Many subscribers hated the music and made this clear during and after the performances,[87] producing what one commentator has described as some of the noisiest scenes ever witnessed at a Philharmonic concert:[88] '[f]uddy-duddies plainly didn't want the avant-garde', as the New York Times remarked subsequently.[89] Many of the performers held a similar view: according to some reports, they took liberties with the music, hissed the composers and damaged Cage's contact microphones, used in his Atlas Eclipticalis with Winter Music.[90] The composers were angered by the reaction of the audience and the behaviour of the performers.[91] And the music press hated not just the four 'Music of Chance' concerts, but the whole series, criticising Bernstein's decision to sweeten each programme with more traditional works and what they regarded as his condescending, misleading or provocative introductions.[92] Atlas Eclipticalis with Winter Music received most of the criticism, but ...Out of 'Last Pieces' was not immune, being described variously as 'half-composed before the concert',[93] 'noisy chaos',[94] 'less bedlam than boredom'[95] and 'a tinkly thing with harp plucks and oboe gurgles, like noodle soup going down a drain'.[96] Even so, Feldman did experience some immediate benefits

---

[85] Leonard Bernstein, 'Aleatory composers', unpublished typescript dated 4 February 1964 with handwritten amendments, Leonard Bernstein Collection, Music Division, Library of Congress. The concerts included spoken comments, which Bernstein seems to have read from this typescript.

[86] [Unsigned: D], 'Is it music?', Newsweek, 2 September 1963, 53.

[87] Morton Feldman, '"I am interested in the commitment". Conversation with Frits Lagerwerff, 4 July 1987', in Mörchen (ed.), Morton Feldman in Middelburg, 830–2.

[88] Humphrey Burton, Leonard Bernstein (London: Faber and Faber, 1994), 342.

[89] Howard Klein, 'The avant garde advances', New York Times, 19 December 1965, X26.

[90] See, for example, David Revill, The Roaring Silence – John Cage: A Life (New York: Arcade Publishing, 1992), 206–7. This has been disputed by some members of the orchestra (Benjamin Piekut, Experimentalism Otherwise: The New York Avant-Garde and its Limits (Berkeley: University of California Press, 2011), 35–9).

[91] See, for example, Feldman, '"I am interested in the commitment"', 830–2.

[92] Burton, Leonard Bernstein, 342.

[93] Miles Kastendieck, 'Electric music wired for boos', New York Journal – American, 7 February 1964, 18.

[94] Winthrop Sargeant, 'Musical events: first causes', New Yorker, 15 February 1964, 126.

[95] [Unsigned: H], 'Sound of cybernetics', Newsweek, 17 February 1964, 88.

[96] [Unsigned: B], 'Composers: far-out at the Philharmonic', Time, 14 February 1964, 80.

from the increased exposure, with the *New York Times* publishing an interview with him in early February and Colombia records releasing a studio recording of . . .*Out of 'Last Pieces'* by the New York Philharmonic on LP record later in 1964.[97]

The King of Denmark, dated August 1964, is Feldman's most frequently performed and recorded graph and, indeed, one of the more frequently performed and recorded works in his catalogue. This popularity is attributable to its reputation as one of the very first important works for solo percussion,[98] its best-known precursors being Cage's *27'10.554"* (1956) – the last of his time-length pieces – and Stockhausen's *Zyklus* (1959). It also reflects the novelty of Feldman's famous requirement that the percussionist should play without sticks or mallets, using fingers, hands or arms, which was evidently intended to minimise audible attack and facilitate the 'extremely low' dynamics specified in the notes with the score. His decision to compose another graph for a solo performer may appear surprising in view of the opportunities they present for sabotage or memory-infected extemporisation,[99] but it would be wrong to infer that a fundamental shift in his stance had taken place. Solo works are more likely to attract performers committed to doing justice to the music they play than orchestral works, for example.

The religiopolitical title – chosen after completion – refers to King Christian X of Denmark, who is alleged to have donned the Star of Israel, which the Jews were forced to wear during the German occupation of his country, in a gesture of 'silent protest'.[100] Feldman saw a connection between this act and the 'silent resistance' offered by his work to 'Stockhausen's expressivity' in *Zyklus* and 'all the noisy music of the world'.[101] Indeed, he portrayed his new graph as 'the American answer

---

[97] 'Feldman throws a switch between sight and sound', interview by Brian O'Doherty, *New York Times*, 2 February 1964, XII, and *Leonard Bernstein Conducts Music of Our Time*, Columbia Masterworks, ML 6133/MS 6733.

[98] Steven Schick, *The Percussionist's Art: Same Bed, Different Dreams* (University of Rochester Press, 2006), 4.

[99] The very first ictus, which specifies an isolated group of seven consecutive sounds in the high register, presents one of many examples.

[100] Feldman, 'An interview with Morton Feldman, Jan Williams', 152. This history has been challenged (Vilhjálmur Örn Vilhjálmsson, 'The King and the Star: myths created during the occupation of Denmark', in Mette Bastholm Jensen and Steven L. B. Jensen (eds.), *Denmark and the Holocaust* (Copenhagen: Institute for International Studies, Department for Holocaust and Genocide Studies, 2003), 102–17).

[101] Eberhard Blum, 'Notes on Morton Feldman's "The King of Denmark"', www.cnvill.net/mfblumking_eng.pdf (accessed 24 June 2015).

to "Zyklus'",[102] and the contrast between the two works in performance – Stockhausen's sometimes frenzied and often loud, Feldman's generally calm and always quiet – is indeed great.

Feldman's graph notation was well suited to a percussion idiom, as he himself once remarked,[103] because many percussion instruments convey only a general sense of register. Such indefinite pitches fit neatly with the register-based classification of sounds in the graphs. In this particular case, he used five designations of register (very high, high, middle, low and very low), and in this respect the work is unique within the series.

Instrumentation is specified in connection with a relatively small proportion of indicated sounds, and even these indications are sometimes rather imprecise ('gongs'). Elsewhere, general guidance ('bell like sounds' or 'skin') is occasionally provided, but more often than not the instrument to be used is entirely at the performer's discretion. Almost certainly, this reflects the unpredictable quality and character of percussion instruments.[104] A consequence is that the number of different instruments used may vary considerably between performances, from 'pocket' configurations, which are more compact and transportable, to 'big band' set-ups.[105] No doubt this aspect of the piece has added to its attraction for many performers, as the almost limitless choice of instruments facilitates a highly individual response. All the same, the chosen configuration must be one that facilitates the production of uniformly quiet sounds of the type specified in the score and at a rate consistent with the chosen tempo.[106]

Tempo is set at 66–92 ictuses per minute. The wide extent of this range probably reflects the latitude given to the performer in selecting instruments, and therefore the associated uncertainty about their physical disposition and decay times. In fact, there is reason to believe that Feldman was even more flexible than the given indication would suggest. Jan Williams, who worked with Feldman on aspects of his performance in the run-up to a 1977 tour of Europe, remembers that their discussions focused on pacing:

> It was obvious to me quite quickly after beginning to work on the piece that the 66–92 tempo was too fast for my realization. Too rushed and frenetic,

---

[102] *Ibid.*   [103] 'An interview with Morton Feldman, Jan Williams', 153.

[104] David P. Shively, Indeterminacy and Interpretation: Three Realizations, unpublished DMA thesis, University of California, San Diego (2001), 9.

[105] Max Neuhaus gave the first performance of his pocket version at Festival Zaj 1 in Madrid on 27 November 1965 (Max Neuhaus to Morton Feldman, postmarked 10 February 1966, Morton Feldman Collection, Paul Sacher Foundation).

[106] For a discussion, see Daryl Pratt, 'Performance analysis: Morton Feldman, *The King of Denmark*', *Percussive Notes Research Edition*, vol. 25, no. 3 (March 1987), 76–9, and Shively, Indeterminacy and Interpretation, 21–4.

I felt. So, I played it at a tempo that felt right for me. We talked about this slower pace and he basically liked what I was doing.[107]

Although dynamics are extremely low, other aspects of the work tend to invite a high degree of physicality in performance, especially when the chosen set-up is large. As David Shively has pointed out, a mallet functions as a mechanical extension of the percussionist's arm, so the embargo on them forces the performer to make larger bodily movements than would otherwise be necessary.[108] This can give performances a powerful visual aspect, which may be another reason for the work's popularity.[109]

The two-stage ending of the work, which juxtaposes its densest and sparsest passages, is perhaps its most memorable aspect. The first stage consists of a short burst of frenetic activity, marked 'as many different sounds as possible'. This is immediately succeeded by a strongly contrasting final stage, eighteen ictuses in length, which includes only two sonorities, played by vibraphone and then glockenspiel or antique cymbal, with specified pitches that are notated on a stave placed under the grid. One commentator has suggested that '[t]he entire work is directed toward' these two sounds,[110] but there is no reason whatever to think that Feldman's piece is goal-oriented in this way or, indeed, in any other manner.

Feldman once explained that he drafted *The King of Denmark* in a single afternoon while sitting on a beach, where he was inspired by 'wisps' of sound, including the 'muffled sound of kids in the distance and transistor radios and drifts of conversation from other pockets of inhabitants on blankets'.[111] Be that as it may, he seems to have been planning it for some time prior to this. The percussionist Max Neuhaus remembered that Feldman came to his studio several times in 1963 to hear instruments and explore techniques and that in 'the second or third session' Feldman was still insisting that the sounds were too loud. Neuhaus continued:

> I suddenly remembered how, as percussion students, we used to practice our parts on stage just before a concert started. In order that the audience not hear us, we used our fingers instead of sticks. I put down my sticks and started to

[107] Jan Williams to David Cline, 31 August 2008 (email).

[108] Indeterminacy and Interpretation, 19.

[109] Some have sought to give their movements an illustrative aspect. For example, Shively has utilised a spatial organisation of the instruments designed to mirror the pitch ordering of the keys on the vibraphone (*ibid.*, 23). In Steven Schick's performances, by contrast, 'the lower the sound the larger the movement, and vice versa' (*The Percussionist's Art*, 172).

[110] John Welsh, 'The secret structure in Morton Feldman's "The King of Denmark" (1964) part two', *Percussive Notes*, June 2008, 32.

[111] 'An interview with Morton Feldman, Jan Williams', 152.

play with just my fingers. Morty was dumbstruck, 'that's it, that's it!' he yelled.[112]

Neuhaus went on to give the first performance at Judson Hall, New York City on 3 September 1964.[113] The *New York Times* reviewer interpreted the unusual performing method as a humorous gesture, describing the work as 'an inaudible satire':[114] hence Feldman's subsequent observation that 'it was considered at the time as an "Emperor's new clothes" piece'.[115]

Finale

Summerspace was performed several times by Cunningham and his company in 1964–5, but Feldman's music continued to encounter some resistance from performers. For example, a problem emerged in the one and only rehearsal for a performance at the New York State Theatre on 3 March 1965. The orchestra was directed by Jorge Mester, who recalled the events as follows:

> It was an unfortunate but sadly hilarious occasion. I dutifully rehearsed the orchestra as best I could, making sure they understood Feldman's instructions. We then proceeded to the pit for the dress (and only) run-through. About eight minutes into the dance, one of the dancers leapt from the wings, whereupon the trumpet player tooted a tune from 'The Grand Canyon Suite' [by Ferde Grofé] – the orchestra fell apart with mirth and was unable to continue.[116]

A different problem emerged the following year, when the New York City Ballet became the first of several other companies to perform *Summerspace*.[117] In the spring and summer, they danced an adapted version, with Rauschenberg's costumes and set and of Feldman's Ixion for chamber ensemble. The production was

---

[112] 'Morton Feldman, *The King of Denmark* (realization date, 1964)', liner notes with *The New York School: Nine Realizations of Cage, Feldman, Brown*, Alga Marghen, plana-P 22NMN.052.

[113] Programme, Second Annual New York Festival of the Avant Garde, Judson Hall, 30 August–13 September 1964.

[114] Howard Klein, 'Music: avant-garde festival closes', *New York Times*, 4 September 1964, 18.

[115] 'An interview with Morton Feldman, Jan Williams', 152.

[116] Jorge Mester to David Cline, 28 September 2014 (email). The actual performance seems to have proceeded without apparent incident (Allen Hughes, 'Dance: at Lincoln Center', *New York Times*, 8 March 1965, 34). The third movement of Grofé's *Grand Canyon Suite* (1931) – 'On the trail' – was well known at this time because of its use on radio and television in advertising Philip Morris cigarettes. Dizzy Gillespie had quoted from it, in May 1953, during a performance of Jerome Kern's *All the Things You Are* (1939) at Massey Hall, Toronto by a super-group that also included Charlie Parker, Bud Powell, Max Roach and Charles Mingus (*The Greatest Jazz Concert Ever*, Prestige 68.319).

[117] Vaughan, *Merce Cunningham*, 112.

overseen by John Braden, but trouble emerged when George Balanchine, the company's artistic director, heard the music and declared it 'a fraud'.[118] The problem, according to Feldman, was that 'he couldn't make any form out of it, he couldn't subdivide it',[119] and it seems to have been this that led to the dance being dropped from the company's repertory.[120]

Based on the tally of works completed, 1965–6 was a relatively unproductive period for Feldman, and neither of his published outputs from this time were graphs. It seems reasonable to suppose that this lower productivity was partly attributable to lecture tours in the UK in the spring and autumn of 1966. That said, it is clear that he began work on *In Search of an Orchestration* during the course of the year,[121] and although the published score is undated, it was almost certainly finished during the first half of 1967. In a letter to Earle Brown dated 16 June 1967, he referred to it by name and implied that it was only recently completed.[122]

Given the high importance that Feldman placed on orchestration,[123] the title he chose for this, the last of his graphs, is unfortunate. 'In Search of an Orchestration' appears to refer to an aspect of the compositional process, but 'search' is not a success verb. Consequently, the bare reference to being 'in search of' an orchestration could be interpreted as an admission of unsuccessful struggle and dissatisfaction with the finished work. Read this way, it would be tempting to connect the title with the fact that this was the last graph.

Nothing could be further from the truth, however. Instead, Feldman meant the title to refer to what he later presented as a normal aspect of his compositional approach, which was the process of discovering an orchestration while composing.[124] On one occasion, he explained that 'the orchestration is never given' and that it 'doesn't materialize usually' until 'about three minutes into the piece'.[125] No doubt he also meant the

---

[118] *Ibid.*, 152.   [119] 'Neither European nor American', 642

[120] Vaughan, *Merce Cunningham*, 152.

[121] An incomplete sketch bears a copyright date of 1966 (James Schuyler Papers, University of California, San Diego). An incoming letter, dated 25 June 1966, includes the following comment: 'I hope the graph piece is progressing satisfactorily' (David Jones to Morton Feldman, 25 June 1966, Morton Feldman Collection, Paul Sacher Foundation). On 16 January 1967, Feldman referred to the work by name as the piece that he was then writing (Cage and Feldman, *Radio Happenings*, 145).

[122] Morton Feldman to Earle Brown, 16 June 1967, Earle Brown Music Foundation.

[123] The fullest surviving account of his thoughts on 'orchestration' appears in 'Unpublished writings: III', in Friedman (ed.), *Give My Regards*, 205–8.

[124] *Ibid.*, 206–7.

[125] 'Twelve tone technique in Varèse's *Déserts*, lecture given at California Institute of the Arts (CalArts) in February 1981', www.cnvill.net/mfdeserts.pdf (accessed 24 June 2015), 9. His

title to allude to the self-conscious process that he sometimes referred to as 'inventing' new instrumentations.[126] Violins are noticeably absent in this work, as they are from all the later graphs, as previously noted.

In fact, Feldman regarded *In Search of an Orchestration* as the culmination of his efforts on graph paper. In a seminar given in Germany in 1984, he described it, tellingly, as his 'Final Solution'.[127] Given that Feldman was Jewish, the black humour in this remark is obvious. Even so, his choice of words demonstrates that he saw *In Search of an Orchestration* as having a special status within the graph series, and they even hint that he may have regarded it – or, more likely, the entire series to that point – as having exhausted the potential of the graph format. Only moments later, in the same seminar, he described it as his 'Opus 24', confirming his high regard for it.[128] The comparison with Anton Webern's *Concerto for Nine Instruments*, Opus 24 (1934) was evidently intended as high praise, given the seminal status accorded to this particular work by serial composers in the 1940s and 1950s.[129]

Feldman also referred to *In Search of an Orchestration* as 'a more complex' ...*Out of 'Last Pieces'* and as ...*Out of 'Last Pieces'* 'five years later',[130] and these comparisons are apt. The instrumentations of the two works are certainly similar, with both graphs scored for rather similar orchestral forces. Moreover, the sound worlds of both are generally similar, combining passages of restless flow with periods featuring lower levels of overall activity and longer time brackets that have a more static aspect. This is underpinned by a more or less identical pacing, with the tempo set at 88 ictuses per minute 'or a little faster' in this new work versus 88 ictuses per minute without qualification in ...*Out of 'Last Pieces'*.

---

preference for discovering the orchestration of a work during the compositional process is a special case of his stated aversion to using preconceived ideas. For this aversion, see for example 'Morton Feldman – waiting, Martine Cadieu, May 1971' [1992], in Villars (ed.), *Morton Feldman Says*, 40, and 'Conversation between Morton Feldman and Walter Zimmermann, November 1975' [1976], in Villars (ed.), *Morton Feldman Says*, 56.

[126] 'Toronto lecture', 143.

[127] 'The future of local music', unpublished transcript of Feldman's week-long seminar at Theater am Turm, Frankfurt, February 1984, 85.

[128] *Ibid.*

[129] See Pierre Boulez, 'Anton Webern', in *Stocktakings from an Apprenticeship*, trans. Stephen Walsh (Oxford University Press, 1991), 299–300, and Karlheinz Stockhausen, 'Weberns Konzert für 9 Instrumente op. 24: Analyse des ersten Satzes' [1953], in *Texte zur Musik – Band 1: Texte zur elektronischen und instrumentalen Musik* (Cologne: M. DuMont Schauberg, 1963), 24–31.

[130] Morton Feldman to Earle Brown, 16 June 1967, and Richard Bjorkman, 'Coming face to face with Feldman', www.cnvill.net/mfbjrkmn.htm (accessed 24 June 2015), respectively.

Where *In Search of an Orchestration* differs most notably from . . . *Out of 'Last Pieces'* is in the less prominent role it bestows on the piano and in its use of elements culled from the two intervening graphs. The principal additions from *The Straits of Magellan* are the much greater variety of timbres and effects, and the design of the ending. Whereas the earlier work ends with a sustained trumpet note emerging from a mass of other sounds, including several that the score specifies as repeated, *In Search of an Orchestration* concludes similarly, with a sustained note from the piccolo emerging from a sound mass, but without any compulsory repetition in this case. Moreover, the percussion part in the newer work incorporates elements from *The King of Denmark*, not only in its greater complexity and augmented scale, but also because the score states that '[f]ingers, hands, forearm, etc. etc. may be utilized'.

A notable development is the inclusion of sliding tones from percussion, strings and harp, which gives this music a more Varèse-like aspect than other works in the graph series,[131] although the dynamic variation that characterises much of Varèse's output is largely absent here ('[d]ynamics throughout extremely low'). Varèse had died in November 1965, just over a year before *In Search of an Orchestration* was completed. Given that Feldman credited him with inspiring his own interest in orchestration,[132] it is distinctly possible that this particular graph was composed with Varèse in mind.

In the letter to Brown dated 16 June 1967 referred to above, Feldman quipped that his new graph 'should really be called In Search of an Orchestra',[133] suggesting that he was finding little enthusiasm for it from potential performers. Details of the first performance may not have survived, but it is clear that this lukewarm reception was a foretaste of things to come, because the work that he regarded as the pinnacle of the graph series has remained largely overlooked, with very few documented performances and only one commercially available recording. The initial lack of enthusiasm for his new graph was one element in a complex web of circumstances responsible for his subsequently declining interest in composing new graph works, or so Chapter 11, which completes the history of the series, will argue.

---

[131] Varèse referred to his interest in 'parabolic and hyperbolic' trajectories of sounds produced by sirens and his use of them in *Amériques* (1921) and *Ionisation* (1931) in 'The liberation of sound', 205.

[132] 'The future of local music' [1985], 170.

[133] Morton Feldman to Earle Brown, 16 June 1967.

3   Notation

Feldman preferred a variety of graph paper featuring perpendicular sets of equally spaced lines of uniform weight that divide each page into a coarse but uniform grid. This is evident in the image reproduced on the cover of this monograph and in Figure 3.1, which shows an excerpt from a sketch of *Projection 1*, presented on facing pages of an early notebook.[1] In one early sketch, reproduced in Chapter 1 (Figure 1.2), he used an engineering graph paper, with contrasting line weights that articulate a hierarchy of grids of different dimensions; this is an isolated example, however, and it is likely that this degree of detail exceeded his requirements in most cases.

The presentation of the graphs – which this chapter begins by addressing – owes much to the printed grid on his preferred paper. This grid is not replicated in published editions of his graph scores, which give prominence, instead, to Feldman's own framework of cells and boxes that he superposed upon it, using it as a template, and within which he placed symbols.

Feldman's symbols typically refer to musical events – usually individual sounds or groups of sounds, but occasionally actions. The character of a symbol gives information about the nature of the designated event, while its horizontal and vertical locations and its length provide additional information, including an indication of its temporal coordinates relative to a pulse. Some of the more important aspects of this scheme of reference and the changes it underwent over the course of the series are reviewed in later parts of the chapter, after purely syntactic aspects of his symbol system and the legibility of his presentation are addressed.

Grid frames

Each sheet of Feldman's preferred paper defined a grid of squares, or *cells*, upon which he drew bounded, rectangular *grid frames* to house his symbols. Many aspects of these grid frames are drawn in on pages of his scores. However, in some graphs, it is evident that the frames have structure that is not explicitly present. These invisible, but implicitly present, aspects are regarded as elements of them in what follows.

---

[1] 'Sketchbook 1', Morton Feldman Collection, Paul Sacher Foundation.

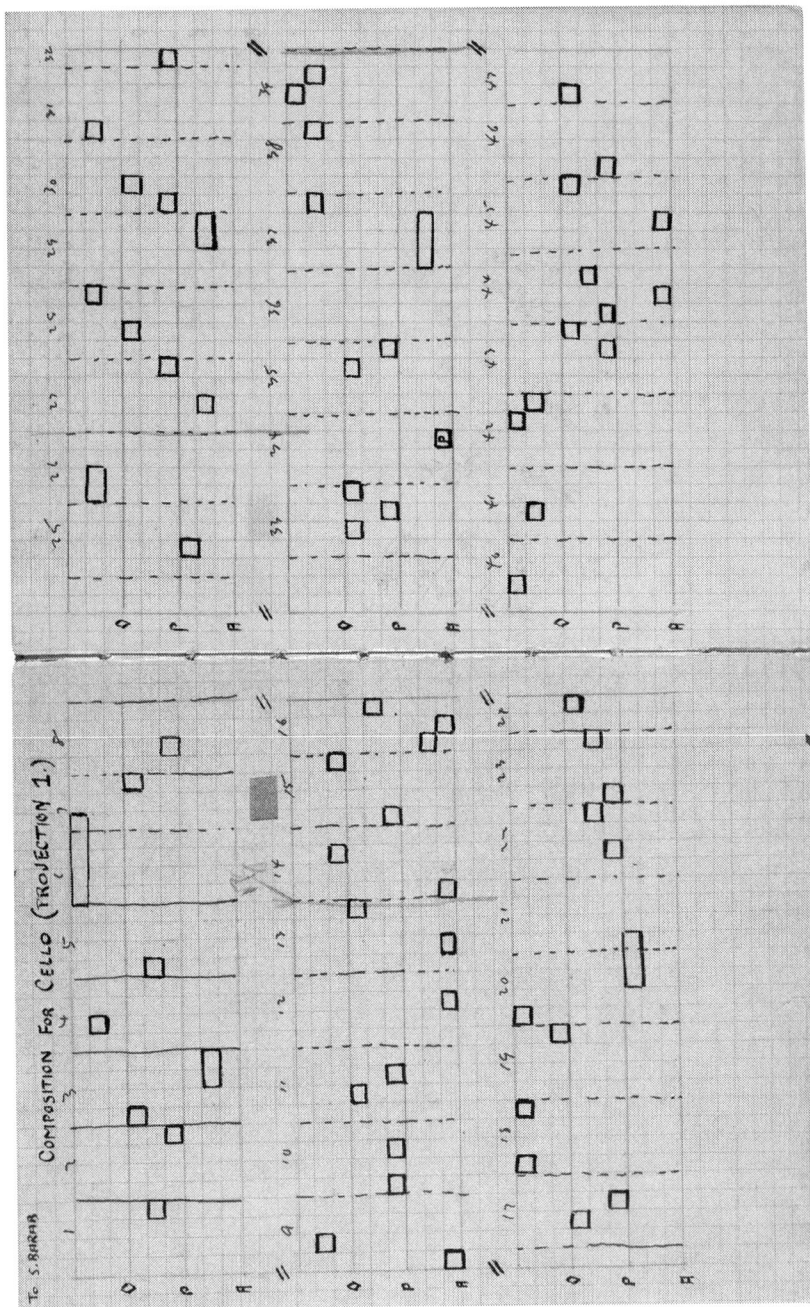

Figure 3.1 *Projection 1*, sketch, pages 1–2

Example 3.1   *Projection 1*, page 2

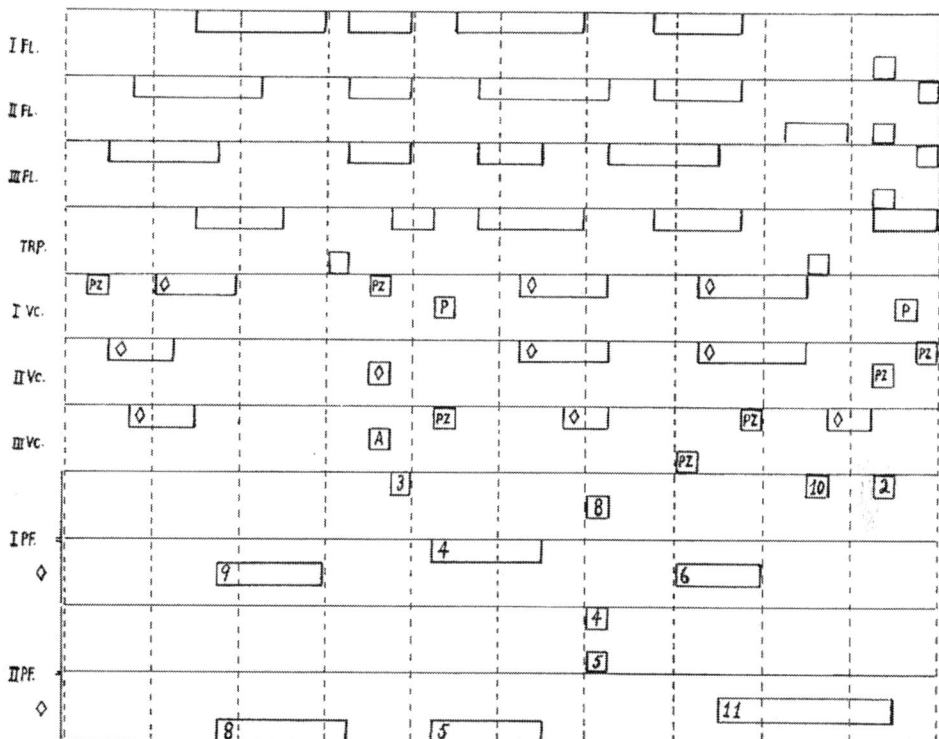

Closely associated with Feldman's grid frames are *labels* and *symbols*. Labels can be viewed as aspects of the grid frames, and are said to be placed on or around them; their purpose is to colour the interpretation of extended areas of the grid frames or to make the score easier to read. Symbols, by contrast, are said to be placed in the frames, and are not aspects of them. Their function is to designate musical events, be they sounds or sound-producing actions.

In the graphs up to and including *Marginal Intersection*, grid frames are divided into a rectilinear network of smaller units that the explanatory notes refer to as *boxes*. Individual cells are not usually delineated, but they evidently underpin the organisation of symbols within boxes and between them. In some cases, lines of boxes are stacked on top of one another without an intervening space in between, but on other occasions a *gutter* is present. For instances of both types of presentation, see Examples 3.1–3.2.

Solid horizontal lines mark the upper and lower edges of boxes, which have dashed vertical lines for sides. Each box is four cells wide, and most

Example 3.2   *Intersection 1*, page 2

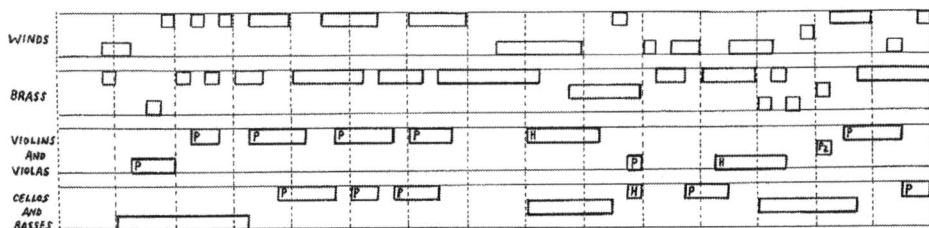

Example 3.3   *Marginal Intersection*, page 3, lower grid frame

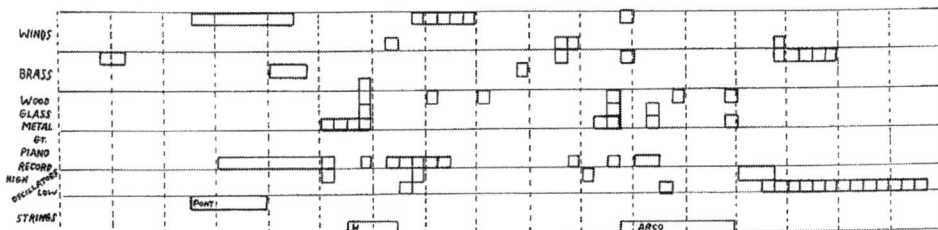

are three cells tall: hence, they contain twelve cells in total. *Marginal Intersection* has a line of boxes that is two cells high, and this is an exception; each of these smaller boxes covers eight cells (Example 3.3). Usually, a label on the left side of the first grid frame allocates an entire row of boxes – and therefore three rows of cells – to a timbre (e.g. pizzicato), instrument (e.g. trumpet), group of instruments (e.g. violins and violas) or instrument type (e.g. brass), and in many cases this label is repeated on subsequent pages. Eight rows in *Marginal Intersection*, including the two mentioned above, are labelled differently, each being allocated to its own instrument.

Sometimes, Feldman omitted (or obscured) parts of this system of boxes, so that it appears incomplete. This phenomenon – evident in Example 1.1 (Chapter 1) – is pronounced in *Projection 1*, *Projection 2* and *Projection 4*. These omissions were cosmetic in character, intended to relieve a starker, more tabular design, which is closer to the one that he would subsequently embrace. They are never radical enough to create confusion, and it is always apparent that an unseen structure is implicitly present. The location of a symbol within the system of boxes – be it explicit or implicit – is always apparent to the naked eye, without recourse to a ruler.

In the published editions of the graphs from *Intersection 2* to *The Straits of Magellan*, Feldman drew cells in his grid frames, as in

Example 3.4 *Intersection 2*, page 6

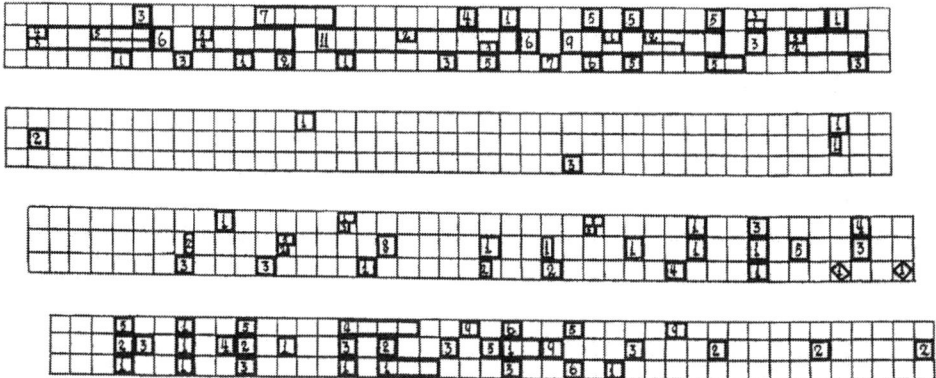

Examples 3.4–3.5.[2] This gives the frames a more tabular appearance, closer to that of his preferred paper. This is underlined by his less frequent intervention in the presentation of these grids, with only one place – *Atlantis*, page 15 – in which elements of the grid frame are obscured. As a rule, in these scores, Feldman marked out the entire grid of cells in a rectangular area on each page. However, in ...*Out of 'Last Pieces'*, he split the last grid frame along a horizontal axis in order to make room for a more conventionally notated piano part; this is presented on two five-line staves without bar lines, which are labelled with clefs, but not time signatures, as in Example 3.6. In the published edition of *The Straits of Magellan*, he included gutters between individual grid rows; this is apparent in Example 3.7.

Normally, in graphs for more than two instruments in this group, individual rows in the grid frame are labelled on their left sides with a mnemonic for an instrument or instrument type. In general, each is associated with a single row, but in *Atlantis* and ...*Out of 'Last Pieces'*, the piano is singled out by being allocated three. In graphs for one or two instruments, comparable labelling is not included.

In a few cases, Feldman highlighted every fifth or tenth vertical line by presenting it differently.[3] This creates a division into blocks that are five or ten cells wide, which contrasts with the division into boxes four cells wide in the graphs up to and including *Marginal Intersection*. From *Ixion* for chamber

---

[2] The page numbering of the latest edition of *Intersection 2*, which forms part of EP67976, differs from that in some earlier editions. Page references cited in this monograph refer to the latest edition, in which the first page of graph notation is page 1.

[3] Every fifth in *Ixion* for chamber ensemble and ...*Out of 'Last Pieces'*. Every tenth in *The Straits of Magellan*. See Examples 3.5–3.7.

Example 3.5   *Ixion* for chamber ensemble, page 4

Example 3.6   ...*Out of 'Last Pieces'*, page 12

ensemble onwards, he added rehearsal marks.[4] These labels are of various types, usually involving Roman numerals with numbers or letters as superscripts, as in Examples 3.5–3.6, and they imply a division of the grid into larger units. In *The Straits of Magellan*, he included a more conventional system, based on an ascending series of Arabic numerals (Example 3.7).

---

[4] In the latest editions of *Intersection 2* and *Intersection 3*, included in EP67976, every tenth column of cells is numbered (sometimes incorrectly). This numbering does not appear in editions published in Feldman's lifetime and was probably added by a third party.

Example 3.7   *The Straits of Magellan*, page 3

Several graphs in this group also include labels that affect the interpretation of areas of the grid frame. Vertical arrows are used thus in both versions of *Ixion* and in . . .*Out of 'Last Pieces'*, as is the word 'low', written underneath an area framed by bold vertical lines in *Atlantis*. *The King of Denmark* includes a system of labels involving dashed lines and names of instruments or sound types; an example ('bell like [*sic*] sounds') appears in Example 3.8.

In *The King of Denmark* and *In Search of an Orchestration*, there is a change in the presentation of certain parts of the grid frames. Although horizontal lines dividing frames into rows are always included, vertical lines dividing rows into columns are not always present. The upshot is rectangular areas within rows that are *undivided*; instances can be seen in Examples 3.8–3.9.[5] In *The King of Denmark*, Feldman appended a short, five-line stave without bar lines below the end of the last grid frame (Example 3.8). A clef is included, but no time signature is given, as in the more conventionally notated piano part on the final page of . . .*Out of 'Last Pieces'*.

Chapter 1 highlighted earlier uses of graphs in Western classical music, but it is feasible that the visual arts were the true source of Feldman's inspiration. His admiration for the works of Piet Mondrian, which he would go on to promote,[6] is documented,[7] and it is credible

---

[5] The published edition of *The King of Denmark* is not paginated.

[6] Feldman selected several pictures by Mondrian for an exhibition at St Thomas University in 1967, as he explained in 'Some elementary questions' [1967], in Friedman (ed.), *Give My Regards*, 64.

[7] 'Studio International interview', 68, and 'Pie-slicing and small moves, Stuart Morgan, Autumn 1977' [1978], in Villars (ed.), *Morton Feldman Says*, 83–4. Feldman included an image of Mondrian's *Composition avec Plans de Couleur sur Fond Blanc*, which depicts a grid of floating rectangles, in 'Crippled symmetry', *Res*, vol. 2 (Autumn 1981), 93. This image is not reprinted in Friedman (ed.), *Give My Regards*.

Example 3.8   *The King of Denmark*, final page

Example 3.9   *In Search of an Orchestration*, page 13

to suppose, as Boulez did,[8] that the visual appeal of the grids of his graphs was, for him, linked to his fascination with the artist's geometric designs. That said, grids, which have been described as 'emblematic' of modernism in the visual arts,[9] and other grid-like rectilinear structures were certainly 'in the air' in the world of painting in which Feldman immersed himself in 1950; they appear in works from this period by Adolph Gottlieb, Barnett Newman and Ad Reinhardt, for example.

Symbols

Feldman placed *symbols* – marks that designate musical events – within his grid frames; some are *basic* in that they do not possess meaningful parts, whereas others are *compound* because they have meaningful constituent elements. Usually, symbols are placed in individual cells or horizontal groups of adjacent cells, although there are exceptions to this general rule. Sometimes, the adjacent cells straddle two consecutive grid frames, as in Examples 3.2 and 3.7.[10]

Clearly distinct periods in the evolution of Feldman's choice of symbols over the course of the series are more difficult to discern than in the presentation of his grid frames. Nevertheless, there is a notable parallel between the general trend towards greater complexity in both the early and the later subseries. As will become clear, in the early graphs (i.e. the *Projections* and *Intersections*), the principal complications that emerge involve the subdivision of cells. In the later subseries, which is initially marked by a renewed simplicity in its symbol resource, the emerging complications stem primarily from a proliferation of new symbols.

In the first seven graphs, up to and including *Marginal Intersection*, squares and rectangles predominate. In some places, they serve as basic symbols, but elsewhere they are parts of compound symbols in which they appear in combination with other elements. Every square and rectangle in *Projection 1* is basic, whereas all those in *Projection 3* are associated with numbers and therefore form parts of compound symbols. In other graphs in this group, they typically serve in both ways, as in Examples 3.1–3.2. Elements associated with them in compound symbols

---

[8] Nattiez (ed.), *The Boulez-Cage Correspondence*, 103.

[9] Rosalind Krauss, 'Grids', *October*, vol. 9 (Summer 1979), 51. This article attributes their emblematic status to their ubiquity in modernist art, which contrasts with their notable absence from the visual art of the nineteenth-century (*ibid.*, 52), and their '[f]lattened, geometricized, ordered' characteristics, which state 'the autonomy of the realm of art' and a withdrawal from nature (*ibid.*, 51).

[10] In Example 3.7, the dashed lines in the first column are elements of compound symbols that straddle pages.

Example 3.10   *Intersection 2*, ictuses 947–55

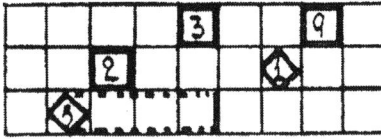

include numbers, letters, the diamond ('◊') and, in *Marginal Intersection*, words and abbreviations (such as 'begin early and gradually fade out' and 'FL'). In all cases, the size and location of a square match those of a single cell in the grid, whereas the size and location of a rectangle match those of a horizontal group of adjacent cells. This alignment highlights the presence of the otherwise invisible grid of cells that underpins the explicit system of boxes.

In *Intersection 2*, complications begin to emerge, as is apparent in Example 3.4, with narrower and shallower rectangles subdividing cells into parts that are clearly meant to be equal in size. Sometimes, these feature in compound symbols with irregular shapes. In three places, a smaller square appears in the corner of a cell, indicating an association with the corresponding quadrant. Two new varieties of symbols involving the diamond also appear, as in Example 3.10.

Square symbols do not appear in *Intersection 3*, and from this point in the series onwards Feldman indicated an association with a single cell simply by placing a symbol within it. This was facilitated by his changed presentation of the grid, with cells now drawn in. In *Intersection 2*, he, or more likely Cage, who recopied the score, included square outlines, which are drawn bolder to make them stand out from cells, which are also delineated, resulting in some rather unattractive redundancy.[11] The rectangles and irregularly shaped outlines, which are also drawn bolder, are not redundant, however, and Feldman continued to use this method of highlighting groups of adjacent cells until . . .*Out of 'Last Pieces'*.

In *Intersection 3*, individual cells are very regularly divided into upper and lower parts but never into narrower subsections. This division is implicit in the placement of numbers, as in Example 3.11. In the score of *Intersection 4*, some cells are divided into two narrower subsections by a dashed vertical line. This graph includes an ambiguous presentation,

---

[11] This redundancy is not present in Feldman's original presentation, seen in [Unsigned: G], *Selections from the Private Collection of Robert Rauschenberg* (New York: Gagosian Gallery, distributed by Rizzoli International Publications, 2012), 127. Feldman remembered that Cage had wanted the presentation to 'float visually' ('The future of local music', unpublished transcript, 89), which suggests that the redundancy was Cage's idea, not Feldman's.

Example 3.11   *Intersection 3*, ictuses 67–9

Example 3.12   *Intersection 4*, ictus 73

shown in Example 3.12. It is not clear whether the vertical arrangement on the right side reflects the restricted space available – in which case the symbol is 'A4', a regular occurrence elsewhere in the score – or the only example of an intended subdivision into quadrants.

Feldman's return to graph music in the late 1950s was marked initially by a renewed simplicity in his choice of symbols, as previously noted; numbers dominate the grid frames in the first few scores, compound symbols are rare or absent, and no attempt is made to divide cells. In both versions of *Ixion*, for example, numbers are the only symbols present, and, within the graph series, only *Projection 1* is as simple in this regard. *Atlantis* includes a few compound symbols with diamonds as constituent elements, but it is not until . . .*Out of 'Last Pieces'* that a greater diversity begins to emerge.

New symbols in . . .*Out of 'Last Pieces'* include Roman numerals and – as mentioned in Chapter 2 – the conventional musical sign for a grace note. A new variety of compound symbol, which straddles horizontal groups of adjacent cells, also makes its first appearance; this consists of one element in a single cell followed by a *dashed extension*, as in Examples 3.6 and 3.13. The five-line staves that split the last grid frame in this case are populated by note heads with incomplete ties, which appear here for the first time in the graph series.

The Straits of Magellan is notable for a material increase in the number of symbol types that are present (see Example 3.7), and further additions

Example 3.13   ...*Out of 'Last Pieces'*, ictuses 280–90, excerpt

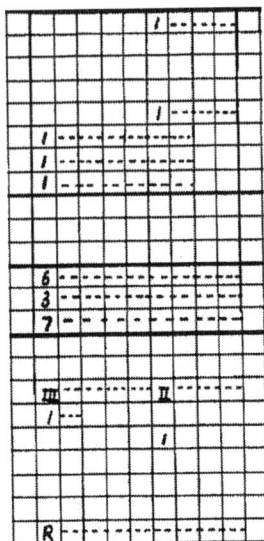

are included in *The King of Denmark* and *In Search of an Orchestration*. All told, the last three graphs in the series make use of an increasingly diverse pool of basic and compound symbols that includes letters, abbreviations, Roman numerals, numbers, shapes, arrows, pictograms, grace note signs and dashed lines, which appear alone or in combinations.

Innovations in the placement of symbols emerge in *The King of Denmark*, with Feldman including cases that straddle more than one row of the grid. Three different types are apparent in Example 3.8, and a fourth is evident in Example 3.14, which also includes a compound symbol, consisting of a grace note and an incomplete tie, that is located on the bottom line. This is one of several symbols located on the outer margins of grid frames, and not within them. Incomplete ties are very common in this particular score; here, as elsewhere, they are regarded as elements of compound symbols.

Split cells re-emerge in the piano part of *In Search of an Orchestration*, albeit only occasionally, but it is, once again, the proliferation of new symbols that is most striking. Among the many new varieties present, two merit highlighting at this stage. One is a *modified* grace note sign, drawn with a minim-like note head; these are prevalent, as is the more conventional grace note sign. Another is a new use of dashed lines; sometimes these precede and follow a third element, usually a modified grace

Example 3.14 *The King of Denmark*, ictuses 185–7

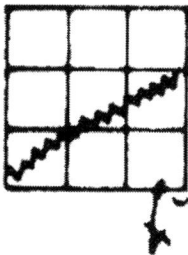

Example 3.15 *In Search of an Orchestration*, ictuses 434–46, excerpt

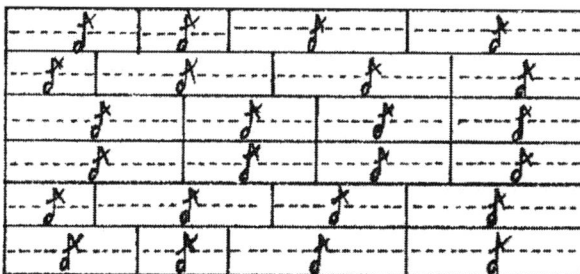

note sign, as in Example 3.15. The dashed line that precedes the grace note is referred to here as a *dashed prefix*.

Legibility

Robert Erickson has written approvingly of the notation of ...*Out of 'Last Pieces'* as follows: 'Morton Feldman has devised a notation for specifying changes of instrumental grouping which is practical enough for orchestral musicians to read'.[12] Apparently, Erickson was unaware of the existence of sets of performance materials for ...*Out of 'Last Pieces'* that include part-books presented in a non-graph format for instruments other than the piano. These are available from Peters. In a performance that uses these materials, only the conductor and the pianist will sight-read from the graph score.

In any case, Erickson's assessment, that the score, as presented by Feldman, is practical enough for musicians to read from, is dubious, and

---

[12] *Sound Structure in Music* (Berkeley: University of California Press, 1975), 91.

Example 3.16 . . .*Out of 'Last Pieces'*, page 8

it is ironic that he singled out for praise a style of presentation that is, arguably, among the least legible in the graph series. A non-standard page from the score is reproduced in Example 3.6, but the difficulties involved in reading from it are more apparent in Example 3.16.

Evidently, Feldman's presentation of the grid makes it difficult to follow by eye. One weakness is the lack of an effective method of subdividing the horizontal axis into subsections, which, like bar lines, might enable performers to relocate their horizontal positions in the score quickly after looking away. Feldman's inclusion of a system of dashed vertical lines, which appear above and below the grid every five ictuses, is too indistinct to perform this role. Moreover, the absence of gutters between instrumental parts gives the score a crowded aspect that hinders relocating one's vertical position. The strong horizontal lines that Feldman included, which divide the orchestra into six sections, are helpful, but not sufficient in themselves as several parts lie away from these divisions and the outer edges of the grid frame.

Used copies of the full score of . . .*Out of 'Last Pieces'* are routinely altered in ways intended to improve their ease of use in performances. For example, Tudor's copy has had a system of coloured lines added, presumably by Tudor himself.[13] A single blue line between the parts for harp and celesta extends through the entire score and was plainly intended

[13] David Tudor Papers, Getty Research Institute.

to provide him with a clearer indication of the vertical location of his parts than offered by Feldman. Furthermore, red vertical lines, which extend from the top to the bottom of the grid have been added every five ictuses, reinforcing the given division; here the intention must have been to provide a clearer system of reference for judging horizontal location. Copland's copy of the score, which was probably the one he used to conduct the San Francisco Symphony Orchestra's performance on 4 February 1967 at the War Memorial Opera House, San Francisco – his only documented involvement with this work – also has strong vertical lines added every five ictuses.[14] Anonymous examples of similar modifications are evident in the defaced performance materials supplied by Peters. Both copies of the full score included in one set are amended in ways intended to facilitate easier relocation. Like Tudor and Copland, a conductor has added a system of stronger vertical lines every five ictuses, whereas a pianist has highlighted the three horizontal lines of the piano part and the sounded ictuses in the celesta part with florescent yellow highlighter pen.[15] All these modifications suggest that Feldman's own presentation is imperfect. That said, the difficulties presented by it are easily remedied with minor modifications such as those mentioned above and, more importantly, they do not impair the ability of the notation to delineate a musical work.

Changes in the presentation of the grid in *The Straits of Magellan*, noted previously and evident in Example 3.7, address these weaknesses. These include the reintroduction of gutters between rows, which are widely spaced on the page and not contiguous, as in *Ixion, Atlantis* and *...Out of 'Last Pieces'*, and the use of a more pronounced system of vertical lines to subdivide the score into horizontal segments, each with a length of ten ictuses. A pre-publication copy of the score that lacks these changes and is therefore more difficult to read still survives.[16] In all likelihood, Feldman became aware of the problems involved in sight-reading from this earlier presentation and modified it accordingly. Another differentiating feature of the published edition is the presence of a conventional system of rehearsal numbers that replaces the clumsy system of Roman numerals with superscripts first used in *Ixion* for chamber ensemble. All told, the published edition of *The Straits of Magellan* is considerably easier to follow – in performance, rehearsal and analysis – than the immediately preceding graph scores.

---

[14] Aaron Copland Collection, Music Division, Library of Congress.
[15] This set bears the stamp of the BBC Symphony Orchestra.
[16] David Tudor Papers, Getty Research Institute.

Significance of vertical location within a grid frame

In the graphs for solo instruments, Feldman used the vertical position of a symbol within its grid frame to specify the register of the event that the symbol designates. Typically, he used three rows per instrument, with the symbol placed within only one, usually to indicate whether the register of the event is 'high' (upper row), 'middle' (middle row) or 'low' (lower row).

In the *Intersections* for solo instruments, some cells are divided – explicitly or implicitly – into upper and lower parts. Feldman's own comments about this aspect of his notation in the notes that accompany these scores are difficult to interpret for reasons explained in Chapter 9. Even so, his intention must have been to signal a division between upper and lower parts of the given register.

The King of Denmark signals finer-grained distinctions between registers using a different method, by allowing symbols to be placed on the outer margins of the grid frame. The explanatory notes indicate that he intended five register designations in this case – namely, 'very high' (on or above the top line), 'high' (upper row), 'middle' (middle row), 'low' (lower row) and 'very low' (on or below the bottom line).[17]

Feldman's use of the words 'high', 'middle' and 'low' indicate that his specifications of register were intended to be vague, not merely relative. Although his explanatory notes often state that the 'limits' of these ranges are to be freely chosen by the performers, he surely meant them to make choices consistent with the absolute connotations of his terms.[18] This constraint rules out many kinds of selection, including those in which narrow ranges adjacent to one another are selected. The division of the pitch spectrum into five parts in *The King of Denmark* is a late innovation with no implications for the interpretation of his tripartite division in earlier works.

In *Projection 1*, the vertical axis is also used to distinguish between three timbres (harmonic, pizzicato and arco), with each timbre allocated its own row of boxes and therefore three rows of cells (high, middle and low). In the graphs for small ensembles, the vertical axis is used to indicate the register and instrument to be used, with each instrument allocated one row

---

[17] At ictus 390, a grace note appears on the line between the middle and upper cells, suggesting a sixth category, but comparison with an alternative presentation (John Cage Collection, Northwestern University Music Library) suggests this was a copying error.

[18] Had he intended his indications of register to be understood as merely relative, without absolute connotations, it is unlikely that he would have labelled them as he did. 'Higher', 'intermediate' (or 'root' or 'basis') and 'lower' are among a range of alternatives lacking absolute connotations that he might have used.

of boxes and therefore three rows of cells. On some occasions, instrumental timbres are allocated their own row of boxes, and piano harmonics in the *Projections* are always treated in this manner.

The intended meaning of the register specification must be different when piano harmonics are indicated. Given the sensitivity of the outputs of such excitations to nuances of the inputs, the performer will struggle to control the register of these sounds. Consequently, it is reasonable to assume that Feldman intended his register indications, in these cases, to be read as tablatures, referring to the position of the keys to be depressed silently, and not to the register of the resulting sounds. That said, the performer will need to avoid keys in the high treble area when the indicated register is high because these do not operate dampers.

Limitations of space on the page would have made it awkward to emulate the presentation used in graphs for small ensembles when composing for larger forces; this may have been a factor in Feldman's decision to use the vertical axis differently in some graphs for larger combinations. In *Intersection 1*, he solved the space problem by using the vertical axis to indicate register (high, middle and low) and instrument type ('[wood]winds', 'brass', 'violins and violas', and 'cellos and basses'), with each instrument of the given type intended to read from the same indications. He used a similar approach in *Marginal Intersection*, which includes rows for '[wood]winds', 'brass' and 'strings',[19] and this is an idea that would subsequently re-emerge in modified form in *Piece for Four Pianos*, one of his first works with fixed pitches and indeterminate durations, in which the four pianists play from identical parts, as previously noted.

A new development in *Marginal Intersection* is that the directions for eight of the eleven instruments or instrumental groups are presented in shallower boxes each containing a single row of cells. This change was attributable to several factors, including Feldman's use of unpitched percussion instruments and the abolition of redundant rows in the parts for high and low oscillators. In other cases, it introduced the greatest degree of indeterminacy of pitch yet seen in the series, with the explanatory notes indicating that the xylophone, vibraphone, amplified guitar and piano are free to choose sounds from any register. This shift towards a greater degree of indeterminacy of pitch was promptly reversed in the next two graphs, *Intersection 2* and *Intersection 3*, in which Feldman sometimes included more precise specifications of register by subdividing his indications of high, middle and low into upper and lower parts.

---

[19] Labelling within parts indicates specific instruments in some places.

The solution to the space problem that Feldman favoured in graphs for larger ensembles from *Ixion* for chamber ensemble onwards was to allocate only one row in the grid frame to each instrument (or instrument type). In these cases, the vertical location of a symbol within a grid frame gives no information about the register of the event that it designates. Some general guidance about registers is given in the explanatory notes provided with these scores. Normally, these indicate that, unless otherwise stated, the high register should be used or, alternatively, that any register is admissible. Additional information is always provided, however. In some graphs, Feldman appended labels to certain areas of the grid that specify that the high or low registers are to be used in those passages (*Ixion* for chamber ensemble, *Atlantis* and *…Out of 'Last Pieces'*). In others, he used symbols containing information about the register of the events that they designate (*The Straits of Magellan* and *In Search of an Orchestration*).[20] Nonetheless, his indications of register in these works tend to be less precise than in the graphs for solo instruments or small ensembles.

Labelling in the score of *Ixion* for two pianos, which includes three rows of cells for each instrument, indicates that the register is 'high' except in a 'low' register intermission. This implies six register designations in this case – a tripartite subdivision between higher, intermediate and lower registers within a coarser bipartite division between high and low registers.

In *The Straits of Magellan* and *In Search of an Orchestration*, no indication of register is provided with the majority of designated events, and the explanatory notes indicate that the registers of these sounds are to be freely chosen by the performer. In *The Straits of Magellan*, 'any register (or registers) may be used' in two-thirds of cases and the corresponding figure for *In Search of an Orchestration* is almost nine-tenths. The implication is that the latter includes the highest overall degree of indeterminacy of pitch found in any graph. This belies the idea that Feldman became progressively less comfortable with indeterminacy as the series progressed, meaning that it would be wrong to see the final break with graph music as prefigured in his treatment of pitch.

These changes in presentation were not solely attributable to space limitations on Feldman's pages; it is reasonable to assume that, in some cases, they were linked to a desire to include differing degrees of indeterminacy. For example, only thirty rows would have been needed to present the score of *Ixion* for chamber ensemble using Feldman's original tripartite division of registers, and it is probable that there was room on his pages to accommodate these. Compare the thirty-three rows used in the published

---

[20] See his use of symbols that include vertical arrows in Examples 3.7 and 3.9.

edition of *Projection 5* and the thirty-one rows used in the published edition of *...Out of 'Last Pieces'*.

Meaning of squares, rectangles and numbers

In many of the earliest graphs, squares and rectangles appear as basic symbols. Ordinarily, these indicate single sounds from each instrument that reads from the part in question, although *divisi* is implied in a few places in the orchestral *Intersections*, in which some parts are read by more than one instrument.[21]

Numbers appear for the first time in the score of *Projection 2*, where they are used in the piano part as elements in a type of compound symbol whose meaning is not explained. Each symbol has two parts: a number; and a square or rectangle. The former is placed within the latter, which is placed directly over one or more adjacent cells.

The explanatory notes with subsequent graphs, up to and including *Intersection 4*, and other surviving materials indicate that in these works numbers specify the quantity of notes to be played simultaneously.[22] The only exception occurs in *Intersection 2*, in which the number 12 is used to refer to a chord containing twelve or more simultaneous notes. Lower numbers are used in this work in the standard way, however. Given the consistency of Feldman's use of numbers in this period, it is safe to assume that they perform the same role in *Projection 2*.

Numbers appear in every subsequent graph except *Intersection 1* which, like *Projection 1*, includes only empty squares and rectangles. One change in the way that numbers are used occurs in *Intersection 3*, where they make their first appearance as basic symbols. This shift was a delayed response to the changed presentation of the grid frames in the graphs from *Intersection 2*, as previously noted.

The explanatory notes with *Intersection 4* state that '[n]umbers indicate the amount of sounds to be played simultaneously (if possible)'. Read one way, this gives no guidance about how the performer should proceed if an instruction proves impossible to execute; it merely recognises the fact that the instructions may be impossible to perform in certain places. The possibility of an alternative and more informative reading is clearer if

---

[21] See *Intersection 1*, brass, ictus 325 and *Marginal Intersection*, [wood]winds, ictuses 546 and 556.

[22] The explanatory notes with the piano *Intersections* state that 'numbers mean how many keys one plays'. However, in a statement published alongside an excerpt from *Intersection 2* in 1963, Feldman wrote that '[n]umbers in each box indicate how many sounds will be played simultaneously' ('Marginal Intersection, Intersection II, Intermission VI' [1963], in Friedman (ed.), *Give My Regards*, 11).

Feldman's instruction is rewritten, with added emphasis, as: '[n]umbers indicate the amount of sounds to be played *simultaneously* (if possible)'. Read this way, Feldman's statement implies that a performer unable to comply may ignore the requirement of simultaneity.

The principal use of numbers in later graphs is different. The notes provided with them state that numbers indicate 'the amount of sounds' to be played or 'how many sounds are to be played', and both these formulations must mean the quantity of consecutive sounds. In *Atlantis*, . . .*Out of 'Last Pieces'* and *The Straits of Magellan*, the piano is treated as a special case, with numbers used as in the early graphs,[23] and this special status is granted not only to the piano, but also to the celesta and harp in *In Search of an Orchestration*. This difference between the earlier and the later graphs was instrumental in producing a noticeably different outcome in performance, as previously mentioned.

In *Ixion* for chamber ensemble, Feldman recognised that the numbers included in the parts for woodwinds, brass and piano are sometimes so high that the indicated quantity of consecutive sounds may not be playable within the specified bracket, and in these cases he indicated the appropriate strategy. For woodwinds and brass, the performer is to 'articulate as many as possible, and flutter or double-tongue the rest, avoiding glissando'; for the pianist, 'the remaining sounds are simultaneous'.

Significance of horizontal location and length of symbol

The horizontal axis of each grid frame refers to units of regular pulse, with successive intercepts designating successive ictuses. It is unlikely that Feldman intended any patterning of emphasis within groups of cells, and, in this regard, all ictuses are equal.[24] Typically, the horizontal location of a symbol within a grid frame locates the designated event within the ictus of the cell in which the symbol is placed or, if the symbol straddles several cells, within their ictuses. Consequently, it locates the associated event within a precisely defined period of elapsed time once the tempo is determined. This period, measured in ictuses or seconds, is the *bracket* in which the event is to occur.

---

[23] The explanatory notes with *Atlantis* state that the piano should be played 'similar in style' to the more conventionally notated, chord-based work *Last Pieces*, suggesting that in its case numbers specify the quantity of sounds to be played simultaneously. In the other works mentioned in the text, Feldman's written remarks state that the notation of the piano part should be understood in precisely this fashion.

[24] A credible explanation of Feldman's decision to abandon the use of boxes is that he came to regard them as potentially misleading, being suggestive of a system of bar lines, a 4/4 time signature and a recurring pattern of emphasis within bars.

No indication of tempo is given in either version of *Ixion*, but indicative guidance is provided in every other case. Sometimes, Feldman's specifications are precise,[25] but it is safe to assume that he intended a degree of flexibility even in these cases, in line with conventional practice. One commentator has suggested the use of a fluctuating tempo in performances of *The King of Denmark*,[26] but this is a mistake. When Feldman expected the tempo to vary, he notated specific fluctuations, as in *Intersection 2* or, alternatively, stated that this was what he had in mind, as in his conventionally notated *Structures* for orchestra.[27] Chapter 1 argued that the transition from the *Projections* to the *Intersections* was motivated, in part, by a desire to mask the rigidity of the temporal organisation of the earlier works. If he had been prepared to accept the use of fluctuating tempos, this would have been unnecessary.

The horizontal location of a symbol also provides additional information about the placement of the designated event within its bracket, but this varies over the course of the series. In the *Projections*, the designated event is to extend throughout the bracket in which it occurs. Consequently, in these works, the square and rectangular symbols that Feldman placed within his grid frames locate the onsets and endings of designated events relative to the pulse, whereas the *lengths* of these symbols (i.e. their horizontal extents), measured in numbers of cells, indicate their durations in ictuses. Some lengths appear to have been drawn free hand, and on occasions these are slightly shorter or longer than an integer number of cells. The discrepancies are usually small, however, and it is safe to assume that integer numbers of cells and therefore ictuses were always intended.

The notation of the *Projections* is therefore proportional, in the strict sense that the horizontal placement and extent of a symbol are related to the temporal coordinates of the designated event (within the period covered by each grid frame) by a linear function. For that reason, the lengths of symbols and spaces between them are directly proportional to the durations of designated events and intervening rests or silences, measured in ictuses and seconds. Hence, the notation provides a transparent visual impression of the temporal organisation of the associated music. The visual correspondence between score and sound is enhanced by the fact that silences need not be marked with symbols, as in conventionally notated music, but can be left blank.

---

[25] Tempo is precisely stated in *Intersections 2–4, Atlantis, . . .Out of 'Last Pieces'* and *The Straits of Magellan*.

[26] Pratt, 'Performance analysis', 72–3.

[27] *Structures* includes the following note: 'Fluctuate between ♩ = 60–69'.

The fact that, in these works, symbols are always associated with integer numbers of grid cells means that Feldman declined to take full advantage of the greater flexibility in specifying locations and durations that his notation afforded. His use of proportionality was *digital* in the sense that he restricted his selections along the horizontal axis to a set of discrete values. This contrasts with an *analogue* treatment in which any point along the axis is regarded as available for use, with the intended location and duration of an event depending upon the precise location and length of the associated symbol.

Feldman's digital approach was by no means compulsory, and an analogue alternative would certainly have increased the notation's expressive power by allowing much finer distinctions between event locations and durations relative to the pulse. In addition, it would have alleviated his persistent concerns about the rigidity of the temporal frame within which he felt he was force-fitting his sounds: with an analogue approach, the outline of the frame is analogous to a ruler against which the sounds are laid, and not a series of adjacent compartments that contain them. Perhaps Feldman's conception of notated rhythm remained too firmly rooted in the idea of counting beats to allow him to take this additional step, which Earle Brown would go on to take in his *Folio* works, *Twenty-Five Pages* and *Four Systems*.[28] He may also have had concerns about legibility, fearing that the difficulty involved in accurately sight-reading fine-grained distinctions between symbol lengths would encourage performers to take measurements and prepare more precisely notated materials in advance of performing, which was not what he wanted. Feldman originally conceived of performers interpreting his instructions spontaneously during the course of a performance, for reasons outlined in Chapters 4 and 8.

Given that Feldman declined to take full advantage of the expressive power latent in the proportionality of his notation, it is fitting to consider why, nevertheless, he may have regarded it as an asset. Clearly, his digital approach has no more expressive power than conventional methods of conveying information about duration with a system of note heads and dots, and the musical content of his presentation could be reproduced easily in a notation that is not proportional, but considerably closer in character to more conventional notation, using note heads and a one-line or three-line stave. In all likelihood, Feldman valued the previously mentioned fact that the horizontal dimension of his notation on the page gives a more literal picture of the development of the music in time than

---

[28] For Brown's account of the circumstances that led him to take this step, see 'The notation and performance of new music', 191–2.

conventional staff notation. Indeed, the divisive method traditionally used in notating shorter durations not only lacks the proportionality of symbol lengths with respect to time found in the additive time notation of the *Projections*, but also possesses an ungainly inverse proportionality, with ever shorter sounds being designated by ever more complex symbols. The importance that Feldman placed on visual aspects of his graph notation, and the reasons why, are highlighted in Chapter 4.

After the *Projections*, the nature of the additional information provided by the horizontal location and length of a symbol is not always so clear, and it is occasionally not possible to be definitive about Feldman's intentions. This is because his explanatory notes are sometimes equivocal, a circumstance at least partly attributable to his penchant for excessively brief explanations. His view was that a composer working with a bespoke notation should avoid lengthy explanations of how it is to be interpreted; this, he felt, 'should be implicit in the score',[29] but one effect of this policy was to obscure the intended meaning of his notation in some places.

A problem of this type emerges from a review of his comments concerning the *Intersections*. Those with the published edition of *Intersection 1* include:

> The performer may make his entrance on or within each given time duration. [. . .] The dynamics are also freely chosen by all players, but once established, must be sustained at the same level to the end of the given time duration.

This statement is almost identical to the one supplied with the published edition of *Marginal Intersection*, and it is very similar to another included in a more general description of the *Intersection* series published in the journal *trans/formation* in early 1952.[30] However, it differs markedly from those provided with the published editions of the remaining *Intersections*. His comments with *Intersections 2–3*, which are very similar to those with *Intersection 4*, are:

> The player is free to choose any dynamic and to make any rhythmic entrance on or within given situation. Sustained sounds once played must be held to the end of the notated duration.[31]

Viewed in isolation, Feldman's comments with *Intersection 1* and *Marginal Intersection* are clear: the designated event can begin at any time within its bracket, but it must be terminated at, and not before, its

---

[29] Cage and Feldman, *Radio Happenings*, 179.   [30] Feldman *et al.*, '4 musicians at work', 168.
[31] The word 'entrance' has been rendered incorrectly as 'entrances' in the typeset notes in the latest editions of *Intersection 2* and *Intersection 3*, which form part of EP67976.

end. One implication is that an event specified in a long bracket may be short if the performer defers entering for a sufficient length of time. Another is that every event – be it long or short – must be held until the end of the bracket in which it occurs. This straightforward reading is not clearly consistent with the comments provided with *Intersection 2–4*, however. These also imply that an event specified in a long bracket may be short, but they insinuate that only '[s]ustained sounds' must be held until the end of the bracket in which they occur and therefore that the performer is free to terminate shorter sounds earlier.

The implied constraints on sounds specified in single ictuses clearly differ, but it will be useful to begin by focusing on longer brackets because in these the differences are likely to be more marked in performance. There is no suggestion in either statement quoted above that sounds specified in extended time brackets must themselves be extended, so it is safe to assume that this need not be the case. Nevertheless, it is initially unclear how Feldman's concept of '[s]ustained sounds', which appears in his comments with *Intersections 2–4*, is to be interpreted. Are these simply sounds occurring in longer brackets or are they, as etymology might suggest, sounds in longer brackets that the performer chooses to play as sustained? The difference between the two readings is considerable. Understood in the first way, sounds specified in longer brackets must always be held until the end of their brackets, and this is consistent with his comments with *Intersection 1* and *Marginal Intersection*. Understood in the second way, sounds in longer brackets may be terminated earlier in the designated period if they are played short. On this reading, a performer playing a sound in an extended bracket is free to play a sustained sound that extends to the end of the bracket or a short sound anywhere within it.

The disparity between the two sets of comments is not attributable to the passage of time. As a rule, the surviving sketches do not include explanatory notes, although there is evidence that notes were originally present in some cases.[32] However, it is clear that the *trans/formation* text and the notes supplied with the published edition of *Intersection 2*, which were recopied by Cage in late 1951 and published subsequently in his handwriting, were produced at around the same time. Yet, they appear inconsistent with one another.

One possibility is that Feldman simply decided to modify the intended interpretation of his graph notation after he completed *Marginal*

---

[32] The residue of a typed set of notes for *Marginal Intersection* is glued to the back of one of the surviving sketches (Morton Feldman Collection, Paul Sacher Foundation). The surviving text does not refer to symbol location and length.

Intersection without applying the revision retroactively to the two *Intersections* that he had, by then, already composed,[33] but several factors argue against this. One is his use of a common term in the titles of works from before and after this alleged change of heart. Another emerges from a review of his comments about *Intersection 2*, which appear alongside an excerpt from the score, in an article issued in 1963, the same year in which the full score was first published:

> The performer may make any entrance within a given time duration, but must hold until end of duration. [. . .] The performer is also free to choose any dynamic at any entrance, but must maintain sameness of volume to end of given duration.[34]

Evidently, these comments are much closer to those in the published editions of *Intersection 1* and *Marginal Intersection* than those with the published editions of *Intersections 2–4*, which seems to suggest that Feldman regarded his two explanations as interchangeable. His use of this alternative formulation also rules out the idea – mooted above – that he intended to allow the performer to curtail a short sound anywhere within an extended time bracket. The implication is that Feldman's references to '[s]ustained sounds' in his comments with the published editions of *Intersections 2–4* actually concern extended time brackets – that is, those with a duration of two or more ictuses.

The preceding analysis has stressed the differences between the two sets of comments. These are marked in theory, but a review of other aspects of these works suggests that they are likely to be less conspicuous in practice. This is because *Intersections 2–4* are unlike their predecessors in the series in being imposing virtuoso works and, in many places, this is bound to constrain the performer's ability to control the terminus of a sound specified as occurring in a single ictus. Perhaps this is why Feldman appears to have been unconcerned by the theoretical differences between his explanations, regarding them as largely equivalent. It may also explain why he preferred to use a different formulation in connection with the virtuoso works for he may have been keen to avoid demanding a degree of control that was not feasible in practice in very many places; hence his insistence, in these cases, on terminating a sound at the end of the bracket in which it occurs only if it is '[s]ustained'. Be that as it may, Feldman's reversion to a form of wording with *Intersection 2* that is similar to the one

---

[33] For this to be credible, Feldman must have completed the *trans/formation* text before finishing *Intersection 2*.

[34] 'Marginal Intersection', 11. A minor error in this edition of Feldman's article has been corrected.

used in the published editions of *Intersection 1* and *Marginal Intersection* strongly suggests that this expresses his true vision of how the virtuoso works should be played where feasible.

Plainly, Feldman's time bracket notation in the *Intersections* would have been difficult to express in a more conventional format without redefining the meanings of standard musical symbols, and although it is not proportional in the strict sense described earlier, it does have proportional aspects. For example, there is a proportional relationship between space on the page and elapsed time in performance, as there was in the *Projections*. Moreover, the temporal locations and durations of brackets are related to the physical locations and lengths of symbols by a linear function while the implied locations of event endings in time are similarly related to symbol endpoints.[35] These aspects mean that the organisation of symbols within the grid frames remains more closely correlated with the temporal organisation of events and silences than in works presented in more conventional notation; hence, it gives a more accurate visual impression of the temporal organisation of the music. This watered-down proportionality with respect to time remained a feature of all subsequent graphs.

In the *Intersections*, symbols are of various lengths, but except in rare cases they are clearly intended to be read as associated with an integer number of adjacent grid cells. This suggests that Feldman continued to interpret the temporal proportionality of his notation in digital fashion; indeed, this was an aspect of its use that never changed. In *Intersection 2* and *Intersection 4*, some symbols divide the lengths of cells into approximately equal parts, as in Examples 3.4 and 3.12, and these were surely intended to be seen as equal, as previously noted. If so, then Feldman's conception was based on a smaller minimum unit of duration, but remained digital even in these cases.

In *Ixion* for chamber ensemble, the next graph in the series, in which every time bracket is a single ictus in length, the notes that accompany the score state that numbers indicate 'the amount of sounds to be played on or within the box'. This explanation does not specify where, within brackets, designated events should end, but the argument presented above strongly suggests that in the immediately preceding graphs, every sound was meant to extend to the end of its bracket wherever possible. Should we ignore history and conclude that the intended meaning of the bracket notation had changed in the five intervening years or should we lean on historical

---

[35] This is not strictly true of *Intersection 2*, in which changes in tempo are specified and proportional relationships hold only within areas in which the same tempo applies.

precedent and regard the explanatory notes with *Ixion* for chamber ensemble as misleading?

In practical terms, the two alternatives will not result in significantly different performances in many places. In this particular work, every event occurs in a single ictus; there are no extended time brackets. Moreover, performers are often asked to play several consecutive notes within a unit of pulse, and where this applies, they will often need to make use of the maximum available span. That said, there are occasions on which the score specifies only one or two notes per ictus where the two readings may result in audible differences.

This may seem a minor issue, but its significance for current purposes is magnified by the fact that the explanatory notes that accompany subsequent graphs do not seem to throw additional light on this matter. For example, those with *Atlantis* are equally unhelpful, stating only that numbers indicate 'the amount of sounds to be played on or within the duration of the beat'. Consequently, our reading of *Ixion* is likely to colour our interpretation of events specified within a single ictus in every subsequent graph.

In my view, the proper course in this case is to ignore history and prioritise a literal reading of Feldman's explanatory notes – that is to say, an event specified in a single ictus can begin and end anywhere within it. One reason is that the five-year gap between *Intersection 4* and *Ixion* is too long to allow us to simply assume an entirely unchanged thought process. Another is his subsequent use of grace note signs as symbols in the graphs from . . .*Out of 'Last Pieces'* onwards, which points to the historical precedent of the *Projections* and *Intersections* having been overturned by this stage. It seems very unlikely that he would have insisted on grace notes being forcibly aligned with the end points of brackets in which they occur.[36]

Every event in *Ixion* is specified as occurring within a single ictus, but subsequent graphs typically specify events occurring in longer periods and these pose new problems of interpretation. For example, six symbols of longer length appear in the piano part of *Atlantis* without any associated commentary. One question that arises here is whether Feldman intended to give the pianist flexibility to curtail these events before the ends of the brackets in which they occur or whether he expected them to be sustained

---

[36] The use of the grace note sign is not explained in . . .*Out of 'Last Pieces'*, but Feldman ordinarily conceived of it as designating a note that is short, but not too short, which is played off the beat. See the written remarks with *The Straits of Magellan* ('[g]race notes should not be played too quickly') and Copland's annotations on his copy of the score of . . .*Out of 'Last Pieces'*, which are headed 'Full conversation with composer' ('not on beat').

until the ends of their respective brackets, as in the *Intersections*. The former answer parallels the reading of shorter symbols, spanning single cells, recommended above, but the latter reading is to be preferred. This is because longer symbols in . . .*Out of 'Last Pieces'* – presented for the first time using dashed extensions – must be interpreted in this way as the explanatory notes provided with the score are clear on this matter. Consequently, *Atlantis* is flanked, on both sides, by graphs in which this reading is appropriate.

Another question concerning the longer symbols in *Atlantis* is whether the performer is free to enter anywhere within the designated bracket, even close to its very end or, alternatively, whether the associated events must be sustained. The former answer mirrors the reading of extended time brackets in the *Intersections* recommended above, but in subsequent graphs, in which the dashed extension is used as the principal means of indicating an extended bracket, a similar reading is doubtful. This is because Feldman's explanations of dashed extensions consistently suggest that these designate events that are themselves 'sustained'. For example, in . . .*Out of 'Last Pieces'*, the explanatory notes state that '[b]roken lines are used to indicate sustained sounds', and similar statements are provided with most subsequent graphs, as will become clear. The implication is that the performer should not defer his or her entrance until the last moment in these cases.[37] The upshot is that *Atlantis* is sandwiched between graphs in which the correct interpretation of extended time brackets differs, making it hard to be sure which was intended in its case. The right course for performers uncomfortable with this uncertainty is to ensure that the events in question are all sustained: this is bound to be consistent with Feldman's wishes because it fits with a reading of his notation that requires this outcome and with one that deems it optional but not necessary.

The explanatory notes with *The Straits of Magellan* state that numbers indicate the amount of sounds to be played 'within the duration of each box' and similar comments appear in the notes with *The King of Denmark* and *In Search of an Orchestration*. As in the immediately preceding graphs, nothing is said about where events designated by numbers should end within brackets and my assumption is, as before, that a performer is free to terminate an event specified as occurring within a single ictus before the end of the bracket in which it occurs. Once again, Feldman was less than clear about how longer symbols, which are common in these last graphs, should be interpreted. For example, in the explanatory notes with *The*

---

[37] This approach is viable in the last two graphs in places in which extended brackets are marked by undivided sections, however.

Straits of Magellan, he wrote that '[b]roken lines [i.e. dashed extensions] are used to sustain one sound until the next'. Similar instructions were to become common in his scores with fixed pitches and indeterminate durations from 1963, but this earlier example is unique within the graph series and unfortunate. In several places in the score, the end of a bracket is followed by one or more empty columns.[38] This means that the score and the accompanying written remarks are inconsistent. In my view, the right course is to prioritise the integrity of the symbolic notation and disregard the written remark.

All we are told on this matter in *The King of Denmark* is that dashed extensions indicate 'sustained sounds'. This leaves it unclear whether the designated event must be sustained until the end of its time bracket, but it does indicate that the performer should not defer entering for too long. This strongly suggests that the same is true of *The Straits of Magellan*, because this particular graph is therefore preceded and followed by others in which this interpretation is compulsory.

There are other reasons to believe that Feldman continued to think of events in extended time brackets as sustained until the ends of the brackets in which they occur, however. For example, he was certainly thinking along these lines some months before completing *The King of Denmark*. In a lecture probably delivered early in 1964, he described a hypothetical graph as having 'a field of time when all the instruments of the orchestra begin anyplace [. . .] and once they begin, hold that particular sound over until the end of the duration'.[39] The implication is that he was thinking of extended brackets – or fields of time, as he referred to them here – in the same way as he had conceived of them in . . .*Out of 'Last Pieces'*, even at this relatively late stage in the series.

The notes with *In Search of an Orchestration*, which are more comprehensive, describe three different types of compound symbol involving grace note signs. One of these involves a modified grace note – one drawn with a minim-like note head – and a dashed extension. Feldman's notes state that this indicates 'a sustained sound, to be held to the end of the given overall duration', and the fact that this symbol is used to indicate a sustained sound held to the end of its bracket must be significant for the interpretation of symbols with dashed extensions in the two immediately preceding graphs. Given that these symbols are known to have been used in

---

[38] Examples appear between the following rehearsal numbers: 19–21; 26–8; 29–31; 38–9; and 40–1. Broken lines are often associated with single sounds, so Feldman's instruction to sustain one sound to the next cannot be interpreted as a call to avoid gaps between sounds within individual brackets.

[39] 'Morton Feldman with Dore Ashton', 7.

a similar way in …*Out of 'Last Pieces'* and *In Search of an Orchestration*, this is a good enough reason for supposing that they were used in similar fashion in the two intervening graphs.

The explanatory notes with *In Search of an Orchestration* also define two other compound symbols involving grace notes, both of which include a dashed prefix as well as a dashed extension. One, which uses a modified grace note sign, indicates 'a sustained sound, to be played at any time within the given overall duration. This sound may be held to the end, or released before the end, of the duration'. The other one, which uses a conventional grace note sign, 'indicates a short sound, played at any time within the given overall duration'. Curiously, there are no instances within the score itself of a symbol of this second type. However, in various places, Feldman included an unexplained symbol involving a conventional grace note sign in an undivided section. Several of these are evident in Example 3.9, and there can be little doubt that they are an equivalent replacement for the absent variety explained in his written remarks.

Undivided sections were used for the first time in *The King of Denmark*, as noted previously in this chapter. Some of these contain symbols of standard size, whereas others contain larger numbers that straddle all three rows of the grid, as in Example 3.8. According to the notes with the score, '[l]arge numbers (encompassing High, Middle and Low) indicate single sounds to be played in all registers and in any time sequence'. In view of the interpretation of undivided sections in *In Search of an Orchestration* outlined above, it is clear that large numbers indicate the quantity of consecutive sounds to be played anywhere within the indicated duration, with the last sound ending before or as the bracket closes.

Less clear is the intended meaning of undivided sections that contain one or more smaller symbols within rows. Feldman did not explain these, but it is probable that they should be understood in an analogous manner, as indicating an event designated by the symbol in the given register, occurring within or throughout the corresponding bracket.

The incomplete ties that regularly appear in compound symbols in *The King of Denmark* are not explained, but must be continuation marks indicating *lasciq̇ vibrare*. The implication is that, in these cases, the performer should refrain from terminating the designated event artificially, so that the music sounds on. Continuation marks, which also appear in the score of *In Search of an Orchestration*, were a significant development in Feldman's graph music. Evidently, brackets associated with these symbols are not meant to circumscribe designated events. They also introduce a new aspect of indeterminacy of duration.

The last grid frame in the score of *The King of Denmark* – shown in Example 3.8 – contains a short section without vertical lines that contains the words 'as many different sounds as possible', which are followed by continuation marks. Here, Feldman's meaning is clear and no additional explanation was necessary. Maximising the number of sounds will involve beginning on the opening beat and continuing to initiate sounds throughout the next five ictuses.

4 Ideology

On some occasions, Feldman portrayed the genesis of his graph music as a spontaneous creative act, performed in Cage's apartment in the winter of 1950–1, rather than the culmination of a search for a format that would satisfy previously defined needs. In comments quoted in Chapter 1, for example, he explained that he 'didn't have any kind of theory' and that he had 'no idea what was going to emerge' when he 'doodled' his first graph.[1] On other occasions, however, he connected the genesis of the format with advantages he claimed for it, suggesting a more calculated mode of discovery, and several examples are discussed below. That said, and as noted in Chapter 1, there is no other evidence – in his surviving notebooks, for example – to suggest that he actively searched for a new notation before finding one. The assumption here is that the original creative act was spontaneous, and that the claimed advantages of the graph format were conceived by him in its aftermath.

These advantages were closely connected with his thinking about music in general. Not every claimed benefit was evident from the outset: some were recognised over time as he gained experience with the notation. Others were consequential upon later innovations, some of which arose in response to problems he encountered in early performances, and, as will become clear, these exerted a profound effect on the resulting sound.

Sound

Many of Feldman's recorded remarks present his use of graphs as a way of giving sole emphasis to 'sound', 'sounds', 'sound itself' or 'sounds themselves',[2] but he rarely addressed these concepts or explained the benefits to be expected from prioritising sound in this way. A useful point of departure in attempting to clarify his views is the following anecdote:

---

[1] 'An interview with Morton Feldman, Jan Williams', 153.

[2] For examples of his use of 'sound itself', see '...Out of "Last Pieces"', G, and 'The anxiety of art' [1965], in Friedman (ed.), *Give My Regards*, 22. For 'sounds themselves', see 'Earle Brown' [1966], in Friedman (ed.), *Give My Regards*, 44, and 'A compositional problem' [1972], in Friedman (ed.), *Give My Regards*, 110. For analogous expressions of enthusiasm for sound, see E. Brown, 'Some notes on composing', 301, 304; Cage, 'History of experimental music in the United States' [1959], in *Silence*, 68–9; and Wolff, 'Immobility in motion: new and electronic music' [1958], in Gronemeyer and Oehlschlägel (eds.), *Christian Wolff*, 24.

I spent the weekend with Karlheinz Stockhausen, and he had a lot of my scores, and he took them to his room and said goodnight. And he came down in the morning and he said, 'I know you have no system, but what is your secret?' And I said to him, 'Well, Karlheinz, I have no secret, but if I could say anything to you, I advise you to leave the sounds alone; don't push them; because they're very much like human beings – if you push them, they push you back. So if I have a secret it would be, "don't push the sounds".' And he leaned over me and he said, 'Not even a little bit?'[3]

The imagery in this passage, of the foolhardy Stockhausen pushing sounds around and of them resisting this pressure, is striking, with sounds portrayed as resistant physical entities or even recalcitrant biological organisms.[4] If presented with it in isolation, it would be tempting to dismiss this imagery as nothing more than poetic licence, included for its undeniably humorous effect, but a review of Feldman's surviving statements reveals that this would be a mistake, for closely related ideas crop up in contexts in which he is clearly in earnest.

For example, Feldman gave the following description of his ideas about sound in a 1964 programme note:

The discovery that sound *in itself* can be a totally plastic phenomenon, suggesting its own shape, design and poetic metaphor, led me to devise a new system of graphic notation – an 'indeterminate' structure allowing for the direct utterance of the sound, unhampered by compositional rhetoric.

Unlike improvisation, which relies solely on memory in selecting the most empirical and sophisticated examples of a style, or styles, the purpose of the graph is to erase memory, to erase virtuosity – to do away with everything but a direct action in terms of the sound itself.[5]

Feldman's idea that sound 'in itself' can suggest 'its own shape, design and poetic metaphor' points, once again, to a conception of sound as capable of acting independently. Moreover, his stated aim of 'allowing for the direct utterance of the sound, unhampered by compositional rhetoric' strongly suggests that he regarded the rightful role of the composer as being to step aside, thereby allowing the sounds to have their say. This interpretation is also encouraged by his occasional references to

---

[3] 'An interview with Morton Feldman, David Charlton and Jolyon Laycock, May 1966' [1967], in Villars (ed.), *Morton Feldman Says*, 28. Compare 'Morton Feldman with Dore Ashton', 5–6; 'Predeterminate/indeterminate' [1966], in Friedman (ed.), *Give My Regards*, 33; and 'Crippled symmetry' [1981], 142–3.

[4] For Feldman's use of the word 'physical' in connection with sound, see, for example, 'Liner notes', 5, and 'Morton Feldman talking to Wilfrid Mellers about his work and the problem of new music', audio recording of BBC broadcast on 28 August 1966, British Library.

[5] '. . .Out of "Last Pieces"', G.

'freeing the sound'.[6] Although these invite a political reading, Feldman was adamant that interpreting his attitudes to sound as 'slogans of [human] freedom' was a misunderstanding.[7]

The idea that the role of the composer is, quite literally, simply to step aside is difficult to swallow, of course, and it is safe to assume that the 1964 programme note, quoted from above, presents an over-simplification of his views, which were more carefully stated in a 1966 interview:

> I think that we [i.e. Feldman and the Abstract Expressionist painters] would allow things to take on their own form, their own poetic metaphor in fact. We were more the observer of the material. And the whole idea was to create a – well one might even call it a precarious balance between the material and its manipulation. And I think it is on that kind of see-saw that a work is accomplished; this balance between the material and those that are involved.[8]

In this more considered statement, Feldman portrayed himself not merely as stepping aside and allowing sounds to speak, but as acting on sounds with due regard for their inherent properties and propensities. His use of the term 'material' in a way that appears to be synonymous with 'sound' is common in his writings and noteworthy because it suggests that he thought of sound as a kind of substance or matter. This is also indicated by his use, elsewhere, in connection with sound, of terminology that is more commonly associated with materials science, such as 'elastic' and 'plasticity', and by his description of it as a 'plastic phenomenon' in the passage from 1964 quoted above, suggesting malleability.[9]

No doubt one element underpinning Feldman's desire to give sound sole emphasis in his compositions from this period was his conviction that the burden of music history is otherwise too great, and that to succumb to history is to allow it to 'crush all that is subtle, all that is personal, in our work'.[10] This line of thinking does not account for his conception of sound as a physical material, with inherent properties and propensities, however, and this aspect of his views probably emerged from his contacts with

---

[6] 'H. C. E. (here comes everybody), Morton Feldman in conversation with Peter Gena, January 1982' [1982], in Villars (ed.), *Morton Feldman Says*, 122. See also 'Liner notes', 6, and 'A compositional problem', 110.

[7] '"Sublimation is the word". Lecture, 2 July 1986', in Mörchen (ed.), *Morton Feldman in Middelburg*, 188.

[8] 'Morton Feldman talking to Wilfrid Mellers'.

[9] For 'elastic', see '. . .Out of "Last Pieces"', G. For 'plasticity', see 'Liner notes', 6. 'Plasticity' is a technical term of materials science that refers to the ability of a material to retain a new shape once the pressure that created it is removed.

[10] 'The anxiety of art', 21. For a discussion, see Kevin Volans, 'What is Feldman?', *Tempo*, vol. 68, no. 270 (October 2014), 9.

Varèse and the Abstract Expressionist painters. According to his own testimony, Feldman spoke with Varèse regularly in the late 1940s,[11] and we can therefore assume familiarity with Varèse's idea of music as 'bodies of intelligent sounds moving freely in space'.[12] This implies that sounds are physical and autonomous, with tendencies of their own, an idea having evident affinities with Feldman's subsequent thinking.

Feldman referred to the influence of Abstract Expressionist painting on his conception of sound in several places, including the passage from the 1966 interview just quoted.[13] Respect for the physical properties of paint was a preoccupation of Abstract Expressionism in the 1940s and 1950s,[14] and in some cases the painters conceived of the paint they used as autonomous and as playing an active role in guiding their work. Pollock famously suggested that 'the painting has a life of its own. I try to let it come through' in an article published in the winter of 1947–8,[15] and years later Feldman himself would suggest that '[a] painter will perhaps agree that a color insists on being a certain size, regardless of his wishes'.[16] In comments published in 1956, Guston maintained that '[t]he very matter of painting – its pigment and spaces – is so resistant to the will'; an observation redolent of Feldman's subsequent advice to Stockhausen.[17]

Feldman recalled that it was Cage who introduced him into the world of the painters in the period after they first met in January 1950.[18] He quickly became one of a small group of composers involved in the Club,[19] and he and Cage also frequented the Cedar Tavern, a favourite haunt of painters

[11] 'Darmstadt lecture, 26 July 1984' [1985], in Villars (ed.), *Morton Feldman Says*, 196.

[12] Varèse, 'The liberation of sound', 204.

[13] See, for example, 'Liner notes', 5, and 'A life without Bach and Beethoven' [1964], in Friedman (ed.), *Give My Regards*, 15.

[14] Meyer Schapiro, '"The liberating quality of avant-garde art", 1957' [1957], in Clifford Ross (ed.), *Abstract Expressionism: Creators and Critics: An Anthology* (New York: H. N. Abrams, 1990), 262, and Robert Goldwater, 'Reflections on the New York School' [1960], in Shapiro and Shapiro (eds.), *Abstract Expressionism*, 135.

[15] '"My painting," *Possibilities*, Winter 1947–48' [1947–8], in Karmel (ed.), *Jackson Pollock*, 18.

[16] 'Vertical thoughts' [1963], in Friedman (ed.), *Give My Regards*, 12.

[17] 'Statement in *Twelve Americans* (1956)' [1956], in Coolidge (ed.), *Philip Guston*, 10. The profound influence of Abstract Expressionist painting on Feldman's ideology and music is well known, but the link between Abstract Expressionism and his graph music has not been explored in detail. More general discussions include: Jonathan W. Bernard, 'Feldman's painters', in Steven Johnson (ed.), *The New York Schools of Music and Visual Arts: John Cage, Morton Feldman, Edgard Varèse, Willem de Kooning, Jasper Johns, Robert Rauschenberg* (New York: Routledge, 2002), 173–215; Amy C. Beal, '"Time Canvases": Morton Feldman and the painters of the New York School', in James Leggio (ed.), *Music and Modern Art* (New York: Routledge, 2002), 227–45; and Boutwell, A Static Sublime.

[18] 'A life without Bach and Beethoven', 15.

[19] Olivia Mattis, 'The physical and the abstract: Varèse and the New York School', in Johnson (ed.), *The New York Schools*, 63.

that was located nearby on University Place. Most probably, it was the comparison between sound and paint that encouraged Feldman's ideas about sounds having malleability. On this point he deviated from Varèse, whose language more often suggested a conception of sound as rigid.[20]

Why did Feldman regard the graph format as particularly well suited to working with sounds conceived of in this way? Clues appear in a set of liner notes for an LP record of his music, issued in 1962, in which he described the beginnings of his graph music:

> The new painting made me desirous of a sound world more direct, more immediate, more physical than anything that had existed heretofore. [...] *Projection II* [*sic*] for flute, trumpet, violin and cello [plus piano] – one of the first graph pieces – was my first experience with this new thought. My desire here was not to 'compose,' but to project sounds into time, free from a compositional rhetoric that had no place here. In order not to involve the performer (i.e., myself) in memory (relationships), and because the sounds no longer had an inherent symbolic shape, I allowed for indeterminacies in regard to pitch.[21]

In this passage, Feldman explicitly connected his earliest thinking about graph music with the Abstract Expressionist painting that was flourishing in 1950–1, pointing to its directness and physicality as inspirations. The terms 'direct' and 'physical' reverberate with this style of painting and Feldman's music of the 1950s and 1960s in a variety of ways. The painting was 'direct' by virtue of its spontaneity and, in many cases, its avoidance of preparatory sketches and preconceived ideas.[22] These properties resonated with Feldman's 'intuitive' approach to composing 'by ear',[23] his stated aversion to using preconceived musical ideas, especially compositional systems,[24] and the fact that he originally envisaged that those performing his graphs would select pitches spontaneously while playing.[25] The painting was 'physical', not only because gestural aspects of the act of painting as practised by some of these artists were especially pronounced,[26] but also because the painters were, in many cases, sensitive to the physical

---

[20] 'The liberation of sound', 197.   [21] 'Liner notes', 5–6.

[22] During a meeting that took place on 21–3 April 1950 at Studio 35, New York City, James Brooks suggested that the art of those present – now known as *Abstract Expressionism* – should be termed '"direct" art' (Robert Goodnough (ed.), 'Artists' session at Studio 35, 1950' [1952], in Ross (ed.), *Abstract Expressionism*, 225).

[23] Feldman, 'Conversations with a young composer', and Feldman's comments in Guston, 'Conversation with Morton Feldman', 92.

[24] See, for example, 'Conversation between Morton Feldman and Walter Zimmermann', 56, and 'Johannesburg lecture 2', 176.

[25] See below and Chapter 8.

[26] See, for example, Dorothy Seiberling, '"Jackson Pollock: is he the greatest living painter in the United States?" *Life*, August 1949' [1949], in Karmel (ed.), *Jackson Pollock*, 63–4, and Elaine de Kooning, 'Hofmann paints a picture', *ARTnews*, vol. 48, no. 10 (February 1950), 38–41, 58–9.

properties of paint, even to the extent of allowing them to steer the compositional process. This resonated with Feldman's own interest in the intrinsic properties and propensities of sound, as previously noted.

Another point of interest is Feldman's suggestion that his aim in *Projection 2* had been 'to project sounds into time'.[27] This statement is remarkable and revealing, both because it highlights his second graph, *Projection 2*, and not *Projection 1*, as his 'first experience with this new thought' – a perspective that this chapter will seek to address – and because it presents his relationship with the sounds of his graph music as unmediated by the actions of performers. Initially, it seems, Feldman preferred to see the creative input of performers as insignificant, which may have been why, in an interview in 1963, he commented that 'in the early days I never really felt that there was any realization involved'.[28]

The immediacy of the relationship that Feldman envisaged between himself and sounds through his *Projections* was doubtless underpinned by the proportional character of his notation, which ensured that these scores presented a clearer picture of the associated music than was possible in conventional notation. It was this immediacy that helps explain why he regarded his graph format as well suited to the task of composing in a way that respected the inherent properties and propensities of sounds. This is because, initially, he conceived of his decision not to enumerate specific pitches and then, in the *Intersections*, entrances and dynamics as allowing the sounds themselves to choose values for these parameters. The following passage, which is also taken from the same 1963 interview, supports this interpretation:

> here was a situation [of] letting the sound just roll along, [. . .] which was a wonderful thing [. . .] to feel, just [as] it was a wonderful thing for [. . .] Jackson Pollock with plenty of equipment and plenty of knowledge to more or less get behind the painting, rather than getting in front of it, or getting behind the sound and watching it become its own shape rather than dictating the shape of the sound. In other words, the whole idea of seeing that sound had a predilection to be heard other than you would think – that was part of the excitement.[29]

Given this perspective on the directness of his relationship to sound through graph music, it was absolutely imperative that performers should

---

[27] He made a similar statement in 'Around Morton Feldman', 3.   [28] *Ibid.*, 2.

[29] *Ibid.*, 11. This passage has been struck out by Feldman in the trypescript in the Morton Feldman Collection at the Paul Sacher Foundation. Note that a copy of the typescript without amendments is in circulation, as is an audio recording of the interview in which Feldman's comments quoted in the text are clearly audible.

make their selections 'at the moment of playing'.[30] Only then could his graphs be viewed as open windows through which he could engage directly with the music. If performers had predetermined their selections, then the sounds would not have been free to choose. In such cases, the performers were creating a barrier between Feldman and sound, thereby severing the direct link that he preferred to imagine having created.

Why did Feldman adopt this unusual perspective? His position was certainly consistent with Varèse's conception of sounds as intelligent, but there is no independent reason to think that he subscribed to this particular aspect of the latter's views. Another possibility is that he was initially agnostic about his graphs being performed – or, perhaps, resigned to them not being performed – in which case he may have conceived of them as 'paper music',[31] in which performers played no part. It is more likely, however, that his view was modelled on the immediacy of the relationship that exists between painters and their paint, and this may be part of the reason why he sometimes referred to his compositions as 'time canvases'.[32]

To be clear, my suggestion is not that Feldman regarded every element of his idiosyncratic view as an empirical truth, although his conception of sounds as having properties and propensities of their own does capture the fact that performers are generally unable to control every aspect of the sounds they produce on conventional instruments. His preferred conceptions of sound as a material substance and of the immediacy of his relationship to sound, in particular, were surely indefensible on that level. It is better to see these elements of his view, instead, as a convenient fiction – an artistic credo – that enabled him to incorporate influences into his thinking about music in a way that he found useful as a source of inspiration.

From Feldman's initially unusual perspective, the link between his graphs and the project of liberating sound is evident – the more that he left out, the more he left for the sounds to fill in. Once this perspective was abandoned, as it became increasingly unhelpful to regard performers as passive elements that could be ignored rather than agents introducing unwanted inputs of their own, this simple link between graph music and the project of freeing sounds was no longer available. Poor performances highlighted the fact that the more that he left out, the more leeway he was giving performers to hijack freedoms never intended for them. As he put it:

---

[30] Programme, Hunter College Playhouse, 21 January 1951.

[31] Feldman, 'Sound, noise, Varèse, Boulez', 1.

[32] 'Between categories' [1969], in Friedman (ed.), *Give My Regards*, 88.

> After several years of writing graph music I began to discover its most
> important flaw. I was not only allowing the sounds to be free – I was also
> liberating the performer.[33]

Even so, it is unlikely that he saw these developments as undermining
every advantage of the graph format. His writings from the early 1960s
allude to other attractions that are not connected with his early perspective
on the immediacy of his own relationship to sounds through graph notation, and these may have formed part of his perspective on graph music
from the outset. Two of the passages in question, from the 1962 LP liner
notes and the 1964 programme note, have already been quoted in this
section, but a third, from 1966, reads as follows:

> Only by 'unfixing' the elements traditionally used to construct a piece of
> music could the sounds exist in themselves – not as symbols, or memories
> which were memories of other music to begin with.[34]

In these three passages, Feldman maintained that the graph format eliminated the action of two undesirable forces in the compositional process –
'compositional rhetoric' and memory – that threatened to shape the
resulting sounds in unnatural ways. For him, 'compositional rhetoric'
was the undesirable outcome of composing with systematic procedures,
and those that he usually had in mind when criticising their use were forms
of serialism, whose popularity steadily increased among composers in the
United States in the years after the Second World War. Feldman had
studied composition with two serial composers – Wallingford Riegger in
the early 1940s and Wolpe – and would surely have been aware of the serial
approach from an early age even though he recalled that neither of them
tried to impose their ideas on him.[35] However, his own view was that
compositional systems were to be avoided, both because they encourage a
preoccupation with compositional technique (what he termed the 'craft' of
composing)[36] and because they involve handing over responsibility for the
music to the system.[37] These consequences, he believed, encouraged a

---

[33] 'Liner notes', 6. For a similar statement, see 'Around Morton Feldman', 1. Unlike Feldman,
Brown and Wolff both cited a desire to give performers greater responsibility in the compositional process as a reason why they employed indeterminacy (E. Brown, 'On December 1952', 7,
and Wolff, '"...something hazardous with which we may try ourselves". Questions' [1964], in
Gronemeyer and Oehlschlägel (eds.), *Christian Wolff*, 52).

[34] 'Predeterminate/indeterminate', 35.

[35] 'Crippled symmetry' [1981], 146, and Claren, 'A Feldman chronology', 256.

[36] 'Predeterminate/indeterminate', 33–4. For 'craft', see 'The anxiety of art', 23.

[37] *Ibid.*, 26–8. This was a standard complaint made by opponents of serialism. For examples of its
use against Darmstadt School composers in the 1950s, see Martin Iddon, *New Music at
Darmstadt* (Cambridge University Press, 2013), 98–9, 112–13. For a contrary view of serialism,

corresponding disregard for sounds, which were at risk of being stymied by systematic input, not only during the compositional process itself but also in the listening experience; hence his view that 'what is heard' when listening to music composed with systems 'is indistinguishable from its process'.[38] His misgivings about memory, which he regarded as an unhelpful distraction, were similar and closely connected with his ideas about the burden of music history, mentioned above. He preferred what he once described as 'handmade' methods of composing that, as he saw it, recognised and reflected the inherent properties and propensities of sounds as they emerged when composing.[39] They also facilitated an unimpeded access to sounds when listening. As he put it: '[s]ound for me is the experience'.[40]

Against this background, advantages of the graph format included the fact that it was incompatible with the use of compositional systems based on pitches and the fact that it prevented him from including remembered melodies in anything other than schematic form. Also, the format lent itself to a way of composing non-sequentially, which undermined the action of all sequentially based systems and memory, but before turning to this aspect of his approach, it will be advantageous to review another aspect of his thinking.

'Time canvases'

In an interview recorded in 1984, Feldman reminisced about the art scene in New York City early on in his career:

> They [i.e. the Abstract Expressionist painters] were creating a new philosophy of painting in the fifties. Some of us were doing the same in music. It was a different approach to space. To understand the compositions that were being developed – both on the canvas and on the sheet – you needed to think about space and time. [. . .] In music that meant pushing tones, octaves, sounds out to the edge, to the periphery.

see Leonard B. Meyer, *Music, The Arts, and Ideas: Patterns and Predictions in Twentieth-Century Culture* (University of Chicago Press, 1994), 240.

[38] 'A compositional problem', 109. Inspired by designs in Near and Middle Eastern carpets and the cross-hatch paintings of Jasper Johns, Feldman looked more favourably on certain types of regulatory system from the late 1970s (Steven Johnson, 'Jasper Johns and Morton Feldman: what patterns?', in Johnson (ed.), *The New York Schools*, 217–47).

[39] See, for example, '. . .Out of "Last Pieces"', G, and 'Conversation between Morton Feldman and Walter Zimmermann', 56. For 'handmade', see 'Darmstadt lecture, 26 July 1984', 208.

[40] 'Introduction by Roger Smalley to "The anxiety of art" – Morton Feldman talks to Andrew Forge', BBC broadcast on 21 April 1967, unpublished transcript, BBC, 8.

'The periphery of what?', asked the interviewer, to which Feldman replied: '[m]aybe human audibility'.[41]

A letter from George Antheil, dated 1 February 1951, confirms that Feldman was preoccupied with ideas about time and space in music early in his career.[42] The letter refers to a conversation between the two men at a concert at which Feldman's music was performed, and Feldman's comments elsewhere suggest that it took place in the apartment of Cage or Virgil Thomson in late 1950 or early 1951.[43] Antheil's letter includes the following:

> I did like your music very much; indeed, your whole point of view. [. . .]
> I think I was the very first composer to write (and compose) about the principle of TIME SPACE which, I maintained then, must ultimately replace the tonal-block system of musical architecture. Moreover, I wrote my 'Ballet Mechanique' [sic] to demonstrate it. [. . .] it is such a joy to see that the younger men, generations later, have 'returned' to the principle, albeit in a new way.[44]

The central importance of time in music had been a key theme in Antheil's writings in the 1920s, when he composed *Ballet Mécanique* (1924). Time, he had written in 1925, is '[t]he most important and least experimented-with part of music', indeed it is 'the stuff of which music is made',[45] and some years later he characterised it as a medium to be considered 'all at once', which should be populated by contrasting blocks of sound placed relative to one another on the basis of 'time values rather than tonal values'.[46] Significantly, for current purposes, he likened this 'time space' to a 'canvas of music' and the compositional process as 'filling out' this canvas.[47] Antheil did not mention this particular aspect of his thinking in his letter to Feldman, but the following remarks, which are taken from another letter, written a few days earlier, to Thomson, suggest that they may have spoken of it:

---

[41] 'Morton Feldman: touch', 142–3.

[42] George Antheil to Morton Feldman, 1 February 1951, Morton Feldman Collection, Paul Sacher Foundation. This letter is a belated reply ('I cannot apologise enough for my long silence') to a message from Feldman ('I deeply appreciated your letter') that appears lost.

[43] 'Give my regards to Eighth Street', 96, and 'Johannesburg Lecture 2', 177.

[44] George Antheil to Morton Feldman, 1 February 1951.

[45] 'Abstraction and time in music, n.d.' [1925], in Mary Ann Caws (ed.), *Manifesto: A Century of Isms* (Lincoln: University of Nebraska Press, 2001), 650–1.

[46] George Antheil to Nicolas Slonimsky, 21 July 1936, Nicolas Slonimsky Collection, Music Division, Library of Congress.

[47] 'My Ballet Mecanique: what it means', *Der Querschnitt*, vol. 5, no. 9 (September 1925), 790, and George Antheil to Nicolas Slonimsky, 21 July 1936, respectively.

Concerning 'the music of the future' I find myself ever more and more interested in the ideas which I commenced to develop with 'Ballet Mecanique' [...] In short, music takes place in time; it is it's [sic] 'canvas'. In the other arts (let us say painting) the question of the spacing on the very medium upon which painting takes place [...] is all-important [...] In music, few people have paid too much attention to the spacing of time [...] I was very interested, when I was in New York, to notice that most of the young composers who had previously been very atonal, made a great point of insisting that they 'had gone through it'; they were no longer brutally systematic, but used this as a help, rather than a hindrance, to go on towards something which had once been utterly familiar to me – 'Time-space'.[48]

As noted above, Feldman would sometimes speak in strikingly similar terms, referring to his own compositions as 'time canvases',[49] and it is possible that his terminology and even his thinking were affected by this early contact with Antheil. The evident affinity between their views is made all the more striking by Antheil's use of lengthy silences towards the end of *Ballet Mécanique*,[50] which invites comparison with Feldman's use of them in several of the earliest graphs, and also by Antheil's description of his compositions as 'projections [...] into musical space'.[51] This is almost identical to the description that appears in the printed programme for the first documented performance of *Projection 2* on 21 January 1951, which explains that the title 'refers to the projection of sounds into space'. As noted in Chapter 1, Feldman heard Varèse use similar terminology at around this time. Even so, Antheil's geometric concept of projection onto a time canvas seems much closer in spirit to Feldman's idea than Varèse's kinetic concept, which involves a form of movement through three-dimensional space.

Despite these remarkable similarities in terminology, Antheil's views appear to be of little use in guiding us to a better understanding of Feldman's views on 'space and time' in the early 1950s. This is because Feldman was sceptical about Antheil's central idea concerning time space – reported by Ezra Pound in his 'Treatise on harmony' – that '[a] sound of any pitch, or any combination of such sounds, may be followed by a sound of any other pitch, or any combination of such

---

[48] George Antheil to Virgil Thomson, 29 January 1951, Virgil Thomson Papers, Yale University Music Library.

[49] 'Between categories', 88.

[50] Cowell, 'Current chronicle', 126–7, and Carol J. Oja, *Making Music Modern: New York in the 1920s* (New York: Oxford University Press, 2000), 82–3. These silences, which steadily increase in length to a maximum of 64 beats, were removed by Antheil in 1952–3 when he revised the score for publication.

[51] 'Abstraction and time in music', 651.

Example 4.1   Schematic diagram included in 'Structure and the Structural Cell'

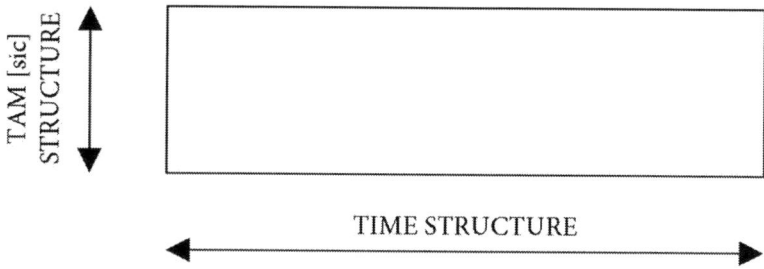

sounds, providing the time interval between them is properly gauged'.[52] It was this idea that underpinned Antheil's conception of time as a canvas, as he made clear in his letter to Thomson – a canvas on which sounds can be arranged relative to one another in a way comparable with a painter placing and rearranging forms.

The following comments, which form part of an undated text in Feldman's handwriting, titled 'Structure and the Structural Cell',[53] which appears to have been composed in the early 1950s, provide valuable clues to his thinking:

> If we think of music in terms of filling out a continuity, with pauses and [...] rests, structure of any kind is then impossible. Structure can not be constructed in this linear fashion but must be seen in its entirety. [...] This time structure then makes it possible to create music as on a canvas [...] Structure then makes us see what the basic materials are and what is unnecessary. Most important structure teaches us that these basic materials are in a state of complete equality. As we also deal with degradations of sound then immediately as we conceive a work we have also a tambre [sic] structure.

Below these comments, Feldman appended a schematic diagram, as shown in Example 4.1.

These materials are highly suggestive, but it is the diagram, which is clearly connected with Feldman's idea of music being 'as on a canvas', which is the initial point of interest, because it appears to portray a vision of music (or, more likely, his music) that has only two dimensions – timbre and time. The last sentence of the text, which refers to 'degradations of sound', suggests that this impression is somewhat misleading, however. If this

---

[52] Ezra Pound, *Antheil and the Treatise on Harmony, with Supplementary Notes* (Chicago: Pascal Covici, 1927), 10. For Feldman's scepticism, see '"I'm not negative, I'm critical". Lecture, 4 July 1987', in Mörchen (ed.), *Morton Feldman in Middelburg*, 852.
[53] 'Sketchbook 2', Morton Feldman Collection, Paul Sacher Foundation.

expression is read as alluding to sounds that are as soft as possible – which exist at the 'periphery [. . . of] human audibility', as he would go on to explain in the 1984 interview quoted from above – then the diagram is rightfully seen as portraying a three-dimensional conception of music in which one dimension – dynamics – which runs perpendicular to the page, is severely attenuated. This idea has obvious affinities with the view that in painting one should avoid illusionistic techniques for representing objects as three-dimensional, thereby rendering pictorial space as flat, which permeated much discussion of Abstract Expressionist painting in the late 1940s and early 1950s.[54]

Feldman's idea that the 'basic materials are in a state of complete equality', which also appears in 'Structure and the Structural Cell', is not explained, but it is clear that insisting on very low dynamics and therefore a flattened conception of music is one way of guaranteeing that the 'basic materials' – namely, sounds and silences – are as similar as possible. With this in mind, we are now in a position to see that Feldman's earliest graph notation, and indeed much of his output throughout his life, has a near-proportional aspect not previously noted, which stems from the fact that the flatness of the score on the page gestures towards the minimal distance between barely audible sound and silence in the music.

The comparison between Feldman's conception of musical space and the Abstract Expressionist view of pictorial space is not idle, for it is highly likely that one of the attractions that very quiet sounds held for him was that it enabled him to envisage his music as flattened and therefore analogous to this aspect of the paintings that he so admired; hence his comment at the Club in 1951 that 'music needs a plane as in painting'.[55] This was why his 'approach to space [. . .] meant pushing tones, octaves, sounds out to the edge, to the periphery [. . . of] human audibility', as he put it in 1984. Moreover, his general preference for sounds with a minimum of attack can also be seen as similarly motivated if the degree of audible attack is regarded as another 'dimension' of music.

It may look like Feldman was taking liberties with the concept of timbre when he drew the diagram reproduced in Example 4.1. For his canvas of music to be genuinely flat, it must have only two extended dimensions, and according to the diagram these are timbre and time. Yet none of his works specify only these two elements if timbre is understood in a conventional

[54] Mark Rothko and Adolph Gottlieb suggested that flatness was the means to 'destroy illusion and reveal truth' ('Rothko and Gottlieb's letter to the editor, 1943' [1943], in Miguel López-Remiro (ed.), *Mark Rothko: Writings on Art* (New Haven: Yale University Press, 2006), 36).

[55] Edgar (ed.), *Club Without Walls*, 161.

manner as distinct from pitch. For example, in the early graphs, register is usually given as high, middle or low, and in all his non-graph music, specific pitches are always indicated. One possibility is that he was operating with an expanded concept of timbre, which includes pitch as well as instrumental colour, in which case it may have been the flattened aspect of one or more elements of the music that was more important to him than the suggestion of only two extended dimensions. Alternatively, he may have had in mind the fact that the use of very low dynamics and a minimum of attack in many of his works – but not the *Intersections* – typically diminish the timbral identity of a sound. This means that the timbral dimension of this music is also flattened, leaving pitch (or register) and time as its only extended elements, although why he would have labelled the vertical axis of his diagram as he did, if he was thinking in this way, is not readily apparent.

For Antheil, the force of the analogy between music and painting stemmed from his view that the placement of sounds relative to one another in time, like the arrangement of forms versus one another on a canvas, is 'all-important'.[56] As noted above, this was not an important part of Feldman's view, which nevertheless seems to have possessed two distinct aspects. One of these, emphasised in this section, was his preference for a flattened conception of his own music. This was his 'obsession with surface', as he once put it,[57] which applied to a great deal of his output, and not just his graphs.[58] The other, applicable only in their case, stemmed from the proportionality of his notation, which ensured that the organisation of the symbols on each page presented a more literal 'picture' of the associated music than is feasible using more conventional notation, and which thereby underpinned his idea of a direct connection between his own self and graph music.

If this was Feldman's perspective, it is initially unclear why he abstained from specifying low dynamics in the *Intersections*. Perhaps we should simply see these works as inconsistent with his painterly conception of much of his music. However, a comment in the printed programme for the first performance of *Marginal Intersection* on 9 November 1952, which states that '[i]n this music, we have arrived at a total concept of space',[59] argues against this. Although the programme note is not attributed, this comment is not one that a third party would have invented, and it is safe to

---

[56] George Antheil to Virgil Thomson, 29 January 1951.   [57] 'Between categories', 88.
[58] 'For Frank O'Hara' [1976], in Friedman (ed.), *Give My Regards*, 127.
[59] Programme, Cooper Union for the Advancement of Science and Art, 9 November 1952.

assume that it was written by Feldman or by another author who was simply reporting Feldman's view.

A peculiarity of *Marginal Intersection* is that it was conceived of as including frequencies that are felt and not heard, and there can be little doubt that the programme note's mention of a *total* concept of space relates to the implied extension of the range of specified sounds beyond the audible spectrum. Even so, the mention of space strongly suggests that he regarded *Marginal Intersection* as fully consistent with his general ideas about time and space in music at this stage in his career. Possibly, he regarded his agnosticism about dynamics – here and elsewhere in the *Intersections* – as creating a new type of flatness, in this case in the musical works themselves, and not in the associated sound. For if dynamics are not specified, then this dimension is simply absent. Consequently, these works are flat simply by virtue of the fact that they lack a dimension that is ordinarily present.

An outstanding question is why Feldman was drawn to the Abstract Expressionist preoccupation with flatness. Clement Greenberg's writings, which were widely discussed at this time, portrayed it as an outcome of the modernist project, which he characterised as an ongoing search for 'purity' – his idea being that each branch of the arts 'should achieve a radical delimitation of their fields of activity', purifying itself by refocusing on its distinguishing characteristics and avoiding those that distinguish other branches.[60] The distinguishing characteristic of painting was, in his view, the flatness it inherited from the two-dimensional character of the painted surface, which should therefore be emphasised at the expense of illusionistic depth – 'imitation' being a distinguishing characteristic of literature, volume a distinguishing characteristic of sculpture.[61]

Feldman's analogical approach was entirely contrary to this assiduously compartmental view. For him, single-point perspective in painting was a methodological device, 'an instrument of measurement' as he put it years later,[62] that interfered with the painter's personal engagement with his materials (paints and canvas) in much the same way in which compositional systems in music hinder the composer's engagement with sound.[63] Consequently, the avoidance of illusionistic space and the attendant embrace of a flattened picture plane facilitated an unfettered contact with these materials and 'a precarious balance' between them and their manipulation that he wished to emulate.[64]

---

[60] 'Towards a newer Laocoon', 69.   [61] *Ibid.*, 71.   [62] 'Between categories', 83.

[63] For an illuminating discussion of Feldman's views on flattened pictorial space in the 1960s, see Boutwell, A Static Sublime, 242–3.

[64] For 'a precarious balance', see 'Morton Feldman talking to Wilfrid Mellers'.

Allover method

In an article published in 1981, Feldman looked back on his early works on graph paper and suggested a more specific parallel with Abstract Expressionism – in this case between the method he had used in composing them and Pollock's method of painting:

> I realize now how much the musical ideas I had in 1951 paralleled his mode of working. Pollock placed his canvas on the ground and painted as he walked around it. I put sheets of graph paper on the wall; each sheet framed the same time duration and was, in effect, a visual rhythmic structure. What resembled Pollock was my 'allover' approach to the time-canvas. Rather than the usual left-to-right passage across the page, the horizontal squares of the graph paper represented the tempo – with each box equal to a preestablished ictus; and the vertical squares were the instrumentation of the composition.[65]

In this passage, Feldman drew attention to an aspect of his technique that he referred to as 'allover'. Typically, this term is used by art critics to refer to an absence of identifiable points of emphasis in some pictures,[66] including many of Pollock's most famous works. However, it is clear that Feldman was thinking of an aspect of Pollock's method and not of a property of his paintings. This was Pollock's practice, from the mid-1940s onwards, of roaming freely around, over and, occasionally, on his canvases, which were placed on the floor, as he painted.[67]

In describing his own compositional technique in the graphs as allover, Feldman was alluding to the fact that their grid-based structure – which he predefined – gave him greater freedom of movement within the score when composing than was normally available when working with conventional notation. For example, in one place, he referred to his ability to carry out what he called 'a retrograde of action' in the graphs,[68] and by this he meant an

---

[65] 'Crippled symmetry' [1981], 147. See also '"I am interested in the commitment"', 786.

[66] For example, Clement Greenberg, 'The crisis of the easel picture' [1948], in *Art and Culture: Critical Essays* (Boston: Beacon Press, 1989), 155.

[67] Pollock, '"My painting"', 17. It is unclear whether Feldman regarded Pollock's practice of dripping, flicking and pouring paint as an aspect of his allover method. This aspect of Pollock's method certainly increased the fluidity of his bodily movements (Jackson Pollock, 'Interview with William Wright, The Springs, Long Island, New York, late 1950, broadcast on radio station WERI, Westerly, Rhode Island, 1951', in Karmel (ed.), *Jackson Pollock*, 22). However, at least one surviving work (*The Key*, painted in 1946), which is known to have been painted on the floor, lacks overt traces of it. In any case, it is doubtful whether dripping, flicking or pouring were integral to the analogy that Feldman had in mind. For evidence that *The Key* was painted on the floor, see Lee Krasner, '"Jackson Pollock at work: an interview with Lee Krasner," *Partisan Review*, 1980' [1980], by Barbara Rose, in Karmel (ed.), *Jackson Pollock*, 41, and Kirk Varnedoe, 'Comet: Jackson Pollock's life and work', in Kirk Varnedoe with Pepe Karmel, *Jackson Pollock* (London: Tate Gallery Publishing, 1999), 47.

[68] '"I am interested in the commitment"', 788.

ability to move right to left on the page during the compositional process. Before the advent of computer technology, this mobility was more difficult to achieve using conventional notation as its bar-based structure was not usually pre-defined, meaning that the pattern of notes tended to be built up, from left to right across the page, in the order in which the notes were to be played.

The ability to carry out a retrograde of action was only one aspect of the allover approach that Feldman nurtured in his earliest graphs and which eventually gave him total mobility along the horizontal and vertical axes of his grids. Once perfected, this approach allowed him to drop symbols in any order, anywhere in the grid on which he was working, with each symbol selected, from the first to the last, capable of being placed in any previously unoccupied location. Like his use of retrogrades of action, this assisted him in avoiding the pull of compositional systems, but it also helped him avoid sequential thinking, from prior cause to subsequent effect – an approach that he regarded as undesirable – by permitting him to work on sounds in any order.

We can now see what Feldman would have regarded as a weakness of *Projection 1*. Evidently, in this case, the predefined grid gave Feldman flexibility to move backwards or forwards while composing to any empty column of cells. However, based on the evidence of the finished work, in which no more than one symbol ever appears in a single column, we can infer that a premise of his approach was that only one sound could be specified in each ictus. This is apparent in Example 1.1 (Chapter 1) and Figure 3.1 (Chapter 3). From this it followed that only one cell in each column could be used, meaning that he was not free to revisit a column once it was occupied. Although he could move backwards and forwards through the grid while composing, he had no free-dom of movement within a column once it contained an entry.

From this perspective, Feldman must have seen *Projection 2* as an advance. The fact that it was scored for more than one instrument allowed him to use several cells in a single column without specifying more than one sound from any instrument in an ictus. This allowed him to revisit columns in which he had already made entries, as shown in Example 4.2. Also, his decision to use only one line of boxes for instruments other than the piano significantly reduced the number of cells within each instrumental part that he was precluded from using. His ability to move around the score was not inhibited by his presentation of the piano part, which is divided into two distinct zones, with one horizontal line of boxes used for specifying struck notes and another used for specifying piano harmonics. At several points, struck notes and piano harmonics are indicated in the same ictus, meaning that the division into two zones did not hinder his ability to revisit columns. Moreover, on four occa-sions the score instructs the pianist to play chords in different registers that

Example 4.2 *Projection 2*, page 6

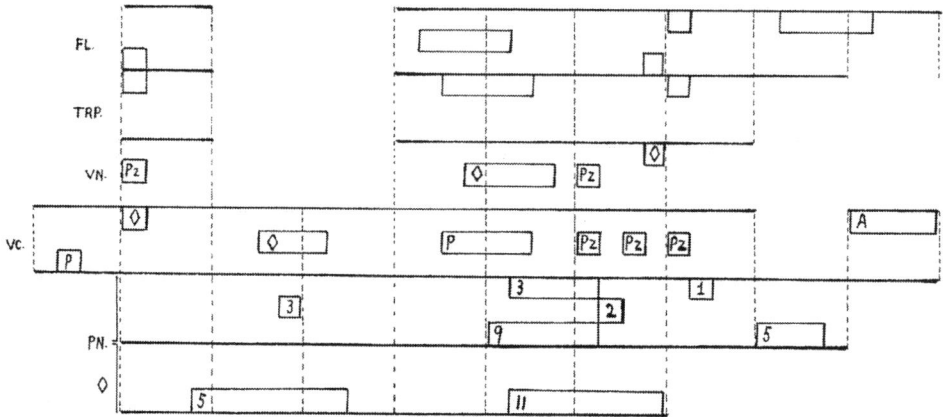

overlap, and each of these involves the use of two cells in some columns in the part for struck notes. The first occurrence of this type, which involves two rectangular compound symbols cohabiting four adjacent columns, can be seen in the example. The implication is that he had given himself the flexibility to revisit columns within this line of boxes, but apparently only once. This device was subsequently reused in *Projections 3–5*.

In the second piano part in *Projection 5*, Feldman included two symbols that straddle the same columns in the boxes used for specifying piano harmonics, as shown in Example 4.3. Clearly, he was, by this time, prepared to allocate more than one symbol to each column in this zone as well as in the one used for specifying struck notes. This resulted in an additional increase in his degree of mobility within the score while composing.

The layout of *Intersection 1* did not facilitate any enhancement of his allover method. However, a change in format in the next graph – *Marginal Intersection* – gave him even more flexibility to roam around the score. This time, in a broad area comprising eight of the seventeen grid rows, he allocated only one row of cells to each instrument, as shown in Example 3.3 (Chapter 3), and indicated in the written notes that accompany the score that the pitched instruments in this group – other than the oscillators, which he designated 'high' and 'low' – were free to choose sounds from any register. Within this area, he was free to use every cell in each column because each cell was allocated to a different instrument. This meant that he could jump around this portion of the score at will, dropping symbols into any of the unoccupied cells in any order. The suggestion made here is that this was intended and an important driver of the change in format.

Example 4.3 *Projection 5*, piano II, piano harmonics, ictuses 21–32

Example 4.4 *Intersection 2*, ictuses 832–43

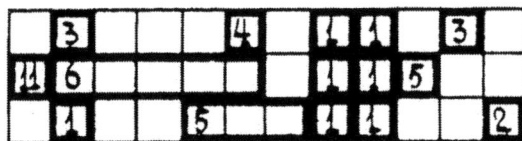

This push towards a more allover approach reached a climax in the subsequent *Intersections* for solo instruments that date from 1951 to 1953. In these, Feldman allowed himself the use of all three cells in each column of his grid frames. Although vertical position was used to indicate high, middle or low registers, as it had been in most previous graphs, he was now prepared to indicate sounds in all three registers in the same ictus, meaning that he could place symbols in all the available cells in a column, as in Example 4.4, which is taken from *Intersection 2*. Consequently, there were no restrictions on his movement within his grid frames when composing these works.

It is useful to compare the distribution of symbols in *Projection 1* with the corresponding distribution in the sketch reproduced in Figure 1.1 (Chapter 1), which may have been the page that Feldman produced at Cage's wild rice dinner party in 1950 and therefore the very first example of his graph music. A similarity between them is that neither includes a case in which more than one symbol appears in a single column. This is not true of any of the graphs known to have post-dated *Projection 1*, which is evidence that the sketch was produced around the same time as *Projection 1*, or earlier, as previously suggested.

It is also useful to compare the compositional method Feldman used in producing *Projection 1* with the one he used three years later in composing *Intersection 4*, his only other graph for solo cello. In *Projection 1*, he permitted himself to move from unoccupied column to unoccupied column, but in *Intersection 4* he gave himself much greater freedom of movement, as can be seen in Example 4.5. In the latter, he was free to jump around the score at will, adding symbols in any unoccupied cells, even those located in previously occupied columns. This was something that he had not thought of doing or chosen not to do in the earlier work. One effect of the changed approach is

Example 4.5 *Intersection 4*, ictuses 63–6

that *Intersection 4* is considerably more difficult to perform as the cellist is regularly required to execute a number of playing actions in the same ictus.

Evidently, Feldman's use of an allover method of composing in a grid frame with three rows of cells – one per register – allocated to each instrumental part was likely to result in works that are difficult to play on many instruments. One way of exerting greater control over the degree of difficulty without compromising mobility while composing would be to abandon the use of three rows in each instrumental part and allocate only one grid row per instrument – that is, to extend the method that Feldman had already experimented with in *Marginal Intersection* to every instrumental part. This is what he did, and, most probably, the reason why he did it, in *Ixion* for chamber ensemble – the graph that marked his return to graph music in 1958 – in which general indications of register are given in the written notes that accompany the score and by labels that appear within it. A page from the published edition is shown in Example 4.6. Although Feldman modified this format in several ways in subsequent graphs – for example, by reintroducing the tripartite division of register in the piano parts of *Atlantis, Ixion* for two pianos and *…Out of 'Last Pieces'* – the changes he made never interfered with this increased freedom to move around the score while composing.

'No-continuity'

As noted above, Feldman suggested a parallel between his allover method of composing and Pollock's allover method of painting. Given that Feldman admired Pollock's art and would have been familiar with his manner of working by the time he composed his first graphs,[69] we are

---

[69] Pollock's methods became common knowledge in 1949, when *Life* highlighted them (Seiberling, '"Jackson Pollock"', 63–4). Early in 1951, Feldman was commissioned to write music for the film *Jackson Pollock*, as previously noted. Feldman's untitled score for two cellos, dated May 1951, is presented in conventional notation. For further details, see Olivia Mattis, 'Morton Feldman: music for the film *Jackson Pollock* (1951)', in Meyer and Zimmermann

Example 4.6 *Ixion* for chamber ensemble, page 9

justified in supposing that this parallelism was no accident, and that it was Pollock's example that stimulated Feldman's development of an analogous technique.[70] However, to see Feldman's method only in these terms would be to underestimate its significance. This is because the method fitted seamlessly with his early aesthetics, and there can be little doubt that this affinity was an important factor encouraging its use and development.

As early as 1944, at the age of eighteen, Feldman set his sights on making a break with musical tradition that would free him from prevailing musical convention and facilitate more spontaneous composition,[71] and part of the appeal of his allover method was that it assisted him in achieving both these aims. For example, the increase in flexibility that the method gave him to move within the score while composing facilitated a more spontaneous way of working by allowing him to shift his focus between locations in the score, as did his decision to refrain from specifying pitches, which reduced the number of possible permutations within an ictus for him to choose from once the instrumentation was decided.[72] Clearly, the graph notation itself was a break with musical tradition, not only because of its unusual syntax, but also because of the associated indeterminacy of pitch. Wolff

(eds.), *Settling New Scores*, 165–7, and Daniel Stern, 'Morton Feldman's glass sequence', in Helen A. Harrison (ed.), *Such Desperate Joy: Imagining Jackson Pollock* (New York: Thunder's Mouth Press, 2000), 305–8. Stern, who performed both cello parts in the recording used in the film, remembered that in 1951 he and Feldman visited Pollock and saw him paint (*ibid.*, 306).

[70] Feldman stated that Pollock's 'walking around' his canvases 'influenced' him in '"I am interested in the commitment"', 786.

[71] This is apparent in his 1944 correspondence with Ernest Bloch (Morton Feldman Collection, Paul Sacher Foundation). This correspondence is described in Boutwell, A Static Sublime, 8–10. Feldman summed up his view of the prevailing alternatives open to him during the 1940s as follows: '[m]usic was either more or less tonal, or more or less atonal, or more or less something in between, like Varèse' ('Morton Feldman Slee Lecture').

[72] Feldman alluded to this advantage in '*Soundpieces* interview', 90.

remembered that many were shocked by this idea,[73] which also precluded the use of tonality or serialism, the two compositional approaches most favoured at that time.

The allover method that Feldman used to populate his grids was also unconventional, of course, not only because it was an alternative to the more traditional method of working left to right across the page, but also because of its associated effects. One of these was that it weakened the influence that his memory of particular sequences of sounds exerted on him while composing.[74] Also, it helped him achieve a state he called 'no-continuity',[75] which involved eliminating what he subsequently referred to as 'cause and effect continuity' from his thinking.[76]

For Feldman, cause and effect continuity involved 'antecedent and consequent building blocks',[77] by which he probably meant any type of sequential organisation that, when present, facilitates the formation of accurate expectations about what will follow and credible *ex post facto* rationalisations of what just occurred.[78] Given that sequential organisation in music is often constructed step by step, left to right along a time axis, the allover method discouraged its presence by giving him greater choice in his order of working.

Feldman's view in the 1950s and 1960s was that sequential organisation was to be avoided. Most probably, this was a lesson that he followed Cage in drawing from Webern's music, which both men and others in their circle heard as less concerned with this type of arrangement than more traditional compositions.[79] Cage's own enthusiasm for 'no-continuity' was reinforced by Wolff's method of composing *For Prepared Piano* in early 1951, going vertically up an down the page despite the fact that it was to be read horizontally,[80] and his emerging involvement in with Zen Buddhism,[81]

[73] 'A chance encounter with Christian Wolff'.   [74] 'Liner notes', 6.

[75] Reported by Cage in 'Lecture on something', 132.

[76] '"I am interested in the commitment"', 786.

[77] 'Morton Feldman', in Varga, *Three Questions for Sixty-Five Composers*, 77.

[78] For a description of cause and effect continuity in tonal music, see Victor Zuckerkandl, *Sound and Symbol*, trans. Willard R. Trask (London: Routledge & Kegan Paul, 1956), chs. VII–IX.

[79] For Feldman on 'just hearing the sounds' in Webern's music and not its 'dialectic', see 'Morton Feldman talking to Wilfrid Mellers'. Cage explained the influence of Webern's music on the New York School composers in terms of its suggesting 'the possibility of [...] music not dependent upon linear continuity' ('Program notes (1959)' [1959], in Kostelanetz (ed.), *John Cage: Writer*, 81). For the influence of Cage's enthusiasm for 'no-continuity' on Feldman, see Morton Feldman and La Monte Young, 'A conversation on composition and improvisation (Bunita Marcus, Francesco Pellizzi, Marian Zazeela)', *Res*, vol. 13 (Spring 1987), 154.

[80] John Cage, 'Remarks before a David Tudor recital (1959)' [1959], in Kostelanetz (ed.), *John Cage: Writer*, 72.

[81] Pritchett, *The Music of John Cage*, 74–6.

which did not appeal to Feldman,[82] who rationalised his view, instead, in terms of the tendency of progressions to become a focus of interest:[83] as previously noted, his self-professed preference was for a focus on 'sound itself'.[84] Avoiding sequential organisation facilitated a different focus in composing and listening, on the properties of individual sonorities and their sum total.

On one occasion, Feldman characterised his emphasis on 'no-continuity' as follows: '[m]y purpose is to take the glue out of music',[85] and in saying this he was echoing a rather well-known remark about the works of all four New York School composers that Cage attributed to Cowell.[86] Neat though it may seem, this turn of phrase – which equates musical continuity in the sense described above with 'the glue' that holds sounds together in a composition – is highly misleading because it implies that they cannot be held together in any other way, an issue taken up in the last section in this chapter.

The allover method minimised the influence of cause and effect continuity on register and, in cases involving more than one instrument or playing method, on timbre, but it did nothing to address other elements of predictability, most notably in dynamics. In the *Projections* and most of the graphs composed after Feldman's return to graph music in 1958, a single dynamic level (typically 'very low' or similar) is specified and this is, without question, a species of continuity in its own right. This may be a reason why he experimented with indeterminate dynamics in the *Intersections*, but even here a single level may be forthcoming. The upshot is that listeners may be able to anticipate this aspect as a performance of any of these works progresses. Feldman was aware of this issue and attempted to address it in *Ixion* for chamber ensemble, in which dynamics are 'low, with an occasional loud sound freely chosen by the performer'.[87] This approach does not seem to have satisfied him, however, because of the attendant upsurge in attack,[88] and he reverted to predictable dynamics in the remainder of the series.

---

[82] Morton Feldman, '*International Times* interview, Alan Beckett, November 1966' [1966], in Villars (ed.), *Morton Feldman Says*, 32–3.

[83] 'Vertical thoughts', 12.   [84] See, for example, 'The anxiety of art', 22.

[85] 'Traffic light music', 24.   [86] 'History of experimental music', 71.

[87] The use of occasional loud sounds in otherwise quiet pieces was a common aspect of Feldman's conventionally notated music from the period 1950–3 (Claren, *Neither*, 61–4).

[88] Cage and Feldman, *Radio Happenings*, 147. He also remarked that it 'created a certain amount of [unwanted] energy that I felt that I had to use' (*ibid.*).

Piano harmonics

Feldman's early perspective on sound and the immediacy of his relationship to it through graph music explains a striking aspect of the *Projection* series from *Projection 2* onwards, which is his frequent indications that the pianists should play 'without sounding (for the release of harmonics)'. The pervasiveness of this device is quantified in Table 4.1, which lists the proportion of the total span of each work during which piano keys are to be held down in this manner. Feldman's scores do not highlight which sounds he expected to trigger sympathetic resonances on the open strings, and it is tempting to assume that he envisaged that the pianist's own playing would generate the necessary excitations. This cannot always be the case, however, and it is not always straightforward to decide what he intended.

In *Projection 2*, for example, the trumpet is instructed to play into the piano, which suggests that it was meant to excite the piano strings in at least some places. Even so, the trumpet and the piano cannot excite the open strings in every case. During one period in which piano keys are to be depressed silently (ictuses 23–7), the trumpet does not sound and no struck notes in the piano part are indicated (Example 4.7). The only sounds scored during this period are from the cello, suggesting that Feldman intended these or ambient sounds in the performing space to excite resonances within the piano.

In *Projection 5*, the sympathetic resonances are never stimulated by the pianist's own playing because struck notes and open strings never coincide (see Example 3.1, Chapter 3). Hence, the intended resonances must be with other instruments in the ensemble or extraneous sound sources. It is true that the explanatory notes that accompany the score specify that the muted trumpet should play into either one of the two pianos. For the chosen piano, this suggests that the principal sympathetic resonances will be generated by the trumpet, which always sounds during periods in which either piano has open strings. However, this leaves the other pianist without a stated counterpart, meaning that any sympathetic resonances that this pianist is able to produce will be excited by the wider ensemble or ambient sounds. It is probably significant that keys are depressed silently through periods in which several instruments are sounding because this increases the likelihood of resonances occurring, even without coordination in pitch selection between performers. The degree of overlap between periods in which piano keys are depressed silently and periods in which other instruments are being played is similar in the two piano parts. Consequently, there is no evident practical reason for recommending that the trumpet plays into one piano in particular.

Let us say that piano harmonics are *primary* when they are excited on the open strings of a piano by sounds from struck strings in the same piano,

Table 4.1. Projections 2–5, *incidence of piano harmonics*

	Proportion of total span in which keys are depressed silently (%)
Projection 2	44
Projection 3 Piano I	19
Projection 3 Piano II	29
Projection 3 Piano I or Piano II	38
Projection 4	16
Projection 5 Piano I	15
Projection 5 Piano II	18
Projection 5 Piano I or Piano II	19

secondary when they are excited by sounds from a second instrument played into the piano, and *tertiary* when they are excited by other sounds. The interpretative problem can then be stated as follows: it is rarely clear whether Feldman intended primary, secondary or tertiary harmonics. No doubt considerable practical importance attaches to these matters for a performer, but there is no evidence to suggest that Feldman gave much thought to them; if he had held a strong view, then this would have emerged in the explanatory notes with the scores or elsewhere, but the surviving record is silent on this topic.

There can be little doubt that Feldman's attraction to piano harmonics in these works was partly attributable to the minimal attack generated by the especially delicate method of excitation involved. The suggestion made here is that he also saw them as a particularly effective way of giving sounds a high degree of control over the audible output of a performance, which is another reason why he regarded *Projection 2*, in which they make their first appearance, as a significant advance on *Projection 1*. When one or more keys is depressed silently, thereby removing the dampers from one or more strings, the pianist has only limited control over the character of any piano harmonics that sound. If the pianist strikes keys while one or more strings are open, then the character of the harmonics will depend upon the instrument being played, its tuning and prevailing atmospheric conditions. Their character may also be influenced by the presence of other vibrations in the vicinity of the piano, including sounds produced by other instruments or ambient sounds, as noted above. And in cases in which no keys are struck during the period in which the strings are held open, the pianist's control over the character of the sounds that emerge is evidently less. Consequently, the uncertainty associated with Feldman's use of this device

Example 4.7 *Projection 2*, ictuses 1–28

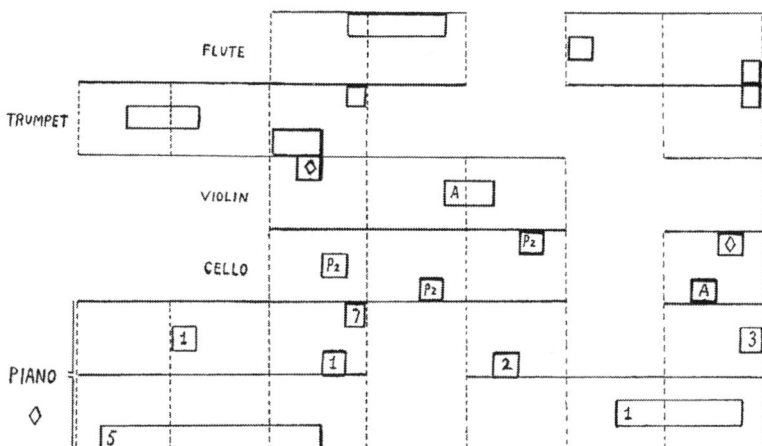

was different in kind, and more robust in the event of intervention by unreliable performers, than the uncertainty associated with his decision not to specify pitches.

A comparison between Feldman's graphs and his more conventionally notated works composed in 1951 reveals a much lesser degree of interest in piano harmonics in the latter. Of the five more conventionally notated works from 1951 that were scored for piano – as a solo instrument or in combinations – that are now published, only one makes use of them. This is *Intermission 3* (1951) for solo piano, which was not made available in Feldman's lifetime.[89] Contrast his apparent enthusiasm for piano harmonics in the graphs: of the six composed in 1951 that utilise a piano, five make extensive use of piano harmonics, *Marginal Intersection* being the only exception. This difference arose from the fact that Feldman's graphs were his principal means of introducing elements not controlled by him in a bid to give sounds freedom of choice. Given his unusual perspective on the relative autonomy of sound, it made evident sense for his interest in piano harmonics, which he saw as giving sounds a particularly high degree of control over the audible output of a performance, to be focused on them, not on his more conventionally notated output.

---

[89] This score was published in 1998 in *Morton Feldman: Solo Piano Works 1950–64*, Edition Peters 67976, in which it is dated 1952, but this appears to be a typographical error. The other works referred to in the text are *Nature Pieces* for solo piano, *Four Songs to e. e. cummings* for soprano, piano and cello, *Variations* and *Extensions 1* for violin and piano.

Silencing the performer

In 1962, Feldman explained that he had returned to graph music, after temporarily abandoning it in the mid-1950s, using 'a more vertical structure where soloistic passages would be at a minimum'.[90] This description was presented as giving his solution to the difficulties he had experienced in performances of the *Projections* and *Intersections*. Elsewhere, he maintained that the choices made by some performers had been merely formulaic, reflecting conditioned responses or remembered sequences, as previously noted.[91]

The 'more vertical structure' of later graphs alluded to in these remarks is evident in Example 4.8, which shows a passage taken from page 6 of *Atlantis*. Feldman's compositional approach was patently 'vertical' in being focused on individual columns of numbers, which were clearly conceived of as units. The connection between this intensified focus on the internal organisation of groups of sounds within single ictuses and his response to the problem of unsatisfactory performances of his early graphs is not so readily apparent, however.

A clearer picture of Feldman's response to this problem emerges in remarks he made in early 1964:

> I no longer would have the areas this long. The areas became much [...] shorter. Everything was more compressed. And we always had the orchestra en masse; we never had soloistic situations.[92]

This indicates that one element of his new strategy was to avoid the presence of long stretches of continuous play by individual instruments, and there can be little doubt that this was intended to limit a performer's scope to inject conditioned responses or remembered sequences. Another element, highlighted in this passage, was his avoidance of unaccompanied playing. On the one hand, this would discourage self-serving virtuosity (the unwanted 'art of improvisation') by limiting the extent to which any one performer was highlighted. On the other hand, it would reduce the audible impact of formulaic choices, made despite Feldman's best efforts, by superposing outputs from different sources.[93] His decision to re-establish greater control of dynamics may have had a similar

---

[90] 'Liner notes', 6. In this text, Feldman stated that he 'returned to the graph' with *Atlantis* and ...*Out of 'Last Pieces'* whereas, in fact, *Ixion* for chamber ensemble marked his return to graph music. For a diagnosis of this oversight, see David Cline, 'Straightening the record: Morton Feldman's return to graph music', *Twentieth-Century Music*, vol. 10, no. 1 (March 2013), 87.

[91] '*Soundpieces* interview', 91, for example.   [92] 'Morton Feldman with Dore Ashton', 9.

[93] This last aspect is mentioned in Claren, *Neither*, 82. Feldman's response would not have concealed a coordinated infringement of his intentions by several performers.

Example 4.8 *Atlantis*, ictuses 196–212

IIa

	1	2	3	4	5	6	7	8	9	10	11	12	13	14
Picc			4				7		5					
1. Fl			1				6						5	
2. Fl			2				9		4					
Cl	9		8		3		4	7					9	
B.Cl	5		3		9		8	6					7	
Bn			5				2		3					
Db.Bn			4				8		7				4	
Tpt			7				2						6	
Hn	4				5		3	2						
Tbn	5				5			2						
Tuba	2				4			2	1				5	
Harp	8		9		7		9						11	
Xyl	6				6		9	7					8	
Vib	9		7		7		8							
Piano										10				
											9		4	
													5	
Vc	3				3				4	5			7	
Cb	2				2				6				2	

motivation. A risk in the *Intersections* is that wayward performers play louder than other members of the ensemble, thereby drawing attention to their unattractive inputs. The reinstatement of equal dynamics – typically 'very low', albeit with occasional loud sounds freely inserted by the performers in *Ixion* – mitigated this risk by purposely de-emphasising individual contributions.

It is now clear that the judicial placement of columns of numbers, which are emphasised by his 'vertical' method of working, could be used to assist him in achieving these aims. Situating them relative to one another in a way that emphasises their status as autonomous vertical units ensures that individual instruments are only rarely permitted to play in consecutive ictuses. Moreover, the emphasis on vertical groupings implies simultaneous activity from several instruments, thereby reducing the scope for unaccompanied playing.

With these thoughts in mind, it is significant that music rehearsals for the first performance of *Summerspace* and the performance at the New York State Theatre in 1965 do not seem to have proceeded smoothly. In the case of the former, for example, Brown remembered Feldman interrupting proceedings in order to criticise a performer for playing pitches that he disliked, even though they were consistent with the notation of *Ixion*,[94] as noted in Chapter 2. The implication is that his selections were not masked by concurrent sounds and that Feldman's solution to the problem of performers making undesirable choices was either not fully formed in

---

[94] See, for example, 'Earle Brown interview with Douglas Cohen'.

Example 4.9 *Ixion* for chamber ensemble, ictuses 601–29

this particular work – the first graph that Feldman composed after the return to graph music in 1958 – or else not entirely successful.

In fact, Feldman's solution does not seem to have been fully formed because, in *Ixion*, performers play throughout extended periods rather frequently and they are sometimes entirely unaccompanied or attended by very few other members of the ensemble. In the passage shown in Example 4.9, for example, the clarinet and trombone both play long sequences of sounds, sometimes simultaneously with one another and at other times unaccompanied. Even if Feldman originally conceived of this passage 'vertically', as a succession of individual columns or ictuses of activity, the use of only two instruments and the placement of columns adjacent to one another leaves scope for the performers to rely on conditioned or remembered sequences and for these to be heard.

In truth, there are many places in *Atlantis* in which Feldman's compositional approach is less patently 'vertical' than in Example 4.8. It is also noteworthy that in this particular work the piano is required to play unaccompanied throughout several extended periods, suggesting that the strategy he outlined in his comments from 1964, quoted above, was still not fully formed at this stage. These aspects leave the work inherently susceptible to the same types of problem in performance that had beset some of his earlier graphs.

These are not the only performance-related risks in *Atlantis*. Feldman's liking for numbers higher than 2 could also be seen as inviting trouble. Except in the piano part, numbers are used to indicate the quantity of consecutive sounds that performers should play within given ictuses, meaning that the inclusion of higher numbers could allow a performer to inject ingrained or remembered sound sequences even within a single unit of pulse. This was a continuing legacy of Rauschenberg's influence, as noted in Chapter 2. In the event of performance-related difficulties of this type, the only line of defence offered by Feldman's work is that they will be made less audible by concurrent sounds from other performers, but there are many places in which instruments are required to play several sounds within a single ictus while unaccompanied. Evidently, this risk is also present in performances of *Ixion*.

Feldman's response to this potential problem began to emerge in *...Out of 'Last Pieces'*. In the score of this particular work, the number 1 is used more frequently than in *Ixion* and *Atlantis*, and several new symbols designating single notes, dyads or chords make their first appearances, thereby reducing the ease with which undesirable sequences can be inserted within a beat. Although this constrained the maximum number of consecutive sounds per ictus from each instrument, the resulting sound remains fluid in many passages, with Feldman compensating for the constraint by using the significantly expanded scale of the ensemble to specify simultaneous activity from a larger number of instruments.

This evolution of Feldman's graph music would continue, with the process culminating with *In Search of an Orchestration*, his self-styled 'Final Solution',[95] in which the vast majority of sounds indicated are single notes or chords. Feldman explained his strategy in this last graph in picturesque fashion in a letter to Brown:

> It's a more complex 'Out of Last Pieces' with <u>no</u> passage – single notes – long or short [. . .] No crawling up and down those little ole white and black notes for us!![96]

Pointillism

In a 1976 interview, Feldman recalled having decided to produce a 'score' that is 'pointillistic' for Cunningham's *Summerspace* after learning that Rauschenberg intended to produce 'pointillistic' costumes and backdrop,[97] and years later he described the intended aural effect of the associated music using similar terminology as 'acoustical pointillism'.[98] Feldman's use of these terms and Rauschenberg's recourse to a design consisting of a dense array of luminous dots of differing colours on a

---

[95] 'The future of local music', unpublished transcript, 85.

[96] Morton Feldman to Earle Brown, 16 June 1967.

[97] *Studio International* interview', 65. The close affinity between set and music in this case is at odds with Cunningham's stated aim of combining dance, decor and music that are placed within the same time structure but are otherwise independent (*The Dancer and the Dance: Merce Cunningham in Conversation with Jacqueline Lesschaeve* (New York: Marion Boyars, 1985), 137).

[98] 'Neither European nor American', 644.

neutral background invite comparison with the masses of dots or small, uniform brush strokes of pointillist painting, exemplified in the works of Georges Seurat. In the late nineteenth century, Seurat placed dots of complementary coloured paints side by side in masses, expecting the colours to mix 'optically' on the retina when the paintings were viewed from sufficient distance.

Underpinning Seurat's approach was the idea of 'optical mixture', a process intended to exploit the brain's ability to combine colours that are presented to it individually. Seurat and his admirers believed that this type of colour addition replicates the actual processes of colour mixture found in nature and therefore is more naturalistic than traditional methods of painting. They also believed that it avoids the loss of light intensity caused by mixing pigments, and that this facilitates a greater degree of luminosity than is otherwise possible.

These claimed advantages of Seurat's method are now discredited,[99] but there is no denying that optical mixture – without an increase in luminosity – takes place when his arrays are viewed at sufficient distance. Moreover, art critics have highlighted other types of perceptual effect created when the dots are viewed at closer quarters. Early scholars focused on a shimmering quality that is observable when the eye has difficulty in resolving the individual dots,[100] whereas more recent scholarship has highlighted the 'finely structured surface' and 'lively texture' that the dots create when they are seen closer up.[101]

Rauschenberg's idea of using dots as camouflage has little in common with Seurat's method of optical mixture, although both involve elements of attempted fusion, albeit of very different types. As noted in Chapter 2, Rauschenberg's plan was that the dancers should seem to fuse with the background when stationary, and his chosen design was evidently not a pre-requisite of achieving this effect.[102] Jasper Johns remembered that the idea of the dots was his and that Rauschenberg's original intention was to

[99] J. Carson Webster, 'The technique of Impressionism: a reappraisal (1944)' [1944], in Norma Broude (ed.), *Seurat in Perspective* (Englewood Cliffs, NJ: Prentice-Hall, 1978), 93–102, and Alan Lee, 'Seurat and science', *Art History*, vol. 10, no. 2 (June 1987), 203–24.

[100] Félix Fénéon, 'From "The Impressionists in 1886" (1886)' [1966], in Broude (ed.), *Seurat in Perspective*, 38, and William Innes Homer, *Seurat and the Science of Painting* (Cambridge, MA: MIT Press, 1964), 171–5.

[101] For 'finely structured surface', see Meyer Schapiro, 'Seurat' [1958], in *Modern Art: 19th & 20th Centuries* (New York: George Braziller, 1994), 102. For 'lively texture', see John Gage, 'The technique of Seurat: a reappraisal', *The Art Bulletin*, vol. 69, no. 3 (September 1987), 452.

[102] Nor is it a pre-requisite of achieving certain other visual effects highlighted in M. Potter, '"A license to do anything"', 9.

paint flowers,[103] which, we can imagine, would have served just as well as a means of concealment.

Of more interest here is the comparison that Feldman drew between pointillist painting and *Ixion*, his music for *Summerspace*. Although there is a tenuous sense in which the visual appearance of the score could be regarded as pointillist – its grids contain masses of adjacent numerals, all of similar size – it seems likely that Feldman was referring to the associated music when he described the score as 'pointillistic', and he certainly had the music in mind when he spoke of 'acoustical pointillism' years later. It is this comparison, between pointillist painting and the music specified by the score, that this section focuses on, for it provides a useful basis for charting important acoustical properties of the graph music and the development of the series over time.

Traditionally, music is regarded as pointillist by virtue of being heard as a somewhat disjointed series of small units that resist smooth sequential integration. In cases in which the listening experience is almost entirely fragmentary – Olivier Messiaen's *Mode de valeurs et d'intensités* (1949) and Boulez's *Structures*, Book I (1952) have been suggested as model examples – the analogy must be with the visual experience of a pointillist painting seen close up, with the small, discrete units heard in the music judged comparable with the clearly discernible dabs of paint.[104] However, when a partially synthesising element is also apparent, as in Webern's use of *Klangfarbenmelodie*, the analogy must be with the visual experience of the painting seen from only somewhat further out. In such cases, the synthesising element in the music – the melodic line in the Webern example – can be regarded as analogous to incipient elements of optical mixture generated by the painting.

Feldman's *Intersections 2–4* are all examples of pointillism of the first type, and *Intersection 3* could, with some justification, be regarded as a paradigm of this genre. The work consists of a quick but regular succession of short, dissimilar chords that are heard as almost entirely discrete, and it will prove useful to reflect on the elements that may be responsible for this impression. One is the lack of overlap between consecutive sounds; only a few time brackets extend over more than one ictus and several of those that are longer do not overlap with others. Another is the sheer variety in the succession of chords, which consist of differing numbers of constituent notes that often

[103] C. Brown, *Chance and Circumstance*, 220.

[104] For the examples, see Robin Maconie, *The Works of Karlheinz Stockhausen* (London: Oxford University Press, 1976), 21.

issue from widely dispersed keyboard locations, and there can be little doubt that this variety inhibits sequential grouping of consecutive sounds by the auditory system, which is typically based upon the detection of similarities.[105] A final element is, surely, the rapidity of the succession, attributable to the fast tempo and the frequent placement of sounds in consecutive ictuses. Studies have demonstrated that the rate at which a succession of tones must be presented for perceptual integration to occur is inversely related to the differences in pitch between them,[106] and it seems likely that the rapidity of the succession precludes integration given the substantial differences in pitch in this case. The net effect of these contributory factors is a highly fragmentary listening experience.

Some of these elements are also in play in the *Projections*, which usually include a preponderance of discrete notes, dyads or chords, the frequent juxtaposition of different registers or timbres and the more frequent occurrence of longer pauses. These contribute to a fragmentary listening experience that also warrants comparison with pointillist painting, but in the *Projections* the sense of fragmentation is mitigated by the 'natural fluidity' that Feldman himself highlighted.[107] The factors that enhance the prospects for sequential integration include slow tempos and, also, uniformly low dynamics, which reduce differentiation. The *Projections* are therefore works that are pointillist, but in which a partially synthesising element – a rarefied melodic line that differs between performances – can nevertheless be discerned.

Arguably, *Intersection 1* and *Marginal Intersection* are unusual from this perspective, even though similarly pointillist performances are feasible, but not obligatory. Both works include many longer time brackets that overlap with periods in which other activity is to occur, and unless performers consistently choose to defer their entrances, these are likely to result in lengthy periods of near-continuous sound in which individual elements come and go. Each of these blocks has a high degree of internal structure that precludes comparison with Seurat's unitary dabs of paint, and neither is reasonably regarded as a pointillist work in the traditional sense outlined above, although individual dots of music will often be audible against a more continuous ground.

Whether Feldman himself would have agreed with this assessment of his *Projections* and *Intersections* is not known, but he is on record as describing *Ixion* as 'pointillistic', as previously noted. This graph is in many ways quite

[105] Albert S. Bregman, *Auditory Scene Analysis: The Perceptual Organization of Sound* (Cambridge, MA: MIT Press, 1990), 58.
[106] *Ibid.*, 461–2.   [107] Cowell, 'Current chronicle', 131.

unlike prior works in the series, however, and it is certainly not 'pointillist' in the traditional sense of that term outlined above. Even so, it has other affinities with Seurat's paintings that make his description of it as 'pointillistic' seem equally appropriate.

As previously noted, Feldman's return to graph music in 1958 was marked by a significant shift in the meaning of his number symbols, which had previously been used to indicate the quantity of sounds to be produced simultaneously. In *Ixion*, he reconceived them as indicating the quantity to be produced consecutively, permitting him to specify more than one, and often many, sounds per instrument in a single ictus. This facilitated a proliferation of shorter sounds within individual units of pulse that invites comparison with Seurat's arrays of tiny dots.

These 'dots' of music are generally too short and too closely spaced in time to be perceived as a disjointed series of small units, however. Consequently, they cannot be regarded as pointillist music in the traditional sense discussed above. Moreover, the synthesising elements are much more prominent in the listening experience than in the *Projections* or Webern's *Klangfarbenmelodie*. Instead, they are perceived as 'a seamless ribbon of sound' that some listeners – including the author – hear as a distinctive experience of sporadic but palpable forward flow.[108] This invites comparison with the more pronounced effects of optical mixture that occur when a pointillist painting is seen at greater distances. Having said that, this 'seamless ribbon of sound' is not entirely smooth. Instead, the music retains a grainy texture attributable to its formation from 'dots', and what is heard is an integrated series of sound particles and not a series of gliding tones. Given the predominance of high registers, this creates the experience of a connected sequence of bright sounds that sparkles as its constituent pitches vary. This effect is comparable with the shimmering quality that early scholarship on Seurat's paintings highlighted at viewing distances just below those necessary for outright fusion. As noted in Chapter 2, this sound world is replicated in *Atlantis* and in partially diluted form in subsequent graphs.

No doubt the psychoacoustic factors responsible for creating such a pronounced sense of movement in the graphs from *Ixion* onwards are complex, but it is not difficult to see some of the elements that may be implicated. To begin with, it is surely significant that each instrument produces bursts of fleeting sounds that typically appear in quick succession. The similarity between the timbral properties of the sounds within

---

[108] For *Ixion* as 'a seamless ribbon of sound', see Jonathan Sheffer, 'The music', liner notes with *Music for Merce*, BMG Music, 09026-68751-2, 12.

each burst and the restrictions that Feldman imposed on register that limit differences between their pitches make it more likely that they will be grouped by the auditory system.[109] Similar factors are likely to encourage grouping of consecutive bursts from the same instrument or group of instruments. In addition, Feldman's renewed insistence on generally low dynamics, which had been abandoned in the *Intersections*, mitigates differences in timbre, and this reduces the likelihood of sounds from some instruments being fully resolvable into identifiable strands, at least in some places. In both versions of *Ixion* and *Atlantis*, the general impression of a single stream of activity is reinforced by the inclusion of low register intermissions. Claren has suggested that the compositional function of these is to disturb the horizontal continuity of register guidance, which is otherwise unchanging. No doubt this is part of the reason for their presence, but it is surely significant that these intermissions force coordinated changes in the pitch selections of every performer. The auditory system will take these as evidence of a single source by the principle of common fate,[110] and this is yet another factor encouraging the formation of a single gestalt.

The re-emergence of extended time brackets, many of which overlap in staggered sequences, in . . .*Out of 'Last Pieces'*, *The Straits of Magellan* and *In Search of an Orchestration* marks a partial retreat from this sound world towards that of the early graphs, especially *Intersection 1* and *Marginal Intersection*, as mentioned in Chapter 2. The retreat is only partial, however, both because the density of sounded ictuses remains very high, as it was in *Ixion* and *Atlantis*, and because the dot-like aspect of a great deal of the music is retained, thereby ensuring a similarly flowing effect in many places, sometimes superposed on a more static ground of sustained sounds. In . . .*Out of 'Last Pieces'* and *The Straits of Magellan*, this dot-like aspect is primarily attributable to the continuing use of numerals higher than '1', which indicate larger numbers of consecutive sounds in individual ictuses, whereas a similar impression is generated by the pervasive presence of grace notes in the score of *In Search of an Orchestration*.[111]

---

[109] For the role played by temporal proximity in grouping, see Bregman, *Auditory Scene Analysis*, 461–2. For the role played by similarities in pitch and timbre, see *ibid.*, 465–6, 470, 478–9. Experimental evidence indicates that the grouping of consecutive tones is not assisted by octave relationships (*ibid.*, 465–6).

[110] For the importance of the principle of common fate in auditory grouping, see *ibid.*, 248–92, 499–500.

[111] Note that the 'natural fluidity' of the *Projections* and earliest *Intersections* and the more kinetic aspect of some of the later graphs are present despite the absence of cause and effect continuity in this music. This is not a contradiction in terms. To equate the 'anti-teleological' with the 'unkinetic' (as in Meyer, *Music, The Arts, and Ideas*, 72) is to overlook the ability of the auditory system to group any sequence of sufficiently similar sounds presented in sufficiently close succession.

With this overview of the pointillist aspects of the graph series now complete, the deficiencies of Cage's assessment of the series after Feldman resuscitated the graph format as being 'disturbingly like what he did nearly 10 yrs. ago' are readily apparent.[112] One can only assume that Cage was thinking exclusively of the similarity of the syntax employed because, as we have seen, the associated sound had mutated, from one that is pointillist in the traditional sense in which this term is used in music, to another that is pointillist in a different, but equally appropriate sense.

---

[112] John Cage to Peter Yates, 6 June 1960.

5 Holism

If, in perfecting his allover method, Feldman's aim was to move freely around his grid frames, dropping symbols into any unoccupied cells in any order, which principles, if any, regulated this procedure? Analysis reveals patterns in the resulting distribution of symbols within graphs, and these suggest that regulatory criteria were operating in many cases. Some criteria appear to have been restricted in scope – they were applied only within a single graph or subset of the series – and these are discussed in Chapters 6–7. Others seem to have had more widespread application, for the patterns that bear witness to their use are found in many graphs. It is these more generally applicable criteria and the more pervasive patterns that were generated by them that are the focus here.

Even-handedness in distributing symbols and activity

The proportional distribution of symbols between register locations in the score of *Projection 4* is shown in Example 5.1, while the corresponding distribution between instrumental parts is shown in Example 5.2. It can be seen that each register location has been allocated a remarkably similar number of symbols, as has each instrumental part.

Registers are not specified for the majority of events in *The Straits of Magellan*, but in this case, Feldman was similarly even-handed in distributing symbols between instrumental parts, with each part receiving a similar number of symbols, as shown in Example 5.3.

Variants of this simple pattern appear elsewhere in the series. One, which shows up in *Intersection 1*, is apparent in Example 5.4. Here, the total number of symbols allocated to each part for string instruments is similar, and the total number of symbols allocated to the strings is similar to the number allocated to the woodwinds and brass.

Another variant involves a balanced allocation that is more restricted in scope. The distribution of symbols over the course of the score in such cases is even-handed within a particular group of instruments, but

Example 5.1 *Projection 4*, distribution of symbols between register locations

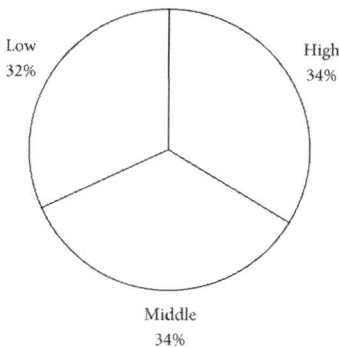

Example 5.2 *Projection 4*, distribution of symbols between instrumental parts

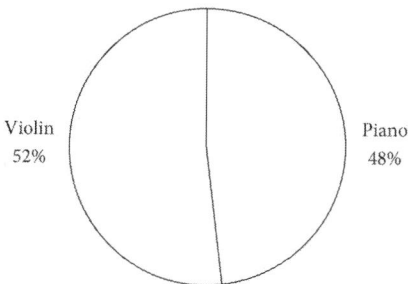

not across the entire ensemble. For example, the various parts for woodwind and brass instruments in *In Search of an Orchestration* include many more symbols than those of other instruments. Nevertheless, the distribution of symbols within this subgroup is equitable, as shown in Example 5.5.

This chapter maintains that these homogeneities were intended by Feldman and that he thought of them as unifying forces within each work. Evidently, the unity they create is not merely syntactic, as even-handedness in distributing symbols between register locations or instrumental parts yields a corresponding even-handedness in distributing musical activity between registers or instruments. The sense in which the term *activity* is used in making this claim is not one that links the degree of activity with the number of notes being played. Instead the level of activity, in the intended sense, is directly proportional to the number of

Example 5.3 *The Straits of Magellan*, distribution of symbols between instrumental parts

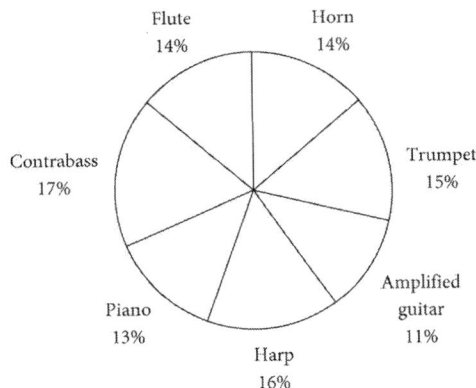

Example 5.4 *Intersection 1*, distribution of symbols between instrumental parts

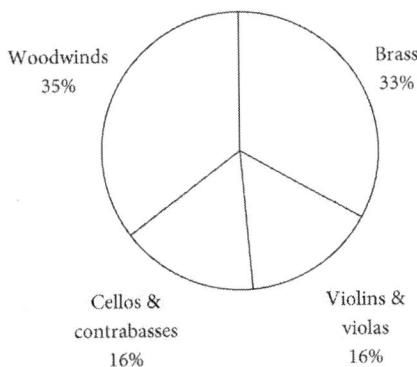

musical events involved, where a musical event is conceived of as a group of sounds or sound-producing actions specified by a basic or compound symbol.[1]

To be clear, the suggestion is not that Feldman actually counted the number of symbols included in each part. It is, instead, that he meant to

---

[1] Events designated by symbols in parts for one instrument involve sounds produced by (or sound-performing actions performed on) one instrument whereas events designated by symbols in parts for more than one instrument involve sounds produced by (or sound-producing actions performed on) more than one instrument.

Example 5.5   *In Search of an Orchestration*, distribution of symbols between parts for woodwind and brass instruments

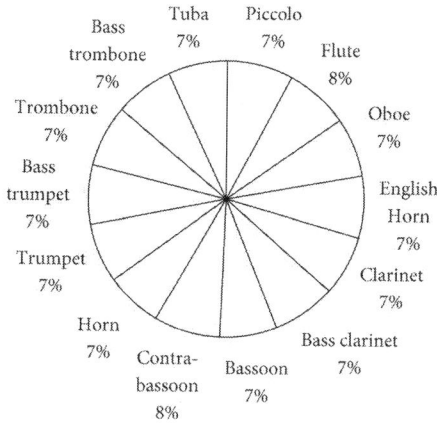

distribute symbols in a broadly balanced fashion, possibly by adding one symbol to each register location or instrumental part in turn. Perhaps the simplest strategy that would produce a balanced effect would be one involving an acutely local scheme in which symbols were equally distributed between register locations and parts within individual columns. However, this type of organisation is relatively uncommon in the works considered above, which must mean that Feldman's method of achieving balance was less circumscribed. This is unsurprising given that his allover method would have enabled him to jump to and fro between columns and even pages, allowing him to balance the placement of symbols in more distant locations.

How pervasive are these homogeneities? Example 5.6 shows the distribution of symbols between register locations in the graphs for solo instruments.[2] The equal treatment of registers is never exact, but the degree of balance plainly increases over time and is near-perfect in *Intersection 4* and *The King of Denmark*. It is not quite as marked in the earlier works, but the thesis that an approximately equal distribution was intended even in them

---

[2] In preparing data for *The King of Denmark*, 'very high' and 'very low' register sounds have been counted as high and low, respectively, whereas symbols that straddle register locations – like those shown in Examples 3.8 and 3.14 (Chapter 3) – have been counted as belonging to every register location that they straddle. The pitches of the two conventionally notated sounds, for vibraphone and glockenspiel or antique cymbal, have been allocated to registers based on their positions within the pitch ranges of these instruments.

Example 5.6   Graphs for solo instruments, in chronological order, distribution of symbols between register locations

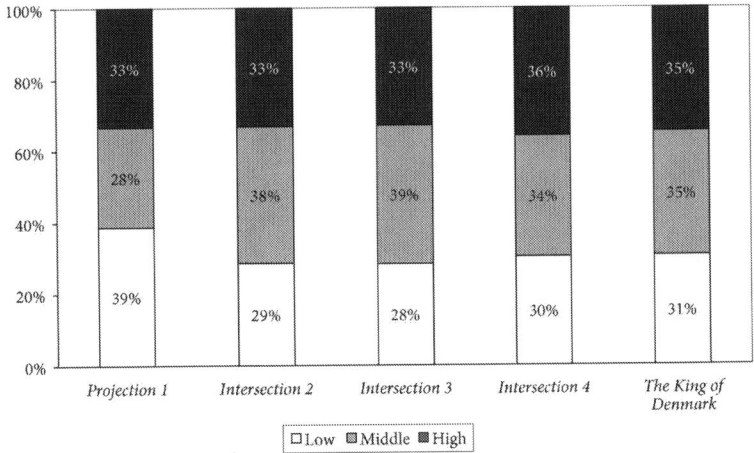

gains weight from the fact that the subseries tends towards a state of almost perfect equilibrium.

Example 5.7 shows the corresponding distribution in other graphs in which register locations are specified by ictus, but here some words of clarification are in order. To begin with, the data shown for *Atlantis* and ...*Out of 'Last Pieces'* only concern their piano parts as it is only in them that register is specified in this way; generic register guidance applies elsewhere in these scores. Moreover, in *Ixion* for two pianos, in which all sounds are in the high register except in a low register intermission, the high, middle and low data points should be read merely as indicating the proportional distribution of symbols within rows of the grid. As noted in Chapter 3, the allocation of rows to registers is somewhat more complex in this case. For example, the upper row of the grid indicates the high end of the high register in the majority of the score and the high end of the low register in the low register intermission. Data for *Projection 4* is excluded because it appeared previously in Example 5.1.

Example 5.7 shows that the distribution of symbols between register locations is almost perfectly equitable in *Ixion* for two pianos and also that a less compelling equity is present in *Atlantis* and ...*Out of 'Last Pieces'*, but not in the four other works in this subgroup. This means that, in total, nine of the fourteen graphs in which registers are specified by ictus could be seen as imprinted with a degree of even-handedness in the allocation of

Example 5.7   Graphs for more than one instrument with registers specified by ictus in at least one instrumental part, in chronological order, distribution of symbols between register locations

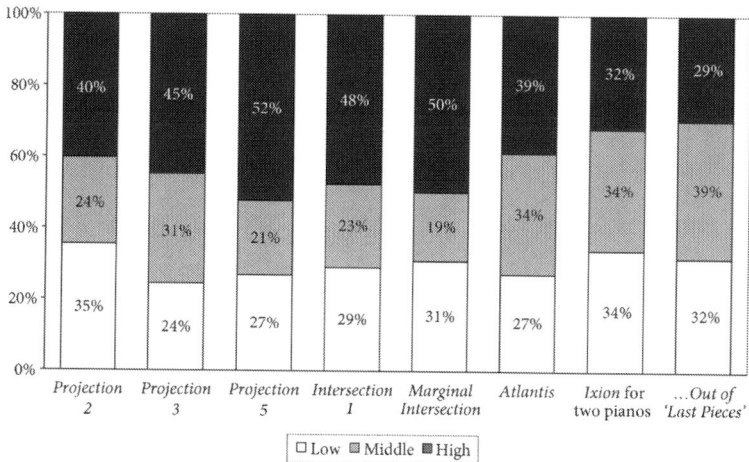

symbols to registers, the exceptions being *Projections 2–3, Projection 5, Intersection 1* and *Marginal Intersection*, all of which were composed in 1951.

Turning to the distribution of symbols between instrumental parts, Example 5.8 shows the proportional mix in graphs for two instruments other than *Projection 4*, which is, once again, excluded. As in Example 5.2, the distributions are remarkably equitable.

The corresponding situation in early graphs for more than two instruments is shown in Example 5.9, from which data for *Intersection 1*, which was previously presented in Example 5.4, is omitted. In none of these graphs is there a simple congruency in the handling of parts. However, there are patterns that are probably traces of deliberate organisation of a related type. Perhaps *Projection 2* is the least compelling example, but even here the instruments fall into two subgroups, the first containing the flute, trumpet and violin, the second containing the cello and piano. Each subgroup has been allocated half of the total number of symbols and within each subgroup the distribution of symbols between instrumental parts is approximately equal. In *Projection 5*, every instrument other than the trumpet is allocated a similar number of symbols. The notes that accompany the score specify that the trumpet should play into either piano, as noted in Chapter 4, and the higher level of activity may be connected with this arrangement,

Example 5.8   Graphs for two instruments, in chronological order, distribution of symbols between instrumental parts

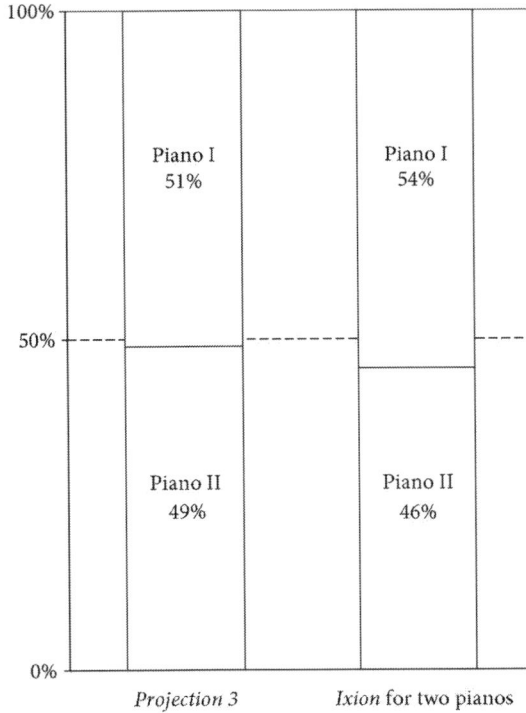

| | Projection 3 | | Ixion for two pianos |

which gives it a pivotal role in exciting piano harmonics.[3] Also noteworthy is the fact that the three flutes receive approximately one-third of the total number of symbols, as do the three cellos. The remainder is evenly distributed between the trumpet, which receives 17 per cent, and the two pianos, which receive 18 per cent between them. This suggests a distribution of symbols analogous to the one previously described in *Intersection 1*. In *Marginal Intersection*, all the eleven instrumental parts fall into one of three subgroups, with the parts in each receiving a similar number of symbols.

Corresponding data for later graphs for more than two instruments except *The Straits of Magellan* are shown in Example 5.10. Symbols in *In Search of an Orchestration* seem evenly distributed within subgroups: Feldman's even-handedness in allocating symbols between woodwinds and brass was highlighted in Example 5.5, but a similar organisation is

---

[3]   That said, a similar arrangement is specified in the written notes with *Projection 2*, in which the trumpet is not allocated a disproportionate level of activity.

Example 5.9 Early graphs for more than one instrument, in chronological order, distribution of symbols between instrumental parts

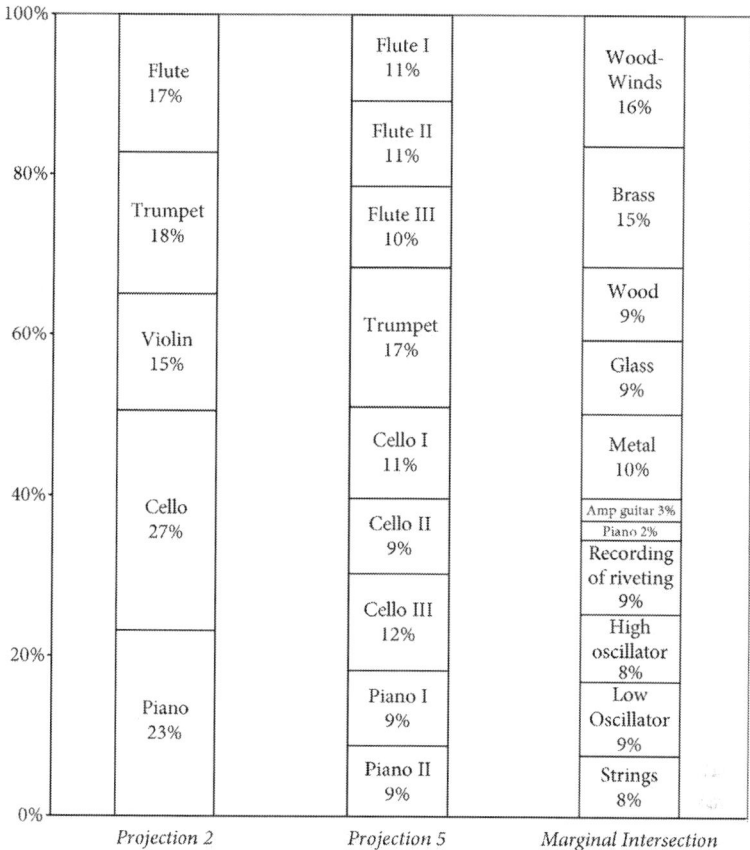

Projection 2	Projection 5	Marginal Intersection
Flute 17%	Flute I 11%	Wood-Winds 16%
	Flute II 11%	
Trumpet 18%	Flute III 10%	Brass 15%
	Trumpet 17%	Wood 9%
Violin 15%		Glass 9%
	Cello I 11%	Metal 10%
Cello 27%	Cello II 9%	Amp guitar 3%
		Piano 2%
		Recording of riveting 9%
	Cello III 12%	High oscillator 8%
Piano 23%	Piano I 9%	Low Oscillator 9%
	Piano II 9%	Strings 8%

also present elsewhere. The most credible division of the other parts is into two additional subgroups, the first including the percussion and harp, the second including the keyboard instruments and strings. Other cases are broadly similar. For example, in *Ixion* for chamber ensemble, the wood-winds each receive a similar allocation of symbols, as do the brass and a third subgroup that includes the remaining instruments.

In *Atlantis* and ...*Out of 'Last Pieces'*, the piano parts include many more symbols than those for other instruments. This is consistent with other factors that also point to the piano having a special status in these works, as noted elsewhere in this volume. For example, in both, the piano is highlighted by being allocated three rows of the grid and a differentiated

Example 5.10 Later graphs for more than one instrument, in chronological order, distribution of symbols between instrumental parts

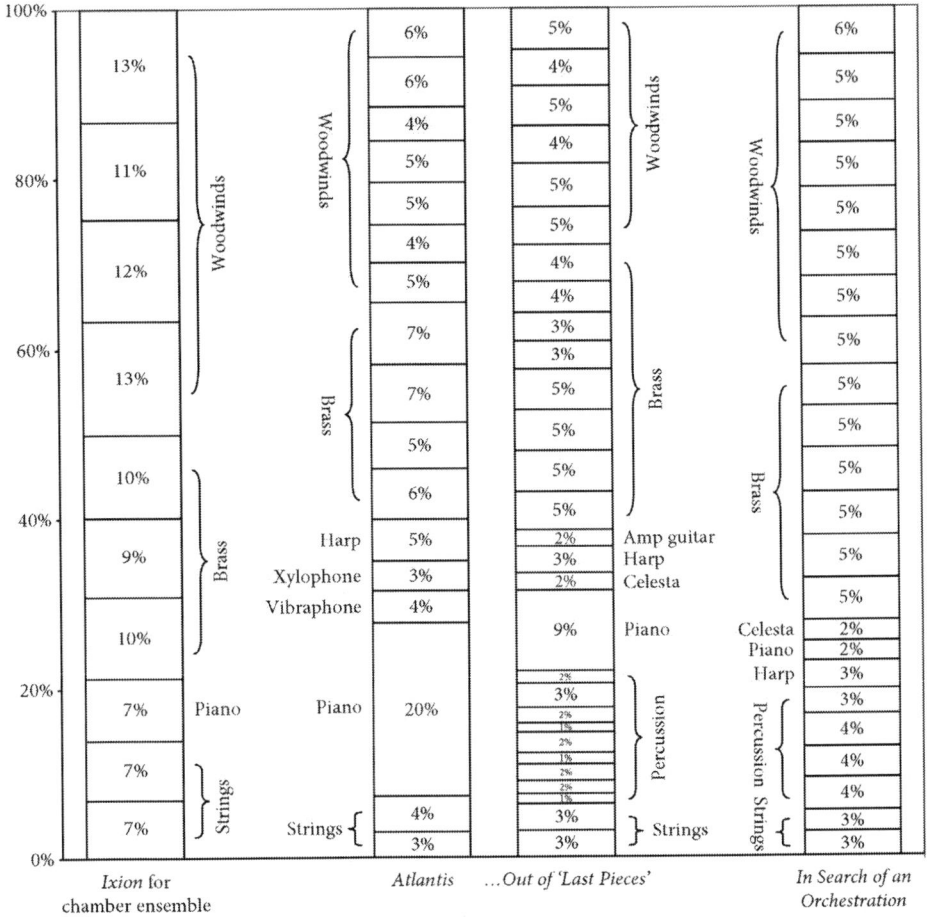

Ixion for chamber ensemble

Woodwinds: 13%, 11%, 12%, 13%

Brass: 10%, 9%, 10%

Piano: 7%

Strings: 7%, 7%

Atlantis

Woodwinds: 6%, 6%, 4%, 5%, 5%, 4%, 5%

Brass: 7%, 7%, 5%, 6%

Harp 5%

Xylophone 3%

Vibraphone 4%

Piano 20%

Strings: 4%, 3%

...Out of 'Last Pieces'

Woodwinds: 5%, 4%, 5%, 4%, 5%, 5%, 4%, 4%

Brass: 3%, 3%, 5%, 5%, 5%, 5%

Amp guitar 2%

Harp 3%

Celesta 2%

Piano 9%

Percussion: 2%, 3%, 2%, 1%, 2%, 1%, 2%, 1%

Strings: 3%, 3%

In Search of an Orchestration

Woodwinds: 6%, 5%, 5%, 5%, 5%, 5%, 5%

Brass: 5%, 5%, 5%, 5%, 5%, 5%

Celesta 2%

Piano 2%

Harp 3%

Percussion: 3%, 4%

Strings: 4%, 4%, 3%, 3%

scheme of reference. Moreover, it receives significant solo space in *Atlantis* and, in ...*Out of 'Last Pieces'*, a conventionally notated insert. Other instrumental parts in *Atlantis* fall into three subgroups, within which each part receives a similar allocation of symbols. These are: trumpet plus horn;[4] woodwinds plus the remaining brass instruments; and, xylophone plus vibraphone and strings. The subgroupings present in ...*Out of*

---

[4] In Example 5.10, these are the parts for brass instruments that each receive 7 per cent of the total number of symbols.

'*Last Pieces*' are perhaps less well-defined and several alternatives are credible. That said, it is clear that the wind and brass parts each receive a similar number of symbols.

Feldman's pages

The regularities highlighted in the preceding section characterise entire works, suggesting that Feldman aimed at a balanced overall effect. They also suggest that he may have worked on his graphs as wholes. Is this second suggestion consistent with other aspects of the surviving record?

Two complete sketches of *Marginal Intersection* consist of individual graph pages, but both sets of pages bear traces of having been laid out and worked on in a continuous run.[5] The earlier of the two, titled 'Marginal Intersection #1', is labelled in a manner that clearly indicates that the entire sketch was viewed as a single entity. Rows in the grid on the first page are labelled in a wide margin on the left side by instrument or instrument group, but no margin is present on the eight subsequent pages, all of which simply begin where the previous page left off.[6] Furthermore, some labelling that applies to the score as a whole appears on the lower right side of the fourth page, which would have been close to the middle of the nine-page sketch had it been worked on as a single unit. Each page has the residue of sticky tape or, alternatively, localised damage where sticky tape has been removed, on its upper edges. Evidently, the pages have been fixed to a wall, and it seems reasonable to assume that Feldman worked on them when they were presented in this way, consistent with his own testimony and Wolff's.[7] Measurements indicate that the total length of the nine pages of the sketch would have been 3.9 metres (12'10").

A second sketch, titled 'Marginal Intersection', has labels on the left side of most pages.[8] However, in this case, Feldman cut the right side of each page except the last to coincide with the end of the grid frame that he drew on it. This was to enable him to fix the end of one page directly over the labelling on the left side of the next page to produce a continuous run. The residue of adhesive tape is evident on all pages in locations consistent with this assessment. Here, though, there is no unequivocal evidence to suggest

---

[5] Morton Feldman Collection, Paul Sacher Foundation.

[6] On these subsequent pages, untidy labelling has been added in red pencil within the graph notation itself.

[7] Feldman, 'Crippled symmetry' [1981], 147, and Christian Wolff, 'Taking chances. From a conversation with Victor Schonfield' [1969], in Gronemeyer and Oehlschlägel (eds.), *Christian Wolff*, 68.

[8] The sixth page has no labelling on the left side and has been cut to coincide with the start of the grid. Additional labelling of some or all of the instrumental parts, in black ink or, alternatively, red or grey pencil, appears within the graph notation, scattered at irregular intervals throughout the sketch.

that the whole was attached to the wall. Perhaps it was laid out on the floor? Measurements indicate that the total length of the twelve sketch pages would have been 4.9 metres (15′11″).[9]

The presence of severe local imbalances in the distribution of symbols that are cancelled out over the course of the score is also consistent with the hypothesis that Feldman worked on this graph as a single unit. For example, the part for glass percussion instruments receives many more symbols than the parts for metal and wood percussion instruments in the first and eleventh grid frames in the published edition, but far fewer in the seventh and tenth, with these local imbalances cancelling each other arithmetically in the score as a whole. Similarly, the piano part has many more symbols than the amplified guitar part in the fifth grid frame, but far fewer in the seventh, whereas the low oscillator part has many more symbols than the high oscillator part in the fourth grid, but fewer in six others. In these cases, an overall balance in the distribution of symbols is achieved. This ironing-out of local disparities strongly suggests that Feldman's allover method of working operated across the entire score and was not restricted in scope by internal boundaries.

Feldman did not always work this way and, on some occasions, he focused on individual grid frames presented on separate pages. An example is ...Out of 'Last Pieces', in which the placement of symbols sometimes creates a remarkable lack of continuity between adjacent grid frames. This is true in the one surviving sketch and in the published edition of the score.[10] A case in point is the disjointed boundary between pages 8 and 9 of the published edition, shown in Examples 3.16 (Chapter 3) and 5.11, respectively. This discontinuity is mirrored in the sketch except that the last four columns shown on page 8 and the three empty columns at the beginning of page 9 are missing. In both versions, the earlier page ends with a mass of symbols that extend as far as the last column, but none of these continues onto page 9, which begins in an altogether different manner, with a much lower density of notated activity. The self-subsistent character of the last page of the sketch and the published edition is emphasised by the presence of the conventionally notated insert, which extends across the full width of the page, and in the published edition, this effect is heightened by

---

[9] This sketch, seen in aggregate, is longer than its predecessor because the grid of its printed graph paper is coarser. Both sketches contain 189 boxes (756 ictuses) of material. In the later sketch, Feldman has added an additional double bar line at the end of the 187th box, thereby truncating the period in which the sound-effects recording of riveting is to be faded out. This change is reflected in the published edition, which includes 187 boxes.

[10] The sketch is located in 'Sketchbook 13', Morton Feldman Collection, Paul Sacher Foundation.

Example 5.11 ...*Out of 'Last Pieces'*, page 9

the presence of a vertical line of grace notes, which runs down its exact centre.[11] Although it is true that the first three pages of the published edition are linked by symbols that straddle the boundaries between them, this is not true of the sketch, in which the same material sits within individual pages.[12]

Trial and error reveals that no reordering of pages generates a material increase in apparent continuity and this rules against the thought that Feldman may have worked on the score as a single unit and subsequently reordered his pages. Although it is possible that he worked on it as a whole and subsequently discarded some of his materials before copying the remaining elements into the surviving sketch, there is no independent reason to think that this is likely.

The thesis that Feldman worked on at least some pages as discrete units is also supported by his surviving remarks. In a lecture he gave just before the New York Philharmonic's performances of ...*Out of 'Last Pieces'* in

[11] This element appears right-of-centre in the last page of the sketch. However, Feldman's annotations indicate that eight additional columns should be added at the end of the page – precisely the number needed to centre it.

[12] There is a fairly close correspondence between the musical content of the first four pages of the sketch and that of the first three-and-a-half pages of the published edition. Thereafter, significant differences emerge. These include the presence of many columns of additional material in the published edition that have been appended to those that appear on each sketch page.

Example 5.12   ...*Out of 'Last Pieces'*, surviving sketch, distribution of symbols between parts for woodwind instruments by page

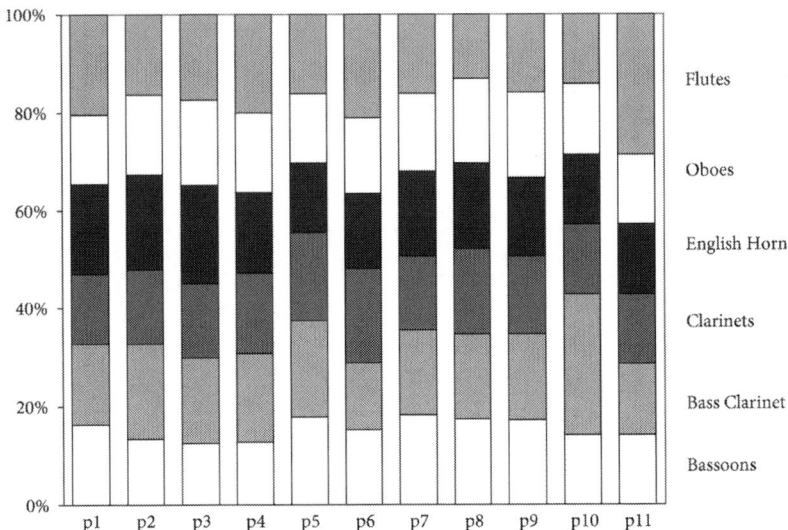

early 1964, he spoke extensively about his graph music and stated that he liked to 'start a fresh page' in order to create a 'fresh situation'.[13] This suggestion is also supported by subsequent remarks, quoted in Chapter 4. In these, he emphasised the importance played by each sheet of graph paper during the compositional process, saying that he had 'put sheets of graph paper on the wall; each sheet framed the same time duration and was, in effect, a visual rhythmic structure'.[14]

For these reasons, it is highly likely that Feldman worked on pages of ...*Out of 'Last Pieces'* as discrete units. The distribution of symbols between instrumental parts on each page is, therefore, of some interest. Examples 5.12–5.13 show how symbols are distributed between the six parts for woodwind instruments in the sketch and the published edition.[15] Clearly, the allocation is broadly balanced on most pages. A similarly balanced allocation within pages is also evident in the surviving sketches and published edition of *The Straits of Magellan* and in the parts for woodwind and brass instruments in the surviving sketch and published

---

[13] 'Morton Feldman with Dore Ashton', 19.   [14] 'Crippled symmetry' [1981], 147.

[15] Symbols that straddle pages have been counted as belonging to both pages on which they appear.

Example 5.13 . . .*Out of 'Last Pieces'*, published edition, distribution of symbols between parts for woodwind instruments by page

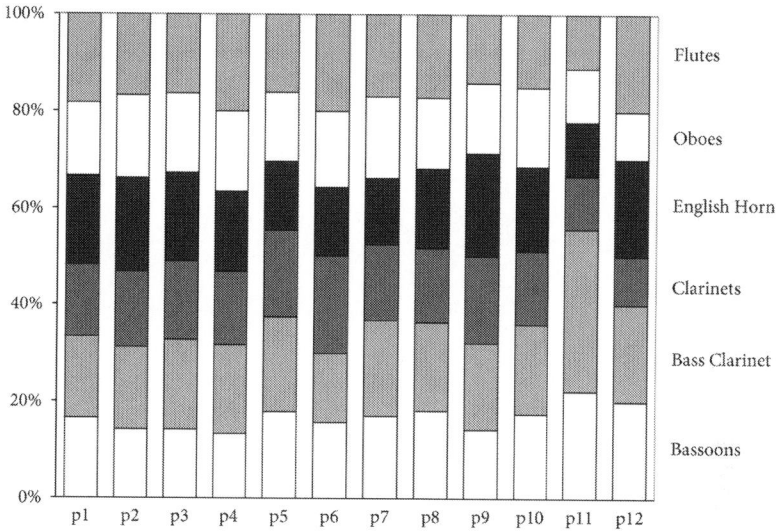

edition of *In Search of an Orchestration*,[16] suggesting that Feldman also composed these works by page.[17]

Projection 4 deserves special mention because it seems likely that Feldman worked on it in four units, each consisting of two adjacent pages in the published edition of the score. The clue to his approach is an abnormality in the presentation of his grid frames in the published edition, which are not uniform. Those on pages 1, 3, 5, 7 and 8 all have ten columns of boxes, whereas those on pages 2, 4 and 6 all have eleven. This suggests that he worked on units containing twenty-one columns of boxes, with the twenty-first box remaining unused in the last unit.[18]

---

[16] For the sketches, see Morton Feldman Collection, Paul Sacher Foundation and James Schuyler Papers, University of California, San Diego, respectively.

[17] For charts showing the allocation of symbols between parts by page in the published editions of *The Straits and Magellan* and *In Search of an Orchestration*, see David Cline, 'Allover method and holism in Morton Feldman's graphs', *Perspectives of New Music*, vol. 51, no. 1 (Winter 2013), 82–3.

[18] If so, then these materials, which are lost, must have pre-dated the only surviving sketch, which is presented on ten pages of graph paper with slight variations in the number of ictuses per page ('Sketchbook 1', Morton Feldman Collection, Paul Sacher Foundation). Like several other items in the same notebook, this sketch includes very few amendments, which strongly suggests that it was copied from an earlier source.

The fact that each two-page unit has a characteristic look lends additional weight to this view. This is evident in Example 5.14, in which the density of symbols on both pages in each unit can be seen to be similar. There are, in addition, more specific factors that bind each page to its partner. For example, pages 3 and 4 are linked by symbols that pass between them, as are pages 5 and 6, whereas the two-page units are not linked to each other in this manner. Also, pages 3 and 4 both include a distinctive type of sequence in the piano part that does not occur elsewhere in the score. This specifies a chord with high and low register notes that is immediately adjacent to a chord in the middle register. It is also noteworthy that the placement of rectangles in the row of boxes for piano harmonics is near-symmetric in all three units in which they feature.[19]

The distributions of symbols between register locations and instrumental parts in each two-page unit are shown in Example 5.15. Evidently, the balanced allocation across the score as a whole – highlighted in Examples 5.1–5.2 – is also present more locally.

Syntactic and semantic balance

The patterns highlighted in this chapter all involve elements of *syntactic balance* – that is to say, near-equality in the distribution of symbols. In some cases, the near-equality applies in the allocation of symbols between instrumental parts, while in others it applies in the allocation of symbols between register locations. In graphs with large numbers of instrumental parts, the syntactic balance may be restricted in scope, applying only across a specific subset of instrumental parts. In examples of this type, more than one variety of syntactic balance may be discernible, with subsets of instrumental parts internally balanced, but with significant differences between subsets. The patterns sometimes appear on individual pages or small groups of pages, and in these cases the same pattern is discernible on most pages or page groups. In other cases, they are not discernible on pages or groups of pages, but only across the entire score.

My contention is that these homogeneities were intended. In theory, it is possible that they were an unintended outgrowth of some other aspect of Feldman's compositional method. Certain types of compositional system might produce a balanced effect. However, there is no trace of anything of

---

[19] Piano harmonics are specified in the lowest line of boxes in the first three units. None are specified in the fourth unit.

Example 5.14 *Projection 4*, published edition, pairs of adjacent pages with page breaks within pairs highlighted

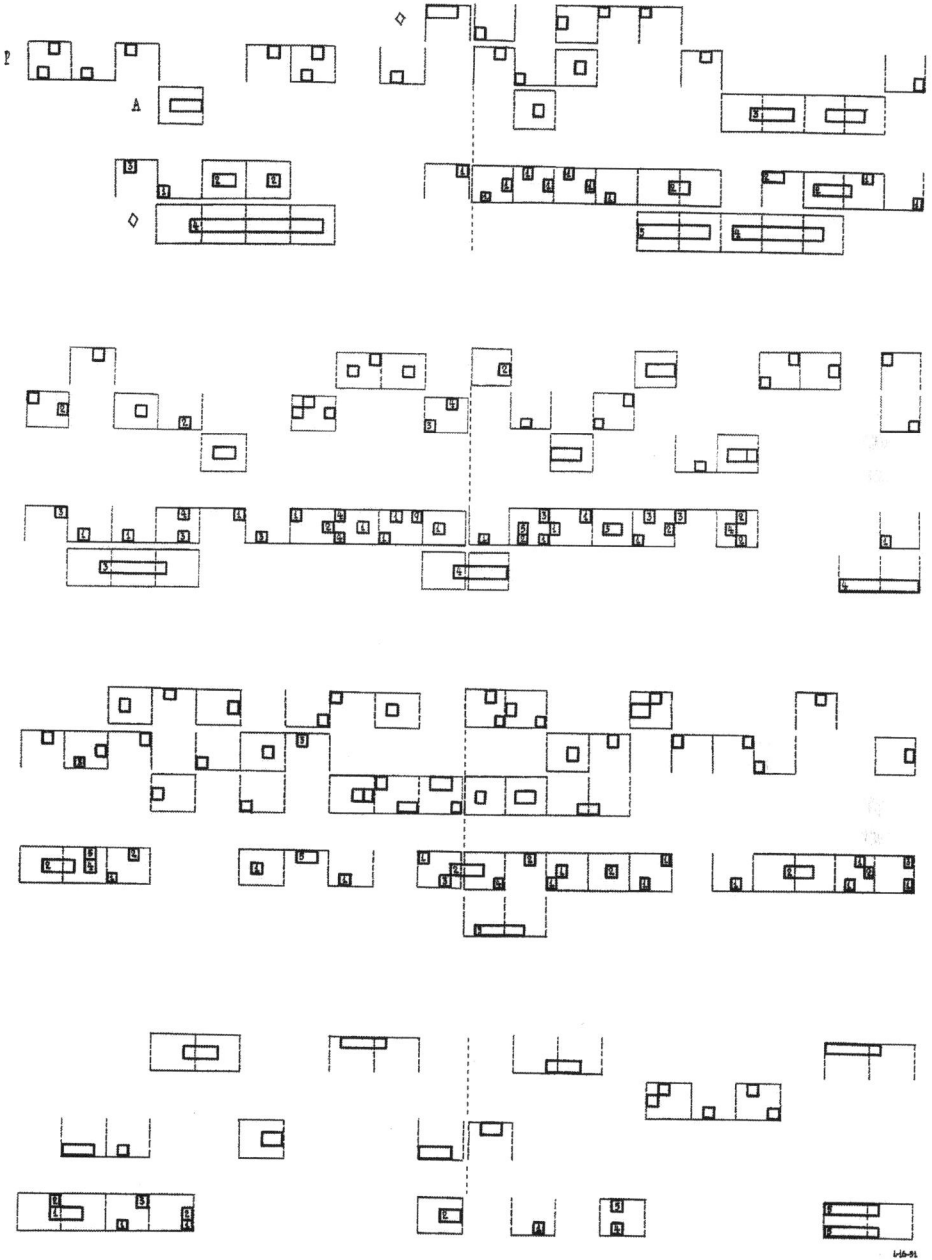

Example 5.15 *Projection 4*, distribution of symbols between register locations and instrumental parts by pair of adjacent pages

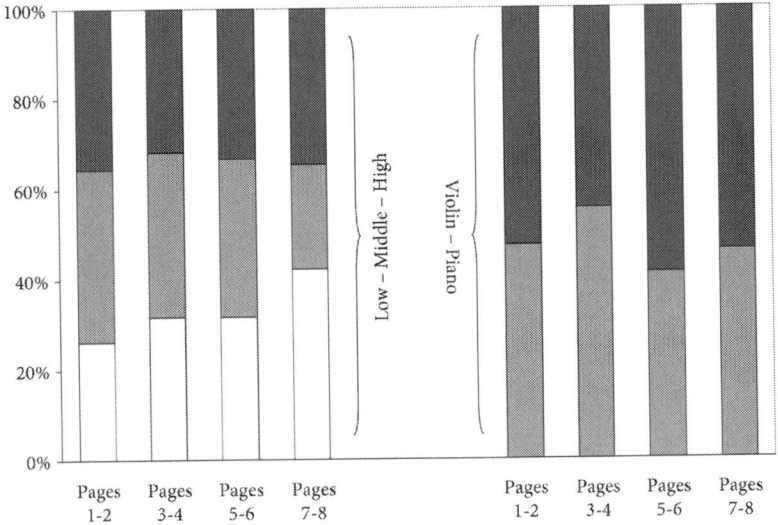

this sort in his working papers, and many of his surviving comments attack the use of compositional systems, as noted in Chapter 4.

Another possibility, which can also be ruled out, is that the homogeneities are purely statistical in origin. One circumstance that argues against this is the high degree of syntactic balance found in some graphs, which is statistically unlikely to have been produced by chance. For example, random distributions of 194 symbols – precisely the number present in the score of *Projection 4* – between three register locations in two instrumental parts exhibit the same degree of syntactic balance found in this score or a higher degree of balance only in one in twenty cases.[20] Another is that given a sufficiently large number of symbols, chance will always tend towards wholesale uniformity and not the more complex patterns found in many of the graphs for larger ensembles.

The unity imparted by these homogeneities is not merely syntactic; it is also semantic, because even-handedness in distributing symbols between register locations or instrumental parts implies *semantic balance* – a corresponding even-handedness in distributing musical activity between registers or instruments. Feldman's recourse to equitable distributions of symbols and activity in these works invites comparison with other aspects of his approach, for it

---

[20] The random distributions discussed in the text were created using the 'RAND(x)' function in Microsoft Excel 2003.

can be seen as paralleling his tendency to specify equal dynamics in graphs other than the *Intersections*. He once declared himself 'against hierarch[ic]al worlds',[21] and both of these aspects of his graph music can be seen as particular manifestations of a general distaste for hierarchies.

Holism, molecularity and atomism

In a text published in 1952, but probably written in the midst of composing the first three *Intersections* in 1951, Feldman wrote:

> What determines the initial conception of my *Projections* and *Intersections* is a weight either reminiscent or discovered. Weight for me does not have its source in the manipulation of dynamics or tensions but rather resulting from a visual-aural response to sound as an image gone inward creating a general synthesis.[22]

A notable aspect of these remarks is that they portray the visual appearances of the graphs as formative in the processes involved in producing them. Feldman's idea appears to have been that a particular combination of visual properties of the score and sonic properties of the associated music were fused in his mind in a synthesis that he referred to as an 'image' and reflected in the work in what he termed 'weight'.[23] The implication is that, at this time, he saw syntactic aspects of his graph scores as formative aspects of the associated music.[24] No doubt this perspective was underpinned by the unusually close relationship that exists between the visual properties of each graph score and its sound in performance.

Also notable is the fact that they characterise Feldman's initial conception of his graphs in unitary terms, describing them not only as a 'synthesis', but also with a variety of other singular terms, including 'weight' and 'image'. Similarly, in a 1963 interview, he stressed the importance of the 'overall image' in his early works:

> I never wanted that building with additions. I always wanted the overall image. My desire at the particular time was not related so much to a music history but very much related to the painting situation that was happening all around me. I was very much involved with the image of a work rather than making up a work out of passages, out of variations.[25]

---

[21] 'The future of local music', unpublished transcript, 224.

[22] Feldman et al, '4 musicians at work', 168.

[23] Feldman's use of the term 'weight' is otherwise unexplained, but its ordinary meaning is suggestive of heaviness or mass or, more likely in this case, density.

[24] Claren's account of this early text omits any reference to visual aspects of the scores and Feldman's use of the term 'synthesis' is unexplained (*Neither*, 123).

[25] 'Around Morton Feldman', 4.

The implication is that, from early on, Feldman conceived of his graphs *holistically* – that is, as integrally unified wholes – rather than as collections of independently viable sounds or sound sequences. A corollary – unstated by Feldman, but implied by his stated views – is that the significance of an individual sound or group of sounds stems from the multiplicity of connections it has with every other sound or group of sounds in the work as a whole.[26]

Elsewhere in Feldman's surviving comments, a somewhat more complex picture emerges. For example, in the lecture he delivered in the run-up to the New York Philharmonic's performances of . . .*Out of 'Last Pieces'*, he described an evolution in his graph music as follows:

> [Previously] I was still thinking very conventionally; that is, music in a sense going along this way, rather than thinking of music as something happening in the whole period of time, which is more my thinking now, the way I work now.[27]

His suggestion in this passage was that his more holistic conception ('happening in the whole period of time') emerged during the course of the graph series, implying that it was absent or not fully formed in unspecified early graphs in which his compositional approach was more conventional ('going along').

Moreover in 1987, Feldman spoke of 'keeping up the same image' through 'movement and mobility':

> What I was looking for was a more . . . unchanging image, where you have this image and there is movement and mobility but essentially it's just the energy of keeping up the same image, so to speak.[28]

This suggests that he thought of the image not just as present in the work as a whole, but also as articulated within it, perhaps diffusely or, alternatively, within well-defined sections.

The account of his compositional focus presented in this chapter fits with all these claims. For example, it points to a preoccupation with syntactic aspects of his graph notation that go beyond its striking appearance and proportional aspect. Also it sheds light on Feldman's remarks about the image associated with each graph, for the singular or overall image of each graph stems from the holistically organised distribution of symbols in the score, which ensures a holistically organised distribution of activity.

---

[26] Compare Michael Dummett, 'The philosophical basis of intuitionistic logic' [1973], in *Truth and Other Enigmas* (London: Duckworth, 1978), 218.

[27] 'Morton Feldman with Dore Ashton', 9.   [28] '"I am interested in the commitment"', 786–8.

Typically, this distribution exhibits elements of equilibrium or balance. Feldman alluded to 'balance' in the *Projections* and early *Intersections* in another text published in 1952 but probably written in 1951, in which he drew a connection between 'weight', 'balance' and 'movement'.[29] He used the term 'balance' in more than one way in later writings, and it is hard to be sure how he intended it in 1951, but it is credible to suppose that it had a visual aspect. In the 1980s, he sometimes used the term in this way. For example, in a 1984 seminar, he described his conventionally notated *Structures* for string quartet, dated March 1951, and *Variations* as follows:

> the grid was the whole page at that time [. . . with *Structures*] I would write something over here and then I would write something over here [. . .] then I would write something over here and then I would write something over here. [S]o you have [. . .] this kind of balance in time. I wrote a piece like that for Merce Cunningham, a piano piece, in which [. . .] there was a chord going down the center of the page [. . . at] a certain angle. So in a sense it was a kind of crazy periodicity of time going down the page.[30]

It is easy to imagine Feldman pointing to different locations in space as he spoke these words about his compositional approach, intending to suggest to his audience that he moved from one side of his page to another to produce a balanced visual effect. My suggestion is that he worked in a similar way when composing his graph music, jumping to and fro within pages, or groups of adjacent pages, or around the score as a whole. Note that his subsequent reference to the 'angle' made by the 'chord' running down the centre of a page of *Variations* strongly suggests that he was speaking of visual aspects of the score of *Structures*.

Two elements of the account presented thus far in this monograph fit with Feldman's suggestion of an evolution from early graphs, in which his compositional thinking was more conventional, to a more holistic approach in subsequent graphs. One is the explanation given in Chapter 4 of changes in the presentation of his graphs up to *Ixion* for chamber ensemble, which portrays them as responses to the needs of his emerging allover method. Another is the analysis presented in this chapter of the ways in which he distributed his symbols, which shows that his holism is more consistently evident in later graphs.

The latter also makes sense of Feldman's remarks about maintaining an image through movement and mobility. In some graphs, this chapter has argued, the overall image of the work, which is reflected in the overall

---

[29] Quoted in Cowell, 'Current chronicle', 131.

[30] 'The future of local music', unpublished transcript, 23. Feldman used the term 'balance' in a similar manner in '"I am interested in the commitment"', 792.

distribution of symbols between register locations or instrumental parts and the overall distribution of activity between registers or instruments, is also imprinted on individual pages or groups of adjacent pages and therefore associated sections of the music. This assists in 'keeping up the same image' because it ensures that the unifying principle underpinning the work as a whole also pervades, informs, and unifies each of its constituent subsections.

This congruency between individual pages or groups of adjacent pages and the score as a whole suggests that, in these cases, Feldman applied his allover method within subsections of the score, which he only subsequently combined to produce the finished whole. Even so, it would be wrong to confuse this molecular aspect of his compositional method with a molecular conception of the associated works, that is to say, one in which the whole is regarded as a juxtaposition of complex units that are themselves entirely self-contained and independently viable. My contention is that the organisation of each subsection was answerable to an overall pattern or image, which was replicated across subsections, meaning that the subsections themselves are not properly regarded as self-contained units. This repeated image is a constitutive link between them that engenders holism even in these cases.

Chapter 4 compared the allover method of working that Feldman evolved in the 1950s with the allover method that Pollock used from the mid-1940s onwards, but Feldman's holism is another link with Pollock's paintings from this period. This is because many of these paintings also possess a notably holistic aspect, despite their apparently chaotic microstructure and their avoidance of traditional illusionistic methods of unifying an image by portraying spatial relationships within it from a single viewpoint.[31] Clement Greenberg described Pollock as 'alone in his power to assert a paint-strewn or paint-laden surface as a single synoptic image',[32] and this holistic aspect of Pollock's works was subsequently discussed by William Rubin, who saw the strength of Pollock's best pictures as depending 'on his having introduced such great variety in their local areas while making them cohere in an organically unified whole'.[33]

In an excerpt from a 1963 interview quoted above, Feldman connected his desire for an 'overall image' in his early graphs with the prevailing

---

[31] For a discussion of these methods, see William V. Dunning, *Changing Images of Pictorial Space: A History of Spatial Illusion in Painting* (Syracuse University Press, 1991).
[32] '"American type" painting' [1955], in *Art and Culture*, 217.
[33] '"Jackson Pollock and the modern tradition," *Artforum*, February–May 1967' [1967], in Karmel (ed.), *Jackson Pollock*, 131.

situation in painting, and it is probable that he would have regarded this aspect of his work as a link not only with Pollock, but also with other painters in his circle that produced single image works, including Guston, Newman and Mark Rothko. Guston was outspoken on this point, explaining that he did not 'want to be stuck with parts' in his paintings and that what he wanted was a 'peculiar kind of unity'.[34]

In an article published in 1981, Feldman described the central importance of the 'scale' of his works and drew a parallel with Rothko's preoccupation with finding precisely the right dimensions for his immense canvases.[35] For Feldman, Rothko's preoccupation with scale was the source of his success in producing a holistic effect; what underpins the unity of these paintings was, for him, 'Rothko's finding that particular scale which suspends all proportions in equilibrium'.[36] By implication, Feldman was, at that time, seeking that particular scale that would suspend the musical proportions of his own works in a holistic balance, creating what he described in the same essay as 'the contradiction in not having the sum of the parts equal the whole'.[37] He seems to have been thinking primarily about his long, late works when he made these remarks, and it is doubtful whether he saw the smaller scale of his graphs as of equal importance in unifying them. The suggestion here is, instead, that he intended holistic elements of balance in the distribution of symbols, and therefore musical activity, within them to achieve a similar effect.

Feldman sometimes portrayed his own efforts in composing his graphs as focused primarily, or even exclusively, on individual sounds. For example, in 1962, he explained that in these works he was 'allowing the sounds to be free',[38] and four years later he suggested that '[o]nly by "unfixing" the elements traditionally used to construct a piece of music [in indeterminate works such as his graphs] could the sounds exist in themselves'.[39] Such remarks, which portray individual sounds as central, are atomistic in character (each sound only for itself) whereas this analysis has uncovered holistic aspects of his music that imply a focus on the overall effect of all the sounds in each work. Atomism and holism are inherently opposed, and to suggest that there were elements of both

---

[34] 'Conversation with Joseph Ablow (1966)' [1994], in Coolidge (ed.), *Philip Guston*, 60.
[35] 'Crippled symmetry' [1981], 137.   [36] *Ibid.*, 149.
[37] *Ibid.*, 137. See Wes York, 'For John Cage (1982)', in Thomas DeLio (ed.), *The Music of Morton Feldman* (New York: Excelsior Music Publishing Company, 1996), 149, and Griffiths, *Modern Music and After*, 280.
[38] 'Liner notes', 6.   [39] 'Predeterminate/indeterminate', 35.

in his graph music would be to imply inconsistency. That said, there was no inconsistency in this case because there was no atomism. The apparently atomistic strand in his thinking was merely an expression of his desire to avoid cause and effect continuity. The sounds were to be free in the sense that they were not to be shackled in predictable sequences, and there is no inconsistency between this position and his holism, which required, nevertheless, that every sound was answerable to an internally balanced, overall design.

6 Compositional methods I

Feldman claimed to compose 'by ear',[1] but what did this involve? He stressed listening and intuition,[2] but there were elements of method as well.[3] These methods are rarely conspicuous in the finished works, and his surviving comments provide us with only occasional clues to their presence. This, it seems, was the result of a deliberate strategy. In an interview from the 1960s, he explained: 'I'm anti-process [...] I'm always burning the process behind me. I don't like there to be a trace of process in the finished work'.[4] No justification was provided, but his comments elsewhere point to a desire to foreground the sound of his compositions by suppressing their formative aspects. As a result, focusing on his methods involves a degree of excavation, and it could, with some justification, be seen as acting contrary to his wishes.

Even so, much can be learned. Close attention to the surviving record suggests that elements of method were often in play. Feldman's allover method of working, outlined in Chapter 4, which assisted him in achieving a holistic balance in the organisation of his material, was one of these, but some graphs and pre-publication materials also show traces of other types of deliberate organisation. Sometimes, these are only suggestive, but, on other occasions, they are sufficiently clear to support firm conclusions about his approach. The following survey, which spans two chapters, follows a broadly chronological course.

Horizontal thinking

In the 1960s, Feldman characterised his early graphs as tainted by a kind of thinking that he termed 'horizontal',[5] and his comments make clear that, in

---

[1] 'Conversations with a young composer', and Feldman's comments in Guston, 'Conversation with Morton Feldman', 92.

[2] 'Conversations with a young composer'; 'Conversation between Morton Feldman and Walter Zimmermann', 55; and 'Johannesburg lecture 2', 176.

[3] Feldman sometimes denied that he knew how he produced his compositions ('Liner notes', 4–5). For a discussion of his tendency to downplay methodical aspects of his approach, see Noble, *Composing Ambiguity*, 23.

[4] 'Morton Feldman', interview, in Brian O'Doherty, *Object and Idea: An Art Critic's Journal 1961–1967* (New York: Simon and Schuster, 1967), 101. The passage quoted in the text does not appear in the abridged version published in 1964 ('Feldman throws a switch', XII).

[5] '...Out of "Last Pieces"', G; 'Around Morton Feldman', 5; 'Vertical thoughts', 12; and 'Morton Feldman with Dore Ashton', 8–9.

his view, horizontal thinking while composing tended to produce cause and effect continuities in the resulting music. He did not describe the horizontal elements in question, but there are suggestive patterns in the placement of some symbols in these works, and he may have come to regard some of these as problematic. In the *Projections*, patterns occur in the *register contours* of some instruments. The latter are ordered sequences of registers in which the disposition of registers matches the order in which they are to be played by a specific instrument. Hence, they ignore durations, silences and nuances of playing method.

The register contour of *Projection 1* is shown in Example 6.1. This is replete with patterns, but it would be unwise to simply assume that these were consciously constructed. A review of similar sequences derived from random register selections reveals that they also contain patterns.[6] That said, a comparison indicates that immediately repeated or reversed *modules* – short sequences of registers (such as low–high–low or low–high–high–middle) – are more common in the register contour of *Projection 1* than in most randomly generated analogues. Groups containing immediately repeated modules are marked 'RPT' in Example 6.1, whereas those containing immediately reversed modules are marked 'RV'.[7] Similar patterns are observable elsewhere in the *Projection* series. For example, in the cello part of *Projection 2*, shown in Example 6.2, reversed modules are common.

A comparison between the resister contour of *Projection 1* and similar, but random sequences also reveals that wide register shifts (from high to low and vice versa) are considerably more frequent in Feldman's graph than in most random analogues, whereas the repetition of registers in consecutive sounds is significantly less common in the former than the latter. This observation can be quantified. Example 6.3 is a summary analysis of relationships between the registers of consecutive sounds in *Projection 1*, showing the relative frequency of three types of association: an unchanged (i.e. repeated) register; a narrow shift to an immediately adjacent register; and, a wide shift (from high to low or vice versa). The analysis ignores differences between the directions of movement; for example, a shift from middle to high is regarded as narrow, as is a shift from high to middle. If Feldman had not attended to aspects of register contour, one would expect to find wide shifts less common than they are because they cannot be made from the middle register, unlike register repetitions and narrow shifts. This is unless he had a pronounced aversion to the middle register, which a measurement of the distribution of

---

[6] The random distributions discussed in the text were created using the RANDBETWEEN function in Microsoft Excel 2002.

[7] Other groupings are feasible. Only those containing four or more elements are highlighted.

Example 6.1 *Projection 1*, register contour of cello

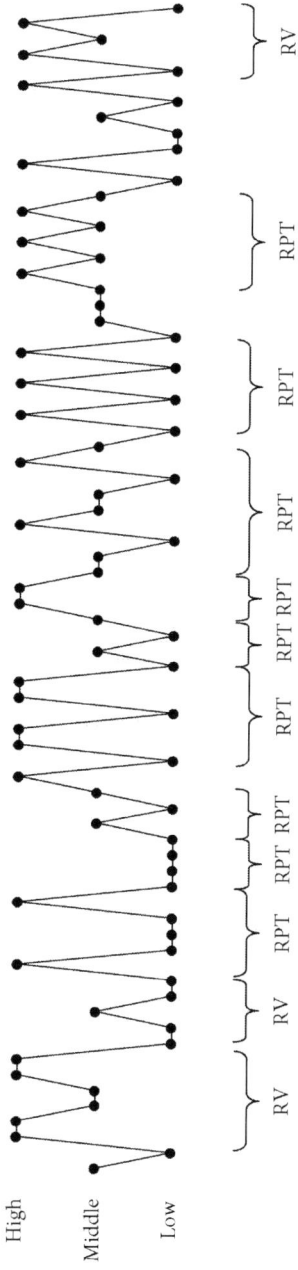

Example 6.2 *Projection 2*, register contour of cello, reversed modules highlighted

Example 6.3 *Projection 1*, changes in register between consecutive sounds

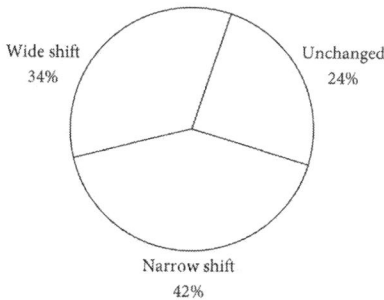

Wide shift
34%

Unchanged
24%

Narrow shift
42%

sounds between registers demonstrates was not the case. Similarly, if he had not attended to aspects of register contour, one would expect to find register repetitions more prevalent than they are. This is because register repetitions, unlike wide register shifts, can be initiated from any register.

How much less frequently would wide shifts be present and how much more frequently would repetitions appear if Feldman had not attended to aspects of register contour? In a random sequence of registers of sufficiently long length, the relative frequencies of repetitions to narrow shifts to wide shifts would be 3:4:2 (i.e. 33 per cent: 45 per cent: 22 per cent). In none of the many randomly derived sequences examined while preparing this chapter was the deviation from this ratio as marked as in the register contour actually observed, which strongly suggests that Feldman actively attended to this aspect of *Projection 1*. His propensity for wide register shifts coupled with his stated desire for 'natural fluidity' may explain why the indicated tempo is slow. This is because an increase in frequency separation between consecutive sounds requires a slower rate of succession if a listener is to perceive the sounds as connected.[8]

Another variety of horizontal thinking is evident in one of the surviving sketches of *Projection 5*, a page from which is shown in Figure 6.1.[9] In the published edition of the score, each cello part is allocated three rows, one for each register, with Feldman indicating the desired timbre using symbols, but in the sketch each cello is allocated three sets of three rows, one for specifying harmonics, a second for specifying pizzicato and a third for specifying either arco or sul ponticello. A striking aspect of this sketch is that on three of the

[8] Bregman, *Auditory Scene Analysis*, 461–2. Elsewhere, Bregman argues that the more-or-less inverse relationship between frequency separation and rate of succession for perceptual grouping is the auditory equivalent of Körte's third law of apparent motion in vision (*ibid.*, 178).
[9] 'Sketchbook 1', Morton Feldman Collection, Paul Sacher Foundation.

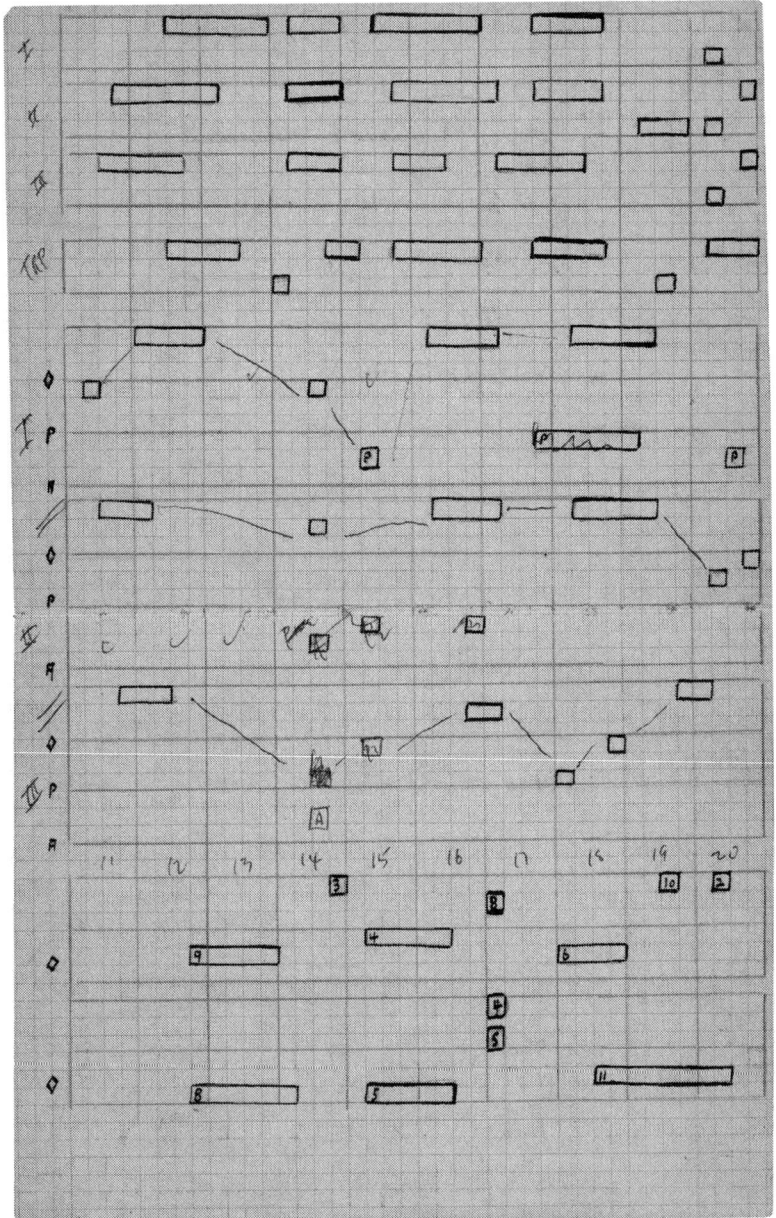

Figure 6.1 *Projection 5*, sketch, page 2

four grid frames Feldman drew rough lines connecting consecutive symbols within each cello part. The lines indicate specific progressions over time – referred to here as *trajectories* – and the fact that he marked them in this way demonstrates that they were a focus of his attention.

This is initially surprising because the course of a trajectory need not be connected in any simple way with the evolution of any one musical parameter. For example, a gradually ascending trajectory might be associated with a movement from a low to a high register, but equally it might be associated with a movement from a high register to a low register in a different timbre. Most probably, he was interested in their visual aspects. This would fit with his self-professed interest, in his earliest writings, in visual properties of his graph scores and with the fact that several early graphs include trajectories, like those in Examples 6.4–6.5, that are optically striking.

These were not the only horizontal aspects of Feldman's approach. Others include deliberate contrasts between adjacent or nearby materials and conscious transmutation of materials that had previously been used. One example of what may have been a deliberate contrast in *Projection 1* has been described by John Welsh as 'an exchange of timbral and registral roles'.[10] Another occurs in the opening moments of *Projection 4*, shown in Example 6.6. The sound that begins in ictus 14 is the first arco sound specified, the first sound specified in the middle register and the first extended sound.[11] The contrast between this sound and those that precede it is therefore pronounced, and it seems highly likely that this was intended.

An example of transmutation occurs in the piano part later in the same score. The first group of symbols shown in Example 6.7 appears on page 3 of the published edition. It specifies a combination consisting of two notes in the middle register followed by a chord consisting of four high and four low notes. The second group, which appears on page 4, specifies a similar combination except that, in this case, the first element consists of four notes in the middle register whereas the second element consists of two high and two low notes. It seems likely that the first group was consciously transformed in producing the second, or vice versa.

Proportional subdivisions of the overall duration

Several authors have suggested that the organisation of certain conventionally notated works composed by Feldman in the early 1950s is based on

---

[10] '*Projection 1* (1950)', in DeLio (ed.), *The Music of Morton Feldman*, 30. See Appendix 2 for discussion.

[11] I owe this observation to Ryan Vigil ('Compositional parameters', 252).

Example 6.4 *Projection 1*, ictuses 105–24

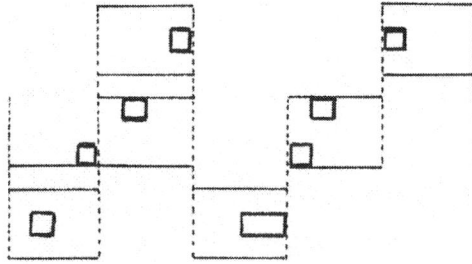

Example 6.5 *Projection 4*, ictuses 41–56

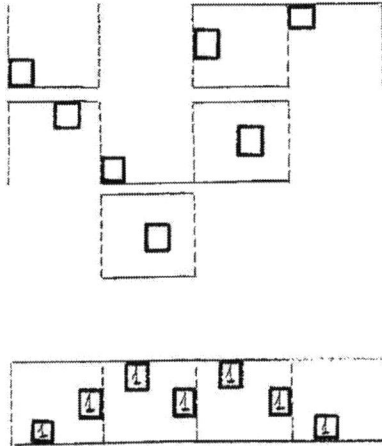

simple proportional subdivisions of the overall duration, into halves, thirds, quarters etc. The evidence for this claim is that significant episodes in the music are often placed at, or around, proportionally significant locations within these works.[12] The undated text 'Structure and the Structural Cell', described in Chapter 4, contains a brief reference to 'exact proportion' that has been struck out by Feldman,[13] but there are no similar comments elsewhere, and his surviving sketches bear no traces of having been partitioned in this way. Neither of these circumstances

---

[12] See K. Potter, An Introduction, 20–1; Gianmario Borio, 'Morton Feldman e l'espressionismo astratto', in Gianmario Borio and Gabrio Taglietti (eds.), *Itinerari della musica Americana* (Lucca: Una Cosa rara, 1996), 121–6; and Noble, *Composing Ambiguity*, 49–55, 88–9.

[13] The deleted text, which reads 'One must then find an the [*sic*] exact proportion', is located between the second and third sentences quoted in Chapter 4.

Example 6.6 *Projection 4*, ictuses 1–28

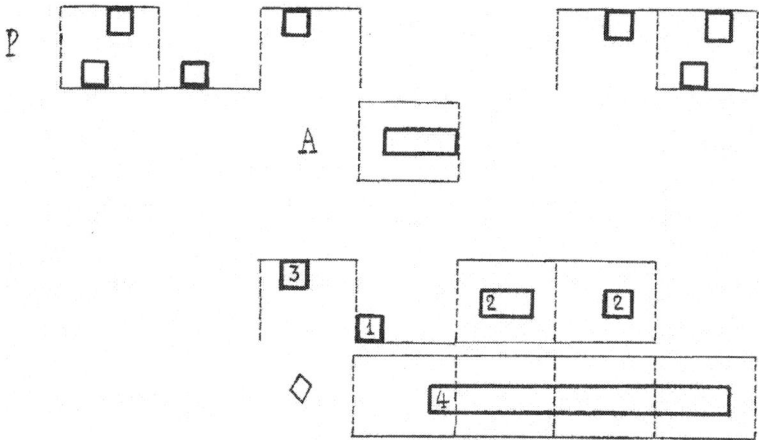

Example 6.7 *Projection 4*, ictuses 112–13 and 150–1, excerpts

counts as a decisive objection, however. He was rarely forthcoming about any aspect of his compositional technique and his own words testify that he deliberately obscured traces of his working methods, as noted above.

Self-consciously working with proportions in his graphs would have been a natural adjunct to his allover method because it would have allowed him to skip to and fro between arithmetically significant locations, modifying activity in one area in the light of modifications made at others. Even so, most of the graphs do not seem to have been deliberately organised in this manner, and Appendix 2 argues that a recent analysis of *Intersection 3* that purports to uncover a formal architecture of this type, based upon aggregate completions, is untenable. Although important events in Feldman's graph music are sometimes located near, or even at, proportionally significant points within the overall duration, this rarely occurs often enough to suggest that Feldman was actively working with proportional divisions that he systematically exploited.

For example, the two longest silences in *Projection 2*, which are prominent in the listening experience, are both located at, or close to, points of proportional significance. The shorter of the two is placed across the boundary between the first and second thirds of the work whereas the longest silence occurs a few seconds after the boundary between the first and second halves. There can be little doubt that Feldman was aware of the arithmetical significance of his choice of these locations and that this was part of the reason why he selected them. Still, this is hardly compelling evidence of systematic manipulation of a network of proportions: the inexactness of the match between the location of the longest silence and the midpoint argues against that hypothesis, as does the absence of similar examples located elsewhere in the work. Instead, it seems properly regarded as an instance of routine thinking about structure.

That said, there is a credible – though not definitive – case for thinking that Feldman did work this way in *Projection 3*. This is because seven of the most prominent events in this particular composition are placed close to proportionally significant locations within the overall duration. Seven may seem a small number, but it represents a significant fraction of the total number of events present in this very short and sparsely populated work. The following analysis ignores sympathetic resonances generated in periods in which Feldman indicates that keys are to be depressed silently. These are often inaudible in available recordings and, as notated, they extend over long periods, meaning that it is only to be expected that many of them straddle points of proportional importance.

A useful place to begin is with the observation that all three registers are sounded simultaneously only twice. The rarity of these chords and other factors to be discussed mean that they are prominent in the listening experience. In the first case of this type, one piano plays two notes in the middle register while the other piano plays three high and four low notes. In the second case, one piano plays five high notes while the other piano plays one low note and three in the middle register. In both cases, nine notes are sounded in a single ictus.

The first of these chords is highlighted in the listening experience in other ways. As well as being the very first sound involving all three registers, it includes the very first low register notes and the largest number of notes yet played; consequently, it may be the loudest sound yet heard. It is also highlighted on the page by being the first occasion on which either pianist plays in more than one register simultaneously and by being the first instance in which both pianos play together. The second chord is highlighted in the listening experience, not just by being only the second sound involving all three registers, but also by being preceded and followed by lengthy silences, which emphasise its individuality.

With these points in mind, it is intriguing that the first chord is played at ictus 27, close to the boundary between the first and second quarters of the time axis, located between ictuses 28 and 29, whereas the second chord is played at ictus 98, which coincides with the exact midpoint of the fourth quarter, between ictuses 98 and 99, which lies seven-eighths of the way through the overall duration. This is evident in Example 6.8, which shows an annotated condensation of the score with both piano parts combined in the same system. This example excludes piano harmonics.

The first of these two chords is perhaps the first prominent event in the work, but the second prominent event follows soon after in ictuses 34–6, in which Feldman specifies an ascending series of registers in consecutive ictuses. This is the only instance of this type of structure and it is also notable because it is placed within a burst of activity centred on the boundary between the first and second thirds of the overall duration.

Another prominent chord extends between ictuses 54 and 58, across the midpoint of the time axis. This chord initially consists of eight high register notes played by one piano and seven low register notes played by the other piano, meaning that it includes a far larger number of notes than in any chord played previously; once again, it is likely to be the loudest sound yet heard. It is also highlighted in the listening experience by the fact that it includes the largest number of high notes and the largest number of low notes yet played.

Closely related observations apply to the massive middle register chord in ictuses 73–6, which straddles the boundary between the second and last third of the overall duration at ictus 74. This sound is likely to be relatively louder, and is also prominent for other reasons, both because it contains the largest number of notes that sound in a single register and because it is preceded and followed by lengthy silences. It is highlighted on the page because it includes the largest number of notes sounded by either pianist and the largest number played by either pianist in a single register.

The locations of the most important silences also merit attention. The work begins with the longest notated silence (four seconds), but there are six shorter silences that are placed within the music that exceed two seconds in length and therefore the empirically established maximum for grouping consecutive sounds (1.5–2.0 seconds).[14] Four of these are located in the last third of the work, where they produce a highly fragmentary listening experience in the closing stages, but it is the locations of the remaining two that are of more interest here. The first is located at ictuses

[14] Paul Fraisse established a threshold for grouping of between 1.5 and 2.0 seconds ('Time and rhythm perception', in Edward C. Carterette and Morton P. Friedman (eds.), *Handbook of Perception, Volume VIII – Perceptual Coding* (New York: Academic Press, 1978), 206). Elsewhere, he suggested a more precise figure of approximately 1.8 seconds ('Rhythm and tempo', in Diana Deutsch (ed.), *The Psychology of Music* (New York: Academic Press, 1982), 156). See also Justin London, *Hearing in Time: Psychological Aspects of Musical Meter* (New York: Oxford University Press, 2004), 29.

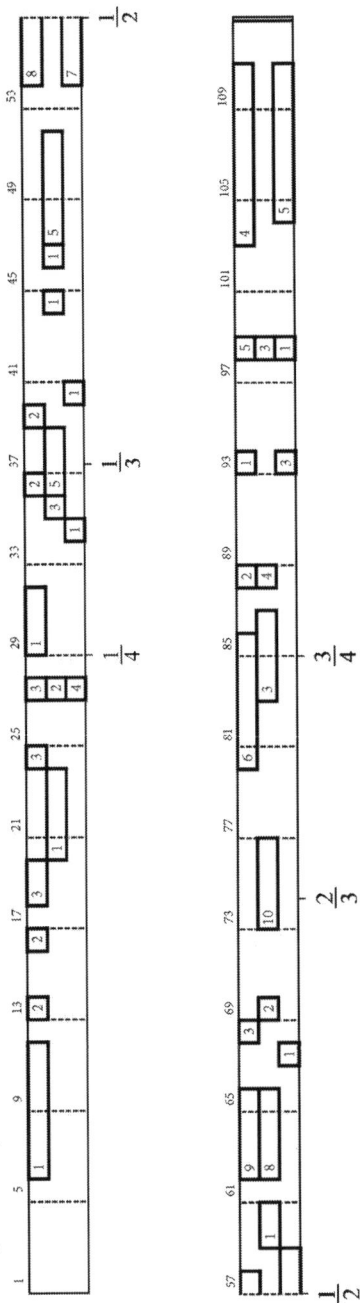

Example 6.8 *Projection 3*, annotated condensation excluding piano harmonics

40–2 and therefore coincides with the midpoint of the second quarter of the overall duration, between ictuses 42 and 43.[15] The second is located in ictuses 70–2, a period that straddles the midpoint of the third quarter of the time axis, between ictuses 70 and 71.[16]

None of these observations is very remarkable in itself, but in combination they add up to a credible case for thinking that *Projection 3* was deliberately organised along arithmetical lines. This case is not definitive, however. One weakness is its inability to account for the location of the largest single chord, consisting of seventeen notes, that is played at ictuses 62–5. True, this chord straddles the point which lies exactly half way between the midpoint of the work as a whole and the boundary between its second and last thirds – that is, the point lying seven-twelfths of the way along the time axis. Even so, it is hard to see an appeal to this as anything other than special pleading; more than half of all cells in the score are located within two ictuses of divisions of the whole into twelve equal parts.

Rhythmic structure

A striking feature of the published edition of the score of *Intersection 1* is that it consists of fifteen graph pages, each of which, except the last, consists of fifteen boxes of four ictuses. The width of the grid on the fifteenth page is sixteen boxes, meaning that the total width of the score is therefore 15^2+1 boxes.

This points to a connection with Cage's working practices. From the late 1930s to the mid-1950s, Cage organised his compositions using what he sometimes referred to as 'rhythmic' structures.[17] These are temporal structures imposed at two distinct levels, both on the duration of the work as a whole and on the durations of its parts; hence Cage's description of the principle underpinning these works as 'micro-macrocosmic'.[18] The resulting isomorphism is expressed as a short, ordered series of numbers – typically integers – that articulate the organisation of durations at both levels.[19]

For example, the isomorphism present in Cage's *Concerto for Prepared Piano and Chamber Orchestra*, which he completed in February 1951, the very same month in which Feldman finished *Intersection 1*, can be

[15] It ends just before the golden section (ictus 43).
[16] It begins just after the golden section (ictus 69).
[17] Most of Cage's concert works composed between 1939 and 1956 use this type of structure (James Pritchett, 'From choice to chance: John Cage's *Concerto for Prepared Piano*', *Perspectives of New Music*, vol. 26, no. 1 (Winter 1988), 54).
[18] 'A composer's confessions', 35.
[19] Cage worked with two distinct types of rhythmic structure (Pritchett, The Development of Chance Techniques, 183). This section focuses on those used in works contemporary with *Intersection 1*.

represented by the ordered series {3, 2, 4, 4, 2, 3, 5}. In this case, the work as a whole is divisible into twenty-three sections of equal size, each containing twenty-three bars. The twenty-three bars in each section are grouped into seven phrases as indicated by the ordered series, while the twenty-three sections in the work as a whole are grouped into seven larger units in similar fashion. Given the unchanging tempo, this organisation implies a similar isomorphism between durations on micro and macro levels.[20]

Any composition that exhibits a rhythmic structure of this type will comprise n^2 elements, where n is the sum of the set of numbers that expresses the isomorphism; hence the potential significance of the fact that the grid of *Intersection 1* comprises 15^2+1 boxes. If such a structure is present, then the isomorphism must operate at the level of the work as a whole and at the level of individual pages (the equally sized sections), in which case the grouping of pages within the score must be reflected in the grouping of boxes within pages.

The presence of an additional box on the last page does not undermine this supposition. A review of the published edition reveals that this box, which is empty, is only clumsily appended; it is narrower than any other box and literally squeezed onto the end of page, suggesting that it was not part of the work's essential conception. Although it is also present in the only surviving sketch in graph notation,[21] other aspects of the sketch point to its being a secondary component. For example, an arithmetical calculation that yields 900 that is also present indicates that Feldman initially intended 900 ictuses (225 boxes), while a tell-tale arrow points at the middle of the 113th box, which marks the exact midpoint of a score with 225 boxes, but not one with 226. Equally significant is the fact that many of Cage's works include codas appended to rhythmically structured core elements; some of these are one bar in length, containing a final sound.[22] Although the last box of *Intersection 1* is empty, its presence is redolent of these single-bar appendages.

---

[20] In the *Concerto for Prepared Piano and Chamber Orchestra*, Cage added another level of organisation by grouping the seven sections into three movements, with the first and second movements each containing three sections and the third movement containing only one. This was not essential to the rhythmic structure of the work, but it was to the project of the *Concerto*, which was to portray an initial opposition and ultimate reconciliation between the prepared piano and orchestra (Pritchett, 'From choice to chance', 56).

[21] Morton Feldman Collection, Paul Sacher Foundation. A sketch of the first few ictuses in a more conventional notation is reproduced and discussed in Chapter 10.

[22] Paul van Emmerik, 'An imaginary grid: rhythmic structure in Cage's music up to circa 1950', in David W. Patterson (ed.), *John Cage: Music, Philosophy, and Intention, 1933–1950* (New York: Routledge, 2002), 219.

These observations are suggestive, but they are not sufficient to establish that a rhythmic structure is present. Another possibility, which cannot be ruled out at this stage, is that the arithmetic properties of the grid frame were deliberately chosen in order to echo Cage's music from this period, perhaps as a kind of homage or ironic gesture, but were not used in organising the music, and it is here that we confront a difficulty in advancing the argument beyond this point. As a rule, Cage drew the performer's attention to the rhythmic structures present in his compositions: the elements of the structure are usually marked in the score by double bar lines, rehearsal numbers or letters,[23] and the ordered series expressing the isomorphism is often highlighted in the accompanying written notes. For example, in the *Concerto for Prepared Piano and Chamber Orchestra*, the ordered series is explicitly stated, the start of each phrase within a section is identified by a rehearsal number and the end of each section is distinguished by a double bar line. No similar markings appear in the published edition of the score of *Intersection 1* or in the sketch. This does not rule against the hypothesis that a rhythmic structure is nevertheless present as Feldman may have had no interest in highlighting its existence to anyone other than Cage, its dedicatee, but it does mean that a simple visual corroboration of the hypothesis is not available. Nor does the organised distribution of symbols between instrumental parts highlighted in Chapter 5 argue against it. There is no inconsistency in the idea that Feldman actively sought to distribute symbols evenly in this way while also attending to aspects of internal structure.

The function of Cage's rhythmic structures evolved during the course of his career.[24] In his earlier works, he meant the structure to be heard; accordingly, he composed melodic lines designed to articulate it, at least in some places. However, even in this early phase, his idea was that the structure should not be too rigidly observed; in a 1944 essay, he emphasised the need for a 'duality' between the 'clarity' of the rhythmic structure and 'grace', which he explained as 'the play with and against' clarity.[25] By 1951, though, he had come to regard the rhythmic structure as an empty template that need not be audible in any way, its purpose being to serve as a frame of reference for organising material using a variety of systematic compositional devices.[26] For example, in the *Concerto for Prepared Piano and Chamber Orchestra*, one role that the rhythmic structure plays is to house Cage's selections of sound gamuts, with most phrases containing gamuts having been obtained by performing a series of predetermined or

[23] *Ibid.*, 218.   [24] Pritchett, 'From choice to chance', 74–5.

[25] 'Four statements on the dance: grace and clarity' [1944], in *Silence*, 91–2.

[26] He outlined this conception in a lecture given at the Club in 1950. This was published subsequently as 'Lecture on nothing' [1959], in *Silence*, 109–27.

randomly selected moves around the rows and columns of grid-like charts of possible outcomes.[27] Be that as it may, gamuts extend over boundaries between phrases in some cases,[28] meaning that, as in earlier works, the outlines of the rhythmic structure are sometimes obscured.

This last observation has important implications for the project in hand. A rhythmic structure used to articulate impermeable boundaries would preclude symbols straddling architecturally significant units and this might be discernible in consistent patterns of placement of material within the score as a whole and on individual pages. Such patterns are not discernible in *Intersection 1*, in which every boundary between boxes is straddled by symbols on some pages. This does not rule out the presence of a rhythmic structure conceived of as a permeable compartmentalisation, however. The presence of this type of structure is likely to result in looser patterns in the organisation of material, and a useful place to begin searching for these is with a review of visual appearances.

The most striking aspect of the score, when it is viewed as a whole, is a dramatic change in texture that occurs at the boundary between pages 10 and 11. The number of symbols drops sharply, from 71 on the former to just 19 on the latter. As shown in Example 6.9, the lower level of activity implied by this shift is sustained throughout the remainder of the score. Indeed, the last five pages all have a characteristic look, not shared by the immediately preceding pages, and this suggests that they should be regarded as a single unit. If a rhythmic structure is present, this indicates that the boundary between pages 10 and 11 is a prescribed division and that the last term of the ordered series that expresses the associated isomorphism is therefore 5, as in the *Concerto for Prepared Piano and Chamber Orchestra*.

If so, then the line separating the tenth and eleventh boxes on each page must also have been conceived of as structurally significant. Given that the boundary between pages 10 and 11 is marked by a change in the density of symbols present, it makes evident sense to look for a similar shift at the corresponding point on each page. A change in density at the boundary between boxes 10 and 11 is evident to the naked eye in most cases, as in Example 6.10.

This is additional evidence that *Intersection 1* possesses a rhythmic structure, but the outstanding challenge is to arrive at a complete account of the isomorphism. One possibility is that the work possesses a relatively coarse structure expressible by the ordered series {10, 5}, meaning that there

[27] For further discussion, see Pritchett, 'From choice to chance', 50–81, and Brett Boutwell, 'Marvelous Accidents': The *Concerto for Prepared Piano and Chamber Orchestra* of John Cage, unpublished M. Mus thesis, University of North Texas (1999), 1–86.
[28] *Ibid.*, 61.

Example 6.9 *Intersection 1*, number of symbols per page

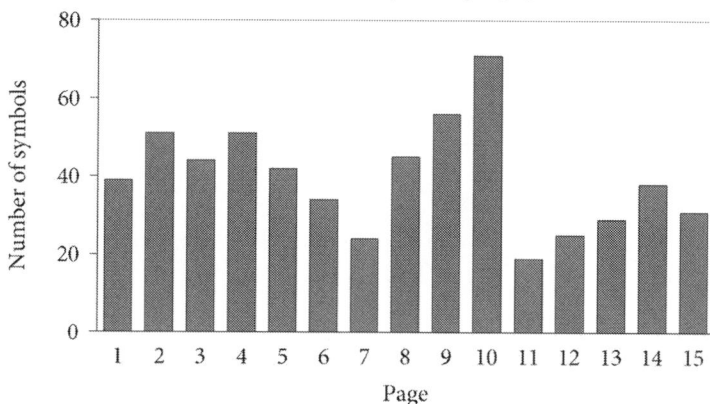

is no more organisation to discern, but this series is shorter than those Cage employed, which points to further detail being present. The larger size of the first term in the series suggests that this should be the focus of attention, as does the apparent homogeneity – to the eye – of the last five pages.

The suggestion that the isomorphism is expressible as the ordered series {5, 5, 5} is consistent with labelling in the sketch, in which every fifth box is numbered (5, 10, etc.).[29] It is tempting to dismiss this numbering, which does not appear in the published edition, as a heuristic device for indicating location within the score, but we should not overlook the possibility that the implied division of pages into three equal parts has a deeper significance. If so, then the boundaries between the fifth and sixth pages of the score and between the fifth and sixth boxes on each page all have architectural significance.

Some pages do appear to be organised in this way, the best example being page 8, shown in Example 6.10, which is clearly divisible into three equally sized parts containing significantly different quantities of symbols – fifteen, six and twenty-four, respectively. However, the difference between the density of symbols present in boxes 1–5 and boxes 6–10 is generally less well defined than the corresponding difference between boxes 6–10 and boxes 11–15, as shown in Table 6.1. Moreover, the boundary between the fifth and sixth pages does not seem to mark a point of inflexion.

An alternative structure is suggested by the account of the listening experience presented in Chapter 1, which portrayed this particular work as divisible into four distinct phases: first quarter; second quarter; first third of the second half; and last third. This implies an isomorphism expressible

[29] Morton Feldman Collection, Paul Sacher Foundation.

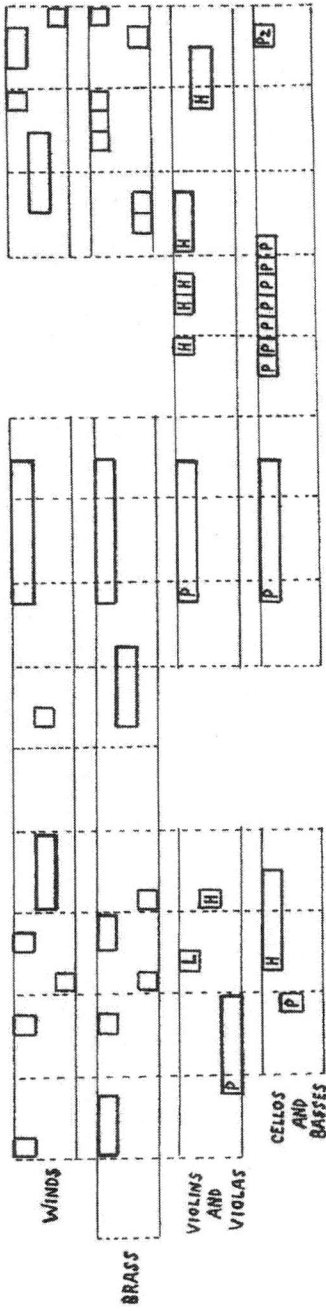

Example 6.10 *Intersection 1*, page 8

Table 6.1. Intersection 1, *numbers of symbols by page and intra-page division*

	Boxes 1–5	Boxes 6–10	Change in density (%)	Boxes 6–10	Boxes 11–15	Change in density (%)
Page 1	19	15	−21	15	5	−67
Page 2	18	13	−28	13	19	46
Page 3	7	16	129	16	21	31
Page 4	21	25	19	25	5	−80
Page 5	7	22	214	22	12	−45
Page 6	11	15	36	15	8	−47
Page 7	6	10	67	10	8	−20
Page 8	15	6	−60	6	24	300
Page 9	16	20	25	20	20	0
Page 10	26	24	−8	24	21	−13
Page 11	6	4	−33	4	9	125
Page 12	15	6	−60	6	4	−33
Page 13	10	11	10	11	8	−27
Page 14	14	15	7	15	8	−47
Page 15	12	13	8	13	6	−54

Note: *symbols that straddle two or more boxes are counted as belonging to the first box in which they appear.*

as $\{3\frac{3}{4}, 3\frac{3}{4}, 2\frac{1}{2}, 5\}$, consistent with the conclusions about the final term of the series reached earlier in this section. This ordered series includes mixed fractions, unlike the one used in *Concerto for Prepared Piano and Chamber Orchestra*, but it cannot be ruled out for this reason.[30] Immediately after completing the *Concerto*, Cage began working on *Music of Changes*, in which the rhythmic structure is expressible as $\{3, 5, 6\frac{3}{4}, 6\frac{3}{4}, 6\frac{3}{4}, 5, 3\frac{1}{8}\}$.

An advantage of this alternative is that it is discernible at the macro level in the listening experience. Although Cage was by this time no longer thinking of rhythmic structures as inherently audible, this is only a weak argument against the alternative proposal because we cannot assume that Feldman conceived of them in identical fashion.

A comparison between the densities of symbols in the four areas on each page implied by this division provides further support for the hypothesis that this series is the one that Feldman used. Measurements reported in Table 6.2 indicate that the densities of symbols in adjacent areas are considerably

---

[30] At the intra-page level, the series is expressible in ictuses in simpler terms as $\{15, 15, 10, 20\}$.

Table 6.2. Intersection 1, *numbers of symbols by page and intra-page division*

	Boxes 1–3.75	Boxes 3.75–7.5	Change in density (%)	Boxes 3.75–7.5	Boxes 7.5–10	Change in density (%)	Boxes 7.5–10	Boxes 11–15	Change in density (%)
Page 1	16	7	−56	7	11	136	11	5	−77
Page 2	14	10	−29	10	7	5	7	19	36
Page 3	4	10	150	10	9	35	9	21	17
Page 4	16	16	0	16	14	31	14	5	−82
Page 5	4	13	225	13	13	50	13	12	−54
Page 6	6	18	200	18	2	−83	2	8	100
Page 7	3	8	167	8	5	−6	5	8	−20
Page 8	12	5	−58	5	4	20	4	24	200
Page 9	8	16	100	16	11	3	11	20	−9
Page 10	19	18	−5	18	13	8	13	21	−19
Page 11	3	6	100	6	1	−75	1	9	350
Page 12	12	4	−67	4	5	88	5	4	−60
Page 13	10	5	−50	5	6	80	6	8	−33
Page 14	9	14	56	14	7	−25	7	8	−43
Page 15	9	14	56	14	2	−79	2	6	50

Note: *symbols that straddle two or more boxes are counted as belonging to the first box in which they appear.*

different on many pages, with the differences between the first and second elements in the structure typically just as well defined as those between its last two elements.

As in the analysis of *Projection 3*, presented earlier in this chapter, it is not possible to say with certainty that the suggested structure is present. Unlike Cage, Feldman did not draw attention to his methods, and the patterns that exist in the organisation of the material are not sufficiently clear-cut to warrant unequivocal conclusions about those he used. Even so, the case for thinking that *Intersection 1* possesses a rhythmic structure is reasonably solid – another reason for thinking that Feldman's method of composing 'by ear' was, on occasions, more methodical than is generally assumed.

Chance processes

Tudor remembered that in 1951 Feldman was impressed by Cage's ideas about using chance in composing *Music of Changes*,[31] Cage's first full-scale

---

[31] 'David Tudor: interview with Peter Dickinson', 82–3.

attempt to apply chance operations in composing an entire work. An intriguing question about Feldman's early methods, therefore, is whether they made use of chance-based processes, such as tossing coins, rolling dice or referring to tables of random numbers. Feldman never admitted to using procedures of this type, and by 1958 he was actively criticising recourse to them,[32] but we cannot legitimately infer that he had always avoided them previously. He disliked being portrayed as one of Cage's disciples and went to considerable lengths in interviews to stress his independence. The use of chance operations defined Cage's music from 1951, so if Feldman had made use of them early in his career, he might have wished to conceal this fact, given that it would have been taken as an unequivocal sign of Cage's influence.

That said, there is no surviving documentary evidence that establishes that Feldman used such processes in composing his graphs and this, in itself, is prima facie evidence that he did not. To probe further, our only course is to look for traces of chance operations in the works themselves. *Intersection 2* is surely the graph to focus on, in addressing this issue, given that it was the first to make extensive use of numbers, which lend themselves to being selected by chance methods in especially direct ways. Moreover, the score is dated August 1951, meaning that Feldman worked on it during the period in which Cage composed *Music of Changes*.[33]

The fact that 12 is the highest number that appears in the graph is immediately suggestive, as is the fact that it is to be interpreted in an irregular way. Lower numbers indicate the precise number of sounds to be played, but 12 means twelve or more sounds. This could point to the use of a compositional process in which 12 was the highest available number, but any suggestion that he might have made his selections by throwing two dice is quickly dismissed. The distribution of numbers that appear in the score (Example 6.11) is quite unlike the distribution that dice would produce. Feldman's selections exhibit a marked bias towards the number 1 and include a much lower incidence of numbers greater than 5 – evidence of sensitivity to the fact that a pianist's hand has five fingers.

The score also includes loose designs in the selection and arrangement of numbers in specific areas that are too common to be consistent with the use of a simple, chance-based mechanism. These involve the presence of several consecutive numbers in a group of adjacent cells that are otherwise empty, so that the terms appear next to one another or separated only by unoccupied cells. Example 6.12 highlights two different types of arrangement of

---

[32] 'Sound, noise, Varèse, Boulez', 1–2.

[33] The four parts of *Music of Changes* are dated as follows: Part I, 16 May 1951; Part II, 2 August 1951; Part III, 18 October 1951; and Part IV, 13 December 1951.

Example 6.11   *Intersection 2*, frequency with which numbers occur

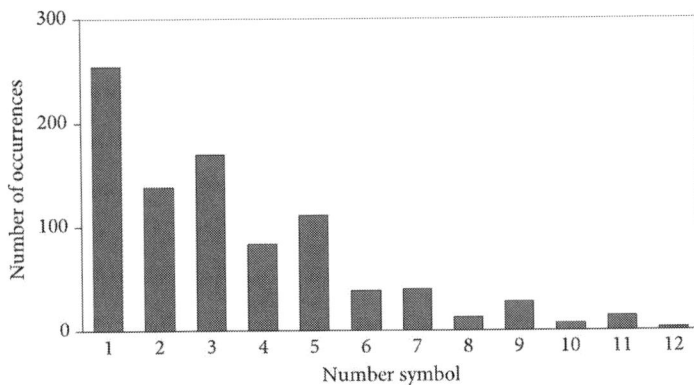

this kind. In the first type of case, the numbers are presented in a horizontal line of grid cells. There are four instances of this type on page 4 of the published edition of the score, one of which straddles two grid frames. A similar arrangement straddles pages 4 and 5 and is therefore only partially visible. All these are highlighted in grey, with the arrangements that straddle grid frames and pages marked with grey arrows. In the second type of case, the consecutive numbers are presented in a rectangular group of cells. There are fourteen arrangements of this type on page 4; these are highlighted in the example with pronounced rectangular outlines. One of these arrangements, marked with white arrows, straddles two grid frames. Many similar patterns of both types can be found elsewhere in the score.

The case for seeing Feldman's tempo guidance as dictated by chance is initially more promising. The first nine pages of the published edition are set at a tempo of 158 ictuses per minute, but the tempo changes four times on the penultimate page, as highlighted in Table 6.3.[34] Years later, Feldman attributed the presence of tempo changes in *Extensions 1*, a conventionally notated work completed two months after *Intersection 2*, to Milton Babbitt's example in *Composition for Four Instruments* (1948),[35] but it is hard to see the frenetic oscillation between two tempo markings in this particular composition as a

[34] The first page of Feldman's original manuscript ([Unsigned: G], *Selections*, 127) indicates a lower tempo of 128 ictuses per minute, suggesting that Feldman revised his guidance prior to Cage re-copying the score in late 1951: Cage's copy, which became the published edition, includes the higher figure of 158 ictuses per minute. The whereabouts of the remaining pages of Feldman's manuscript are not known, so it is unclear if the tempo changes in the published edition were originally present.

[35] *'Soundpieces* interview', 87.

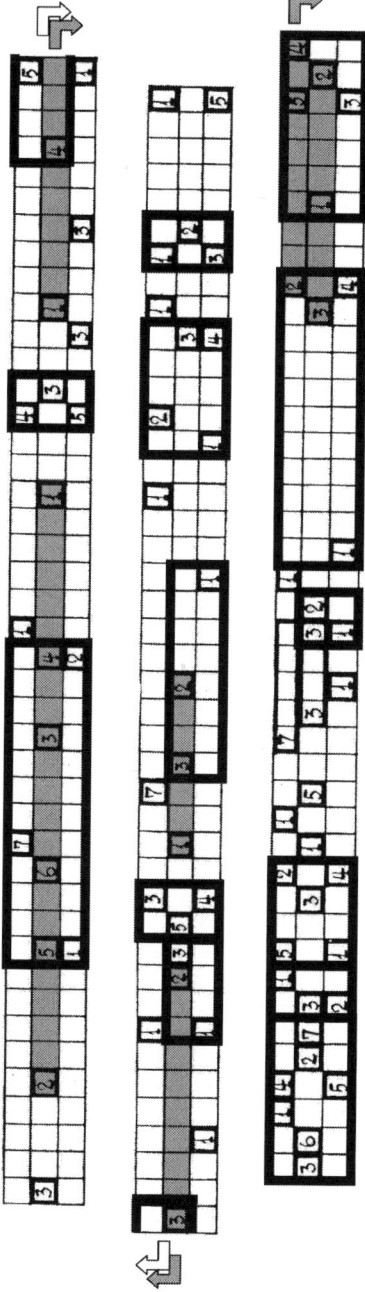

Example 6.12 *Intersection 2*, page 4 with numerical patterns highlighted

Table 6.3. Intersection 2, *indicated tempos*

Ictuses per minute	Tempo applied from (ictus number)	Tempo applies for (ictuses)	Tempo applies for (seconds)
158	1	1,249	474
198	1,250	38	12
172	1,288	7	2
276	1,295	16	3
178	1,311	152	51

model for Feldman's much less frequent shifts between multiple tempos in *Extensions 1* or, indeed, *Intersection 2*.[36] Moreover, a striking aspect of the changes notated in the graph has no precedent in Babbitt's composition and seems to point, instead, to their selection by chance. This is the seeming redundancy of the third tempo indication, which applies to a short period containing no sounds. This period has a theoretical duration of 2.44 seconds, which could have been represented instead by eight cells at the immediately preceding tempo of 198 ictuses per minute (2.42 seconds) or eleven cells at the subsequent tempo of 276 ictuses per minute (2.39 seconds).

The tempo of *Music of Changes* also fluctuates at irregularly spaced intervals. Although there is nothing analogous to Feldman's soundless tempo change in the first three parts of the score, there are two apparently redundant tempo changes on the last page of part IV, which Cage worked on after Feldman had finished *Intersection 2*. The presence of a similar anachronism in both scores could point to a similar method of construction. Given that Cage is known to have used chance processes in selecting his tempo values, the similarity in outcome is circumstantial evidence that Feldman also had recourse to chance.[37]

These arguments are ultimately inconclusive, however, for there is another possibility, which seems equally likely – namely, that Feldman deliberately chose varying tempos for a didactic purpose. As noted in Chapter 1, Boulez included a long and sustained attack on Feldman's graph notation in a letter to Cage in December 1951. His principal

---

[36] Claren has noted the difficulty in establishing a clear connection between *Composition for Four Instruments* and *Extensions 1* (*Neither*, 64).

[37] For Cage's use of chance in selecting tempos in *Music of Changes*, see Pritchett, *The Music of John Cage*, 83. There is little overlap between the tempo values used in *Intersection 2* and *Music of Changes* and there is no simple arithmetical relationship between the two sets of values.

argument against the format was that it was incapable of specifying irrational durations:

> the fact of tempo indicated by a scale in seconds signifies a constant metric unity which is 60, and this for all the works. I am willing that one have metric unities which may be multiples or divisions of 60. But I do not see why one would have only that. [. . . This] is to refuse all the fractional values by relation to 60 (a simple metronome is then perfect for him); and to refuse again all the irrationals of the divers kinds.[38]

This letter appears to have been written after *Intersection 2* was completed, but it is clear that Wolff had relayed Boulez's reservations about the graph format previously, after visiting him earlier in the year.[39] Consequently, it is distinctly possible that Feldman learned of Boulez's position before finishing his graph, in which case he may have chosen to include varying tempos in order to demonstrate the limits of Boulez's argument. Evidently, it is not possible to specify irrational divisions of the pulse using the graph format, but as *Intersection 2* makes clear, it is possible to specify irrational divisions of time by selecting an appropriate tempo. This is because each tempo indication specified in the score implies a unit of pulse equal to an irrational fraction of clock time. For example, a tempo of 172 ictuses per minute implies a duration of 15/43 seconds per ictus.

The case for seeing the placement of diamond symbols as based on chance is also inconclusive. These are used in the *Projections* to signal harmonics on stringed instruments and the silent depression of piano keys for the production of sympathetic resonances, as previously noted. Accordingly, it is natural to assume that the unexplained use of the same symbol in *Intersection 2* was meant to be interpreted in the second of these ways, yet eighteen of the twenty-four entries with diamonds occur in periods in which the score indicates no other sounds. There appears to be nothing – except ambient sounds in the performing space – to excite sympathetic resonances in these cases. This is precisely the kind of unusual outcome that one might expect to see if their placement had been determined by chance.

---

[38] Nattiez (ed.), *The Boulez-Cage Correspondence*, 115. Boulez's critique ends as follows: 'I think of these Intersections [. . .] that they let themselves go dangerously to the <u>seduction of graphism alone</u>. [. . .] willingly I would ask Feldman [. . .] not to satisfy himself with a seductive exterior aspect' (*ibid.* 116, with Boulez's underlining). This was a misunderstanding. As noted elsewhere in this volume, visual aspects of the graph scores are closely related to audible properties of the music. For Feldman, attending to the former was therefore tantamount to attending to the latter. In none of the surviving graphs is the tempo set at 60 ictuses per minute.

[39] *Ibid.*, 110.

In his notes to the most recently published edition of the score, Volker Straebel has suggested that the diamond symbol 'might indicate harmonics, produced by lightly touching the string while pressing the key'.[40] The advantage of this reading is that it aligns the interpretation of the entries with diamonds in *Intersection 2* with Feldman's use of diamonds in the *Projections* to signal harmonics from stringed instruments. Be that as it may, there is no other example in Feldman's works from any period in which he instructs the pianist to play inside the piano.

A connected reason for rejecting Straebel's suggestion and, instead, interpreting the diamond symbols as indicating the silent depression of keys, is that the latter course allows us to see the greatest possible degree of continuity in Feldman's notation for piano in his graph series. Diamonds reappear without being explained in the piano parts of two subsequent graphs, *Atlantis* and *...Out of 'Last Pieces'*. There is no difficulty involved in interpreting them as indicating the silent depression of keys, as these symbols always occur when the piano or other instruments in the ensemble are sounding. However, in the next graph, *The Straits of Magellan*, the use of the diamond is explained in the accompanying notes as '[f]ingers down without sounding, using sustaining pedal', which connects the meaning of the symbol in this score with its use in piano parts in the *Projections*.

The implication is that in *Intersection 2* Feldman notated actions that may not directly affect the sounds to be produced. This could point to the use of a chance procedure in their selection, but other explanations are also feasible. One is that he was interested in the indirect effects of his seemingly redundant instructions, such as the associated increase in difficulty involved in complying with every aspect of his notation and the indirect impact on other sounds caused by making the performer's playing more rushed. Another is that the deviant symbols were intended as a humorous touch. *Intersection 2* was dedicated to Tudor and the only copy of the score was given to him as a 'personal' gesture,[41] so it is possible that it included a private joke. Cage's *Suite for Toy Piano* (1948) also contains what may have been intended as humorous elements, and these may have inspired Feldman to try something similar. The humorous elements include Cage's specification of a wide dynamic range, which

[40] 'Morton Feldman: early piano pieces (1950–1964): notes on the edition', in Volker Straebel (ed.), *Morton Feldman: Solo Piano Works 1950–64*, EP67976 (New York: C. F. Peters, 1998), 60.

[41] Morton Feldman to Cornelius Cardew, 25 April 1961, Cornelius Cardew Papers, British Library.

cannot be produced on a toy piano and, significantly, his use of diamonds to indicate piano harmonics, which a toy piano cannot produce.[42]

Number strings

Numbers are used sparingly in *Projections 2–5*, but they are by far the most frequently used symbols in the piano *Intersections* and several later graphs, and in some of these number-soaked scores, simple numerical patterns that this study will refer to as *number strings* or, more succinctly, *strings*, regularly recur. Strings are groups of three or more different numbers, such as {1, 3, 2, 4}, that are all terms in a sequence of consecutive integers. Every term in the sequence must appear once, and only once, for the sequence to count as a string, but the terms need not appear in ascending or descending order. The sequence may begin with the number 1, as in the example just given, but this need not be the case. For example, the group {9, 7, 8} also qualifies as a string.

In several graphs, beginning with *Intersection 2*, Feldman regularly placed the terms of a string within a group of adjacent cells containing no other numbers, so that the terms appear next to one another or separated only by empty cells. Example 6.12 (above) highlights cases in which the string is presented in a horizontal line of grid cells and others in which it is presented in a rectangular group of cells. Henceforth, strings placed in horizontal or vertical lines are referred to as *linear* – or, where this is more appropriate, *horizontal* or *vertical* – whereas those placed in rectangular groups of cells are referred to *areal*. This facilitates the follow-ing observation: the score of *Intersection 2* includes many horizontal and areal strings, but very few that are vertical.

Strings can be singled out and therefore counted in different ways, so an explanation of the method to be used is necessary. As the term 'string' is used here, a particular number can count as a member of one areal string, one horizontal string and one vertical string; this may seem arbitrary, but grounds will emerge in what follows. Even so, there are still choices to be made. For example, if the six numbers from one to six appear in order in a single row of cells, they can be counted as one longer string, {1, 2, 3, 4, 5, 6}, or two shorter strings, {1, 2, 3} and {4, 5, 6}. The approach used here is to single out the longest possible strings, even if this means excluding num-bers that could otherwise be seen as terms in shorter groupings, on the grounds that longer strings have a lower probability of being present by

---

[42] The explanatory notes with the score state that the work can also be played on an ordinary piano, with which sympathetic resonances could be made to sound.

accident. Many of the longest strings found in the graph series straddle two or even three grid frames or pages.

The score of *Intersection 2* includes only three vertical strings, but in the much shorter score of *Intersection 3*, there are seventeen. Vertical, horizontal and areal strings that appear on the first page of the published edition are highlighted in Example 6.13, as are two irregular string types, marked with pronounced, non-rectangular outlines that interlock with one another. Arrangements that straddle grid frames are marked with arrows. The higher incidence of vertical strings in this case may be connected with the more frequent use of grid cells that are subdivided into upper and lower parts. These gave Feldman greater scope to include longer strings – up to six numbers in length – in individual columns.

Feldman employed number strings more frequently in *Ixion* for chamber ensemble, *Atlantis* and . . .*Out of 'Last Pieces'*. For example, *Ixion* contains approximately 350 linear strings, of which more than 100 include five or more terms. Some are particularly long, with the two longest both containing the nine terms from 1 to 9. Strings are most frequently present towards the end of the score, and are especially prominent on pages 18–19 of the published edition. Horizontal, vertical and areal strings on page 18 are highlighted in Examples 6.14–6.15. As before, parts of strings that straddle one or more adjacent grid frames are marked with arrows.

In *Atlantis*, there are approximately 400 linear strings, of which almost 100 include five or more numbers. Again, some are long, being up to eight numbers in length, with the longest including eight terms, 1–8, 2–9 and 4–11. Strings on page 1 are highlighted in Examples 6.16–6.17.

In . . .*Out of 'Last Pieces'*, strings are also common, especially on pages 1–7, but they are rather less prevalent overall. There are approximately 200 linear strings in total, of which almost forty include five or more terms.

The frequent appearance of strings and their long lengths in some cases strongly suggest that they are not present simply by chance. What they point to, instead, is a compositional method, employed by Feldman, which involved distributing a 'row' of consecutive numbers within an otherwise empty line of cells or an otherwise empty rectangular or irregular area of the grid. Perhaps he silently counted out the sequence in ascending or descending order, placing each number in turn as he counted.[43]

Analysis reveals no clearly recognisable patterns in Feldman's choice of numbers for use in strings, and it also suggests that he had no favoured way

---

[43] The score also contains many near-instances of horizontal and areal strings in which the terms of a string plus or minus a number are present. It is possible that, on some occasions, Feldman initially included a string and then added or erased a term.

Example 6.13 *Intersection 3*, page 1 with number strings highlighted

Example 6.14 *Ixion* for chamber ensemble, page 18 with horizontal strings highlighted

Example 6.15 *Ixion* for chamber ensemble, page 18 with vertical and areal strings highlighted

Example 6.16 *Atlantis*, page 1 with horizontal strings highlighted

1a

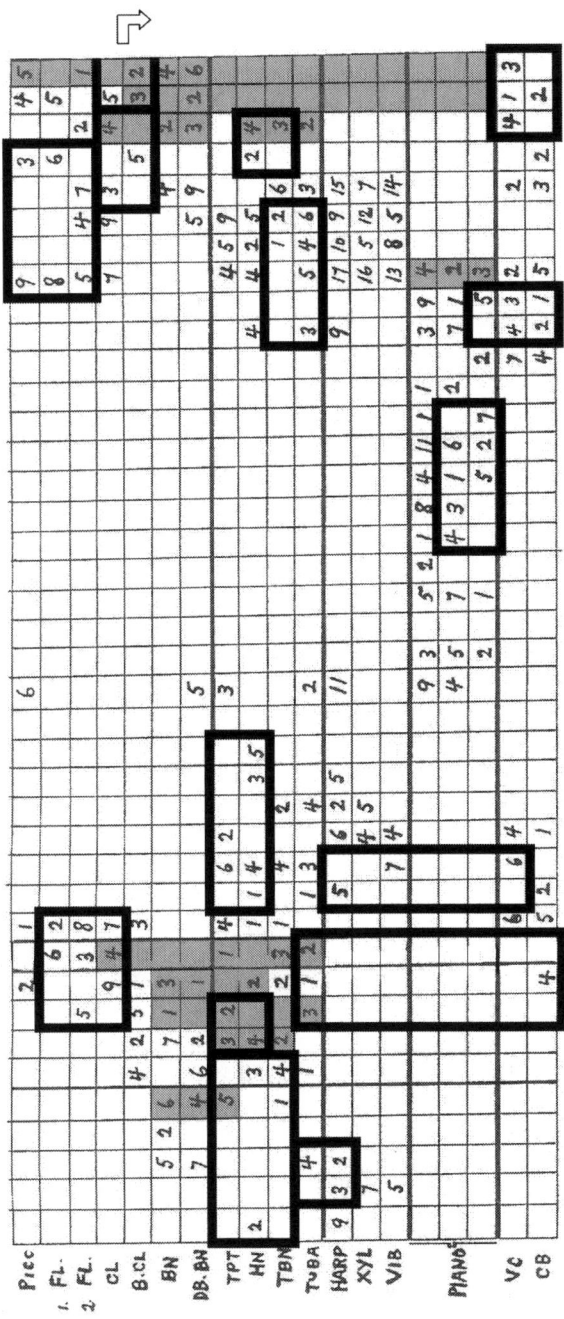

Example 6.17 *Atlantis*, page 1 with vertical and areal strings highlighted

Example 6.18 '15 sec Structure for piano'

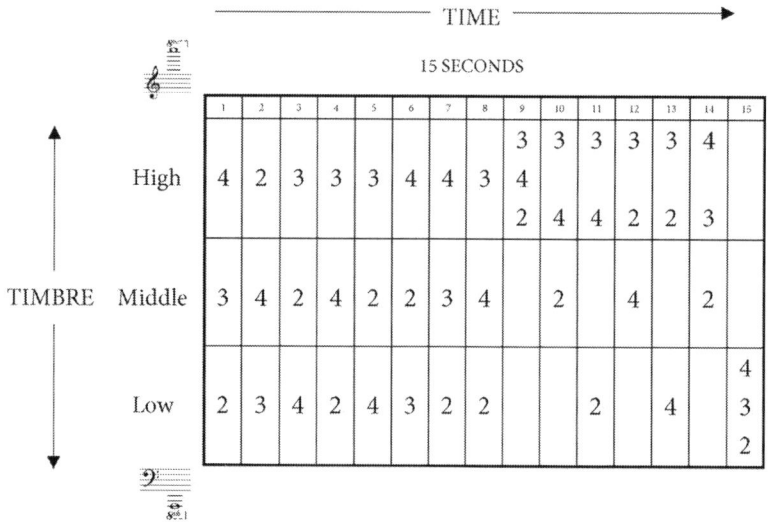

TIME →

15 SECONDS

TIMBRE	1	2	3	4	5	6	7	8	9	10	11	12	13	14	15
High									3	3	3	3	3	4	
High	4	2	3	3	3	4	4	3	4						
High									2	4	4	2	2	3	
Middle	3	4	2	4	2	2	3	4		2		4		2	
Low	2	3	4	2	4	3	2	2		2		4			4
Low															3
Low															2

of ordering their terms. Some numbers are terms in more than one string and sometimes this may have been an unintended, but not necessarily unwelcome, by-product of his placing strings next to one another in his grid frames. If so, then it is impossible to determine in these cases which strings were primary, and this is a reason why linear strings were not prioritised over areal strings or vice versa in the above. Another reason is that the simultaneous use of some numbers in several strings may have been intended by him in some cases.

Further evidence that Feldman manipulated strings quite deliberately appears in a handwritten note, titled 'Aim: <u>Method</u> of variabilities',[44] which may date from 1952, although this is uncertain.[45] This note includes a preliminary sketch of a '15 sec Structure for piano' – possibly a graph – replicated in Example 6.18. Several factors make it difficult to form a complete explanation of the purpose and meaning of this sketch,[46] but its significance for current purposes stems from the blatant use of

---

[44] Feldman's underlining.

[45] Morton Feldman Collection, Paul Sacher Foundation. The note appears on the back of a folded flyer/programme for Tudor's Cherry Lane performances on 1 January and 10 February 1952, which is placed inside 'Sketchbook 3'. The title '15 sec Structure for piano' appears to the right of the sketch, but is struck out.

[46] One is why Feldman labelled the vertical axis 'timbre', and not 'register'. Another is the meaning of an obscure note that appears immediately below the sketch.

vertical strings containing the terms 2, 3 and 4 in every column. The juxtaposition of different vertical distributions of these three terms produces horizontal strings in some places, but in this particular instance, it is evident that vertical strings are primary and horizontal strings largely derivative.

Why was Feldman attracted to using number strings? One possibility is that he regarded them as having numerological appeal,[47] but an argument against this is that their numerological interest appears to be rather limited. A more credible suggestion, perhaps, is that he enjoyed the loose connection that the presence of these patterns forged with serialism. Although the strict application of serial techniques would become one of his bêtes noires on the grounds that the system, not the sounds, was in control, it is evident that this criticism would not preclude a controlled allusion to serial method,[48] and it cannot be ruled out that he might have conceived of such an approach as irony.

That said, he may have regarded the presence of strings as having more concrete benefits. To begin with, the inclusion of horizontal and areal strings in *Intersections 2–3* usually results in a significant increase in difficulty for the performer. In an area of the score that includes a horizontal string, the performer is constantly forced to alter the number of notes played simultaneously with each hand or arm and therefore not allowed the luxury of reusing the same hand or arm position in consecutive attacks, and this is typically, though not always, the case in areas that include an areal string. Perhaps this increase in difficulty was the effect that Feldman intended. The piano *Intersections* were written for Tudor and the many challenges that they present indicate that Feldman actively sought to produce works that were exceptionally difficult to perform.

This is unlikely to be the reason why he included so many vertical strings in *Intersection 3*, however. It is true that some of those that he included – like the one shown in the middle column in Example 6.19 – are particularly awkward to play. Even so, it is hard to see why the use of a string is integral to the difficulties involved, which derive instead from the very large number of constituent notes in widely distributed registers. More likely, Feldman used vertical strings as a way of creating subtle gradations of

[47] Nicholls has argued that Feldman relied on numerological factors to determine some aspects of his more conventionally notated scores from 1950 to 1951 ('Getting rid of the glue: the music of the New York School', in Johnson (ed.), *The New York Schools*, 30).

[48] The suggestion that he worked this way also gains support from a review of sketch materials for some later works, such as *Violin and Orchestra* (1979) and *For Samuel Beckett* (1987), at the Paul Sacher Foundation. These include lists of twelve pitches that in some cases have been ticked off, presumably as Feldman systematically included each one, as noted in Noble, *Composing Ambiguity*, 124.

Example 6.19   *Intersection 3*, ictuses 296–8

register within chords by emphasising constituent elements to differing extents, and a similar idea probably underpinned his use of vertical strings in *Ixion, Atlantis* and *...Out of 'Last Pieces'*. These produce subtle gradations of overall timbre by requiring different instruments to play different numbers of sounds within an ictus; this results in instrumental contributions being emphasised to differing extents.[49]

Similar reasoning suggests that the use of horizontal and areal strings in these works was meant to introduce delicate differences between timbres in adjacent and nearby ictuses, and Feldman's surviving comments about rhythm in his graph music indicate that ensuring the presence of such variations was indeed one of his principal aims in his later graphs, as will now become clear.

Comments by Feldman, published in a review article in 1952, highlight his early thinking about rhythmic aspects of his graph music:

> My Projections and Intersections is a weight either reminiscent or discovered. Weight for me does not have its source in the realm of dynamics or tensions, but rather resulting from a visual-aural response to sound as an image gone inward creating a general synthesis. Weight involves the finding of a pulse which allows for a natural fluidity. Discovered weight implies discovered balance. Discovered balance implies discovered movement from this pulse.[50]

The opening of this quotation is a variant on a passage, quoted in Chapter 5, from another article published in the same year, but the last three sentences are important additions. They suggest not only that Feldman

---

[49] Listeners have a natural propensity to attend more closely to attacks than subsequent aspects of sounds, meaning that they listen more closely to timbres that sound more often, all else being equal. This is an instance of a more general phenomenon, sometimes referred to as the 'orienting response', which is the natural tendency of perceivers to attend to changing aspects of their perceptual environment (Sloboda, *The Musical Mind*, 174). Another reason is that differences in the numbers of notes are likely to affect relative dynamics. It is more difficult, on some instruments, to play a rapid sequence of short notes as quietly as a less hurried sequence of longer notes.

[50] Cowell, 'Current chronicle', 131.

aimed at creating 'natural fluidity' or 'movement' in his earliest graph music,[51] but also that he believed that creating this effect depended only upon selecting the right pulse for the work in view of the overall quantity of scored activity. His description of the fluidity as 'natural' could suggest a contrast with fluidity of an 'unnatural' type. Given the importance of cause and effect continuity in generating movement in tonal music and its intended absence in his graphs, it is not unreasonable to suppose that this unnatural type of fluidity was one attributable to tonal relationships.

More than a decade later, in 1963, Feldman returned to the issue of 'movement' in a letter to Bernstein, in which he denied the presence of 'rhythm' in his more conventionally notated *Structures* for orchestra and . . .*Out of 'Last Pieces'* while insisting on the presence of 'movement':

> I was struck by the fact that you felt a lack of 'rhythmic interest' in this piece [i.e. *Structures*], because what I was actually after was an atonal rhythm, or, more precisely, no rhythm. It is the juxtaposing of various weights of sound which make for the movement, rather than any rhythmic design. This is equally true of 'Out of Last Pieces,' [*sic*] and is in fact one of the basic ideas throughout my work.[52]

Evidently, Feldman's insistence that *Structures* and . . .*Out of 'Last Pieces'* lack 'rhythm' was shorthand for the claim that they lack tonal rhythm; here again, there can be little doubt that he would have connected this with the intended absence of cause and effect continuity. His position was, instead, that they possess 'atonal rhythm', which is the source of a different type of apparent 'movement'.

Feldman seems to have discussed the intended character of the perceptible movement in . . .*Out of 'Last Pieces'* with Copland in the run-up to a performance of this work by the San Francisco Symphony Orchestra, conducted by Copland, in early 1967. Copland's handwritten notes on his copy of the score, written during or after a conversation with Feldman, mentioned in Chapter 3, contain the remark 'drifts by like a river'. Most probably, this is how Feldman described the intended effect. Feldman's simile of a river does not quite capture the somewhat erratic character of the perceptible forward movement, which ebbs and flows, as is evident when listening to the available recordings. Perhaps a

---

[51] The text certainly pre-dated *Intersections 3–4* and it may have been written before Feldman completed *Intersection 2*. Chapter 4 argued that many passages in *Intersections 2–4* are heard as a succession of short, dissimilar chords that are almost entirely discrete.

[52] Morton Feldman to Leonard Bernstein, 19 June 1963, Leonard Bernstein Collection, Music Division, Library of Congress. The letter was written after a telephone conversation with Bernstein's assistant, Jack Gottlieb. Bernstein's handwritten notes on his copy of the letter indicate that Gottlieb had misrepresented his reaction to *Structures*.

comparison with the more hesitant flow of a rivulet or stream might have been more apt.[53] A less flattering description of the movement, which nevertheless registers its prominence in the listening experience, had appeared in a review of one of the New York Philharmonic's 1964 performances of ...*Out of 'Last Pieces'*, in which an anonymous critic echoed a fashionable description of Pollock's painting as 'noodle soup' by characterising the sound of Feldman's work as 'like noodle soup going down a drain'.[54]

There is no question of either of the similes of the rivulet or the stream being applicable to the early graphs. The velocity of apparent motion audible in the available recordings of the *Projections* is too low and too punctuated with lengthy silences to make it appropriate to describe it in this way. As noted above, experimental psychology has concluded that sounds that are separated by 2.0 seconds or more cannot be grouped by human auditory systems, but *Projection 1*, which is a relatively short work lasting around three minutes, includes sixteen silences that last longer than this at the given tempo. Lengthy silences are common elsewhere in the *Projections* and in the *Intersections* except *Intersection 2* and *Intersection 3*. This implies a somewhat fragmentary listening experience, which is quite unlike the impression of erratic but unbroken flow generated by recorded performances of many of the later graphs.

Based on the evidence of the available recordings, the pace of the audible movement is somewhat faster in *Intersection 1* and *Marginal Intersection*, and this may be attributable to generally higher densities of sounds, and, in *Marginal Intersection*, the use of a sound effects recording of riveting, which is discussed in more detail below. However, in the *Intersections* for solo instruments, the dominant impression is of chaotic (i.e. energetic but essentially static) activity, not linear or forward motion, as noted in Chapter 4.

Feldman's earlier view was that the sense of movement generated by the *Projections* and earliest *Intersections* was attributable to an overall weight – this being determined by, or even equivalent to, the overall density of activity specified in the score. One problem with this theory is that it overlooks the role played by local factors in generating or inhibiting forward flow, such as the overlapping of sounds and the regular presence of long silences. Feldman's subsequent view – that the sense of movement generated in the later graphs arose from the juxtaposition of different 'weights' – has the

---

[53] The analogy of a river flowing was used by Varèse in describing his musical ideal as early as 1936 ('The liberation of sound', 197).

[54] [Unsigned: B], 'Composers', 80. For 'noodle soup' as a nickname for Pollock's paintings, see Frederick Gore, *Abstract Art* (London: Methuen, 1956), 60.

advantage of highlighting local factors, but it seems incomplete as a theory of the apparent movement audible in these works. Changes in weight are not a prerequisite of producing apparent flow of the type that is prominent in some of the graph music. An example clearly attributable to other factors can be heard in *Marginal Intersection*, in which the frequent intervention of a sound effects recording of a riveting machine operating at high frequency creates a strong sense of forward flow. Evidently, this is a grouping phenomenon heard in any succession of sufficiently similar sounds when the lengths of the intervals between them are set within certain limits.[55] Chapter 4 highlighted several reasons why Feldman's later graph music is especially susceptible to horizontal grouping and therefore capable of generating a pronounced experience of apparent motion, but the changing weights emphasised by Feldman were not among them. Changing weights – attributable to the presence in the score of horizontal and area strings, for example – are responsible for varying inter-onset intervals between sounds; consequently, they are more pertinent to changes in the apparent velocity of this perceived movement than to its basis.[56]

Number strings do not reappear in the graphs from *The Straits of Magellan* onwards, and this was probably connected with Feldman's use of an increasingly complex array of symbols, described in Chapter 3. In the immediately preceding graphs, where strings are most prevalent, numbers dominate Feldman's grid frames, but in *The Straits of Magellan* and the graphs that followed, other types of symbols are also given a prominent role, and this must have interfered with his ability to include strings by reducing the number of groups of otherwise unoccupied cells in which they might be located. For example, on the first page of *The Straits of Magellan*, almost half of the symbols present are of these alternative types. Compare the corresponding figure of only 3 per cent on first page of . . .*Out of 'Last Pieces'*, the immediately preceding graph.

In a 1983 interview, Feldman explained that one of the problems he experienced with 'the early grid' was its tendency to be 'too design-oriented' and he went on to explain that '[i]t was very easy to make wonderful designs on the page'.[57] Which designs he had in mind is not documented, but candidates include his striking use of horizontal and

---

[55] For a discussion, see L. van Noorden, *Temporal Coherence in the Perception of Tone Sequences* (Eindhoven: Druk vam Voorschoten, 1975).

[56] For the impact of inter-onset intervals on the velocity of apparent movement, see Zohar Eitan and Roni Y. Granot, 'How music moves: musical parameters and listeners' images of motion', *Music Perception: An Interdisciplinary Journal*, vol. 23, no. 3 (February 2006), 221–47, and Steve Larson, *Musical Forces: Motion, Metaphor, and Meaning in Music* (Bloomington: Indiana University Press, 2012), 138.

[57] 'An interview with Morton Feldman, Jan Williams', 153.

vertical groups of square symbols in *Marginal Intersection*, evident in Example 3.3 (Chapter 3), which may have been intended to evoke the horizontal and vertical lines of coloured squares in Mondrian's last two paintings, *Broadway Boogie-Woogie* and the unfinished *Victory Boogie-Woogie*, as well as some of the more ornate trajectories highlighted earlier in this chapter. He may also have been thinking of the striking optical effect of his string-based designs. If so, then a main purpose of radically expanding his resource of symbols in *The Straits of Magellan* may have been to wilfully inhibit his ability to include them.

7 Compositional methods II

The closing stages of Chapter 6 included commentary on several later graphs, but there is more to say about the compositional methods employed in some of these later works. Consequently, this chapter begins by rewinding the clock back to 1958, before recommencing a broadly chronological review of other aspects of the methods Feldman employed up until 1967.

The opening section begins with a puzzle about tempo in *Ixion*. The solution developed through an analysis of unpublished materials exposes a complex history that is justly classified as compositional method, but only in a rather different sense from most other aspects of this and the preceding chapter, for reasons that will become apparent. The discussion also touches on aspects of performance practice, which are so intimately connected with the arguments presented in this chapter that they sit better here than in Chapters 8–9, where performance-related matters are the focus.

Derivation from a precursor with elastic form

The immediate cause of Feldman's decision to recommence composing graph music in 1958 was a request from Cunningham for a composition to accompany his dance production *Summerspace*. As noted in Chapter 2, Cunningham originally envisaged a dance of fixed duration ('about 15 minutes long'), but his view evolved. For practical reasons outlined by him in the following text, his subsequent vision was of a dance with a duration that might vary between performing spaces to a greater extent than he typically envisaged:

> in this dance, the lengths of time were enlarged. previous to this, the lengths of the dances had been fixed in short time periods, one minute, 2½, up to 5 minutes, or according to the musical phrase. here I decided to have a dance roughly 15 to 17 minutes long. the time has never been fixed closer than that. different size stages make the lengths different, and extend or diminish the time. mr. feldman's score allows for this. if we did fix it to a length as being 'what it should be,' in trying to reproduce this exact length on the next stage, we would be imitating and approximating something. i decided to let it be what it was each time.[1]

[1] *Changes* [n.p.], with Cunningham's punctuation.

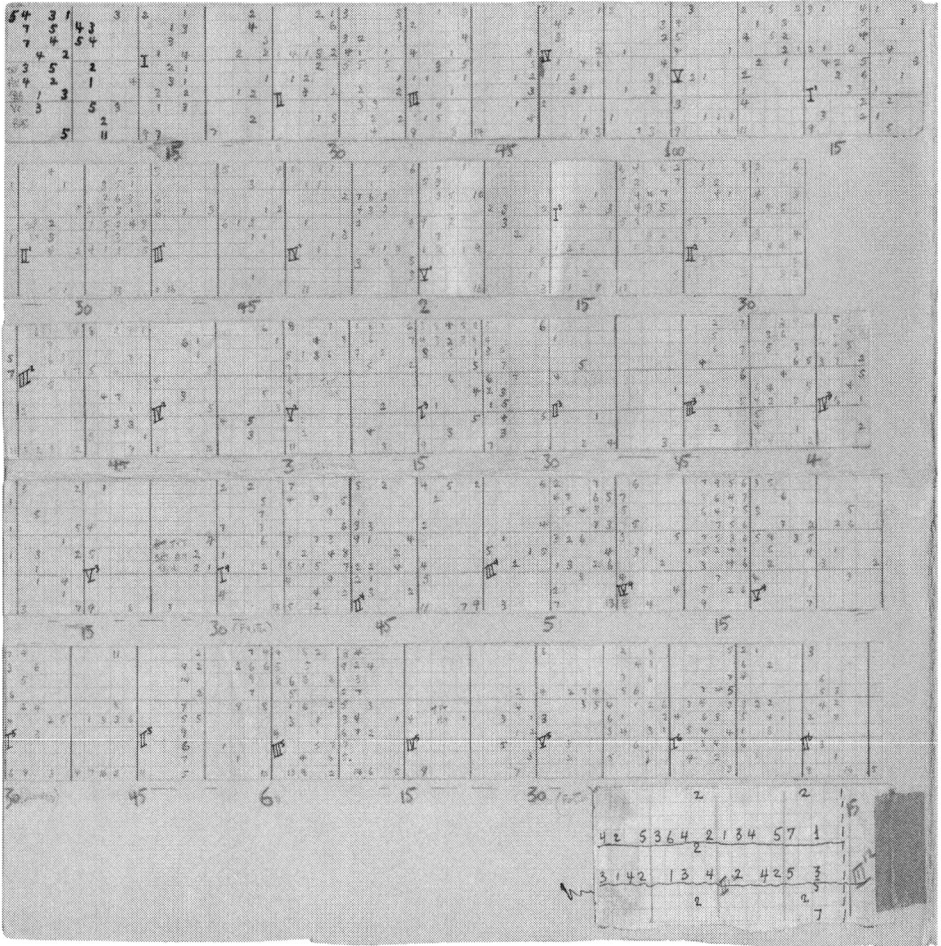

Figure 7.1 *Ixion* for chamber ensemble, paperboard score

A puzzling omission from *Ixion* for chamber ensemble – the music that Feldman composed for *Summerspace* – that distinguishes it within the graph series is any indication of tempo,[2] and it is tempting to suppose that this was Feldman's response to Cunningham's request for music with an adjustable span.[3] Although Feldman may have resorted to this simple device when preparing the score for publication

---

[2] The written notes that accompany the published edition of the score state that 'each box' is 'equal to MM [*sic*] or thereabouts'.

[3] The only other graph that, in its published form, lacks tempo guidance is *Ixion* for two pianos, which he subsequently transcribed from the version for chamber ensemble. This transcription was also for use with *Summerspace*.

several years after the work was first performed, the suggestion to be defended here is that his initial response was more involved. In fact, pre-publication copies of the score, described below, circulated with a typed set of notes that differ from those issued with the published edition. These include explicit indications of tempo that seem to have been removed before publication.

A clearer picture begins to emerge from a study of a revealing document, reproduced in Figure 7.1 and referred to hereafter as the 'paperboard score' of *Ixion*.[4] This is presented on a large sheet of paperboard, to which graph

[4] John Cage Collection, Northwestern University Music Library.

Example 7.1   *Ixion* for chamber ensemble, paperboard score, schematic diagram

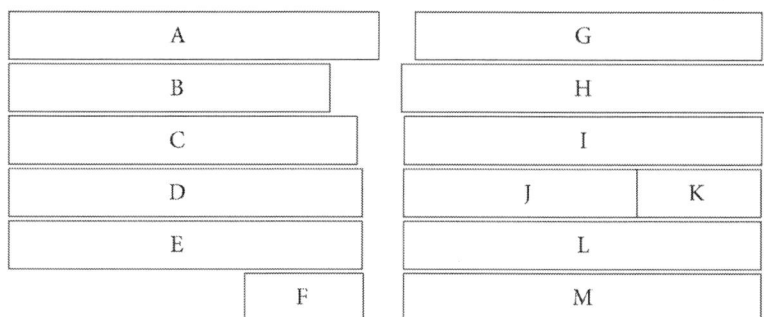

notation has been glued in two columns, one on each side of a central fold, with each column containing six systems. All but one of these are of similar length. The organisation of the paperboard score is shown schematically in Example 7.1, with each system labelled for ease of reference in the following discussion.

Examination reveals that the paperboard score incorporates three different types of materials:

• Ten longer strips of graph paper (A–E, G–I and L–M), which are fairly similar in length. These strips contain numbers that are written in pencil in Feldman's handwriting and they appear to have been carefully cut from larger pieces of graph paper. Faint traces of numbers that are otherwise erased appear in some of these strips and are still legible in many cases.

• Three shorter strips of graph paper (F, J and K), which appear to have been torn from larger sheets in an untidy manner. Numbers on these are written in black ink, with no corrections, and they are not in Feldman's handwriting. One of these shorter strips is the short system at the bottom of the first column on the paperboard. The other strips sit side by side and form the fourth system in the second column.

• Markings of various types in black and red ink that appear to have been superposed on and around the graph paper. Some of these markings, such as 'Entrance' and 'Carolyn entrance', clearly concern Cunningham's dance, while others, such as the labels that indicate elapsed time every fifteen seconds, primarily concern Feldman's music.

The ordering of the instrumental parts within each strip differs from the one found in the grid frames of the published edition. Nevertheless, comparison reveals that their musical contents are similar, and it is therefore likely that the paperboard score is the original source from which the published edition was copied. Numbers differ in relatively few places (eighteen entries, from a total of more than 2,600 are different), and these disparities are accountable as copying errors; none involves a patently deliberate revision. The only substantial differences concern tempo and duration. These are unspecified in the published edition, as previously noted. However, in the paperboard score, the given indications of elapsed time imply a total duration of fifteen minutes and a range of tempos that vary between subsections. Some verbal guidance of tempo within subsections ('Slower', 'Faster') is also given.

The provenance of the paperboard score is not documented, but the reference to 'Carolyn' (i.e. Carolyn Brown) points to its having been worked on during rehearsals for the first performance of *Summerspace* on 17 August 1958, and it seems safe to assume that it was used by Cage when conducting the work on that occasion.[5]

Another aspect of the published edition of *Ixion* that distinguishes it within Feldman's graph series is that the score includes lengthy repeated or near-repeated passages. The first case involves the exact repetition of a complex sequence of 254 symbols, shown in Example 7.2, which spans more than two pages.[6] This sequence begins on page 12 at ictus 460 and extends over sixty-seven ictuses to end on page 14 at ictus 526, and it is immediately repeated, beginning at ictus 527. The second case involves the near-repetition of a sequence of thirty-two symbols, which begins on page 15 at ictus 594, immediately after the second occurrence of the passage shown in Example 7.2, and extends across eighteen ictuses, ending at ictus 611 on page 16. This sequence is immediately repeated from ictus 612 except that in its second occurrence, one of the thirty-two symbols is omitted. Both occurrences of this passage are shown in Example 7.3. The missing symbol is the number 2 in the top row (allocated to one of the three flutes) that appears at ictus 609. This is not repeated at the corresponding point in the restatement.[7] The locations of these passages within the published edition are shown schematically in Example 7.4.

The two passages in the published edition that repeat or near-repeat immediately preceding material correspond to J–K and F in the paperboard score. J–K corresponds to the second occurrence of the longer passage shown in Example 7.2, whereas F corresponds to the near-repetition of the shorter passage shown twice in Example 7.3. J–K and F are the untidily torn strips of graph paper, and it is likely that these were

---

[5] The records of the Merce Cunningham Dance Company indicate that *Summerspace* was performed with *Ixion* for chamber ensemble only twice during Carolyn Brown's tenure with the company: at the premiere and at the Phoenix Theatre, New York City on 16 February 1960.

[6] Rows allocated (top to bottom) as follows: flute I; flute II; flute III; clarinet; horn; trumpet; trombone; piano; cellos; and double basses.

[7] In Example 7.3, this symbol and the location it would have occupied had the repetition been exact are highlighted in grey. Note that the allocation of rows to instruments is as in Example 7.2.

Example 7.2 *Ixion* for chamber ensemble, published edition, sequence occurring at ictuses 460–526 and 527–93, with repeated constituent elements highlighted

Example 7.3 *Ixion* for chamber ensemble, published edition, sequence occurring at ictuses 594–611 and its near-repetition at ictuses 612–29, with difference highlighted

Ictuses 594–611   Ictuses 612–29

Example 7.4 *Ixion* for chamber ensemble, published edition, schematic diagram showing locations of passages that are repeated or near-repeated

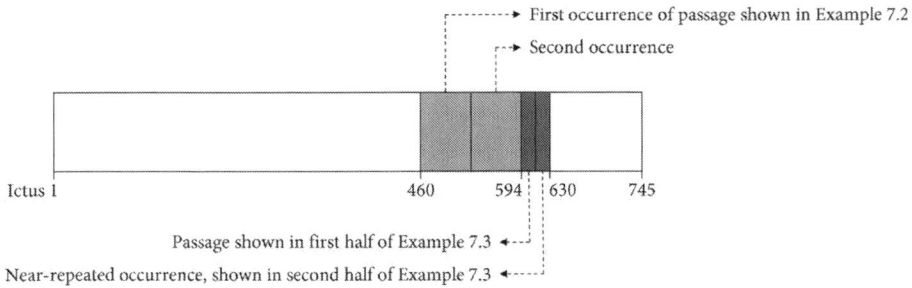

introduced at a different stage of the compositional process from the other materials. An excerpt from K is shown in Figure 7.2 in order to highlight the handwriting. The unusual presentation of the number 7 in this excerpt, which features a short but pronounced vertical line suspended from the left end of the horizontal element, is a hallmark of Cage's calligraphy. A similar presentation of the number 7 is found in the published edition of *Intersection 2*, which is known to be in his hand.[8]

Two of the added elements in the paperboard score, J and K, appear side by side and form the fourth system in the second column of graph notation, as previously noted; these exactly reproduce the numbers in the third system, I, suggesting that Cage copied the third system to produce the fourth. The other added element, F, which appears at the bottom of the first column, exactly reproduces the numbers at the start of the fifth system, L, in the second column. Given that L probably followed on from I in Feldman's original materials, it is likely that Cage copied two adjacent sections of the grid from Feldman's original materials; these sections now makes up I and the beginning of L. Although F is pasted at the base of the first column, labels in Cage's handwriting indicate that it should be understood as appearing within L, immediately after the section it reproduces.[9] Consequently, the intended ordering of the materials in the paperboard score is: from A to E; then from G to the end of the first part of L; then F; then the remainder of L; and then, finally, M.

Interestingly, the musical content of F does not differ from that of the material in the first part of L, on which it is based, unlike the corresponding

---

[8] See the upper system in Example 3.4 (Chapter 3) and all three systems in Example 6.12 (Chapter 6). In the published editions of his own scores, Cage usually added a short, transverse bar across the oblique element in the number 7.

[9] The labels are terms in an ascending series of Roman numerals with Arabic numerals as superscripts. The reason why F was pasted away from its intended location is not apparent.

Figure 7.2 *Ixion* for chamber ensemble, paperboard score, excerpt

passage in the published edition, which lacks one symbol present in the immediately preceding passage. Although it is possible that Feldman deliberately introduced a discrepancy when producing the published version of the score, the omission may have been a copying error, in which case an exact replica of the preceding passage was intended. In the corresponding passage in *Ixion* for two pianos, which was transcribed from *Ixion*, the repetition is exact. This suggests that the omission in *Ixion* was indeed a copying error.

These factors suggest that the paperboard score was put together by Cage from Feldman's original materials, with the repetitions in Cage's handwriting added by him in order to lengthen the overall duration. This implies that, strictly speaking, Cage was a co-author of *Ixion* in its published form. Although it is possible that Cage used his own initiative in lengthening the score that Feldman prepared for Cunningham, this is unlikely, for reasons that will become clear. Most probably, Cage acted as he did because the work that Feldman presented to Cunningham, which was in all likelihood named 'Ixion', but which will be referred to here as 'Ixion*' to avoid confusion with the derivative graph now bearing that name, licensed him to do so.

Although it is not known if Feldman's instructions about how to lengthen the materials that he presented to Cunningham were written or oral, or if he identified which sections were repeatable, we can reasonably assume that eliminating Cage's repetitions, which were optional additions, will take us closer to the original core of *Ixion**. The resulting form is

Example 7.5 *Ixion**, schematic diagram of possible core

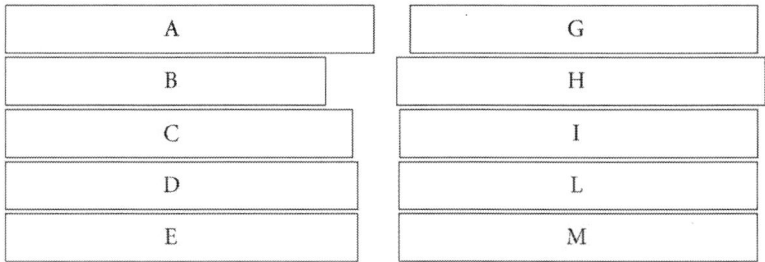

A		G
B		H
C		I
D		L
E		M

shown schematically in Example 7.5, which should be read from A to E, then from G to I, and then from L to M.

As a matter of fact, Example 7.5 may be identical with the original core of *Ixion**, but this is not certain. One possibility is that original material was discarded by Cage. Although this would be consistent with small variations in the lengths of systems A–E, G–I and L–M, it is unlikely that substantial cuts were made given that extensions – F, J and K – were deemed to be necessary. Another possibility is that the intended ordering of the ten systems in *Ixion** was indeterminate, in which case their placement in *Ixion* may be only one of many legitimate arrangements. This is difficult to rule out, but nothing points unambiguously to them having been presented originally in a different order. Also, the material in M has the character of an ending, which is where it is located in the paperboard score. The density of indicated sounds rises steeply to a peak of 101 in its last ictus, far above levels found elsewhere in this work, consistent with this being fashioned as a concluding climax.

A striking aspect of the first passage that Cage chose to repeat is that it contains four occurrences of a substantial group of symbols; these are highlighted in grey in Example 7.2. This element of repetition may have been intended to signal that the passage as a whole or, perhaps, elements of it could be duplicated if an extension of the work were deemed necessary, although this would make it unclear why Cage repeated the first half of Example 7.3. If so, then the three areas, of increasing length, towards the end of the score in which the number 1 appears in every cell might also be a signal of a similar type. These are shown in Example 7.6.[10] A study of the paperboard score suggests that Cage chose not to take advantage of any implied offer in their case.

There is independent reason to think that Feldman intended these three areas as expandable and retractable. In 1976, he likened *Ixion* to an 'oilcloth'

---

[10] The allocation of rows to instruments is as in Examples 7.2–7.3.

Example 7.6 *Ixion* for chamber ensemble, published edition, ictuses 628–78

because it had 'plenty of material to work with, to either shorten or lengthen'.[11] This remark argues against the suggestion that Cage acted on his own initiative in lengthening Feldman's original score. Its reference to *Ixion* as a work that can be made shorter, as well as longer, is also significant. Perhaps he was thinking of the flexibility attributable to the absence of tempo guidance in the published edition, but his reference to there being 'plenty of material to work with' would then appear out of place. His remark reads more naturally if he was thinking of *Ixion** and the fact that he had envisaged that certain passages might be shortened or even excluded. That being so, it is reasonable to assume that he regarded those in Example 7.6 in which the number 1 appears in every cell in this way. Although these passages occupy only thirty-eight ictuses in total and would therefore allow only a modest shortening of the whole, this facility would have been useful in fine-tuning the overall duration after replicating longer sections.

In 1937, Cowell proposed a closer alignment between music and dance through the production of works with what he called 'elastic form'.[12] His idea was that a composer writing music for dance should produce musical compositions with adjustable elements.[13] This would allow the music to be altered, without undermining its integrity, in response to changes in the dance during rehearsals.[14] Cowell went on to suggest several ideas for introducing this type of elasticity. These included the use of melodic phrases or whole sections that could be repeated, rearranged, expanded, contracted or otherwise altered (within given limits).[15] He also suggested the use of flexible instrumentations that would allow performances using a variety of solo instruments and instrumental combinations.[16] These ideas, which Cowell applied in several works, had special utility for him given that at this time he was forced to write music for dance at arm's length. This was due to his incarceration in San Quentin prison.[17]

Feldman's method of dealing with Cunningham's request to write music for *Summerspace* appears so similar to the one that Cowell recommended that one cannot help but wonder whether he had Cowell's ideas in mind. In

---

[11] '*Studio International* interview', 65.

[12] 'Relating music and concert dance' [1937], in Dick Higgins (ed.), *Essential Cowell: Selected Writings on Music* (New York: McPherson, 2001), 229.

[13] He also suggested the creation of dances with adjustable elements that can be altered in order to improve their fit with the associated music (*ibid.*).

[14] *Ibid.*, 227, 229.   [15] *Ibid.*, 230.   [16] *Ibid.*, 230–1.

[17] Cowell was incarcerated in 1936–42. For details, see Michael Hicks, 'The imprisonment of Henry Cowell', *Journal of the American Musicological Society*, vol. 44, no. 1 (Spring 1991), 92–119, and Joel Sachs, *Henry Cowell: A Man Made of Music* (New York: Oxford University Press, 2012), 275–349. Leta E. Miller has identified five compositions with elastic forms composed in this period ('Henry Cowell and modern dance: the genesis of elastic form', *American Music*, vol. 20, no. 1 (Spring 2002), 1–24).

all likelihood, Feldman would have been familiar with Cowell's thoughts on these matters. Cage had known of Cowell's innovations since the late 1930s,[18] and would go on to write about them in an article published in 1959,[19] the year after *Summerspace* was premiered. Feldman composed several works that would accompany dances in 1950–1,[20] making it probable that he and Cage discussed Cowell's ideas in the early stages of their friendship, and Cowell's active support for their music at the time makes this even more likely.[21] Feldman, who had been introduced to Cowell by Cage in the early 1950s, remembered that they 'talked for hours' when they first met.[22]

This account of Feldman's return to graph music, which portrays *Ixion* as the result of a two-stage process, gains weight from the fact that *Ixion** was not Feldman's only work with elastic form for dance. For example, the unpublished *Figure of Memory* for solo piano, prepared for Merle Marsicano's dance with the same name, also has expandable elements. The one-page score, which is undated but probably contemporary with *Ixion**, consists of three short phrases, each consisting of two identical bars.[23] Initially, these are to be played in order, with each phrase repeated three times before the next is played and each repetition 10–15 seconds apart. Thereafter, Feldman's handwritten notes indicate that the identical elements are to be played 'in random order, always about 10–15″ apart, in units of 3 or 5 measures'. An unpublished dance work for solo piano, which appears to be considerably older, can also be elongated. The conventionally notated score,[24] addressed to Cunningham, includes a handwritten note that states that the first eight bars can be '[p]lay[ed] over as many times as needed', with Feldman adding that '[f]or me 3 times sounds just right'. Although this item is also undated, a loose leaf sketch of the same work is tucked inside one of Feldman's earliest surviving sketchbooks,[25] which contains materials from 1951 to 1952.[26]

[18] Leta E. Miller, 'Henry Cowell and John Cage: intersections and influences, 1933–1941', *Journal of the American Musicological Society*, vol. 59, no. 1 (2006), 68.

[19] 'History of experimental music', 71.

[20] These include *Three Dances* (1950), *Variations* and *Nature Pieces*.

[21] For Cowell's support, see his 'Current chronicle', 123–36, and Francis D. Perkins, 'New School recital', *New York Herald Tribune*, 3 May 1952, 8.

[22] 'Give my regards to Eighth Street', 94.

[23] Morton Feldman Collection, Paul Sacher Foundation.

[24] Untitled 'tune' for Merce Cunningham, John Cage Collection, Northwestern University Music Library.

[25] 'Sketchbook 3', Morton Feldman Collection, Paul Sacher Foundation.

[26] In addition to these points, it is noteworthy that in the early 1950s Feldman experimented with mobile works that prefigure aspects of *Ixion** (Cline, 'Straightening the record', 79).

Example 7.7   *Ixion* for chamber ensemble, 'John Cage tempo changes'

Moderato
V^2 Slower
I^4 Moderato
I^5 Slower
V^5 Faster
IV^6 Slower on second measure
V^6 Lento at second measure at "low"
III^7 Slightly faster at "high"
II^8 Fast
V^8 Faster
III^{12} Suddenly slow
II^{13} Accelerando on second measure
III^{13} Fast to end

As noted above, pre-publication copies of the score of *Ixion* circulated with a set of notes that differ from those with the published edition, and how these fit into the preceding account is an outstanding question.[27] Whereas the notes that accompany the published edition do not specify tempo, the pre-publication set specifies two different scenarios, one of which is explained thus:

> Numbers indicate the amount of sounds to be played on or within the box, each box being equal to MM92 or thereabouts.

An 'alternative' scenario, described as '[t]he John Cage tempo changes', gives verbal indications of tempo in each of thirteen subdivisions of the work, which are presented as in Example 7.7.[28] The fact that these variations in tempo are attributed to Cage suggests that they did not reflect Feldman's initial conception – indeed, Chapter 3 argued that the use of fluctuating tempos was contrary to his conception of these works. Nevertheless, it is probable that they were used in the first performance in August 1958; several are marked on the paperboard score and all are marked on the two surviving instrumental part-books that were prepared by Cage for use in the premiere.[29] It is tempting to suppose that they were introduced at Cunningham's request in order to underpin changes in the tempo of the dance, but Carolyn Brown, who danced in the premiere, has stated categorically that changes of rhythm in the dance are unrelated to Feldman's music.[30]

---

[27] This set of notes is reproduced in Cunningham, *Changes* [n.p.].
[28] The numerals in this list refer to specific locations in the score that are similarly labelled.
[29] John Cage Collection, Northwestern University Music Library.
[30] 'Summerspace: three Revivals', *Dance Research Journal*, vol. 34, no. 1 (Summer 2002), 75.

There are several puzzling aspects of this early set of notes. One is the suggested steady pace of approximately 92 ictuses per minute. This fits with Feldman's aim of melting into the decor for *Summerspace*, for a performance played at this tempo is bound to be saturated with musical dots that have an evident affinity with Rauschenberg's luminous dabs of paint, but it is surprisingly fast given the length of the score and the anticipated duration of Cunningham's choreography.[31] At this pace, the 745 ictuses of *Ixion* would extend only a little over eight minutes, but performances of *Summerspace* are considerably longer than this. For example, timings marked on the paperboard score suggest that the first performance lasted fifteen minutes, as previously noted;[32] this is consistent with Cunningham's initial conception, set out in his letter to Rauschenberg, as 'about 15 minutes long' and his more mature vision of the dance as 'roughly 15 to 17 minutes long'. A video recording of the Merce Cunningham Dance Company's 1999 revival of *Summerspace*, shot in 2001, lasts a little over twenty minutes.[33]

A remote possibility is that 92 ictuses per minute was the intended tempo if the work were to be played on a stand-alone basis, although why Feldman would have wished it to be played faster without Cunningham's dance is not clear. A much more likely scenario is that this was the tempo originally intended for *Ixion**, in which case Feldman may have anticipated a greater number of legitimate repetitions than were actually used in creating *Ixion*. If so, this raises the subsidiary question of why a smaller number came to be used. The most probable explanation is that members of the ensemble that played at the premiere were incapable of performing the work at the indicated pace, necessitating the use of a slower tempo and a smaller than intended number of repetitions.

This explanation is credible. With a tempo of 92 ictuses per minute, *Ixion* is a challenging work to play, with performers regularly asked to produce large numbers of consecutive sounds within single ictuses each lasting only 0.65 seconds. The extent of the difficulty is evident from a review of the maximum number specified per ictus in each instrumental part, shown in Table 7.1. Feldman's notes with the published edition explain how most of the performers should respond if they prove unable to play the indicated number of consecutive sounds in the designated span,

---

[31] It has been suggested that *Ixion* has a tempo of approximately 92 ictuses per minute (e.g. Claren, *Neither*, 82). This view may have been based on the indication given in the early set of notes.

[32] Tempo varies between 16 and 80 ictuses per minute. Approximately two-thirds of the score is played at tempos between 40 and 60 ictuses per minute.

[33] *Merce Cunningham Dance Company: Robert Rauschenberg Collaborations – Three Films by Charles Atlas*, DVD, ARTPIX, 2011.

Table 7.1. Ixion *for chamber ensemble, maximum number of consecutive sounds per ictus, by instrument*

Instrument(s)	Maximum number of consecutive sounds per ictus
Flute I	12
Flute II	14
Flute III	19
Clarinet	12
Horn	8
Trumpet	11
Trombone	9
Piano	24
Cellos	12
Double basses	7

Table 7.2. *Graphs for larger ensembles composed in 1959–67, indicated tempos*

Year dated	Work	Tempo (ictuses per minute)
1959	*Atlantis*	92
1961	*...Out of 'Last Pieces'*	80
1961	*The Straits of Magellan*	88
1967	*In Search of an Orchestration*	88 or a little faster

but it is hard to believe he intended these get-out clauses to be exercised frequently in an optimum performance.

An examination of the tempos recommended by Feldman in the four graphs for larger ensembles composed after *Ixion* lends additional weight to the view that he originally intended the materials he prepared for Cunningham to be played at 92 ictuses per minute and a greater number of repetitions than Cage included. As shown in Table 7.2, tempos indicated in three of these works are close to, or identical with, this rate.

A premise of the preceding account has been that Cage used *Ixion** as Feldman intended it to be used, to derive a performable work with an appropriate duration, but at least some of the evidence is consistent with the theory that Cage used his own initiative in cannibalising the materials that Feldman prepared. However, this theory leaves important questions unanswered. For example, why did Feldman prepare materials that appear so short with the tempo guidance of 92 ictuses per minute specified in the pre-publication set of notes? If a slower tempo was originally envisaged, why did he single out 92 ictuses per minute as an appropriate rate? And why, years later, did he suggest that he had provided Cunningham with 'plenty of material to work with, to either shorten or lengthen'? The alternative account outlined above, which presents both Cage and *Ixion* in a considerably more favourable light, answers these questions and is therefore preferable.

Why did Feldman choose not to recreate *Ixion** for publication? Undoubtedly, it was different in type from other graphs that he published in that, unlike them, it was designed to give others the means to construct a range of performable works of varying lengths. Although the unspecified tempo of *Ixion* marks it out within his output of graphs, indeterminacy of tempo is not only more common in Western classical music in general, but also commonplace in Feldman's works with fixed pitches and indeterminate durations, meaning that *Ixion* fits more neatly with the rest of his published output. This may have been a factor in its eventual promotion over its less characteristic parent.

Another possibility is that Feldman's confidence in the utility of *Ixion** was undermined by the inability of the performers at the premiere to play the work at the originally intended pace. If this is what happenned, then he may have come to see that a sufficient degree of indeterminacy of overall duration could be obtained without resurrecting *Ixion** by taking the derivative work that had been produced from it, with the extensions added by Cage, allowing the performers to select a tempo that was much slower than originally envisaged and accepting a lower density of sound per second than he had originally intended.

Perhaps this account will be of interest to those intending to perform Feldman's music for *Summerspace*, because it implies that those performing *Ixion** can legitimately tamper with *Ixion* in certain ways. This will not result in a performance of *Ixion*, but it may still count as a performance of *Ixion**, provided that the performers do not alter *Ixion* in ways that transgress the limits originally set by Feldman. These are not known, but three interpretative strategies are likely to be consistent with them: the elimination of Cage's repetitions; the inclusion of additional repetitions identical in kind to those that Cage introduced; and the expansion and contraction of the areas in Example 7.6 in which the number 1 appears in every cell. The first strategy is likely to be within the limits set by Feldman because it probably takes us closer to the original core of *Ixion**, as previously discussed. The second strategy is likely to be consistent with the limits he set because it duplicates repetitions that Feldman licensed. This strategy would be undermined if Feldman's instructions with *Ixion** had limited the number of legitimate repetitions to those included by Cage, but there is no good reason to think that this is likely.

As noted above, some performances of Cunningham's dance have lasted longer than twenty minutes. Performing *Ixion* for this length of time would involve playing it at a steady tempo of less than 40 ictuses per minute. Reverting to the precursor work from which it was derived and expanding its length by adding and, if necessary, subtracting elements in the ways suggested above is a method of producing music of longer duration consistent with Feldman's original intention of melting into Rauschenberg's decor.

Corollary

The grid frame on page 4 of the published edition of *Atlantis* is unusually short, having only thirty-five columns versus a norm of forty columns per page elsewhere in the score. However, the corresponding page of Tudor's copy, which pre-dates Feldman's contract with the C. F. Peters Corporation, has the standard number, and a comparison reveals that the last five columns on this page have been excluded in the published edition. The contents of these missing columns exactly match those of the first five columns on page 5 in both versions. In Tudor's copy, the word 'omit' appears above these, but they are present in the published edition (Example 7.8), and it is the immediately preceding material that has been cut. This implies that the score originally contained an instance of substantial repetition that was edited out. A second notable aspect of the score, which, in this case, is present in Tudor's copy and the published edition, is the inclusion of six adjacent columns of identical material on page 9, shown in Example 7.9.[34]

These aspects of *Atlantis* invite comparison with features of *Ixion* for chamber ensemble that the previous section attributed to its intended use with *Summerspace*. Their presence suggests that Feldman may have conceived of *Atlantis* – or, more precisely, *Atlantis**, the predecessor work set out in Tudor's copy of the score, from which *Atlantis* may have been derived – as like *Ixion** in having elastic form and in being composed for dance; hence, its classification with *Ixion* for chamber ensemble and *Ixion* for two pianos in Chapter 2. If so, then Feldman's purpose in including the repeated passage that he subsequently removed was to introduce an element that might be played any number of times, thereby facilitating a lengthening of the total duration without the need for a corresponding reduction in tempo. This facility was not needed in the first performance, however, in which the

---

[34] The allocation of rows to instruments is as in Example 7.8.

Example 7.8 *Atlantis*, ictuses 156–60 (first five ictuses on page 5)

Example 7.9 *Atlantis*, ictuses 345–50 (page 9)

'alternate' version was presented as a stand-alone work, with Tudor at the piano. Consequently, the repeated element was struck out, and it was this somewhat truncated, less indeterminate version of the original composition that Feldman selected for use in the published edition. As in the passages in *Ixion* in which the number 1 appears in every cell, his original purpose in including the six adjacent columns of identical material may have been to introduce an expandable or retractable element in case of a need to fine-tune the total duration; this element was retained in the published edition.

The full version of *Atlantis* is scored for seventeen instruments: a larger ensemble than one might expect to find with a modern dance troupe in 1959–60. This does not rule against the idea that it was, indeed, a dance work, however. The chamber ensemble version of *Ixion* for *Summerspace*, composed in 1958, is scored for thirteen to nineteen instruments and there is reason to believe that Feldman created an orchestral work for a Paul Taylor dance in 1959 or 1960, as will soon become clear. Moreover, the suggestion that *Atlantis* was originally conceived of for dance neatly explains Feldman's decision to specify an 'alternate' version for a smaller ensemble: this was attributable to his sensitivity to cost and logistical issues.

These points are suggestive only. Achieving a higher degree of certainty would involve identifying the specific dance that *Atlantis** was designed to accompany, and it is here that we confront a serious difficulty. This is because precise details of Feldman's rather extensive involvement with dance in the 1950s and 1960s – his music is known to have been used by a long list of dancers and choreographers, including Shirley Broughton, Cunningham, Jean Erdman, Pearl Lang, Katherine Litz, Marsicano and Taylor – are sometimes hard to determine. As Claren has pointed out, documentation associated with a named dance often cites Feldman as the composer without indicating the name of the specific musical composition used.[35] Unsurprisingly, in such cases, the omission is replicated in the few reviews that refer to the music.

A brief survey of Feldman's work with Taylor, who danced with Cunningham's company in 1953–4 before leaving to establish his own troupe, illustrates the issues involved. To begin with, Taylor is known to have used several of Feldman's pre-existing works in conventional notation for solo piano with his *Images and Reflections*, which was first performed, with costumes by Rauschenberg, in late 1958. Happily, the works in question – *Illusions* (1948), *Intermissions 1–5* (1950–2) and *Extensions 3* (1952) – are listed in the printed programme.[36] However, Taylor's own testimony suggests that he went on to commission Feldman to compose a brand new work to accompany a re-choreographed version of his *Meridian* for an expanded ensemble of six dancers.[37] This version of the dance was first performed, by an 'Italian orchestra',[38] at the Spoleto Festival of Two Worlds in Italy in the summer of 1960. Initially, it seems, Rauschenberg agreed to provide the costumes and set, but Alex Katz stepped in at the last minute after a disagreement with Taylor led to his exit.[39]

The printed programme for the event indicates that the music played with *Meridian* was Feldman's,[40] but no title is provided here or in other sources, and no work by Feldman titled 'Meridian' is documented. The thought that the composition in question was, in fact, *Atlantis** gains weight from Taylor's description of the dress rehearsal: 'some of the trumpeters in the pit show their distaste for *Meridian*'s delicate and far-out score by flutter-lipping too often, but, like good sports, they play the performance almost as if they can

[35] Claren, *Neither*, 237.   [36] Programme, Kaufmann Concert Hall, 20 December 1958.

[37] Paul Taylor, *Private Domain: An Autobiography* (New York: Alfred A. Knopf, 1987), 96. *Meridian* was originally scored for three dancers with costumes by Louise Thompson and music by Boulez (*Le Marteau sans maître*). See Angela Kane, 'A catalogue of works choreographed by Paul Taylor', *Dance Research: The Journal of the Society for Dance Research*, vol. 14, no. 2 (Winter 1996), 16.

[38] Taylor, *Private Domain*, 96

[39] Mark Steinbrink, 'Why artists design for Paul Taylor', *New York Times*, 3 April 1983, section 2, 24. A collage by Katz illustrating his set design is reproduced in Seán Kissane (ed.), *Vertical Thoughts: Morton Feldman and the Visual Arts* (Dublin: Irish Museum of Modern Art, 2010), 301.

[40] Souvenir programme, 3rd Festival of Two Worlds, Spoleto, Teatro Nuovo, 8 June–10 July 1960.

bear it'.[41] This appears significant, in view of the problems encountered in rehearsals of *Ixion* and the fact that Feldman's explanatory notes with *Atlantis* indicate that the brass should double-tongue sounds that they are unable to articulate. However, a sheet of notes in Taylor's handwriting indicates that Feldman's music was unlike *Atlantis* in being scored for a full orchestra and in being structured in three distinct movements, spanning eleven minutes in total, the first and longest of which (seven minutes) was repeated after the third movement was played.[42]

Transcription

Each system in *Ixion* for two pianos consists of a grid with six rows (Example 7.10). This is divided into two parts – three rows for each piano – by a pronounced horizontal line. The use of three rows per part implies a tripartite division of register, but this cannot be interpreted as between high, middle and low. This is because Feldman's labelling indicates that all pitches are in the high register except in a central section in which low registers are to be used. Consequently, in this particular work, his tripartite indications must be read as specifying subdivisions of the pitch spectrum within a coarser bipartite partitioning. These three subdivisions are *higher, intermediate* and *lower* in what follows.

A review of the process used by Feldman in creating the transcription from the original work for chamber ensemble gives a vivid glimpse of his working methods, although the problems he was addressing were, in this case, more circumscribed than those involved in free composition. This is because a comparison between the two makes it possible to track elements of his thinking in each ictus. As will become clear, the comparison reveals that his method had more and less methodical aspects.

The gist of Feldman's approach is apparent from a comparison between page 1 of the published edition of the original work and the first forty ictuses of the transcribed version, both shown in Example 7.11. In every case, the entries in a given column of the original clearly served as the basis for those in the corresponding column in the transcription. No single method of transposition was used, however, and several are apparent in these early entries. Others make their first appearance elsewhere, and a discussion of these is deferred until later in this section. It seems likely that Feldman devised new alternatives as he worked his way through the original score from start to finish.

---

[41] *Private Domain*, 98   [42] Paul Taylor Dance Company.

Example 7.10 *Ixion* for two pianos, page 1, first grid frame

I								II							III						IV		
5	7		5	1			11		9	7		4		7		6	3		3	7	6		7	9		1	8	7	14		7	4	2
	3	3		5	9					2							1	1	2	3		3	2	1	1		1				1	5	1	2
	4	1			3			4		2		3	2	4	3		4	3	2	5		4					7		1
	7		7		7	3	2											4				3
																3	8	7		1		1	7	5		1	6	1	1
	4		3		2	3		1		6		4	1	4	4		1	2	4		1	2

In fifteen columns, Feldman simply redeployed all the numbers present in the original in the corresponding column of the transcription, while in eight others he proceeded similarly but added two or more numbers from the original before redeploying their sum. In four more columns, in which the original lacks entries, he proceeded in parallel fashion, leaving the corresponding column in the transcription blank. In all these columns, the sum of the numbers present in the original equals the sum of the entries in the corresponding column of the transcription.

In nine cases, he proceeded in more selective fashion, redeploying a subset of the entries that appear in the original, with or without prior summation, meaning that the sum of the entries in the source is greater than the sum of entries in the transcription. This leaves three columns unaccounted for. In one of these (ictus 13), the original is populated, but the corresponding column is left blank. This could be seen as a special case of selective redeployment, in which the subset of entries selected for redeployment is empty. His decision on whether to make a selection rather than redeploy all the numbers present, with or without prior summation, seems to have been driven, at least in part, by the magnitude of their sum. Typically, he proceeded thus only in cases in which this total is large, although there are examples involving large totals in which he persisted in redeploying all the numbers present.

Two columns have yet to be accounted for and require individual commentary. At ictus 26, the original score contains the numbers (3, 3, 4, 5) whereas the corresponding column contains (4, 6, 8). This might look like a case in which one of the entries in the former is used twice in calculating entries in the latter (3 + 3 = 6, 3 + 5 = 8), but this method is not prominent elsewhere in the score. Consequently, it seems more likely that Feldman simply misread the 5 as an 8. The entry at ictus 35 appears similar, but only at first sight. The published edition of the score for chamber ensemble contains the numbers (1, 3, 4) whereas the transcription has (1, 5, 7), suggesting that the number 4 was summed twice (4 + 1 = 5, 4 + 3 = 7), but this is incorrect. The numbers contained in the corresponding column of the paperboard score, shown in Figure 7.1, are (1, 3, 4, 5). This indicates that Feldman

Example 7.11 *Ixion* for chamber orchestra vs *Ixion* for two pianos, ictuses 1–40, annotated restatement

Example 7.12 *Ixion* for chamber ensemble, ictuses 1–40, register destinations in *Ixion* for two pianos (where identifiable)

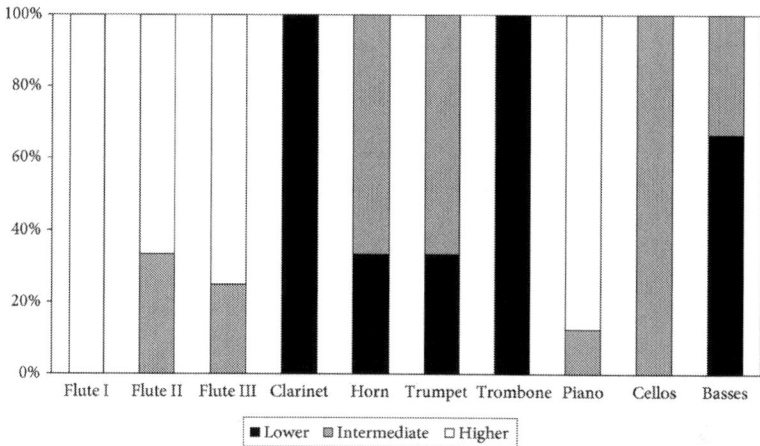

worked from the paperboard score while preparing the transcription and strongly suggests that the absence of a 5 in the published edition was a copying error.

These remarks have focused on Feldman's methods for determining an appropriate set of numbers for use in the transcription, but his associated methods for distributing them between instruments and register locations have yet to be considered. An initial observation is that they favour Piano I, which receives many more entries and most of the biggest numbers.[43] This suggests that Feldman meant the part for Piano I to be more difficult to play. As will become clear in Chapter 9, Tudor would go on to play this part in early performances while Cage would play the easier part for Piano II. It is safe to assume that this was the outcome that Feldman intended.

Feldman's method of selecting appropriate register locations in the transcription becomes clear if we focus only on cases in which there is no uncertainty about source and destination. Example 7.12 classifies those in the first forty ictuses by source instrument and destination register. In cases in which two numbers in the original score are summed before redeployment, both are counted as sources of the corresponding entry in the transcription.

---

[43] These patterns are typical of the score, although the disparity between quantities is less marked elsewhere.

Table 7.3. Ixion *for chamber ensemble, theoretical ranking of high register ranges of instruments by pitch (highest first), versus most frequent register destination in* Ixion *for two pianos, ictuses 1–40*

	Theoretical ranking	Most frequent destination
Piano	1	Higher
Flutes	2	Higher
Clarinet (B♭)	3	Lower
Trumpet (B♭)	4	Intermediate
Cellos	5	Intermediate
Horn (in F)	6	Intermediate
Trombone (Tenor)	7	Lower
Contrabasses	8	Lower

It can be seen that, in this sample, Feldman usually assigned numbers from a given instrumental part in the original to a particular register in the transcription. For example, those from the flute and piano parts were typically assigned to the higher register rows, whereas, in general, numbers from the horn, trumpet and cello parts were allocated to the intermediate register locations. Numbers from the parts for clarinet, trombone and contrabasses were assigned to the lower registers, by contrast. These patterns are confirmed by a more wide-ranging survey of comparable data taken from elsewhere in the two scores, except that the part for the third flute is treated less consistently than in Example 7.12, with numbers originating in this part being allocated to all three register locations in broadly similar proportions.

Let us tentatively assume that Feldman's aim in distributing activity between registers in the transcription was to preserve, in broad outline, the register contour of the original work. Then it would be reasonable to expect his allocations to reflect an intuitive ranking of the high register ranges of the instruments in the original. If we can devise a ranking of this type, then this expectation can be tested by seeing whether it suggests a distribution of activity similar to the one he produced.

One way of ranking the high register ranges of the instruments used in Feldman's original work for chamber ensemble is to derive an ordering based on the mid-point pitch of the upper third of each instrument's total compass. This implies the ranking shown in Table 7.3,[44] which also

---

[44] The pitch ranges used to determine this ranking are as indicated in Alfred Blatter, *Instrumentation and Orchestration*, 2nd edn (New York: Schirmer Books, 1997).

indicates the most common register destination of numbers in the opening ictuses of the transcription, by instrument.

Although the distribution found in the transcription is broadly consistent with the theoretical ranking shown in the table, Feldman's treatment of numbers originating in the clarinet part was not. The suggestion that he was thinking of a bass clarinet is not completely satisfying. This is because the mid-point of the upper third of its pitch range falls between those of horn and cello, which would suggest the intermediate registers as more appropriate destinations. The anomaly is not peculiar to the opening ictuses, but is consistently present throughout the transcription, and it presents something of a puzzle. This is worth dwelling upon because its solution clarifies oddities in the surviving record.

It will be helpful at this point to reflect, once more, on the paperboard score of *Ixion*. The labelling of the instrumental parts in the top left corner is incomplete, but a comprehensive set of labels appears at the start of the right column, and these are the focus of interest. Most of the list is presented in pencil in Feldman's handwriting, but the fourth entry has been overwritten in black pen in handwriting that is difficult to identify; it may have belonged to Feldman or Cage. The amendment reads 'Cl' but the original entry – 'TUBA' – remains clearly visible underneath. The implication is that Feldman originally envisaged the work being performed by an ensemble that included a tuba but not a clarinet, and that he or Cage subsequently revised his original conception. A review of the printed programme for the first performance of *Ixion* for chamber ensemble with *Summerspace* provides a clue as to why this revision may have been necessary, for no tuba player is listed among the personnel of the Eleventh American Dance Festival's orchestra.

The suggestion that the instrumentation of Feldman's work was revised gains additional weight from a review of the two surviving instrumental part-books in Cage's handwriting.[45] One of these, which is marked 'Tuba' and parenthetically labelled 'Optional', presents the material that appears in the fourth row of each grid in the paperboard score, which is replicated in the clarinet part in the published edition. The other surviving part-book in Cage's handwriting is labelled 'Flute III'. The printed programme for the first performance of *Summerspace* lists only one flute and one piccolo, suggesting that the third flute part was not played, and this is consistent with the fact that the corresponding part-book – and the part-book for tuba – remained in Cage's possession.

---

[45] John Cage Collection, Northwestern University Music Library.

We are now in a position to reconstruct the events that culminated in Feldman's initially puzzling approach to transcribing the contents of the clarinet part when preparing *Ixion* for two pianos. Originally, it seems, the clarinet part was intended for tuba, but no tuba player was available and a decision was taken to allow the tuba part to be performed by a clarinet. When Feldman worked on the transcription, however, he operated with his original conception. Given that his aim was to distribute activity between registers in the transcription so as to preserve, in broad outline, the register contour of the original work, this implied that the materials in the clarinet (né tuba) part should be redeployed in the lower registers. For reasons that are unclear, he subsequently decided not to reinstate the tuba when preparing the ensemble work for publication.

This concludes the review of the first forty ictuses of the transcription, which represents only a little more than one-twentieth of its total length of 746 ictuses. A survey of the processes employed in the remaining ictuses would, no doubt, be of interest to some readers, but it would probably test the endurance of others, especially given that it would not add greatly to the purport of the preceding remarks. For what is already clear is that Feldman's approach combined more and less methodical aspects. Its more methodical elements included his recourse to simple algorithms for transforming the contents of a given column in the original and his organised approach to redeploying their outputs in a way that would preserve, in broad outline, the register contour of the original work. Its less methodical elements included his personal choice of which algorithm to use in a particular case and his avoidance of a slavish recourse to rules that would dictate one particular register for every number drawn from a given instrumental part. The importance of retaining some flexibility in this area is evident if, as Chapter 5 suggested, his aim was to achieve the holistic balance in the distribution of symbols between registers across the work as a whole highlighted in Example 5.7 (Chapter 5).

That said, a number of observations about the remaining ictuses are warranted. As previously noted, Feldman seems to have supplemented his methods for transforming the contents of columns in the original into material suitable for redeployment as he worked through the transcription process. The most commonly used addition makes its first appearance at ictus 41, in which the numbers (2, 7) in the original score are paired with (1, 1, 7) in the corresponding column of the transcription. Evidently, in this case, Feldman reconceived the 2 as 1+1 and then demerged its constituent elements for subsequent redeployment. The use of this demerger process makes it considerably more difficult to track Feldman's thinking with any certainty in some later columns because its availability creates multiple routes from source materials to outputs.

A second observation concerns Feldman's method of redeploying material in the low register intermission in ictuses 357–81. One might expect to find a modified method of redeployment here because a ranking of the low register ranges of instruments in the original is not a mirror image of a ranking of their high register ranges. For example, the piano is capable of producing both the highest and the lowest notes in the ensemble, meaning that it would be natural to redeploy materials originating in the piano part of the original to lower register locations in this section. In fact, a review of the data does not confirm this expectation, although it does show that his method of redeployment is noticeably less consistent in this area than in the first forty ictuses.

Feldman's handling of the long, repeated and near-repeated sequences in the original also merits commentary. The exact repetition of the long sequence shown in Example 7.2 resurfaces as a near-repetition in the corresponding columns of the transcription. The transcription of the first occurrence of the sequence, which extends between ictuses 461 and 527, is near-repeated in ictuses 528–94, with two minor alterations in ictuses 528 and 549, which may be copying errors. By way of contrast, the near-repetition shown in Example 7.3 resurfaces as an exact repetition in ictuses 595–612 and 613–30, providing further evidence that Feldman worked from the paperboard score. As previously noted, the single difference between the two occurrences of the passage in question in the published edition of the original work for chamber ensemble is not replicated in this source, which includes two identical occurrences. Not every structural feature of the original is replicated, however. Notable absentees include the three areas of increasing length, towards the end of the original score, in which the number 1 appears in every cell, which are not mimicked in the transcription.

The locations given in the previous paragraph differ by one ictus from those cited previously for the corresponding passages in the original. This is due to the presence of an extra, blank column in the transcription at ictus 382, immediately after the end of the low register intermission. It seems highly likely that this addition was added simply to enhance the visual appearance of the derivative score. The end of the intermission is marked in the original with an arrow between ictuses 381 and 382 and the label 'HIGH' above ictus 382. Feldman added an arrow in the same location in the transcription, but ictus 382 is the last column in the ninth system in this new version, meaning that there was insufficient room for him to add the label without it extending beyond the end of the system, thereby spoiling the vertical alignment on the right side of the page. His solution was to leave the last column in the ninth system blank, thereby adding an extra ictus, while including the label above the very next column – the first in the tenth system.

Collage

The practice of utilising more than one notational format in a single score would become common in Feldman's non-graph works composed in 1963–9, in which he typically combined passages presented in one or more of his notations for fixed pitches and indeterminate durations with passages presented in conventional staff notation. As noted in Chapter 2, however, he mixed different notations for the very first time in . . .*Out of 'Last Pieces'*. Through much of this graph, the piano part is allocated three rows in each grid frame, but on the last page – reproduced in Example 3.6 (Chapter 3) – it is presented on two five-line staves. Within these staves, which lack bar lines and time signatures, stem-less note heads with continuation marks appear without intervening rests, specifying a series of sound events of definite pitch and indeterminate duration.[46] The practice of mixing notations also recurs at the very end of *The King of Denmark*, in which two sounds of definite pitch and indeterminate duration are specified on a five-line stave.

Feldman's decision to specify pitches at the end of . . .*Out of 'Last Pieces'* and *The King of Denmark* indicates a conception of their closing stages that was less flexible than those of their other components. In the former case, but not the latter, which is too short, it may also have had a pedagogical aspect. Two years previously, Brown had composed *Hodograph I* (1959), whose score combines passages in a proportional variant of conventional notation with occasional 'line drawing[s]' (squiggles) that are meant to suggest 'the trajectory and the character' of an improvisation.[47] In this case, Brown explained that he expected the less flexible material to inform the performers' interpretations of the line drawings,[48] and it may be that in . . .*Out of 'Last Pieces'* Feldman had something similar in mind.

This section argues that Feldman's decision to begin mixing notations was also connected with contemporary developments in the visual arts, for he worked on . . .*Out of 'Last Pieces'* during a period of intense interest in collage and the closely related technique of assemblage in art circles in New York City. For example, in February 1961, a month before Feldman

---

[46] The staves are sandwiched between upper and lower areas of the grid frame. This implies temporal locations for the sonorities specified on the staves versus those specified in the surrounding frame.

[47] E. Brown, [Untitled, on notational problems], 12.

[48] *Ibid.*, and 'An interview with composer Earle Brown', 309–10.

completed his graph, Cage finished an article on Rauschenberg,[49] arguably the leading practitioner of assemblage at that time, in which he praised the latter's 'combines', artworks in which photographic images, newspaper clippings and three-dimensional objects, including stuffed animals, were included in otherwise abstract paintings. Later that year, Rauschenberg went on to contribute two of these works to a major exhibition, titled 'The Art of Assemblage', dedicated to assemblage and its historical precursors, including all forms of collage, at the Museum of Modern Art.[50] In the catalogue, William Seitz, who organised the exhibition, wrote of the 'current wave' of interest in these areas, explaining that they had become 'the language for impatient, hypercritical, and anarchistic young artists'.[51] A preview had previously noted that 'interest in this new kind of expression is in the air' and it included an impressively long list of associated shows featuring collage and assemblage at commercial galleries in New York.[52]

In view of this backdrop, we can assume that Feldman introduced the five-line staves at the end of . . . *Out of 'Last Pieces'* as a collage-like gesture, combining radically different notational formats in a single work, thereby echoing the latest fashion among painters. In fact, the five-line stave is physically glued in place in a surviving sketch,[53] suggesting that he may have intended it to be viewed as an 'intruder' object in his grid.[54] If so, then the inclusion of an unusual ending had an intentionally visual aspect and the final page of the score should be seen not just as a page from a score, but also as a papier collé.

It is not clear whether Feldman composed the intruder object specifically for use in . . . *Out of 'Last Pieces'* or cannibalised it from previously composed materials. If he extracted it from materials he originally composed for use in *Last Pieces* – a piano work with fixed pitches and indeterminate durations, completed in April 1959 – then this would explain his unusual

[49] 'On Robert Rauschenberg, artist, and his work' [1961], in *Silence*, 98–108.

[50] The exhibition ran from 2 October to 12 November 1961. Rauschenberg contributed *Canyon* and *Talisman*. Feldman described his more conventionally notated works *Crippled Symmetry* (1983) and *String Quartet II* (1983) as assemblages ('"I'm reassembling all the time". Lecture, 2 July 1985', in Mörchen (ed.), *Morton Feldman in Middelburg*, 58, and 'String Quartet II' [1984], in Friedman (ed.), *Give My Regards*, 196), but there are no records of similar comments about his graphs.

[51] William C. Seitz, *The Art of Assemblage* (New York: Museum of Modern Art, 1961), 87.

[52] Dorothy Gees Seckler, 'Gallery notes: start of the season – New York', *Art in America*, vol. 49, no. 3 (1961), 84–6, 128, 130, 132, 134.

[53] Morton Feldman Collection, Paul Sacher Foundation. The insert in the sketch does not include the last two sonorities specified in the corresponding insert in the published edition.

[54] For the use of 'intruder' objects in collage, see Eddie Wolfram, *History of Collage: An Anthology of Collage, Assemblage and Event Structures* (London: Studio Vista, 1975), 19.

choice of title for the graph. It would also connect . . .*Out of 'Last Pieces'* with a technique used sporadically by Pollock of physically recycling parts of previous works to produce new ones.[55] This method was subsequently used more intensively by Lee Krasner, Pollock's wife, who cannibalised her own art and left-over fragments from Pollock's, to serve as materials for new paintings.[56]

It is doubtful that . . .*Out of 'Last Pieces'* counts as a musical collage in the more commonly accepted sense in which the third movement of Luciano Berio's *Sinfonia* (1969) might be regarded as a prime example. In such cases, the diverse elements that are juxtaposed, superposed or melded are often audibly distinct,[57] but this is not true of Feldman's work. Although the notation of the intruder object is markedly different – visually – from that of other parts of the graph score, its audible content is not differentiated: the fragment indicates dyads and chords to be played by the piano, an instrument used elsewhere in the work; the notated sounds are sustained, which is common in other passages in the piano part; and the fragment does not include any indication of dynamics, suggesting that it, like the rest of the graph, is subject to the general guidance given in the notes (i.e. 'very low').

The lack of continuity between several pages in the score, highlighted in Chapter 5, which can now be seen as another collage-like gesture, provides additional support for this interpretation, as does the presence of a column of grace notes that (literally) bisects the horizontal axis of the last page. This element is surely appropriated from Feldman's *Variations* for piano, which was intended to accompany performances of Cunningham's similarly named dance *Variation*. The score of this more conventionally notated work features a single column of grace notes, distributed between six identical chords, that bisects an otherwise sparsely populated page, creating a striking visual image, shown in Example 7.13.[58] In both cases, Feldman's use of this device may have been meant to refer to the

---

[55] Francis Valentine O'Connor and Eugene Victor Thaw (eds.), *Jackson Pollock: A Catalogue Raisonné of Paintings, Drawings and Other Works, Volume 4: Other Works, 1930–1956* (New Haven: Yale University Press, 1978), 97–117.

[56] Ellen G. Landau, 'Channeling desire: Lee Krasner's collages of the early 1950s', *Woman's Art Journal*, vol. 18, no. 2 (Autumn 1997–Winter 1998), 27.

[57] J. Peter Burkholder, 'Collage', Grove Music Online, Oxford University Press. For the elements combined in the third movement of *Sinfonia*, see David Osmond-Smith, *Playing on Words: A Guide to Luciano Berio's* Sinfonia (London: Royal Musical Association, 1985), 39–71.

[58] This example is taken from a copy of the score at the New York Public Library that includes annotations by Cage. These have been removed using publishing software. The published edition of the score, which is engraved, replicates the unusual aspects of Feldman's original presentation.

Example 7.13 *Variations*, page 4

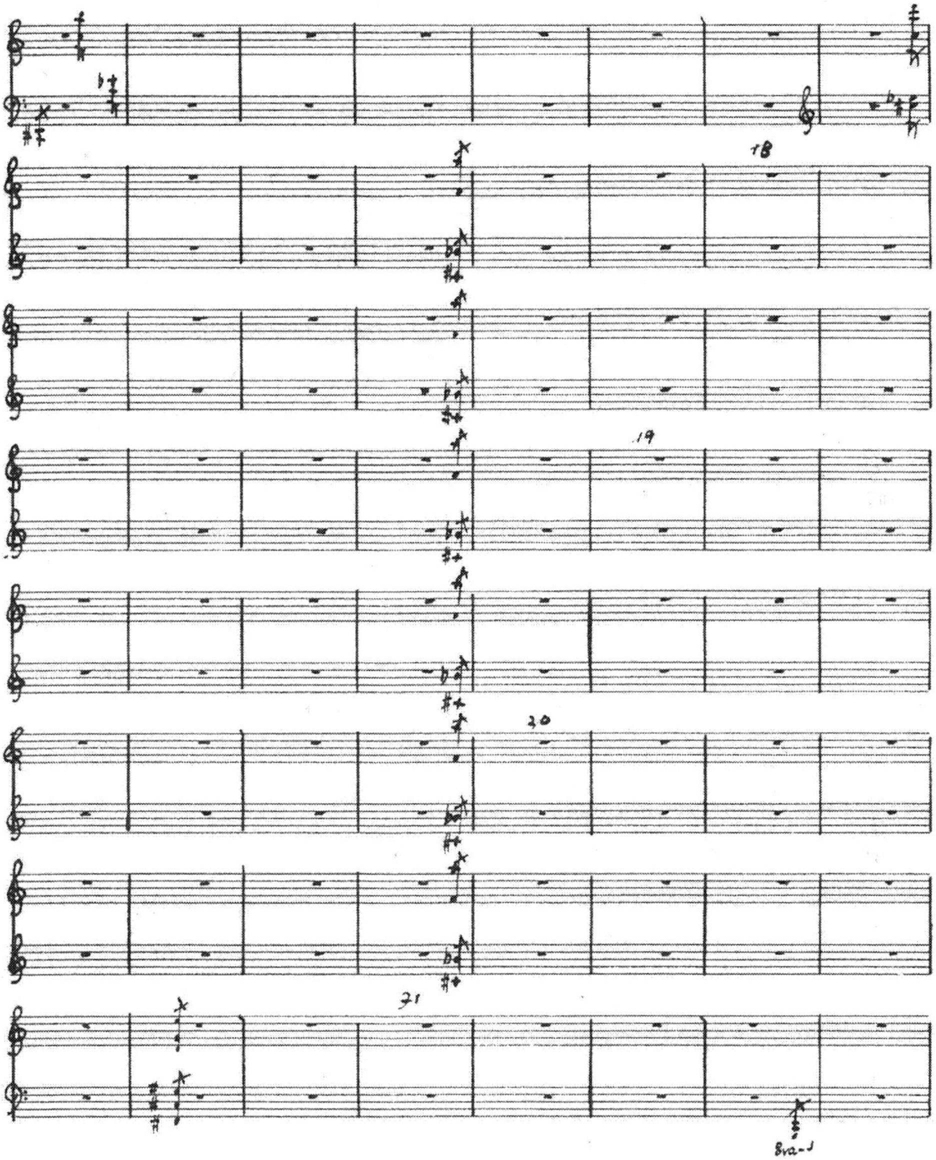

narrow vertical stripes or 'zips' that bisect some of Newman's otherwise monochromatic canvases – most notably in his *Onement* series, painted in 1948.[59] However, in . . .*Out of 'Last Pieces'*, the zip also refers back within Feldman's own catalogue, to *Variations*. Unlike the more conventionally notated ending in the piano part of . . .*Out of 'Last Pieces'*, this column of grace notes is written into the grid in the sketch mentioned above and not glued in, so it is not an example of papier collé. Nonetheless, it appears to be an example of a closely related method of syntactic quotation, akin to paintings in which intruder objects are painted into the picture, and not inserted.[60]

Feldman's long-standing interest in 'no-continuity' was fully compatible with the ideological basis of collage – namely, 'setting one thing beside the other without connective'.[61] Nevertheless, 'no-continuity' does not seem to have been the driving force underpinning his use of collage and collage-like methods in this particular case, which was driven instead – as on other occasions – by contemporary work in the visual arts.

Superimposition

Page 7 of the published edition of *In Search of an Orchestration* is formally related to pages 1, 2 and 4. The relationship is best described with a thought experiment. Imagine that each of these previous pages is drawn on a transparent sheet and that these sheets are placed on top of one another. Pages 2 and 4 are stacked so that their grid frames align, but the grid of page 1 is displaced by ten columns to the left along the horizontal axis, so that its first ten columns are not superimposed on the grids of the two other pages. An empty grid frame is then placed on top of the stack so that it aligns with those of pages 2 and 4. The content of each of its cells is then set equal to the content of one of the two or three cells directly below it – referred to here as the *corresponding* cells – or left blank. If the selected content is part of a symbol that straddles more than one cell in the source frame, then the remainder of the symbol is also selected for inclusion in the covering page. Only twenty-eight symbols on page 7 out of a total of 263 cannot be accounted for in this

---

[59] Feldman lived in the same house as Newman in 1956 (Claren, 'A Feldman chronology', 263), but it is likely that they became acquainted in 1951 (*ibid.*, 259).

[60] That said, the meaning of the column is different. In *Variations*, it straddles six systems and the designated notes are played in six distinct chords, whereas in . . .*Out of 'Last Pieces'*, the designated sounds are all played in a single ictus. The pitches of the constituent sounds are specified in *Variations*, but not in the graph.

[61] Roger Shattuck, *The Banquet Years: The Origins of the Avant Garde in France, 1885 to World War I: Alfred Jarry, Henri Rousseau, Erik Satie, Guillaume Apollinaire*, revised edn (New York: Vintage Books, 1968), 332.

way. Of these, twenty-five appear to be closely related to symbols presented at corresponding points in pages 1, 2 and 4, whereas only three appear to be unrelated to this earlier material.

Symbols on pages 1, 2 and 4 that are reused on page 7 are highlighted in Examples 7.14–7.16. Example 7.17 shows how these symbols reappear on page 7 using the same system of highlighting. The displacement of the material from page 1 is also marked. Symbols that cannot be strictly determined by the method described above are not highlighted. In two places, symbols that appear on page 7 are identical to those in corresponding cells on two previous pages. In these cases, the symbols on page 7 are marked with two types of highlighting.

The utility of this thought experiment suggests a possible connection with Cage's works that use transparent sheets, such as *Fontana Mix* and the derivative works he composed with them – the progeny of *Fontana Mix* being *Aria* (1958), *Sounds of Venice* (1959), *Water Walk* (1959) and *Theatre Piece* (1960). Although we can assume that Feldman was adept at transferring his scores to onionskin paper to facilitate photoreproduction, there is no concrete evidence to suggest that he actually superposed materials of this type in the compositional process, and he may have worked, instead, by comparing and copying non-transparent sheets.

It would be premature, at this stage, to conclude that page 7 must have been created by a process using selective superimposition of materials presented in previous pages. This is because the formal relationships that exist between the pages are also consistent with Feldman working in the reverse order, from the later page to the earlier pages using a process of selective decomposition. If he worked this way, then his method involved deriving source materials for pages 1, 2 and 4 from a three-way division of page 7. Given Feldman's allover method of working, this cannot be ruled out on the grounds that it implies a compositional process that runs against the flow of the music.

Having said that, there is reason to believe that Feldman's direction of working was from the earlier to the later pages – that is, from pages 1, 2 and 4 to page 7. In interviews conducted by Paula Ames in the early 1980s, he described a similar phenomenon at work in his more conventionally notated *Piano* (1977) as 'superimposition'.[62] This suggests that in *Piano* and, by implication, in his last graph, the compositional process involved combining multiple sources. This is confirmed by his comments in a conversation recorded in 1983 in which he mentioned the fact that in

---

[62] Paula Kopstick Ames, '*Piano* (1977)', in DeLio (ed.), *The Music of Morton Feldman*, 104.

Example 7.14   *In Search of an Orchestration*, page 1, with material that reappears on page 7 highlighted

Example 7.15 *In Search of an Orchestration*, page 2, with material that reappears on page 7 highlighted

Example 7.16 *In Search of an Orchestration*, page 4, with material that reappears on page 7 highlighted

Example 7.17 *In Search of an Orchestration*, page 7, with material from pages 1, 2 and 4 highlighted his graphs he would sometimes 'superimpose the same grid on another grid'.[63]

Feldman's use of a superimposition process is, almost certainly, yet another case in which his working methods were directly affected by the visual arts. In another conversation, this one recorded in 1985, he suggested that Cage's use of transparencies in the late 1950s and early 1960s was inspired by Rauschenberg methods, and he went on to suggest that he too had 'been thinking about' these methods 'for many years'.[64] By 1967, the year in which *In Search of an Orchestration* was composed, Rauschenberg had been superposing material in his artworks using a variety of techniques, including solvent transfer, lithography and silkscreen printing.[65] Precisely which of these methods Feldman had in mind is unclear, however.

There are several other examples of selective superimposition within *In Search of an Orchestration*. For example, one in four of the symbols in the parts for woodwinds and brass on page 7 reappear in the same grid locations on page 8, whereas the symbols in a short section in the percussion part on page 7 reappear, with only minor adjustments, on page 8, but displaced by twenty columns to the left.[66] Additionally, most of the materials in the parts for percussion and strings in the first nineteen columns of page 12 reappear in the last nineteen columns on page 13.

This is the earliest documented instance of this procedure in Feldman's catalogue, but it is not unique within his output. Ames has highlighted its use in *Piano*,[67] and Claren has described the application of similar techniques in *On Time and the Instrumental Factor*, a conventionally notated work for orchestra completed in 1969, and in several later works in conventional notation, including *Chorus and Orchestra (II)* (1972), *Neither* (1977) and *Flute and Orchestra* (1978).[68]

In one conversation with Ames, Feldman referred to his superimpositions as 'functional collage', but in another he qualified this assessment:

> It's not really a collage. My definition of a collage is when you have two obviously different [kinds of] material. I feel that these are vertical structures creating a more dense [texture].[69]

[63] 'The Johannesburg Masterclasses, July 1983: Session 9', www.cnvill.net/mfmasterclasses09.pdf (accessed 24 June 2015).

[64] 'Interview, Saturday, June 29, 1985, Middelburg', by Paul van Emmerik, unpublished transcript.

[65] Branden W. Joseph, *Random Order: Robert Rauschenberg and the Neo-Avant-Garde* (Cambridge, MA: MIT Press, 2003), 180.

[66] This creates formal links between the materials on page 8 and those on pages 1, 2 and 4 (David Cline, Morton Feldman: Dimensions of Graph Music, unpublished PhD thesis, University of London (2011), 251–3).

[67] 'Piano (1977)', 132–7.   [68] *Neither*, 140, 145–6.   [69] Ames, '*Piano* (1977)', 104.

The superimposition process, as Feldman used it, typically did produce an increase in the density of the resulting music, as in Examples 7.14–7.17. Feldman may also have viewed it as creating a degree of unity within a score, in which case the process seems more closely associated with his holism than his collage-based methods. That said, it is highly unlikely that any of the individual elements that are reused in the score of *In Search of an Orchestration* will be discernible in a performance, unless the orchestra recognises the compositional processes involved and deliberately seeks to highlight the connections between the source materials and their subsequent reappearance. This is because the selectively repeated materials include indeterminate elements, meaning that performers are entitled to play different occurrences of selectively superimposed material differently.

'No-continuity' and holism revisited

Several compositional methods outlined above and in Chapter 6 establish relationships between adjacent, nearby or even distant materials within graphs. To what extent are these inconsistent with Feldman's more general position outlined in previous chapters?

The presence of horizontal thinking in the *Projections* certainly appears at odds with his aim of 'no-continuity' between sounds, at least in some cases. For example, in *Projection 4*, the differentiating aspects of the sound that begins at ictus 14 (see Example 6.6 in Chapter 6) do facilitate a credible *ex post facto* rationalisation for its presence – namely, as forming a deliberately marked contrast with the immediately preceding material. This is surely the reason why Cage objected to Feldman's decision to finish *Marginal Intersection* with 'a real cadence (dim poco a poco)'.[70] Elsewhere, Cage listed 'ascending or descending linear passages' and 'crescendi and diminuendi' as among 'the most banal of continuity devices'.[71]

In other cases, the presence of horizontal thinking appears to be less clearly an issue. Even though Feldman attended to register contour in at least some of the *Projections*, the contours he selected do not seem to include easily recognisable patterns, and this severely constrains the listener's ability to construct backward-looking explanations or make forward-looking predictions.

As noted elsewhere in this volume, Feldman came to view the presence of horizontal thinking in his early graphs as potentially problematic, presumably for the reasons given above, but there is no documentary evidence to suggest that he worried about the possible presence of continuity in his

[70] Iddon, *John Cage and David Tudor*, 15–16.   [71] Cage, 'History of experimental music', 75.

later graph music. It is true that his use of horizontal strings is not sufficiently systematic to provide the listener with any predictive capability. However, they do appear to provide a rationale for the presence of some sounds as deliberately contrasting with immediately preceding materials. Perhaps this was another reason why Feldman actively avoided them in the graphs from *The Straits of Magellan* onwards.

His use of elastic form in *Ixion** and large-scale repetition in both published versions of *Ixion* appear more subversive, given his general outlook. This is because the presence of large-scale repetitions could provide listeners with predictive capability, especially when performers choose the same rhythm and pitches for use in different occurrences of a repeated passage.[72] The associated risks seem less marked with his use of superimposition in the score of *In Search of an Orchestration*, but, even so, its use could facilitate backward-looking explanations if the orchestra chooses to play different occurrences of selectively superimposed material in the same manner.

The homogeneities highlighted in Chapter 5 demonstrate that Feldman's more local methods did not compromise his holism, but they do point to a genuinely molecular aspect of his approach in some places. There is no question of any congruency between these molecules – the numbers in a horizontal string, for example – and the works in which they occur, as there was between pages and scores in some cases. The implication must be that he distributed his molecules in ways commensurate with his holism, meaning that elements of molecularity coexist with, but were, in the end, answerable to his holism in these works.

---

[72] It would be wrong to conclude that this was a reason why Feldman chose not to recreate *Ixion** for publication, as this would make it unclear why he chose to retain substantial repetitions in the published editions.

8 Non-notated preferences

Feldman's 'official' position was that those performing his graphs are free to select any notes of their choice, provided that they play in the given registers, except in the more conventionally notated inserts in ...*Out of 'Last Pieces'* and *The King of Denmark*, in which exact pitches are specified. This permissive stance is explicitly stated in an unattributed text in the printed programme for the first performance of *Marginal Intersection* in late 1952:

> The playing musicians are the final judges of what notes they shall play.
> [...] they can pick, in the indicated register, any note they may choose.[1]

Even if someone other than Feldman penned this text, it is clear that it reflects his view, for a verbatim report of comments he made from the stage that night confirms that this was his official position:

> When asked by a curious member of the audience, 'How do you indicate on such paper which note is to be played?' Feldman replied, 'I don't, it doesn't matter. Any sound will do so long as the player does something at the point marked for his entry.'[2]

This apparent agnosticism would remain his official stance. For example, in an interview published in the *New York Times* in 1964, he spoke about an unspecified graph and remarked that '[a]ny note will do as long as it's in the register'.[3]

In reality, Feldman's official position was something of an over-simplification. We know that he was sometimes unhappy with the specific choices that performers actually made, and it will be useful to recap the examples highlighted in Chapters 1–2. To begin with, he was upset by an early performance of one of the *Intersections* for orchestra in which the brass section conspired to play 'Yankee Doodle' in a way that complied with his written indications in the score. We also know that he disliked the xylopho-nist's playing in an early performance of *Marginal Intersection* ('what he actually played was of such a horrendous nature')[4] and that he openly criticised

---

[1] Programme, Cooper Union for the Advancement of Science and Art, undated [9 November 1952].
[2] Glanville-Hicks, 'Music in the Making at Cooper Union', 35.
[3] 'Feldman throws a switch', XII. [4] 'Morton Feldman with Dore Ashton', 8.

a performer's note selections, even though they were consistent with his written indications, in a music rehearsal for *Summerspace* in 1958.

Speaking about the 'Yankee Doodle' case, Feldman described the act of deliberate sabotage by the musicians involved as 'murder' and contrasted it with what he called '[m]anslaughter'.[5] The latter term was clearly meant to apply in cases of serious but inadvertent deviation from his intent, and the other examples mentioned above may have been of this type, although we cannot be sure that the divergences involved were not deliberate, as they had been in music rehearsals for *Summerspace* in 1965.

It cannot be coincidence that all these problem cases involved graphs for larger ensembles. Typically, Feldman's graphs for solo instruments or small combos were initially targeted at specific individuals, often friends and acquaintances, who would have been familiar with his music, interested in understanding his preferences and committed to rehearsing thoroughly. By contrast, his arm's-length relationship with a large ensemble was bound to carry more risk, especially in the 1950s, when notational innovation and heightened performer choice were genuinely new and likely to encounter resistance from conservative musicians; as late as 1967, Feldman suggested that the increased freedom given to performers by his music 'scares them to death'.[6] No doubt union rules on pay exacerbated the problem by restricting rehearsal time.[7] Although the rehearsal schedules for the specific performances mentioned above are not documented, we know that there was only one rehearsal of . . .*Out of 'Last Pieces'* before the premiere in March 1961, for example.[8]

Feldman's official agnosticism about which notes performers should play led Cage to portray him as a 'hero' in his 'Lecture on something' in 1951 – Cage's idea being that 'the accepting of what comes without preconceived ideas of what will happen and re-gardless of the consequences' constitutes a form of heroism.[9] By the same token, it seems safe to assume

---

[5] 'Around Morton Feldman', 14.

[6] 'Far-out composer Feldman says: "think of it as an environment"', interview by Ann Holmes, *Houston Chronicle*, 13 March 1967, Section 2, 4.

[7] C. Brown, *Chance and Circumstance*, 187.

[8] Howard Shanet to Morton Feldman, 9 March 1961, Morton Feldman Collection, Paul Sacher Foundation. This indicates that the rehearsal took place at 4pm on the day of the performance. To be fair, concerts in this series were themselves regarded as public rehearsals (Broekman, 'Music in the making', 10), as noted in Chapter 1. The New York Philharmonic's higher profile performances of the same work in 1964 were somewhat better rehearsed, with two sessions specifically dedicated to rehearsing Feldman's music (4–5 February), which would also have been played in the last rehearsal session (6 February) in a run-through of the entire programme. See Joan Bonime to Morton Feldman, 28 January 1964, Morton Feldman Papers, Music Library, State University of New York at Buffalo.

[9] 'Lecture on something', 136. Cage's punctuation, without his unusual spacing.

that it was Cage's experiences conducting *Ixion* for *Summerspace* that caused him to retract this assessment publicly in 1959. As he put it in a passage quoted from in Chapter 2:

> On paper, of course, the graph pieces are as heroic as ever; but in rehearsal Feldman does not permit the freedoms he writes to become the occasion for license. He insists upon an action within the gamut of love, and this produces (to mention only the extreme effects) a sensuousness of sound or an atmosphere of devotion.[10]

Cage's description of the characteristics that Feldman insisted on in rehearsals, poetic as it may be, is too elusive to be of much help in deciphering Feldman's predilections. This chapter aims at a clearer statement, but it is not only concerned with the question of which pitches the performer should play; examination of Feldman's explanatory notes and other sources reveals a variety of other preferences, and these are also highlighted. Previous chapters have described one of his pet dislikes – his aversion to self-serving virtuosity; hence his comment that 'a musician has to be extremely intelligent to know that I don't want his intelligence. He just needs to be humble and fantastically proficient'.[11] Therefore, this is not addressed.

The aim of the chapter is simply to tease out other aspects of what Feldman wanted, or preferred not, to hear. More theoretical issues lurk in the background, to be sure. Among these are questions about which properties are essential to the identity of these works and must be present if a performance is to count as of Feldman's music. The discussion steers clear of these, not because they are unimportant, but because they are contentious in their own right and can only be addressed within a broader investigation of the nature of musical works.

Perfection of tone

A review of available sources reveals that Feldman expected performers to produce sounds with specific characteristics that are usefully classified under the general heading 'perfection of tone'. As will become clear, this encompasses 'purity', 'anonymity' and 'sourcelessness'. Producing sounds with all these traits is not always feasible. However, Feldman's general position seems to have been that they should be present wherever possible.

To begin with, Feldman's earliest published writings indicate a desire for what he called a 'pure (non-vibrating) tone'.[12] This statement equates

---

[10] Included in the prefatory remarks with 'Lecture on something', 128.
[11] 'Traffic light music', 24.
[12] Feldman *et al.*, '4 musicians at work', 168–72. See also Cowell, 'Current chronicle', 131.

purity with the absence of vibrations, and other evidence suggests that this was a call to avoid unnecessary variations in pitch and, in some cases, dynamics within individual sounds. A desire for the least possible variation in pitch surfaced in the written notes with *Intersection 1* and *Marginal Intersection*, in which he specified a minimum of vibrato, and his comments elsewhere indicate that he was uncomfortable with vibrato effects for much of his career.[13] A reason emerged in a 1986 lecture, in which he told of a concert in which vibrato was prominent and 'all of these pieces to a certain degree sounded the same'.[14] Evidently, his idea was that vibrato is so distinctive that it masks a sound's other aspects.

Feldman stated his desire for the least possible variation in dynamics in the explanatory notes with *Intersection 1, Marginal Intersection* and *Intersection 4*.[15] These specify that the dynamic level of each sound is to be freely chosen by the performer, with Feldman adding the proviso that the chosen level should be sustained until the end of the sound in question. A similar comment was not needed in the notes with *Intersections 2–3* because the pianist has less control over this aspect of the music. Feldman's general preference for avoiding unnecessary variations in dynamics within tones also surfaced in his dislike of the tremolo effect produced by a vibraphone motor. In four of the five graphs in which a vibraphone appears (*Atlantis, . . .Out of 'Last Pieces', The King of Denmark* and *In Search of an Orchestration*), he specified that the motor be turned off.[16] That said, he seems to have become more amenable to variations in dynamics within sounds in later graphs, and even invited them on occasions. Flutter tonguing is highlighted as an acceptable strategy in some circumstances in *Ixion* and *Atlantis*. Moreover, string tremolo effects, flutter tonguing and percussion rolls are explicitly notated in the last three graphs.

Feldman's desire for more anonymous instruments and timbres is a common theme in his writings,[17] and is informed by logic similar to that used in connection with vibrato. For example, his reason for disliking the sound of the oboe in the 1950s and 1960s was that he found the timbre so idiosyncratic that it masked its other aspects.[18] More generally, Feldman disliked instruments possessing what he called 'too much

---

[13] 'Morton Feldman talks to Paul Griffiths, August 1972' [1972], in Villars (ed.), *Morton Feldman Says*, 48, and 'The barrier of style. Conversation with Iannis Xenakis, 4 July 1986', in Mörchen (ed.), *Morton Feldman in Middelburg*, 328.

[14] 'Lecture in USC Composition Forum, April 4th, 1986', unpublished transcript.

[15] See also 'Morton Feldman talks to Paul Griffiths', 48.

[16] The exception is *Marginal Intersection*.

[17] For a representative example, see 'An interview with Morton Feldman, David Charlton and Jolyon Laycock', 27.

[18] *Ibid.*

personality'.[19] No doubt this was another reason why, throughout his career, he tended to prefer dynamics that were very low. The waveform of any note played softly tends to emphasise the fundamental tone, with the relative intensity of higher harmonics increasing as the dynamic level is raised.[20] Given that the composition and relative intensity of the higher harmonics determine the instrumental character of a tone, emphasising low dynamics will tend to reduce heard differences between notes played on different instruments.

One commentator has interpreted Feldman's preference for anonymous sounds as a desire for sounds that 'blend into an unidentifiable timbre',[21] but this seems too extreme. It makes nonsense of Feldman's professed emphasis on the importance of instrumentation, discussed below, and his occasionally idiosyncratic instrumental line-ups. More likely, Feldman enjoyed subtle variations in instrumental 'hue'.

Having said that, it is clear that a performer intent on playing as Feldman would have liked will generally refrain from accentuating differences in timbre by artificial means. A bizarre choice of trumpet mute on the first recording of *The Straits of Magellan* yields just the sort of effect that Feldman would have wished to avoid.[22] The use of a mute is specified in the score, but here it results in an idiosyncratic sound remarkably similar to one closely associated with Miles Davis on many of his famous recordings.[23] As early as 1939, Copland had predicted that at least some of the growing number of types of mute being used in jazz were likely to be introduced into the symphony orchestra.[24] Whether Feldman was unaware of their variety or simply chose to ignore it (at his peril) is unclear. Surely, what he had in mind was a mere method of attenuating the overall sound level, but none of the common mutes have only this effect. A study contemporary with the earliest graphs demonstrated that the

[19] 'The future of local music', unpublished transcript, 220.

[20] James Jeans, *Science & Music* (Cambridge University Press, 1937), 149.

[21] Clemens Gresser, (Re-)Defining the Relationships Between Composer, Performer and Listener: Earle Brown, John Cage, Morton Feldman and Christian Wolff, unpublished PhD thesis, University of Southampton (2004), 48.

[22] *Music Before Revolution*, EMI, C 165-28954/7.

[23] Perhaps the trumpeter's choice of mutes explains why Sabine Feisst suggested that *The Straits of Magellan* 'conveys a jazzy character' ('Morton Feldman's indeterminate music', liner notes with *Morton Feldman: Indeterminate Music*, Mode Records, mode 103). Davis' sound has been attributed to his use of a metallic Harmon mute with its stem removed. His first use of this device on record derives from a 1954 recording session (Ian Carr, *Miles Davis: The Definitive Biography* (London: HarperCollins, 1998), 81). The resulting sound has been characterised as 'full and breathy in the lower register and thin and piercing in the upper' (*ibid.*).

[24] *What to Listen for in Music*, revised edn (New York: McGraw-Hill, 1957), 94.

timbral quality, pitch range and sound field of the instrument are also affected.[25]

'Sourcelessness', by which he meant 'with a minimum of attack', is another characteristic that Feldman expected performers to deliver. This is explicitly stated in the written notes with ...*Out of 'Last Pieces', The Straits of Magellan* and *In Search of an Orchestration*, and Peter Dickinson observed him requesting it in a public rehearsal of *Projection 2* in 1966.[26] These comments reflect a general bias against audible onset effects that applies across most of his output,[27] although the performer's freedom to choose louder dynamics in the *Intersections* must mean that he regarded them as exempt, at least to some extent. Undoubtedly, this bias is connected with his preference for anonymous sounds because onset characteristics are important distinguishing factors between timbres.[28] It therefore comes as no surprise that his argument for sourcelessness is similar to those highlighted above in connection with his other preferences – namely, that a pronounced attack tends to become a focus of attention, thereby masking a sound's other aspects.[29]

Fixity of specified instrumentation

An ongoing debate about whether the given instrumentation of a musical work should, in general, be regarded as one of its essential properties hangs on the question of whether there is, or was, a performance tradition of interpreting guidance about instrumentation as flexible.[30] Whatever the outcome of this general dispute, there is no doubt that Feldman intended performers to observe the given instrumentations of his graphs, although care is needed in interpreting the word 'given' in this statement, for reasons that will become clear. Feldman, like Varèse, typically placed great emphasis on the instrumentations of his works, and this is an important theme of many of his surviving statements.[31]

---

[25] Martin J. Kurka, A Study of the Acoustical Effects of Mutes on Wind Instruments, unpublished M. Mus. thesis, University of South Dakota (1950).

[26] 'Feldman explains himself during his first visit to Europe in 1966, Peter Dickinson, April/May 1966' [1966], in Villars (ed.), *Morton Feldman Says*, 21. The performance took place in London (Programme, College of St Mark and St John, 1 May 1966).

[27] For a representative statement of his position, see 'The anxiety of art', 25.

[28] Winckel, *Music, Sound and Sensation*, 34.   [29] 'The anxiety of art', 25.

[30] Stephen Davies, *Musical Works and Performances* (Oxford: Clarendon Press, 2001), 60–71, and references therein.

[31] For example, 'Unpublished writings: III', 205–8, and 'The future of local music' [1985], 160, 191–2. For Varèse's views on instrumentation, see Edgard Varèse and Alexei Haieff, 'Edgard Varèse and Alexei Haieff questioned by 8 composers', *possibilities*, vol. 1, no.4 (Winter 1947/8), 97.

Feldman emphasised the importance of the specified instrumentations of his graphs in several places, and in 1987 he explained that the absence of precise specifications of pitch necessitated a strict adherence to their specified aspects, including instrumentation:

> When I was a younger man I got a letter from Cornelius Cardew that he was putting on a concert and he didn't have the right instruments for the pieces – my chamber graph pieces – and he asked if he could use any kind of instruments he wanted. And I said, 'No, please, don't. Because those pieces don't exist without this instrumentation.' The instrumentation is everything. [...] At that particular time I didn't give the pitch. I needed the other compensating things to glue the piece together. [...] I needed my instruments because I didn't have the pitch.[32]

Feldman's memory of this exchange, which took place in 1961, was not entirely accurate. In reality, his missive about instrumentation was ambiguous and consequently misunderstood by Cardew.[33] Even so, the intended message – that the given instrumentation is sacrosanct – is clearly stated in his comments quoted above.[34] This means that a recently released recording of *Projection 1* played on contrabass is inconsistent with his wishes.[35]

In view of the uncompromising tone of Feldman's comments on this issue, it is initially surprising that he experimented with different instrumentations of finished graphs on a number of occasions. His transcription of *Ixion* for two pianos is a case in point, but others are perhaps less well known. For example, in 1968 Feldman replied to Gerd Zacher's request for a work for organ by suggesting a rendition of *Intersection 3*. This piece was, Feldman enthused, 'still the most "modern" piece ever written', and might make a 'brilliant realization for the organ'.[36] Around the same time, he suggested to Bertram Turetzky the idea of performing *Intersection 4* on contrabass, despite the fact that this work was conceived for cello.[37] Feldman, as the composer, was entitled to make changes, of course, but

---

[32] "'I'm not negative, I'm critical'", 852.

[33] Feldman wrote: 'No "versions"!!' (Morton Feldman to Cornelius Cardew, 25 April 1961). Cardew replied: 'It will be interesting to try & memorise "Intersection #2" still without making a "version"!' (Cornelius Cardew to Morton Feldman, 18 May [1961], Morton Feldman Collection, Paul Sacher Foundation).

[34] See also 'Unpublished writings: III', 206.   [35] *Edges*, +3DB Records, +3DB010.

[36] Morton Feldman to Gerd Zacher, July 1968, Gerd Zacher. For a recording of Zacher's version, see *Gerd Zacher, Organ*, Deutsche Grammophon, 139 442.

[37] Programme notes for Turetzky's 1969 performances of *Intersection 4* state that the idea of adapting the work for contrabass was suggested by the composer (Programme, University of Michigan School of Music, 8 April 1969, and Programme, USCD Music Department, 8 December 1969).

others are not entitled to do so if their aim is to perform as he would have wished.

That said, he did give performers some freedom of choice in certain cases. The most notable of these is *The King of Denmark*, in which the instruments to be used are typically – though not always – at the performer's discretion, although those chosen must be suited to the task in hand – namely, of producing sonorities of the type that Feldman notated. In this particular case, instrument selection is a vitally important preparatory task that facilitates a highly individual response to the work, as noted in Chapter 2. Set-ups mentioned in the literature include: Williams' 'capsule' version,[38] which used a fairly restricted set-up to make 'the compositional structure (form) clearer' by encouraging the use of the same instrument to produce sounds designated by different occurrences of the same symbol, and facilitate international touring;[39] Shively's larger set-up, which was designed to ensure a formal isomorphism between symbols and sounds, with similarities and differences between types of symbols reflected in corresponding similarities and differences between timbres in performance;[40] and the even larger configurations apparently favoured by Daryl Pratt, which are designed to meet a number of self-imposed constraints, including the avoidance of repeated sounds and sound sequences.[41]

Spontaneity

In sympathetic comments published in 1952, Cowell described an excerpt from an otherwise lost graph, labelled 'Intersection #3', as 'a plan for the control of improvisation'.[42] This is one of several indications that Feldman initially intended performers to make spontaneous decisions during the course of a performance about which pitches to play and, in the *Intersections*, about when to begin playing them and how loud they should play. The alternative strategy of preparing selections in advance was one that Feldman did not originally intend, but seems to have come to accept subsequently.

---

[38] Mentioned by him in Feldman, 'An interview with Morton Feldman, Jan Williams', 153.

[39] Jan Williams to David Cline, 14 July 2008 (email) and 29 November 2010 (email).

[40] Shively, Indeterminacy and Interpretation, 18, 21, 25. Williams' idea of making 'the compositional structure (form) clearer' is similar, but a review of his annotated scores indicates that he did not insist on a formal isomorphism between instruments and symbols – the same instrument was sometimes used to produce sounds designated by different symbols, and different instruments were sometimes used to produce sounds designated by the same symbol (Jan Williams Collection of Annotated Scores, Music Library, State University of New York at Buffalo).

[41] Pratt, 'Performance analysis', 78.   [42] 'Current chronicle', 131.

An earlier indication of Feldman's preferences appeared in the printed programme for the first performance of *Projection 2*. An uncredited author wrote: '[t]he title of this work refers to the projection of sound into space. What particular sounds these are is left to the choice of the musicians at the moment of playing'.[43] It is possible that this note was penned by somebody other than Feldman, but it almost certainly reflects his views. One indication of this is that it ends as follows: '[s]ince each performance of this composition is different, yet essentially the same, it will be played twice in succession'. The decision to include successive performances was surely intended to showcase the variability in the resulting sound produced by incorporating spontaneous choices, and it is most unlikely that it would have been taken without Feldman's approval.

Cage's comments on Feldman's music in a lecture given at the Juilliard School of Music in 1952, while Feldman sat with him on stage, confirm that this was his position. Cage spoke of Feldman's *Projections*, saying that '[a] player is free at the instant of playing to play any note in the register indicated'.[44] Cage had by this time completed his shift to non-intention and developed a dislike for improvisation, which makes it highly unlikely that he was misrepresenting Feldman on this issue.[45]

That spontaneous decisions were originally intended is not surprising, given the context in which the graphs emerged. Feldman was intimately familiar with the culture of spontaneity that permeated contemporary American art in the late 1940s and early 1950s through his links with the New York School painters.[46] Given that he admired many of these artists and their works, it is not surprising to find him interested in assimilating elements of their approach. More importantly, as noted in Chapter 4, Feldman's general thinking about sound, as capable of acting independently, necessitated the use of spontaneous decision-making.

Even as late as 1964, Feldman continued to think of performers selecting pitches spontaneously as they played. In the printed programme for the New York Philharmonic's performances of ...*Out of*

---

[43] Programme, Hunter College Playhouse, 21 January 1951.

[44] 'Juilliard lecture' [1967], in *A Year from Monday: New Lectures and Writings by John Cage* (London: Marion Boyars, 1968), 102. For Feldman's being on stage, see Cage's prefatory remarks (*ibid.*, 95).

[45] For Cage's views on improvisation, see Sabine M. Feisst, 'John Cage and improvisation: an unresolved relationship', in Gabriel Solis and Bruno Nettl (eds.), *Musical Improvisation: Art, Education, and Society* (Urbana: University of Illinois Press, 2009), 38–51, and Rebecca Y. Kim, 'John Cage in separate togetherness with jazz', *Contemporary Music Review*, vol. 31, no. 1 (February 2012), 63–89.

[46] For a discussion of this context, see Daniel Belgrad, *The Culture of Spontaneity: Improvisation and the Arts in Postwar America* (University of Chicago Press, 1998).

'Last Pieces', he wrote: '[u]nlike improvisation, which relies solely on memory in selecting the most empirical and sophisticated examples of a style, or styles, the purpose of the graph is to erase memory, to erase virtuosity – to do away with everything but a direct action in terms of the sound itself'.[47] The contrast with improvisation makes it natural to read this passage, which was also quoted in Chapter 4, as about performing, not composing. Feldman's idea was that, in performance, graph music transcended freely improvised material in important ways. Like free improvisation, it is spontaneous, involving formative decisions at the time of playing. However, the restrictions imposed by the score disrupt the influence of conditioned responses and memories, neither of which is allowed free rein, and this facilitates a more direct, or unfettered, connection with sound.

Nevertheless, the surviving record suggests that Feldman came to accept the alternative approach of preparing selections before playing, the first known examples of which are Tudor's 1954 performances of *Intersection 3*. Arguably, the many challenges that this particular work presents make it something of a special case, but even so Brown remembered Feldman being uncomfortable with Tudor's modus operandi.[48] Later on, Feldman's general mistrust of performers may have made him more amenable to this type of approach. As noted elsewhere in this study, his avoidance of graph notation in 1954–7 was driven by discomfort with some spontaneous performances. Even if, originally, he had regarded this type of approach as the only one acceptable, the subsequent discovery that it was inviting an 'art of improvisation' may have unsettled his confidence to such an extent that he was willing to accept an alternative – even one that negated his earlier conception of a direct relationship between him and the resulting sound.[49] Hence, Dickinson's testimony that Feldman 'did not object to the players working out their parts in advance' during the public rehearsal of *Projection 2* in 1966, mentioned above.[50]

The upshot is that either approach to performing was acceptable from Feldman's latter-day perspective. Be that as it may, it seems highly likely that he continued to prefer spontaneously created performances that avoid unwanted excess on the ground that they – and they alone – were consistent with his original ideals.

---

[47] '. . .Out of "Last Pieces"', G.

[48] 'Earle Brown and Frans von Rossum', April 1990, unpublished transcript, Earle Brown Music Foundation.

[49] For 'art of improvisation', see 'Liner notes', 6.   [50] 'Feldman explains himself', 21.

Avoiding lazy choices

Dickinson's report includes another pertinent observation, which is stated and interpreted by him in the following passage:

> The pianist was rebuked for playing a close-position minor triad in the middle register, although there are of course no written instructions to the contrary.
>
> It became clear that Feldman is working within common practice stemming from Webern where intervals of the ninth, seventh or tritone dominate, and a suggestion of tonal relations would obviously be out of place.[51]

A difficulty with Dickinson's reading of the rebuke is that it jars with other evidence, such as Cage's prior assessment of Feldman's openness to sounds with tonal characteristics:

> At the present time, a twelve-tone time, it is not popular to allow the more common garden variety of tonal relations These latter are dis-criminated against. Feldman allows them to be if they happen to come along. [...] the only reason for his being able to allow them is by his acting on the assumption that no tonal relations ex-ist, meaning all tonal relations are acceptable.[52]

More importantly, Dickinson's reading sits uncomfortably with the individual freedom of performers to make their own choices about which notes to play. In the ensemble graph works, this is bound to result in a proliferation of intervals, including consonances, which makes it hard to see why their presence in an individual contribution should be of special concern.

An alternative reading of Feldman's intervention, consistent with Cage's assessment, is that he objected not so much to the particular chord that the pianist played, but to the way in which it was chosen. He generally disliked 'lazy' choices: '[j]ust concentrate on not making the lazy move' was how he summed up his own approach in composing his long, late works, for example.[53] In similar fashion, he disliked performers resorting to conditioned responses or remembered sequences, preferring what he saw as a concentrated focus on the sounds being produced and a sensitive

---

[51] *Ibid.*

[52] 'Lecture on something', 133. Cage's punctuation, without his unusual spacing. Compare E. Brown's attitude: 'I was especially annoyed by the idea that, in twelve-tone counterpoint, one avoided consonances. I liked the idea of "the liberation of dissonance" but did not agree that it should mean the enslavement of consonance: the substitution of one prejudice for another' ('Transformations and developments of a radical aesthetic', *Current Musicology*, nos. 67–8 (Autumn 1999), 39).

[53] '*Soundpieces* interview', 92. As John Tilbury put it to me, in conversation: there should be no 'free-wheeling' when playing Feldman.

engagement with them on their terms. This is surely why, in the public rehearsal, he emphasised 'listening'.[54] What this concentrated engagement amounts to in practice is initially unclear, but if he felt that the pianist had simply resorted to a familiar pitch combination, if the selection process amounted to nothing more than a technical reflex, then this would account for his stance. Interpreting his response this way, a minor triad, or any other combination, was acceptable in principle, provided that it was deliberately chosen in some as-yet unaccounted-for way based on the performer's listening experience.

Another advantage of this reading is that sits better with Feldman's statements quoted at the beginning of this chapter, which suggest that performers are free to select whichever notes they choose. These are blatantly inconsistent with a desire to promote certain intervals while suppressing others, but the clash of ideas is less pronounced if his view was not that performers should promote or avoid specific outcomes, but only that they should choose in a particular way or, alternatively, avoid a particular way of choosing.

The matter is clinched by a letter in which Feldman sought to clarify his views on the pianist's playing:

> 1. If she <u>heard</u> it – out of a maze – so to speak
> 2. If she <u>heard</u> it even as a <u>tonal</u> resolution
> 3. If she <u>heard</u> it as a color (or the <u>COLOUR</u>)
> 4. If – in fact – she <u>heard</u> it
> THEN–
> O.K.!!
> But, I'm afraid her 3rd can best be described as a … tick.[55]

In other words, the pianist was not 'listening'. Feldman's description of her triad as a 'tick' shows that he saw it as a conditioned response, and his comments indicate that he would have withdrawn his criticism – albeit reluctantly – if this assessment had been mistaken.

The idea that, for Feldman, it was not just the performer's selection that mattered, but also the manner in which the selection was made, gains additional support from the fact that it paralleled his views on painting. We know that he saw the painter's concentrated engagement with materials during the creative process as a vital ingredient in the finished work. Where such engagement was absent, the painting was, for him, of lesser value, as the following anecdote about an unnamed painter makes clear:

---

[54] Dickinson, 'Feldman explains himself', 21.
[55] Morton Feldman to Peter Dickinson, 27 June 1966, in Villars (ed.), *Morton Feldman Says*, 22–3.

I was asked to write a film music on him. So, I looked at the film and he is in a studio [. . .] and as he is painting [. . .] his little daughter walks in [. . .] and he turns to her and he smiles. As he is smiling he is still smearing. [. . .] I wouldn't write the film because of that one moment [. . .] I didn't want to be associated with that.[56]

In music and painting, Feldman's view was that the quality of the perceptible product depends upon what might be termed the 'authenticity' of the creative act, which invites the question of whether he regarded this authenticity as necessarily manifest in the finished work. Would the pianist's selection have sounded better if chosen differently? Feldman did not say, but a negative response would imply that sonically identical performances might be of different qualities, which would fit uncomfortably with his insistence on the priority of sound. The alternative view, that he held that the authenticity of a creative act is always manifest, is therefore preferable. If so, then Feldman's position must have been that the pianist's selection sounded bad.

'[S]imilar in style to "Last Pieces"'

The explanatory notes with the score of *Atlantis* state that the '[p]iano is notated to be played in the high, middle or low register, similar in style to "Last Pieces"'. This presents us with an immediate puzzle about the meaning of numbers. *Last Pieces* – one of Feldman's works with fixed pitches and indeterminate durations – is chord-based, whereas the explanatory notes with *Atlantis* begin with the statement that '[n]umbers indicate the amount of sounds to be played on or within the duration of the beat'. This implies that they specify quantities of consecutive sounds, and this is confirmed by Feldman's specific comments about instruments other than the piano. For example, the harp, xylophone and vibraphone are all instructed to '[a]rticulate as many single sounds as possible', and for most instruments he indicates how the performer should proceed if there are too many sounds to play. However, there is no such guidance with the piano part, despite the fact that it includes very large numbers. Compare *Ixion*, in which the notes state that '[i]f there are too many single sounds for the piano to play, the remaining sounds are simultaneous'.

It is hard to be sure, but the right strategy in this case, I suggest, is to interpret Feldman's reference to *Last Pieces* as over-riding his initial statement about numbers, but only in connection with the piano. This fits with the absence of guidance about how the pianist should proceed if the

---

[56] 'The future of local music', unpublished transcript, 55.

demands made by the score prove excessive and is supported by comparison with . . .*Out of 'Last Pieces', The Straits of Magellan* and *In Search of an Orchestration*. The explanatory notes with these explicitly state that this is how numbers in their piano parts should be interpreted, as noted in Chapter 3.

That said, there is no question of this exhausting the significance of Feldman's remarks about *Last Pieces*, which are among the most helpful that he made about the intended interpretation of his graph music. This is because they guide the pianist to consult a contemporary work in which pitches are specified as a stylistic model of how the piano part should be played. The aim of this section is to try to distil the salient messages.

There can be little doubt that at this time Feldman regarded *Last Pieces* as a pivotal work in his output. It was the first of his compositions published by the C. F. Peters Corporation,[57] the only one published in his lifetime that the company would engrave, the only composition of his own that he would refer to in the title of another work (. . .*Out of 'Last Pieces'*) and the only composition that he cited as a stylistic model. It comprises four distinct 'pieces' that it will be convenient to number: the first (henceforth *Last Pieces* 1) is to be played '[s]low' and '[s]oft'; the second (*Last Pieces* 2) '[f]ast' and '[s]oft'; the third (*Last Pieces* 3) '[v]ery slow' and '[s]oft'; and the fourth (*Last Pieces* 4) '[v]ery fast' and '[s]oft as possible'. Durations are 'free', but *Last Pieces* 4 is highlighted by the following twist: both hands are to start together but '[d]urations are free for each hand'.

A one-page note, in Tudor's handwriting, titled 'Feldman's program note for Last Pieces', ends with the following statement:

> I compose by ear – I discover my sound, & then go on to discover the next – always aware that I'm hearing what I'm doing, rather than composing.[58]

The implication appears to be that each sound was chosen individually and selected, primarily, for its individual properties. This is tantamount to atomism and if the account of Feldman's holism presented in Chapter 5 is correct, it is not strictly applicable to his graph music. Even so, the statement is suggestive because it implies a high degree of disjunction between successive elements. This manifests Feldman's interest in 'no-continuity', highlighted in Chapter 4.

---

[57] Walter Hinrichsen to Morton Feldman, 17 June 1963.

[58] This document appears to be a transcript of Feldman's original programme note for the first performance of *Last Pieces*, which Tudor gave in 1959. Other parts of the note are reproduced in the printed programme (Programme, The Village Gate, 26 April 1959). The elements quoted in the main text are not included, however. Tudor's transcript is presented in block capitals throughout. This element of his presentation is not replicated in the printed programme or above.

If the piano part in *Atlantis* is to be played in a similar style, it would seem that the pianist's selections should highlight the individuality of each sound, versus those immediately adjacent to it, and not its associative links. No doubt a degree of sonic particularity can be imparted through the judicious use of various playing techniques that are not explicitly notated, including voicing and pedalling. It is safe to assume that Feldman would have wished the pianist to utilise these devices where appropriate, but his reference to *Last Pieces* indicates that he had more than this in mind and that the music as written should serve as a guide.

In a study of *Last Pieces* 3, Thomas DeLio has argued that its constituent sonorities initially appear unconnected, but that as the music proceeds, perceptible relationships between them proliferate, thereby linking them over time.[59] Be that as it may, Feldman's comments suggest that the appearance of particularity was his primary concern, and this is confirmed by remarks he made about a contemporary work, *Durations 1* (1960) for alto flute, piano, violin and cello:

> In *Durations 1* the quality of the particular instruments together suggested a closely written kaleidoscope of sound. To achieve this I wrote each voice individually, choosing intervals that seem to erase or cancel out each sound as soon as we hear the next.[60]

A corollary is that a pianist playing *Atlantis* should make choices that minimise associative links between successive sounds wherever possible.

In a study of *Last Pieces* 1, Robert Morris has argued that sonic particularity is achieved through a variety of means.[61] His views are pertinent to the issues under review, and it will prove useful to proceed by highlighting several aspects of his discussion. Morris notes that only two of the forty-three sound events notated by Feldman are single tones – the second (F3) and the thirty-first (D1) – and that these are therefore highlighted.[62] The remainder are dyads and chords that are *wide* because the number of semitones from bottom to top – henceforth the *width* – is always large (19–64 semitones in this case).[63] These elements include multiple instances of every pitch class, but a considerable number of specific pitches are rare, meaning that they, when present, are also highlighted.[64]

Morris also reviews the intervallic spacing within chords, with similar results. Some 'spacing types' have multiple instances.[65] These include

[59] '*Last Pieces #3*', in DeLio (ed.), *The Music of Morton Feldman*, 39–68.   [60] 'Liner notes', 7.
[61] 'Aspects of performance practice in Morton Feldman's *Last Pieces*', presented at the Third Biennial International Conference on Twentieth-Century Music, University of Nottingham, 29 June 2003.
[62] *Ibid.*, 7.   [63] *Ibid.*   [64] *Ibid.*, 8.   [65] *Ibid.*, 9.

Example 8.1 *Last Pieces 1*, width and centre, by numbered sonority, and pitch contours of the outer voices

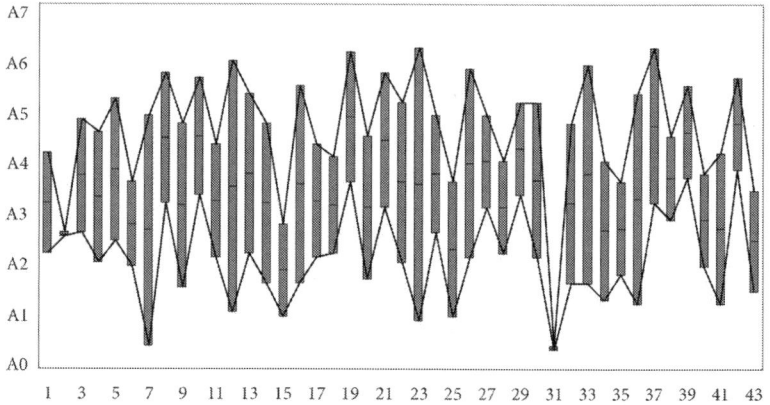

'overtone' spacing, in which intervals become narrower at the upper end of a chord, and 'barbell' spacing, in which two groups of neighbouring pitches are situated at the top and bottom of a chord with a wider interval between the two groups.[66] However, two spacing types stand out because they are uniquely represented: only one chord (the fourteenth sound event) has 'centred' spacing, with mirror symmetry around its centre, and only one (the seventh) has 'inverse-overtone' spacing, in which intervals between adjacent notes are narrower at the lower end of the chord.[67]

These factors highlight singular elements within the work as a whole, but Morris draws attention to others that imply a degree of local disjunction between adjacent events. For example, the pitch contours of the outer voices are noticeably discontinuous, thereby ensuring that adjacent events cannot be connected 'by anything like traditional voice-leading'.[68] Also, no two adjacent events have the same centre, where this is defined as the pitch or semitone dyad mid-way between the highest and lowest pitches.[69] We might add that non-adjacent events with identical centres are well dispersed and that this introduces a somewhat longer-range element of disjunction. Many of these elements are discernible in Example 8.1, which shows the pitch range and centre of each of the forty-three sonorities, presented in the order in which they occur, and the contours of the highest and lowest pitches.

Morris mentions the occasional use of fermatas and arpeggiation.[70] These also highlight specific sonorities, but given that durations are free, his focus is understandably on the pitch-related factors outlined above.

---

[66] *Ibid.*   [67] *Ibid.*   [68] *Ibid.*, 10.   [69] *Ibid.*, 9.   [70] *Ibid.*, 6–7.

Nonetheless, these elements also serve to highlight certain dyads and chords and thereby assist in promoting sonic particularity.

If Feldman intended us to see *Last Pieces* as an organised continuity in which a complex network of vertical and horizontal relationships are integral to the intended effect – as DeLio portrays *Last Pieces 3* – then it is a mystery how he could have expected a pianist to construct a similar degree of organisation spontaneously, during the course of playing *Atlantis*. Achieving a similar effect would surely involve superhuman mental dexterity or, alternatively, working out which notes to play in advance, and then playing from memory or a written-out version. If so, his preference for spontaneous note selection seems little more than wishful thinking.

The significance of the alternative to DeLio's view, outlined above, is not just that it suggests how a pianist performing *Atlantis* might decide which notes to play – namely, those that emphasise sonic particularity in the ways highlighted. They also suggest a possible answer to the question of how it might be feasible to make appropriate selections spontaneously during the course of a performance. This is because many of the highlighted features can be correlated with bodily aspects of the pianist – the width of a chord by the relative placement of the hands; its centre by the placement of the hands relative to the keyboard; the spacing type by the shape of each hand and their placement relative to one another; and the location of the outer voices by their shapes and positions. Consequently, achieving sonic particularity becomes amenable to a bodily approach to chord selection, with a constantly changing bodily configuration and placement relative to the keyboard generating a constantly varying succession of shapes and sizes of chords that differ markedly.

This approach is bound to produce a proliferation of intervallic relations, including consonances, within and between sonorities, but this is fully consistent with Feldman's known preferences, as discussed in the previous section. More importantly, consonances are common in *Last Pieces*, which is to serve as our model. For example, five of the forty-three sonorities in *Last Pieces 1* include at least one simultaneous octave and adjacent octaves are present in many more cases.[71]

With these points in mind, it is instructive to review the more conventionally notated insert at the end of the piano part in . . .*Out of 'Last Pieces'*, which Chapter 7 suggested may have been included as an indication of how the graphed elements should be played. This insert includes eleven sonorities: three single notes; three dyads; and five chords. As in *Last Pieces 1*, the

---

[71] Simultaneous octaves appear in the thirtieth, thirty-third, thirty-fourth, thirty-sixth and thirty-seventh sonorities.

Example 8.2   . . .*Out of 'Last Pieces'*, last page of piano part, width and centre, by numbered sonority, and pitch contours of the outer voices

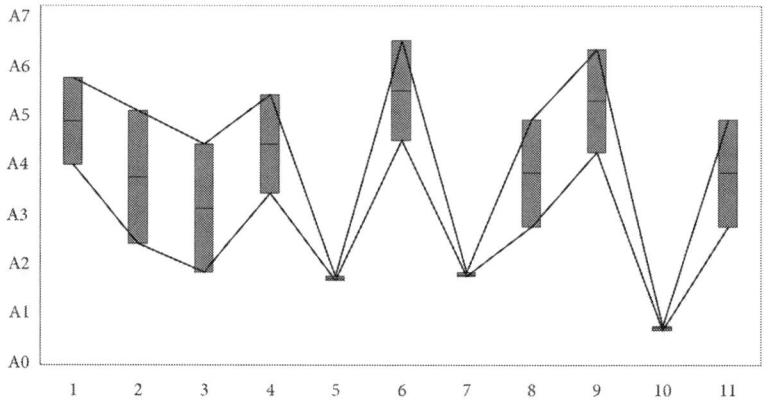

dyads and chords are all wide, with widths ranging from 21–32 semitones in this case. The three single notes are highlighted, not only by being single, but also by being the three lowest pitch notes in the insert.

There is no discernible pitch specificity. Every pitch class is represented, with D♯ and A most common and B and F occurring only once. Although many specific pitches are absent, this is attributable to the relatively small size of the sample, which includes only thirty-seven notes in total. No specific pitch appears in consecutive sonorities, but there are several adjacent octaves, and simultaneous octaves are present in two of the five chords. One chord is repeated, meaning that there are four distinct chord types, of varying shapes. Two have inverse overtone spacing, one is centred and one exhibits an approximately even distribution of notes within its span.

The high degree of disjunction between adjacent events is highlighted in Example 8.2. The centres of most adjacent sonorities are distant from one another and the contours of the outer voices are noticeably discontinuous, as in *Last Pieces 1*. Consequently, the intended message of the insert appears to be broadly similar to the one communicated by the reference to *Last Pieces* in the explanatory notes with *Atlantis*: the pianist should vary the shapes, sizes and keyboard locations of sonorities and their centres as a means of generating sonic particularity. However, the presence of a repeated chord clearly indicates that the sounds selected need not be unique within the context of the whole and that the pianist's primary objective should be to ensure a more restricted form of particularity that is applicable on a local level.

The importance of these observations for a pianist performing *Atlantis* or ...*Out of 'Last Pieces'* is clear, but my view is that they have wider implications within a study of Feldman's graph music because they strongly suggest that Feldman would have regarded local particularity as an appropriate aim for any performer, and not just the pianist.

Listening

Feldman explained his reasons for being dissatisfied with conventional notation in the late 1950s in the following passage:

> Between 1953 and 1958 the graph was abandoned. I felt that if the means were to be imprecise the result must be terribly clear. And I lacked that sense of clarity to go on. I hoped to find it in precise notation; i.e., *Extensions for Three Pianos*, etc. But precision did not work for me either. It was too one-dimensional. It was like painting a picture where at some place there is always a horizon. Working precisely, one always had to *generate* the movement – there was still not enough plasticity for me.[72]

These reservations are best understood in terms of an inability to predict aspects of the morphologies of actual sounds with sufficient accuracy. Feldman's aim was to create a natural sense of flow or movement by harnessing these morphologies, but the difficulty he faced was that the properties he hoped to use are, in practice, partially unpredictable. This is because they depend on contextual factors, such as the character of the instrument being played, the way in which the performer plays the instrument, properties of the performing space and prevailing atmospheric conditions.[73]

From this perspective, placing sounds relative to a regular pulse in conventional staff notation was tantamount to force-fitting unpredictable, potentially irregular elements into a contrived regularity, riding roughshod over aspects of their 'shape' that he wished to harness in creating a natural sense of flow; hence his comparison with the suffocating effect of traditional illusionistic methods of unifying an image by portraying spatial relationships within it from a single viewpoint. It was in this sense that he conceived of conventional notation as lacking what he termed 'plasticity', thereby forcing him to 'generate' movement, rather than allowing him to discover it in the sounds.

[72] 'Liner notes', 6. The *Extensions* for three pianos referred to is *Extensions 4* (1953).
[73] Feldman did not use the term 'morphology', which was favoured by Cage. However, he sometimes referred to the 'shape' ('...Out of "Last Pieces"', G) and 'proportions' of sounds ('Vertical Thoughts', 12).

The solution favoured by Feldman in 1957 was to reduce substantially the precision with which durations were specified in pieces with precisely notated pitches. Feldman said very little in print about how this was supposed to help, but his idea must have been that it would allow each individual performer to determine a rhythm that was tailored to the morphologies of sounds that he or she was producing.[74] If performers listened closely enough and were sufficiently sensitive to what they heard, then this would enable them to discover for themselves the natural sense of movement that he was seeking.

What was the link between morphology and movement that Feldman envisaged? This is not addressed directly in his surviving comments, but he sometimes made a suggestive comparison between the desired effect and 'breathing', which implies a slow, but continuous periodicity.[75] The account favoured here is that the 'breathing of the sound itself' was to derive from the periodic variation in the amplitude of a sequence of sounds from a single instrument each of which is allowed sufficient space for its decay to be heard – or, at least, to begin being heard – when they are presented as a contiguous series. The amplitude of each individual sound begins high or rises to a maximum level and subsequently fades away gradually. Consequently, a contiguous sequence generates a slowly undulating envelope of sound. It was these undulations, from low to high amplitude and gradually back to low amplitude, which I suggest typically underpinned the natural sense of movement that he was seeking.[76] For example, this conception is implicit in the notes provided with many of the works he produced in 1963, which generally included words to the effect that each instrument should enter when the preceding sound begins to fade. A virtue of this reading is that it connects the desired effect with his interest in the decay of sounds, which was something of a preoccupation in the 1960s.[77]

On this account, the role of listening in the performance of these pieces is clear enough, but to what extent is a similar idea in operation in his graph

---

[74] This implies a degree of spontaneity in any appropriately sensitive performance, which is consistent with the following remark about *Four Instruments* (1965) for chimes, piano, violin and cello: 'the actual duration between sounds is determined at the moment of playing by the performer' ('Four Instruments' [1965], in Friedman (ed.), *Give My Regards*, 20).

[75] For 'the breathing of the sound itself', see 'Vertical Thoughts', 13. Feldman suggested that sounds should 'breathe' in 'Conversation between Morton Feldman and Walter Zimmermann', 56.

[76] Interpreted this way, Feldman's idea exemplifies one that Fritz Winckel once described as intentionally making use of 'inner generative powers for the flow of a series of tones' (*Music, Sound and Sensation*, 41).

[77] For a representative statement, see 'The Anxiety of Art', 25.

music? It is true that all the graphs from the *Intersections* onwards allow performers some latitude in deciding where to enter, but the degree of flexibility made available is generally limited, and it is not credible to suggest that he had a similar idea in mind, in my view. For example, in *Intersection 3* the pulse is set at 176 ictuses per minute and there are few sounds that extend over more than one ictus, whereas in *Atlantis* most instruments are regularly asked to play several, and sometimes many, sounds per ictus at a tempo of 92 ictuses per minute. Plainly, these performers will have insufficient freedom to tailor the placement of their sounds to generate the effect of an undulating sequence.

The previous section argued that Feldman wished for sonic particularity in performances of his graph music, but it is clear that total disjunction, which is readily imparted by surrounding any sound with long silences, was not the effect that he intended. His earliest writings reveal a desire for 'natural fluidity', suggesting that consecutive sounds were meant to be heard as connected with one another in sequential groups, and we have seen that there is reason to believe that he hoped for – and, based on the evidence of the available recordings, achieved – a 'flowing' effect in his later graph music. Therefore, the suggestion made here is that it was a delicate balance between sonic particularity, on the one hand, and sequential grouping, on the other, that Feldman intended performers to aim for through a concentrated focus on the sounds being produced.

Evidently, the work involved in ensuring fluidity or flow will depend upon the extent of the differences between consecutive sounds as well as other factors, including their inter-onset intervals. In a performance in which sounds are chosen spontaneously, the extent of these differences is not pre-planned. Hence, the means necessary to ensure that they are grouped with one another in the listening experience – which may involve nuances of timing and dynamics, and instrument-specific playing methods – cannot be anticipated; they can only be ascertained by listening while playing.

9 Tudor's performances

Analysis of Tudor's performances is facilitated by his habit of filling in some of the indeterminate elements left open by Feldman in annotations on scores or in fully fledged written-out versions. These items reveal aspects of his approach that would be difficult to discern from the available recordings of him playing. The following discussion is highly selective, focusing only on some of its more surprising aspects, which challenge a straightforward reading of Feldman's notation and, in some cases, support or contradict the account of his non-notated preferences presented in Chapter 8.

Pitch selections in the piano *Intersections*

Tudor's papers at the Getty Research Institute include a more conventionally notated version of *Intersection 3* in his handwriting.[1] This lacks time signatures and bar lines but is otherwise complete, with pitches and durations fully notated on staves. Tudor's version is not dated, but it is distinctly possible that it was prepared in advance of the first performance, which Tudor gave on 28 April 1954, and that he played from this version, not Feldman's graph score, on that occasion. For reasons that will become clear later in this chapter, it is highly likely that he played from his more conventionally notated version on the only two occasions on which his performances were recorded. Although it is possible that he prepared his more conventionally notated version after the first performance, but before the recordings were made, there is no evidence to suggest that this is likely.

John Holzaepfel maintains not only that Tudor played from his written-out version of *Intersection 3* at the premiere, but also that this was the very first time that Tudor had approached any composer's music this way; consequently, it was an important turning point in his career, because he went on to approach many other works in a similar fashion.[2] Holzaepfel remarked in passing that Tudor's materials blur Feldman's

---

[1] David Tudor Papers, Getty Research Institute.
[2] *David Tudor and the Performance of American Experimental Music*, 78, and 'Painting by numbers: the *Intersections* of Morton Feldman and David Tudor', in Johnson (ed.), *The New York Schools*, 161.

indications of high, middle and low.[3] This section takes a closer look at this phenomenon, which is apparent in Examples 9.1–9.4 and Table 9.1. Each example corresponds to one of the four pages in the published edition of Feldman's score and shows the range of Tudor's pitch selections for each register by ictus. Table 9.1 lists the ranges he used by page and in aggregate.[4]

In many places, a single cell in Feldman's graph score includes two numbers, one placed above the other. Clearly, both numbers were intended to designate sounds in the same register and this is how these split cells have been treated in preparing the data. Two additional conventions observed in preparing Examples 9.1–9.4 are that grace notes in Tudor's written-out version are presented as crotchets, both in terms of duration and placement relative to the pulse, and that the range of pitches associated with a sound of longer duration is allocated to each ictus during which Tudor's materials indicate it is to occur.

An initial observation is that Tudor used pitch ranges that are consistent with the ordinary meanings of the terms 'high', 'middle' and 'low', that is to say, broadly in accordance with a division of the piano's compass into three parts each containing an equal number of semitones, shown with horizontal lines in Examples 9.1–9.4. Also evident is the overlap between his selections in adjacent registers, with those for middle and low overlapping in a range two semitones wide (D3–E3) and those for middle and high overlapping in a range that extends over nine semitones (C♯5–B♭5).

A similar pattern, not noted by Holzaepfel, is discernible in an incomplete version of *Intersection 2*, which is also among Tudor's papers. The presentation of these materials is similar to that of the written-out version of *Intersection 3*, although those for the earlier work are laid out within bars, with most columns in the published edition equivalent to one bar in the written-out version. When and why these materials were created is not clear, but their incomplete state argues against them having been used in

---

[3] David Tudor and the Performance of American Experimental Music, 72–3, and 'Painting by numbers', 166–7.

[4] Tudor specified alternative pitch selections in two places. At ictus 238, only the selection that is presented as primary is included. At ictus 351, he specified one selection in the high register and two possible selections in the middle register. Neither of his middle register selections contains the correct number of notes, and neither is included. Four other selections (ictus 140, middle register; ictus 235, middle and low registers; ictus 351, middle register; and ictus 360, high register) are excluded because they are difficult to reconcile with Feldman's indications. The regular division given in Table 9.1 partitions the piano's pitch range into parts containing an equal number of semitones.

Example 9.1   *Intersection 3*, pitch ranges specified by Tudor in connection with page 1 of the published edition, by ictus

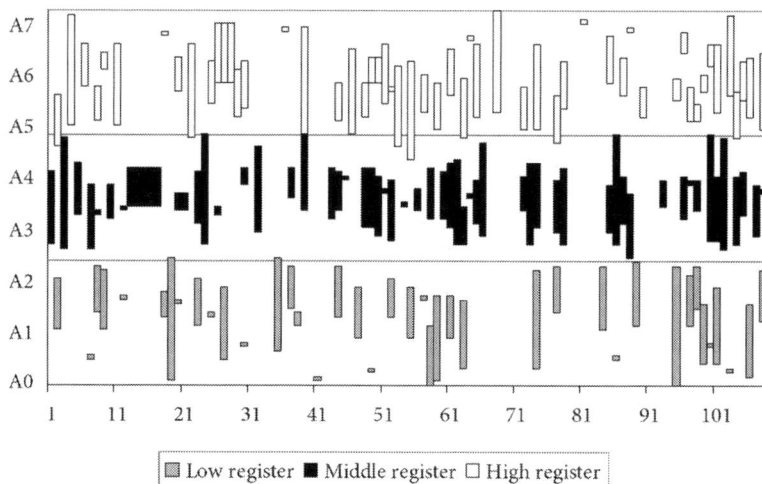

Example 9.2   *Intersection 3*, pitch ranges specified by Tudor in connection with page 2 of the published edition, by ictus

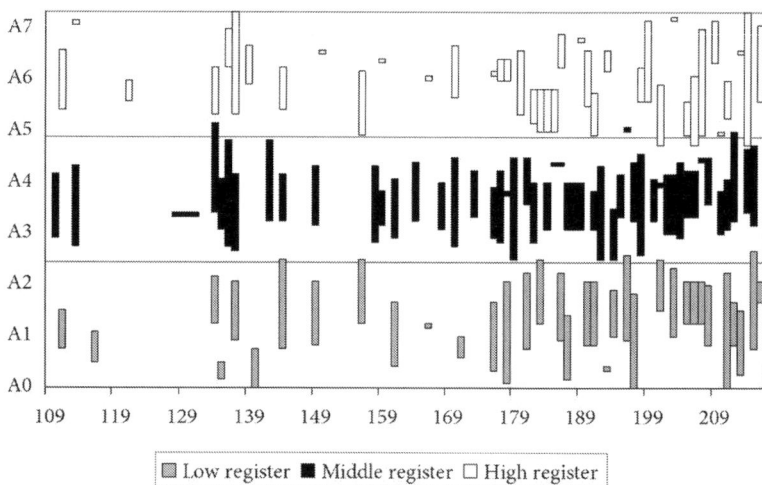

Example 9.3 *Intersection 3*, pitch ranges specified by Tudor in connection with page 3 of the published edition, by ictus

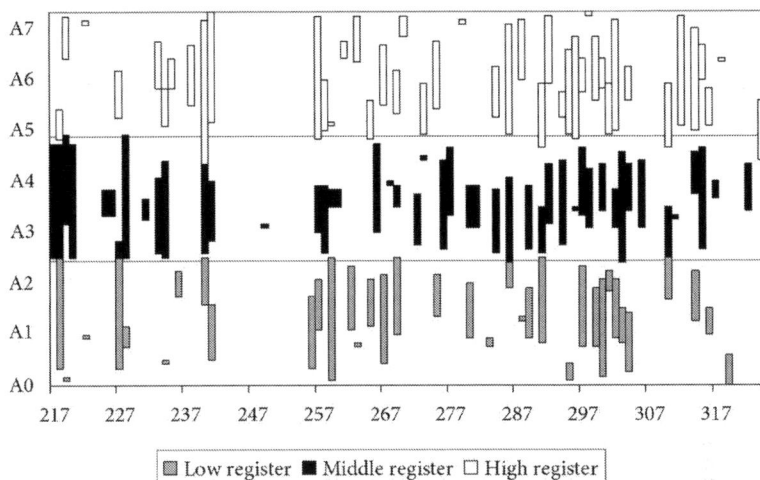

Example 9.4 *Intersection 3*, pitch ranges specified by Tudor in connection with page 4 of the published edition, by ictus

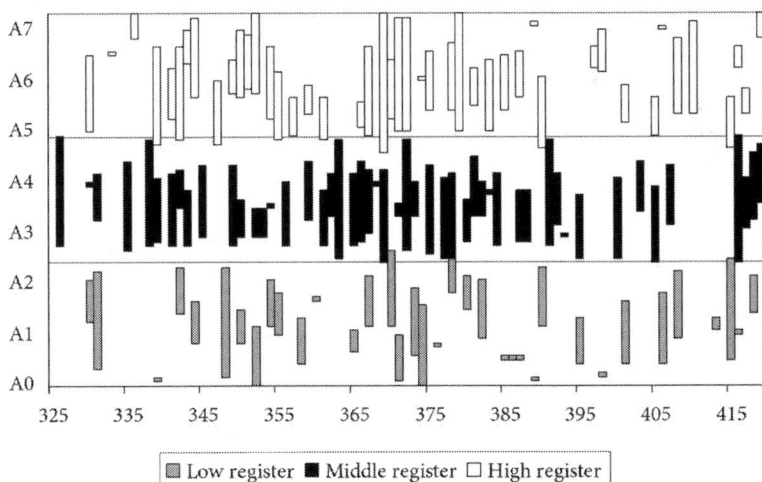

Table 9.1. *Intersection 3, pitch ranges specified by Tudor, by register and by page of the published edition of Feldman's score*

	p1	p2	p3	p4	pp1–4	pp1–4 (s/tones)	Regular division
High	D5–C8	F♯5–C8	C♯5–C8	E5–C8	C♯5–C8	35	G♯5/A5–C8
Middle	D♯3–G5	D♯3–B♭5	D3–G5	D3–G5	D3–B♭5	32	D3/D♯3–G5/G♯5
Low	A0–D3	A0–E3	A0–D3	A0–E3	A0–E3	31	A0–C♯3/D3

performance.[5] In the late 1970s, Tudor sought funding for a project titled 'Documentation and annotation of 90 musical compositions by 22 composers performed 1950–1970 by David Tudor', and it is possible that he began preparing a written-out version of *Intersection 2* in connection with this; Feldman's name was on the list of the twenty-two composers in question.[6]

Despite this uncertainty, Tudor's incomplete version is of considerable interest. This is because his selections, like those he made in connection with *Intersection 3*, blur Feldman's indications of register. Feldman's score extends over eleven pages and Tudor's selections are too numerous to present in full. However, the blurring is apparent in Example 9.5, which shows the range of Tudor's pitch selections by register and ictus on the first page of the published edition.[7] Table 9.2 lists the pitch ranges Tudor used by page and in aggregate.[8]

In this case, Tudor used pitch ranges less evidently in accordance with the ordinary meanings of the terms 'high', 'middle' and 'low'. Indeed, in

[5] Although it is possible that Tudor left sections incomplete to facilitate spontaneous decision-making while playing, the character of the omissions, which do not always correspond with more straightforward passages in Feldman's score, argues against this.

[6] David Tudor to John Simon Guggenheim Memorial Foundation, 1 October 1979, David Tudor Papers, Getty Research Institute. Holzaepfel, who drew my attention to this document, has suggested that Tudor may have worked on his version of *Intersection 2* in the late 1950s ('Painting by numbers', 169), but the evidence he cites is not compelling.

[7] Tudor specified an extra note at ictuses 47 and 108. In both cases, the range recorded in Example 9.5 encompasses all the notes that he specified. He regularly presented alternative selections above and below those on the printed staves and these are excluded. Other conventions are identical to those used in preparing Examples 9.1–9.4.

[8] Sometimes, Tudor specified one too many notes, or one too few: the ranges used in preparing the table encompass all notes specified in these cases. Occasionally, his selections are more difficult to reconcile with Feldman's notation (ictus 684, middle register; ictus 1,099, high register; and ictus 1,204, high and middle registers) and these are not included. As before, the regular division indicated in the table partitions the piano's pitch range into parts containing an equal number of semitones.

Example 9.5 *Intersection 2*, pitch ranges specified by Tudor in connection with page 1 of the published edition, by ictus

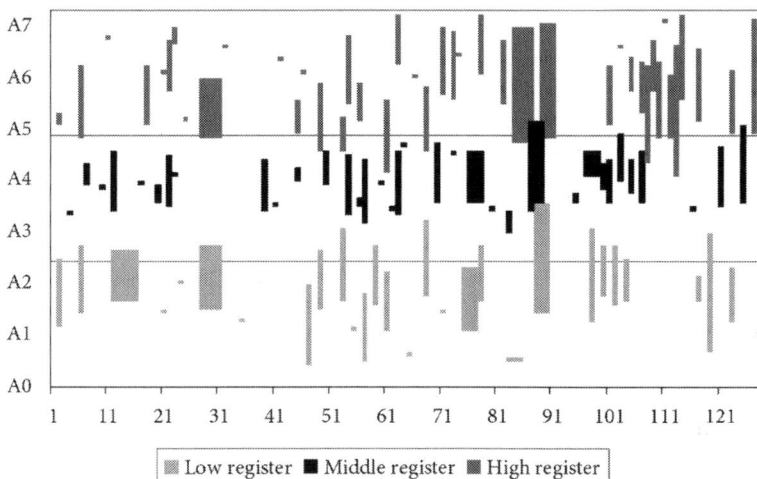

Table 9.2. Intersection 2, *pitch ranges specified by Tudor, by register and by page of the published edition of Feldman's score*

	p1	p2	p3	p4	p5	p6	p7
High	B♭4–B7	E5–C8	D5–B7	G♯5–B7	G♯5–C8	F♯5–C8	C5–B♭7
Middle	A3–B♭5	E3–C6	F♯3–C6	D♯3–G♯5	F♯3–F5	A3–D6	B♭3–C6
Low	D1–D♯4	B♭0–B♭3	D♯1–B♭3	D1–F3	C1–B3	D1–B3	D♯1–F♯4

	p8	p9	p10	p11	pp1–11 (s/tones)	pp1–11	Regular division
High	B5–G7	C5–B♭7	D♯5–A7	D5–B7	B♭4–C8	39	G♯5/A5–C8
Middle	G3–F♯5	G3–G5	A3–D5	G♯3–C5	D♯3–D6	36	D3/D♯3–G5/G♯5
Low	F♯1–G♯3	D1–B♭3	B0–F3	D1–A3	B♭0–F♯4	45	A1–C♯3/D3

some places, such as ictuses 88–90, in which he specified a pitch higher than middle C for use in a low register chord, there are significant discrepancies. Also, his ranges overlap to a greater extent. This is particularly noticeable in his choice of pitches for several extended sounds in ictuses 83–91.

Blurring boundaries between registers cannot have been what Feldman envisioned, and to see why, it will be helpful to begin by reflecting on the everyday use of the terms 'high', 'middle' and 'low'. These terms – like 'young', 'middle-aged' and 'old' – are vague, that is, there are borderline cases in which there is no definite answer to the question of whether or not they apply.[9] No doubt this is why Feldman used them. His idea was to give the performer room to sharpen his indications; hence his comment in the explanatory remarks with the published editions of the earliest graphs that the limits of his indicated pitch ranges may be 'freely chosen' by the performer.[10]

Although Feldman gave no other guidance about how the terms 'high', 'middle' and 'low' are to be interpreted, this does not mean that performers have free rein. His labels carry absolute connotations that he must have expected them to observe: 'high', 'middle' and 'low' are not merely relative terms. For example, the performer is not free to set all three ranges in what would ordinarily be regarded as the high register of the instrument, just as it would be incorrect to classify everybody as young. If Feldman had meant his indications to be understood as merely relative, he would surely have labelled them differently or explained that this was the case in his written remarks.[11]

The vagueness of Feldman's terminology means that it may be appropriate to classify a pitch differently in different contexts. For example, G$\sharp$5 could legitimately be classified as a high register piano note in some contexts and a middle register piano note in others. However, it would be wrong to classify G$\sharp$5 as both a high register note and a middle register note within the same context, just as it would be wrong to describe a fifty-year-old as both middle-aged and old. Based only on these observations, we can conclude that Tudor's approach, which permitted certain pitches to be classified as both low and middle or as both middle and high, was inconsistent with Feldman's notation. This is because there is no reason – other than the fact that Tudor proceeded as he did – for thinking that the register indications given in the scores are to be applied consistently only within subdivisions of the scores.

The mutually exclusive character of Feldman's register indications is implied by his layout, which utilises a single horizontal row of cells per register and a consistent placement of rows relative to one another within systems, with his high and middle register indications always above those for the middle and low registers, respectively. The idea that the pitch of a middle register selection might be higher than that of a high register selection or lower than that of a low register selection fits unnaturally

---

[9] Other comparable classifications are: 'short', 'medium height' and 'tall'; and 'child', 'adolescent' and 'adult'. For an alternative to the standard view of vague statements, assumed in the main text, as neither true nor false, see Timothy Williamson, *Vagueness* (Oxford: Routledge, 1994).

[10] See those with the graphs that pre-date *Intersection 2*.

[11] As noted in Chapter 3, an alternative set of labels that lacks absolute connotations is: 'higher'; intermediate (or 'root' or 'basis'); and 'lower'.

with this presentation in which the organisation of the vertical axis obviously reflects an ordering by pitch.

The precedent of conventional staff notation, which involves a rigid ordering by pitch along the vertical axis of a staff, reinforces the conviction that this is how Feldman's notation should be read. True, the significance of vertical location within a staff can be altered by a change of clef, but this requires an explicit indication that the clef has changed. Consequently, it is only natural that Feldman would have expected his alternative presentation to be read similarly. Had he intended something else, he would have known that this needed to be explained. The only legitimate course is to assume that a similarly rigid ordering by pitch was expected, contrary to Tudor's interpretation.

Contrast the case of split cells with upper and lower parts, which are most naturally read as signalling a mutually exclusive work-wide division between higher and lower pitches within the given register. In their case, Feldman's written remarks with the published editions of *Intersections 2–3* state that '[w]here there are two numbers for one register any part of the register can be used'. Precisely what Feldman had in mind when he wrote these words is not clear, but it is certain that he intended to subvert the most natural reading of this aspect of his notation. The fact that he did so here, but did not qualify his coarser divisions, strongly suggests that they should be interpreted in the most natural way – that is, as mutually exclusive.

This reading of Feldman's presentation is also supported by a review of the written remarks that he did provide; although it is unclear which, if any, of these Tudor would have seen, they represent the clearest available evidence of Feldman's intent. Those with the published editions of *Intersections 2–4* state that '[e]ach system is notated vertically as regards pitch: high, middle, low', which indicates that the vertical axis is being used to specify an ordering by pitch. Although Feldman's wording restricts the scope of his exposition to '[e]ach system' (i.e. to each grid frame), it is highly unlikely that he intended his pitch ranges to be applied consistently only within individual systems and very probable that he intended them to be held fixed. A survey of Feldman's sketches and autograph scores reveals that in some cases, including *Intersection 4*, he varied the number of ictuses per system, often in response to the size or orientation of the pages he used, which strongly suggests that the width of each system was not integral to the meaning of his notation.[12] Moreover, in many graphs, including

---

[12] One of the two surviving sketches of *Intersection 4* consists of pages presented in portrait orientation, with twenty ictuses per system (Morton Feldman Collection, Paul Sacher Foundation). The published edition consists of pages presented in landscape orientation, with forty ictuses per system.

Example 9.6 *Intersection 3*, mid-point of the pitch ranges specified by Tudor in connection with page 1 of the published edition, by ictus

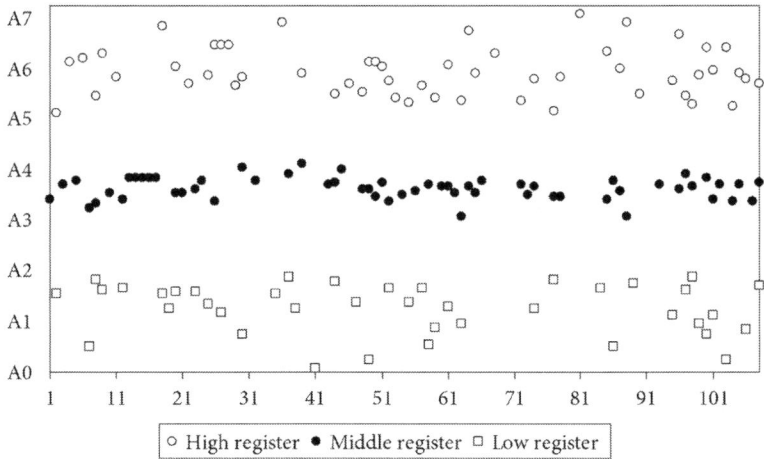

Intersection 2, symbols straddle systems and some indication of how to deal with these would have been needed if performers were free to reinterpret register indications between systems, but none was given.

Additional evidence is provided by the following statement, which appears in the written remarks that accompany all the graphs composed before *Intersection 2*: 'relative pitch (high, middle, low) is indicated'. If Feldman had envisaged overlapping pitch ranges, then this statement can be true only if interpreted as restricted in scope, as applying to each individual ictus or within sections. We have no reason to read it this way other than the fact that Tudor proceeded as he did. If the note is read literally, as a general statement applying within and between ictuses, then overlapping ranges are precluded.

Several interpretative strategies would account for Tudor's error. One is that he interpreted Feldman's register indications incorrectly as applying to entire sonorities. If so, then what counted in his mind would have been some measure of the overall pitch of a sonority, such as the mean or median pitch of its component notes or the mid-point of the pitch range over which it extends. If this were permissible, then the performer would be entitled to include a pitch h in a high register chord H that is below a pitch m in a middle register chord M, provided that H is higher pitched than M. Example 9.6 shows the mid-points of the pitch ranges Tudor specified in connection with page 1 of the published edition of *Intersection 3*. Evidently, the degree of separation between registers is greater than in Example 9.1.

Only in one place, at ictus 196, in which Feldman specified one middle register sound (plus nine in the low register), is there overlap. For the middle register component Tudor notated A5, so the mid-point pitch for this selection must also be A5. However, at ictus 210 he used G♯5 in connection with Feldman's indication of a single high register sound, and at ictus 324 he used (D5–D♯6), with a mid-point between G♯5 and A5, for a group of eight notes in the high register. This minimal overlap cannot be eliminated by selecting an alternative measure of overall pitch because two of the data points concern single pitches; hence it would have to be seen as a local error in execution.[13]

Even if Tudor proceeded this way, it would not have excused his choices. To begin with, this reading has unpalatable implications. For example, if the mid-point of the range of pitches present in a sonority determines its register, then the dyad (A0, C8) will count as in the middle register, as will the chord (A0, E4, C8), which will also be deemed middle if the register of a chord is determined by its mean or median pitch. Neither would ordinarily be regarded as having a definite register. Furthermore, although it is true that this reading is consistent with Feldman's statements cited above, it is inconsistent with others, which clearly indicate that his specifications of register apply to individual notes. For example, the written remarks with the published editions of the graphs that immediately preceded *Intersection 2* include the statement that '[a]ny *tone* within the ranges indicated may be sounded'.[14] It follows that a reading that focuses on the overall pitch of a sonority is inconsistent with Feldman's notation.

Other interpretative strategies would account for Tudor's recourse to overlapping pitch ranges: one sees him consistently applying a set of overlapping ranges whereas another sees him working with a set of mutually exclusive ranges that he periodically reformulated. Most probably, Tudor adopted the latter course. As will become clear, there can be little doubt that this hypothesis has the greatest explanatory power. Holzaepfel described Tudor's reading of Feldman's register indications as 'mobile',[15] suggesting that he also interpreted Tudor as proceeding in this manner.

If Tudor applied a set of mutually exclusive ranges that he periodically reformulated, how frequently did he reformulate them? An initial thought

---

[13] The merits of interpreting Tudor's approach to *Intersection 2* in this way are similar. Once again, there is only one place (ictus 665) in which Tudor's selections would have to be seen as in error.

[14] Emphasis added. This statement appears in the written remarks with the published editions of *Projection 4*, *Intersection 1* and *Marginal Intersection*. A similar statement appears in the published edition of *Projection 5*.

[15] *David Tudor and the Performance of American Experimental Music*, 72–3, and 'Painting by numbers', 166–7.

is that he may have interpreted Feldman's indications of register as mutually exclusive only within systems. This can be tested because Tudor's papers include the materials that he must have worked from when producing his version of *Intersection 3*. The original manuscript of the graph score that Feldman presented to him has seven systems, with the first extending to ictus 64, whereas a copy in Tudor's own handwriting has eleven systems, with the first extending to ictus 39. A glance at Example 9.1 reveals that Tudor's pitch selections overlap within the first thirty-nine ictuses. Indeed, the first instance of overlap occurs very early on, between ictuses 2 and 3. This argues against him having systematically divided the score into sections within which he treated Feldman's indications of pitch as mutually exclusive.

Tudor's papers do not include a copy of Feldman's score of *Intersection 2*. However, the first page of Feldman's original presentation and the published edition in Cage's handwriting both include forty-three ictuses per system;[16] consequently, it is safe to assume that Tudor worked with a score organised in this fashion. This looks significant because the complex series of overlapping pitch ranges used in ictuses 83–91, evident in Example 9.5, correspond to materials that straddle the boundary between the second and third systems. Even so, the overlap cannot be accounted for in this way. For example, Tudor's middle register selection at ictuses 87–9 (D4–B♭5) overlaps several of his high register selections elsewhere in this same system, including G5–A7 at ictuses 89–91. It also overlaps his low register selection at ictuses 88–90 (D2–D♯4), which in its turn cuts across his middle register selection in the same system at ictus 116 (D4). There are, in addition, many other comparable overlaps within systems elsewhere in his version.

A more credible account of Tudor's choices emerges from a review of his thinking on musical continuity. In 1972, he explained that his 'musical perception' changed in 1950–1 while he was preparing to perform Boulez's *Deuxième Sonate* and then Cage's *Music of Changes*:

> The Boulez was where I learned I really had to change the way I thought about musical continuity, and that you don't necessarily go on in a linear progression. When I came to the Cage I had to work on the moment-to-moment differences. *Music of Changes* was a great discipline, because you can't do it unless you're ready for anything at each instant. You can't carry over any emotional impediments, though at the same time you have to be ready to accept them each instant, as they arise. [. . .] I had to learn how to be able to

---

[16] The first page of Feldman's original presentation is reproduced in [Unsigned: G], *Selections*, 127.

Example 9.7   *Intersection 2*, ictuses 345–54

cancel my consciousness of any previous moment, in order to be able to produce the next one.[17]

These events pre-date Tudor's written-out versions of *Intersections 2–3*, but the suggestion made here is that he was thinking along similar lines while working on them, relying on only loosely defined notions of the pitch ranges he would use for each register as he worked through the scores. These notions were imprecise, but broadly consistent with everyday uses of the terms 'high', 'middle' and 'low' in most cases, and they were crystallised over and over again as he reformulated his choices while self-consciously seeking to avoid being influenced by his previous selections, resulting in differences of detail between his ranges.

In case the reader remains unconvinced that this practice was inappropriate, it may be helpful to review its implications in a passage like the one shown in Example 9.7. It is easy to imagine changes to the applicable pitch ranges immediately before and after the high register selections are played that would result in these being allocated lower pitches than the surrounding middle register selections, thereby imposing a progression in pitch that is inconsistent with the evidently intended contour.

The extent of the overlap between the pitch ranges used by Tudor, quantified in Tables 9.1–9.2, gives one measure of the extent of his deviation from the type of interpretation implied by Feldman's notation and explanations, as outlined above. Calculating the minimum number of ictuses in which his pitch selections would need to be altered in order to produce a rigid demarcation between ranges gives another. In the case of *Intersection 3*, this figure (35) equals 11 per cent of the total number of ictuses in which activity is indicated whereas the corresponding figure for *Intersection 2* (74) is equal to 13 per cent of the total number of ictuses in

---

[17] 'From piano to electronics', 24. See also 'David Tudor: interview with Peter Dickinson', 90–1. Elsewhere, Tudor explained that the change in his thinking about musical continuity was triggered by reading Antonin Artaud's *The Theatre and its Double* ('Composing the performer: David Tudor remembers Stefan Wolpe', interview by Austin Clarkson, *Musicworks*, no. 73 (Spring 1999), 31). For a discussion, see Eric Smigel, 'Recital hall of cruelty: Antonin Artaud, David Tudor, and the 1950s avant-garde', *Perspectives of New Music*, vol. 45, no. 2 (Summer 2007), 171–202.

which Tudor's materials include selections. In neither case, on either measure, is the degree of deviation insignificant.

Selecting pitches in advance of performing *Intersection 3*

Tudor must have known that Feldman originally conceived of performers taking any decisions left to them spontaneously as they played. He must also have known that this was not a superficial aspect of Feldman's thinking about his graphs, but that it was, for reasons discussed in Chapters 4 and 8, central to his conception of them at this time. Consequently, we can justly assume that by playing from his written-out version of *Intersection 3* he was knowingly acting contrary to Feldman's wishes.

Feldman alluded to the mismatch between his initial conception of how his graph music was to be performed and Tudor's approach in a 1963 interview in which he stated that 'while David will "realize" a Bussotti score, or a John Cage score (say the imperfections on the paper), in the early days I never really felt that there was any realization involved'.[18] I read these remarks as referring to Tudor's practice of preparing a written-out version from which he would play, in which case their gist is that early in his career he had not regarded this type of approach as either necessary or appropriate. Brown was more forthright in his assessment of Tudor's working methods. In a monologue recorded in 1970, he stated that Tudor's method of preparing a conventionally notated version of *Four Systems* 'didn't interest' him,[19] and elsewhere he stated that he 'didn't want that'.[20] He also recalled Feldman being uncomfortable with Tudor's general procedure,[21] as noted in Chapter 8.

In a liner note for an LP record devoted to Feldman's music issued in 1959, Frank O'Hara wrote of *Intersection 3* as follows:

> Feldman here successfully avoids the symbolic aspect of sound which has so plagued the abstract works of his contemporaries by employing unpredictability reinforced by spontaneity [. . .] the actual notes heard must come from the performer's response to the musical situation. [. . .] Where a virtuoso work places technical demands upon the performer, a Feldman piece seeks to engage his improvisatory collaboration, with its call on musical creativity as well as interpretative understanding. The performance on this record is proof of how beautifully this can all work out; yet, the performer could doubtless find other beauties in *Intersection III* [*sic*] on another occasion.[22]

---

[18] 'Around Morton Feldman', 2.   [19] E. Brown, 'On December 1952', 8–9.

[20] 'Earle Brown and Frans von Rossum', April 1990.   [21] *Ibid.*

[22] 'New directions in music: Morton Feldman' [1959], in Friedman (ed.), *Give My Regards*, 213.

O'Hara was a close friend of Feldman's,[23] and it is likely that his comments, which emphasise the performer's spontaneous response to Feldman's graph notation and the resulting differences between performances, were fully aligned with Feldman's own views at this time. This is ironic given that the recording of *Intersection 3* is of Tudor playing his written-out version.[24]

One tell-tale sign of this is an audible defect in Tudor's performance at ictus 282, which coincides with a page turn – between the third and fourth pages – in his written-out version. Feldman's score indicates a pause of one ictus, equivalent to one-third of a second at the given tempo, but the recording includes a much longer pause, 2.5 seconds in length.[25] A recording made subsequently by Tudor includes a different defect in exactly the same place.[26] In this case, the pause lasts one second and the immediately preceding sonority, which the score indicates should be no more than two ictuses or two-thirds of a second in length, is held for 2.5 seconds.[27] The conclusion that he was playing from his written-out version is corroborated by a comparison between his pitch selections on these recordings,[28] which are very similar not only to one another, but also to those that he had written out. This establishes that he played the same written-out version in both recording sessions.

The fact that Tudor's papers do not include a written-out version of *Intersection 2* that is complete suggests that he performed this particular work from Feldman's graph score, selecting values for the indeterminate elements left open by Feldman spontaneously during the course of his performance. Why, then, did he ignore Feldman's wishes and prepare a more conventionally notated version of *Intersection 3*? Tudor's own testimony suggests that his approach in the early 1950s was always to read from the composer's notation where possible,[29] and various sources attest to his

[23] Morton Feldman, 'Frank O'Hara: lost times and future hopes' [1972], in *Give My Regards*, 103–8.

[24] This recording, made in New York City in late 1958 or early 1959, was issued on *New Directions in Music 2/Morton Feldman*.

[25] This pause begins at 1'43.5" on the recording.

[26] This subsequent recording was made for radio broadcast in Germany in 1959 and appears on *Morton Feldman*, Edition RZ, ed. RZ 1010.

[27] This sonority begins at 1'55.5" on the recording.

[28] This is assisted by the Sonic Visualiser software developed at the Centre for Digital Music at Queen Mary, University of London, with the MATCH Vamp plugin, developed by Simon Dixon. This combination correlates a selected element of one recording with the corresponding element of one or more other recordings of the same work. For an outline of the software, see Chris Cannam, Christian Landone and Mark Sandler, 'Sonic Visualiser: an open source application for viewing, analysing, and annotating music audio files', *Proceedings of the ACM Multimedia 2010 International Conference* (New York: Association for Computing Machinery, 2010), 1467–8.

[29] 'Reminiscences of a twentieth-century pianist: an interview with David Tudor', by John Holzaepfel, *The Musical Quarterly*, vol. 78, no. 3 (Autumn 1994), 633.

exceptional proficiency as a sight reader.[30] This suggests that he was unable to produce a satisfactory rendition by making his selections during performances in this case, meaning that writing out his selections was a *sine qua non* of performing the work in a manner that he regarded as satisfactory.

Although both piano *Intersections* present the performer with a plethora of choices, the density of activity specified in *Intersection 3* is much higher than in *Intersection 2*, as noted in Chapter 1. Performing *Intersection 2* at the tempos given in the published edition involves depressing six keys per second on average but the corresponding figure for *Intersection 3* is a staggering twenty-three keys per second. This makes *Intersection 3* the more difficult of the two works to perform and explains why Tudor may have felt forced to approach them differently. Whether the issue he confronted in attempting to play spontaneously was an inability to produce a sufficiently accurate rendition or discomfort with some other aspect of the resulting sound is not documented. Frank Denyer has suggested that '[b]ecause of the very high [...] note densities Feldman has specified [in *Intersections 3–4*], it is no longer feasible for the performer to even consider choosing the notes spontaneously during the performance, and other strategies become necessary';[31] another possibility is that Tudor was unable to avoid clichéd selections or others he deemed inappropriate.[32]

Playing chords in *Ixion* for two pianos

Tudor's papers include an incomplete version, in his handwriting, of one of the two piano parts of *Ixion* for two pianos. His presentation utilises four staves per system, with two systems containing consecutive material on each page. Systems are subdivided into bars, with each bar equivalent to one column in Feldman's score. The first page of Tudor's version is shown in Figure 9.1.[33]

In the first stave in each system, Tudor reproduced Feldman's tripartite indications from the first of the two piano parts, whereas in the fourth stave he included the similarly structured indications from the second piano part. Sandwiched between these elements, on the second and third staves, is Tudor's written-out version of the materials presented in the

[30] Harold C. Schonberg, 'The far-out pianist', *Harper's Magazine*, June 1960, 50.

[31] 'Feldman's search for the ecstasy of the moment', 7.

[32] Martin Iddon has speculated that 'his hands naturally fell into familiar patterns, which prevented anything unexpected happening, from his perspective' (*John Cage and David Tudor*, 60).

[33] 'Tudor's realization of Morton Feldman's piece Ixion, page 1, 1960', David Tudor Papers, 1884–1998 bulk 1940–96, Getty Research Institute, Los Angeles (980039).

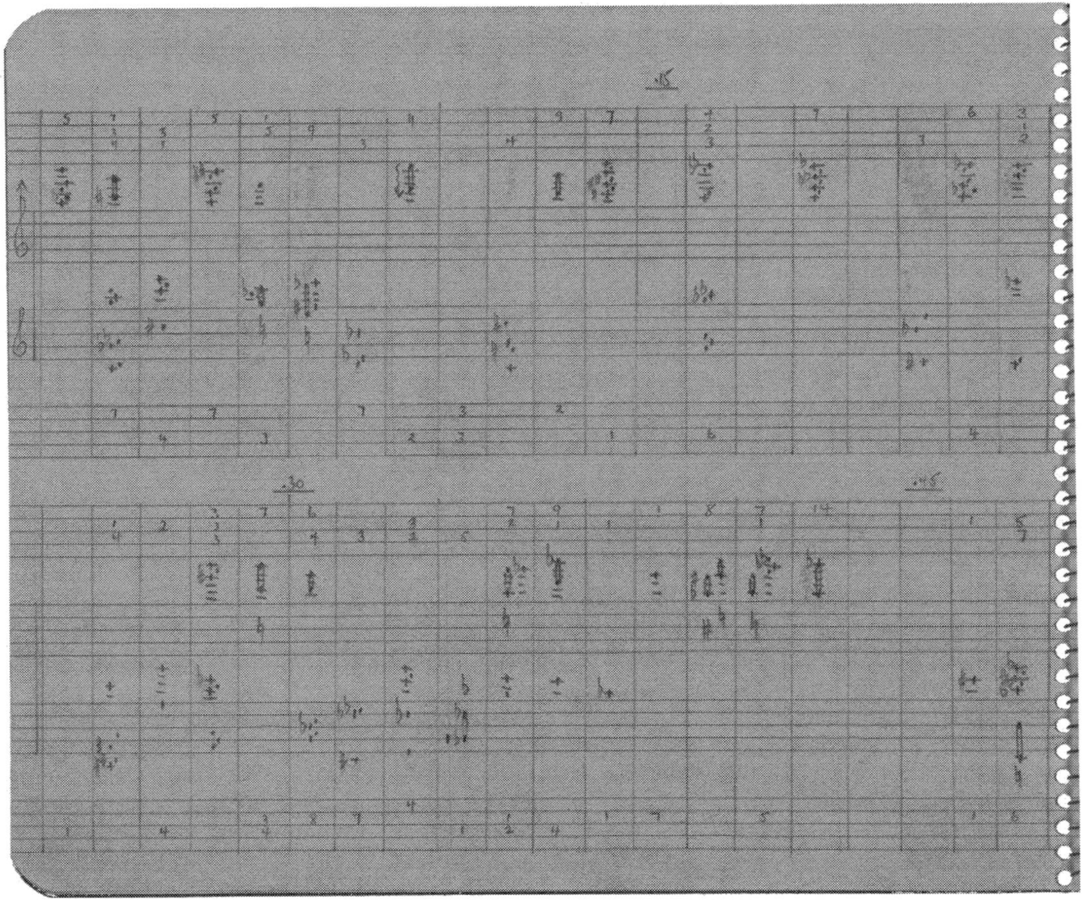

Figure 9.1 *Ixion* for two pianos, Tudor's written-out version, page 1

first stave. A written-out version of those presented in the fourth stave is not included.

The first ten systems, which correspond to somewhat less than one-third of Feldman's score, are complete. The eleventh and twelfth systems both include some written-out materials, but they also include empty bars, apparently awaiting entries. In the next eight systems, only Feldman's tripartite indications appear. Even these disappear in the twenty-first system, leaving nothing but pre-ruled bars, awaiting entries, thereafter.

The second stave in each system is preceded by a treble clef with an upward arrow drawn through it to signal *8va sopra*, whereas the third stave is preceded by a conventional treble clef. This labelling may appear odd given that Feldman's tripartite indications in previous graphs specify not only high and middle but also low register pitches. However, in *Ixion* for two pianos, they cannot be interpreted this way because labelling elsewhere in the score indicates that all pitches are in the high register except in a central section in which low registers are to be used. Consequently, in this work, his tripartite indications specify a subdivision of the pitch spectrum within a coarser bipartite division between high and low registers, as previously noted.

Tudor's written-out materials do not extend as far as the low register section, so they deal exclusively with subdivisions of the pitch spectrum within the high register. His pitch selections in different subdivisions overlap in only three places.[34] All three are visible in Example 9.8, which shows his selections in connection with the first page of the published edition by ictus. The dearth of overlapping selections and the small degree of overlap involved (one or two semitones) suggest that those present may have resulted from unintended errors in applying a mutually exclusive demarcation between subdivisions.

Table 9.3 shows the pitch ranges that Tudor used and the implied ranges if the three cases of possible error are excluded. Tudor's choice of middle C as the lowest pitch is consistent with Feldman's instructions in an unpublished set of explanatory notes in his handwriting with Tudor's copy of the score. These notes, which are reproduced in Figure 9.2,[35] state that low register sounds in the central section of the work should be below middle C.[36]

Once again, it is not clear when or why Tudor produced these materials, or why he suspended or abandoned work on them, but their incomplete state

---

[34] Ictuses 110, 138 and 157.

[35] 'Ixion for Two Pianos, explanatory notes, 1960', David Tudor Papers, 1884–1998 bulk 1940–96, Getty Research Institute, Los Angeles (980039).

[36] This rules against the thought that Feldman's tripartite indications of register in *Ixion* specify a subdivision of the pitch spectrum within a coarser tripartite division between high, middle and low registers.

Example 9.8 *Ixion* for two pianos, pitch ranges specified by Tudor in connection with subdivisions of the high register in the first piano part on page 1 of the published edition, by ictus

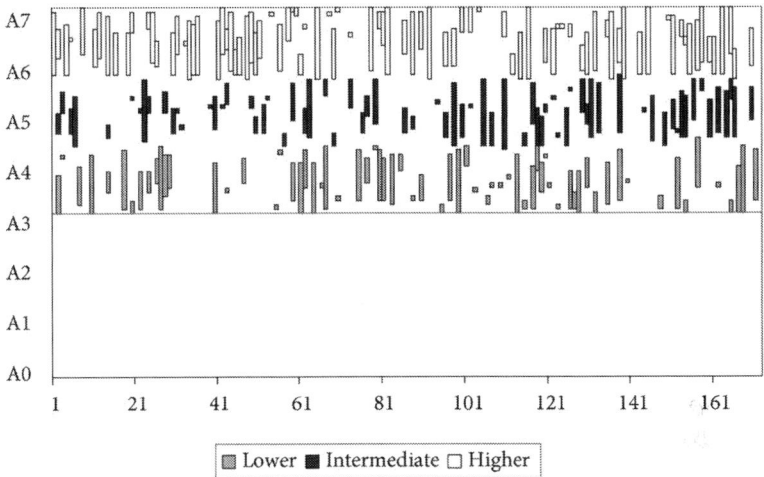

argues against them having been used in performance. Even so, they highlight a surprising aspect of Tudor's interpretation. Usually, pitches are presented in vertical columns within bars, indicating that he envisaged playing groups of notes simultaneously. This approach is consistent with the one that Feldman required in earlier graphs, including *Intersections 2–3*. Nevertheless, it is surely not what Feldman would have expected in this case. This is because a high density of attacks was central to his original conception of *Ixion* for two pianos and the earlier work from which it was transcribed, which is why the unpublished set of written remarks with Tudor's copy of the score also state that performers should play '[a]s many single sounds as possible' (Figure 9.2). The implication is that Feldman intended numbers to be interpreted, where possible, as specifying quantities of consecutive sounds and not numbers of notes played simultaneously.

As noted in Chapter 2, Feldman composed *Ixion* for chamber ensemble intending to 'melt into the decor',[37] consisting of dense arrays of luminous dots, which Rauschenberg was designing for Cunningham's *Summerspace* (see Figure 2.1 in Chapter 2). His use of a dense succession of fleeting sounds was his method of achieving the desired outcome and it is clear that he meant to create a similar effect in the subsequent transcription. Given that the mean value of numbers included in the first piano part of *Ixion* for two

---

[37] '*Studio International* interview', 65.

Table 9.3. Ixion *for two pianos, pitch ranges specified by Tudor in connection with subdivisions of the high register in the first piano part*

Subdivision	Range	Range (semitones)	Range excl. possible errors	Range excl. possible errors (semitones)
Higher	G♯6–C8	17	G♯6–C8	17
Intermediate	D♯5–G♯6	18	E5–G6	16
Lower	C4–F5	18	C4–D♯5	16

pianos is 5.77, Tudor's chord-based approach inevitably involved a very much smaller number of individual sounds than Feldman had envisaged.

Some indication of the impact of Tudor's decision on the resulting sound can be gauged by comparing a recorded performance by Tudor and Cage from the early 1960s, which appears to be the one used by the Merce Cunningham Dance Company to accompany its performances of *Summerspace* in recent years, with a much later recording by Kristine Scholz and Mats Persson, made in 2000. Whereas the performance by Tudor and Cage emphasises chords – typically they play a single sound, dyad or chord in each ictus on this recording – the performance by Scholz and Persson avoids dyads and chords, except in the low register inter-mission where it emphasises them, and is played at a considerably faster tempo.[38] Whereas the former is languid, the latter has an energetic – even scintillating – quality that seems much closer in spirit to Rauschenberg's costumes and decor.[39]

Elapsed time is marked on Tudor's materials and implies a tempo of only 50 ictuses per minute, so his alternative approach cannot be explained on the grounds that the tempo was too fast to allow him to produce more sounds consecutively. More likely, he proceeded as he did because Cage was unable to play as many consecutive sounds as indicated. Unlike Tudor, Cage was not a virtuoso pianist.[40] Also, he was by this time suffering from

---

[38] These recordings appear on *Morton Feldman: Complete Works for Two Pianists*, Alice Musik Produktion, ALCD 024, and *Music for Merce (1952–2009)*, vol. 2, New World Records, 80712-2, respectively.

[39] The performance by Scholz and Persson proceeds at a steady tempo of around 100 ictuses per minute – that is, close to the figure of 92 ictuses per minute that Feldman initially proposed for his earlier version of *Ixion*, for chamber ensemble. Consequently, the performance lasts only approxi-mately 7'30"; it is therefore too short to be of use with *Summerspace*. The recording by Tudor and Cage, by contrast, is played at a variable, but consistently much slower, tempo and lasts a little over 20'. A recorded performance of this length that avoids chords is not currently available.

[40] For Cage's abilities as a pianist, see William Fetterman, *John Cage's Theatre Pieces: Notations and Performances* (New York: Routledge, 2010), 190–1.

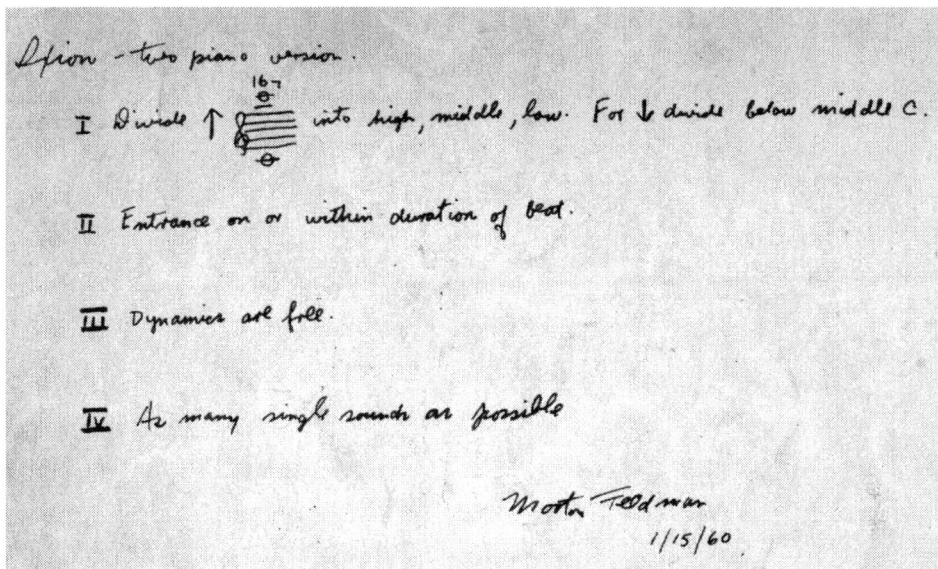

Ixion – two piano version.

I Divide ↑ into high, middle, low. For ↓ divide below middle C.

II Entrance on or within duration of beat.

III Dynamics are free.

IV As many single sounds as possible

Morton Feldman
1/15/60

Figure 9.2 *Ixion* for two pianos, explanatory notes with Tudor's copy of the score

arthritis, which caused him considerable discomfort while playing.[41] This suggests that the two men decided to present a modified version of Feldman's work that was easier to perform. Although Tudor was perfectly capable of performing his part fully in accordance with Feldman's original wishes, he and Cage probably decided that their performances would blend better if he too played dyads and chords.

Pitch selections in *Atlantis*

Tudor's papers include a copy of the score of *Atlantis* with annotations in his handwriting. The latter are presented in an invented notation and give additional information about what to play. The first example appears in the lower part of Figure 9.3.[42]

Tudor's notation is unexplained. However, it is clear that each symbol or group of symbols, in the supplementary grids that he drew beneath Feldman's, depicts a particular type of selection of piano keys and not a

---

[41] Gordon Mumma, 'Cage as performer', in David W. Bernstein and Christopher Hatch (eds.), *Writings through John Cage's Music, Poetry, and Art* (University of Chicago Press, 2001), 116.

[42] 'Feldman's score of Atlantis, with annotations (realization of piano part) by Tudor, 1959', David Tudor Papers, 1884–1998 bulk 1940–96, Getty Research Institute, Los Angeles (980039).

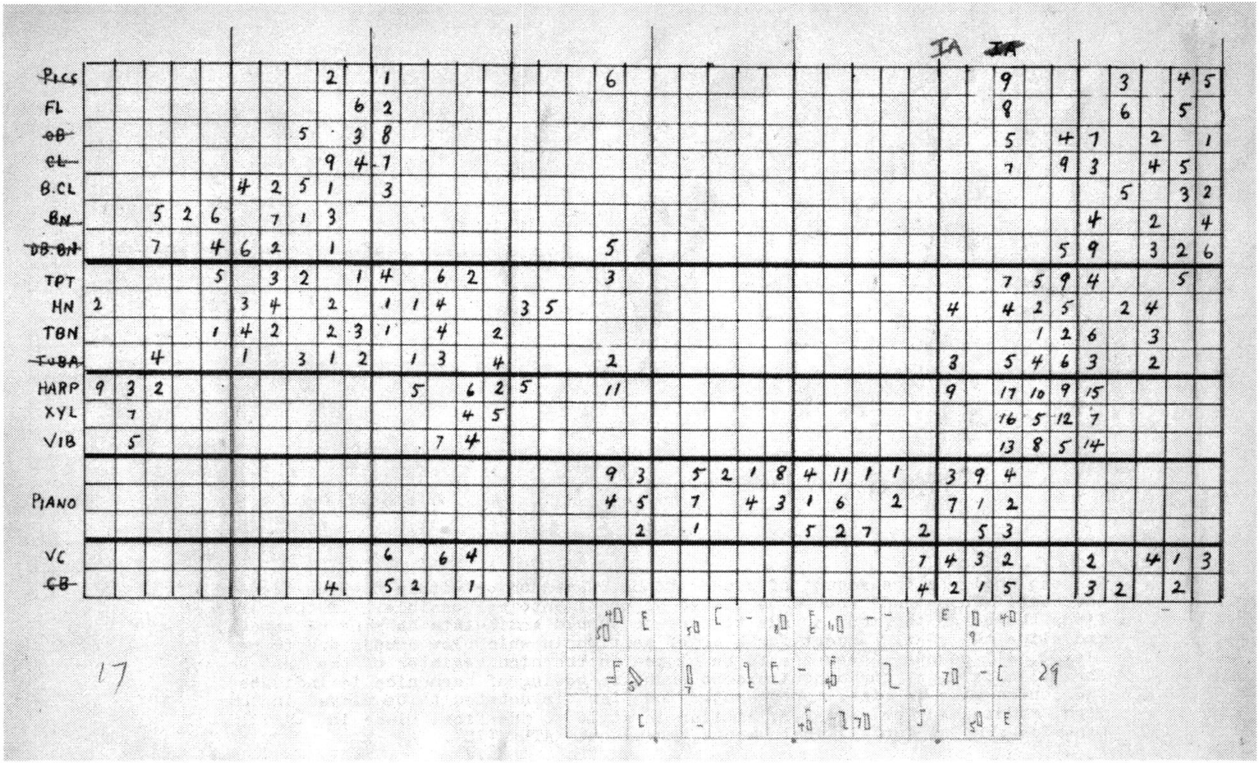

Figure 9.3 *Atlantis*, Tudor's copy of the score with his annotations, first grid frame

particular group of notes. Consequently, the notation is less precise than the conventional staff notation he used in his written-out materials for the piano *Intersections* and *Ixion* for two pianos. It narrows the range of possibilities that Feldman's score leaves open, but goes only part way towards specifying a particular selection of pitches.[43]

Why Tudor proceeded in this manner is not documented, but it may have been connected with a more general shift in his approach to preparing indeterminate works in the late 1950s. Martin Iddon has noted that Tudor ceased preparing determinate versions of Cage's works in 1958 and began preparing partially indeterminate versions of them for use in performance. This shift, he suggests, was initially attributable to Tudor's busy touring schedule, which necessitated him producing versions more quickly.[44]

The interpretation of individual symbols in Tudor's notation is a matter for debate. However, a plausible reading of those in the first occupied column in his supplementary grid is that they specify a chromatic cluster of five notes in the high register played with two notes in the middle register, with this combination to be followed by a chromatic cluster of four notes in the high register (all higher than the five high register notes in the previous chord) with two notes in the middle register (both higher than the two middle register notes played previously).

Tudor's annotations indicate that he envisaged prioritising chords over individual notes. This invites comparison with his interpretation of *Ixion* for two pianos, but it is doubtful that he was usurping Feldman's expectations in this case. For reasons explained in Chapter 8, it is highly likely that Feldman intended the pianist to utilise a chord-based approach in *Atlantis*. Other noteworthy aspects of Tudor's annotations include the fact that they evidently concern the shape of the sonorities that he expected to play and the fact that the indicated shapes vary by ictus. This suggests that he interpreted the piano part in much the same way as Chapter 8 suggested, as inviting a bodily approach to achieving sonic particularity.

A separate page of notes on *Atlantis* in Tudor's handwriting throws additional light on his interpretation. These include three staves specifying contiguous ranges (A0–D3, D♯3–G♯5 and A5–C8) that span the entire compass of the piano. The logo of the Hotel Lamoine, Macomb, Illinois is printed on the back, and this assists in dating these materials. As noted in Chapter 2, Tudor and Cage premiered *Ixion* for two pianos at a performance

---

[43] '17' indicates the number of ictuses that precede the passage notated by Tudor; '29' indicates the number of ictuses until the beginning of the next passage he notated. The reason why several labels in the left margin are struck out is that the score was used in the premiere of the 'alternate' version for ten instruments.

[44] *John Cage and David Tudor*, 138–40.

Example 9.9   Tudor's notes on *Atlantis*, excerpt

3.	+2
4.	−3
5.	+3
6.	4
7.	+4
8.	5
9.	−6
10.	+6
11.	−7
12.	+7
13.	8
14.	−9
15.	+9
16.	−10
17.	+10

of *Summerspace* in Illinois on 28 January 1960. This was just nine days before Tudor played in the premiere of the 'alternate' version of *Atlantis*, which took place on 6 February 1960 in New York City. Given the close proximity of these two dates, it is reasonable to assume that Tudor stayed in the Hotel Macomb while performing *Ixion* and that he prepared his materials for *Atlantis* around this time for use in its first performance.

It is tempting to read the contiguous pitch ranges as specifying fixed limits for Tudor's pitch selections in the high, middle and low registers. However, an adjacent list of numbers, shown in Example 9.9,[45] in Tudor's handwriting complicates interpretation as it could represent a scheme of perturbations from the specified limits. For example, the first entry in the list may indicate that in the third system of Feldman's score, the limits specified in the adjacent staves are to be raised by two semitones, whereas the fourth entry may indicate that the limits specified for the sixth system are to be raised or lowered by four semitones. The absence of entries for the first and last two systems (there are 19 in all) could then be read as indicating the absence of perturbations in their cases.

There is no evidence to suggest that Tudor applied a similarly mechanical scheme of perturbations either in preparing his written-out versions of other graphs or in actual performances. That said, if the scheme is indeed

---

[45] 'Tudor's notes regarding Morton Feldman's piece Atlantis, 1959', David Tudor Papers, 1884–1998 bulk 1940–96, Getty Research Institute, Los Angeles (980039).

one for use in perturbing the adjacent indications on staves, then this is another case in which his approach would have surprised Feldman who, we have seen, intended a fixed system of mutually exclusive pitch ranges to be applied throughout a performance.

Undreamed-of possibilities

In a long article about Tudor, titled 'The far-out pianist', published in June 1960, Harold C. Schonberg observed that 'many consider him one of the great keyboard technicians of the present day'.[46] Schonberg's own assessment was that Tudor was 'the unsurpassed keyboard executant of the new music', a music he described as sometimes 'arcane and rarefied' and sometimes 'the noisiest, brashest, and most eccentric music composed today'.[47] The music in question, Schonberg noted, was that of Cage, Feldman, Wolff, Brown, Stockhausen, Boulez, Sylvano Bussotti, 'and several other experimentalists'. Consequently, it was fitting that his article should include several comments from interviews with Feldman and Cage.

Schonberg described Feldman's working relationship with Tudor as follows:

> Normally he [i.e. Feldman] graphs his music instead of notating it, leaving it up to the performer to translate. He doesn't even bother to work with Tudor. He gives him the music and the instructions. 'Then I go to the concert and hear a miracle. This kind of music is more than merely a specialty of Tudor's. In some ways he's entirely responsible for it. Meeting David enabled me to hear and see possibilities I never dreamed of.'[48]

Tudor's independence from composers while preparing performances is well documented,[49] and it is not this aspect of Schonberg's remarks that is the focus here. This section focuses, instead, on Feldman's statement that Tudor had made him able to hear undreamed-of possibilities. This was something of a volte-face. In the early 1950s, Cage reported that Feldman 'is associated with all of the sounds [of his graph music], and so can foresee what will happen even though he has not written the particular notes down as other composers do';[50] so, what had happened in the intervening years to make him change his view?

Feldman had, of course, discovered his graph music's 'most important flaw', which was that it had inadvertently succeeded in 'liberating the performer', thereby fostering reliance on conditioning and memory and encouraging an unwanted 'art of improvisation', and this was why he 'abandoned'

---

[46] Schonberg, 'The far-out pianist', 50.   [47] *Ibid.*, 49–51.   [48] *Ibid.*, 52.
[49] Holzaepfel, David Tudor, 56–8.   [50] 'Lecture on something', 130.

graph notation in 1953, before returning to it in 1958.[51] However, this cannot have been what he had in mind when speaking to Schonberg. The tenor of his remarks about Tudor was enthusiastic. Moreover, Tudor appears to have become a somewhat reluctant improviser, preferring instead to play from partially or fully written-out versions, as previously noted.

Another possibility is that Feldman was thinking of Tudor's virtuosity and the fact that it enabled him to compose works with a high degree of difficulty. *Intersections 2–3* were certainly intended to challenge Tudor's capabilities. Both demand exceptional dexterity from the performer, who is regularly required to play long sequences of large and sometimes gigantic chords within consecutive beats of a brisk pulse. But why would this warrant describing Tudor as *entirely* responsible for this music?

More likely, Feldman was alluding to another aspect of Tudor's performances of his graphs, which was their propensity to surprise him, and not because of Tudor's ability to successfully negotiate music that most others would be unable to perform, but because his interpretations defied Feldman's expectations and even his original intentions in some cases. This is not because Tudor misunderstood Feldman's expectations, but because he wilfully deviated from what he knew Feldman expected. It was, perhaps, no coincidence that *Ixion* and the 'alternate' version of *Atlantis* were premiered just a few months before Schonberg's interview was published or that the first LP of Feldman's music was issued only the previous year. This was why Feldman regarded Tudor as 'entirely responsible' for some of the graph music that he played, for this was music that Feldman had not envisaged being performed the way Tudor played it.

In 'The far-out pianist', Schonberg reported that Tudor 'is meticulous in observing the instructions of the composer, no matter how complicated they may be'.[52] In view of the evidence presented above, this was an oversimplification, and this is confirmed by a review of other sources. To begin with, studies of Tudor's interpretations of Cage's music have highlighted irregularities. For example, Holzaepfel has argued that Tudor's decision to superpose his readings of some of the pages in *Winter Music* was not as Cage intended,[53] whereas James Pritchett has suggested that Tudor's 'simplification' of the measuring system outlined in *Variations II* (1961) takes his version 'away from Cage's conception and into a wholly unexpected realm'.[54] More recently, Iddon has

---

[51] 'Liner notes', 6.   [52] 'The far-out pianist', 50.

[53] 'Cage and Tudor', in Nicholls (ed.), *The Cambridge Companion to John Cage* (Cambridge University Press, 2002), 181.

[54] 'David Tudor as composer/performer in Cage's "Variations II"', *Leonardo Music Journal*, vol. 14 (2004), 13.

maintained that the second of Tudor's two versions of *Solo for Piano*, the solo piano part from *Concert for Piano and Orchestra* (1958), exhibits 'an almost perverse reading of the idea that the duration of a performance [...] is represented by the left-to-right proportions of its notations' and 'entirely disregards the idea [indicated in Cage's instructions] of each page representing a single system'.[55] In a similar vein, Tudor's interpretation of *Theatre Piece* 'breaks Cage's rules for the piece',[56] and Cage's restriction on the duration of *Extended Lullaby* from *Four³* (1991) 'is ignored [by Tudor] from the outset'.[57]

Tudor's own comments are also significant. For example, in a 1972 interview, he explained:

> [T]here is a paragraph in [Ferruccio] Busoni which speaks of notation as an evil separating musicians from music, and I feel everyone should know that this is true. I had been completely indoctrinated with the idea of faithfulness to notation in the early days, and if you think of notation as being complete then you see what Busoni meant – it can't possibly be complete. Notation is an invention of the devil, and when I became free of it, through pieces like Cage's *Fontana Mix* and *Music Walk*, and later Bussotti's *Piano Piece for David Tudor* No 3, it really did a lot for me.[58]

Busoni's view was that the 'rigidity' of notation makes it imperfect as a means of 'catching an inspiration',[59] witness the fact that '[g]reat artists play their own works differently at each repetition'.[60] From this he inferred that '[w]hat the composer's inspiration *necessarily* loses through notation, his interpreter should restore by his own'.[61] The implication was that the interpreter should not be subservient to notation, but should instead aim to see beyond it and grasp the essence of the music that it may reflect only imperfectly.

In his comments cited above, Tudor connected his liberation from notation with three works composed in the late 1950s. However, aspects of his approach to Feldman's graph music suggest that he began looking beyond notation at an earlier date. This would explain why he applied the mode of thought he had developed in connection with Boulez's *Deuxième Sonate* and Cage's *Music of Changes* when selecting pitches in *Intersections 2–3*. We know that in the early 1950s Feldman was aiming at 'no-continuity', and the suggestion made here is that Tudor saw Feldman's use of a rigid division between registers as implying a connection between sounds that was not only

[55] *John Cage and David Tudor*, 66.   [56] *Ibid.*, 151.   [57] *Ibid.*, 206.
[58] 'From piano to electronics', 24.
[59] Ferruccio Busoni, *Sketch of a New Esthetic of Music*, trans. Theodore Baker (New York: Schirmer, 1911), 15.
[60] *Ibid.*, 17.   [61] *Ibid.*, 16. Busoni's emphasis.

inconsistent with Feldman's own aesthetics but also dispensable; hence his decision to ignore this aspect of the notation and apply the method of working that he had previously developed and still preferred.[62] The implication is that he saw his treatment of registers in the piano *Intersections* – possibly also in *Atlantis* – as more consonant with the composer's general ideas about 'no-continuity' than the treatment of them specified in these works.

It seems likely that Tudor's decision to produce a chord-based version of *Ixion* was driven by practical necessity. In this case, it was simply not possible, given the available resources, to perform the work as Feldman envisaged. Whether he or Cage consulted with Feldman is not known – he may have felt justified in proceeding as he did simply on the grounds that Feldman had specified as many single sounds *as possible* – but we do know that the resulting performances were audibly different in character and less well matched with Rauschenberg's costumes and decor than Feldman planned. If Tudor played from his more conventionally notated version of *Intersection 3* because he could not produce a sufficiently accurate rendition making spontaneous choices, then this aspect of his approach was also of this type, but if he proceeded this way to avoid clichéd selections or others he deemed inappropriate, then this would be comparable with his treatment of register.

Cage relished Tudor's propensity to deliver surprises; hence Schonberg's remark that:

> [o]nce Cage finishes a score he lets the performer work it out any way he pleases; and if what comes out may be entirely different from his original concept, that's all right with him. There is nothing invigorating, he says, about 'a situation where you know precisely what is right and what is wrong.'[63]

Feldman's attitude to the undreamed-of possibilities revealed by Tudor is less clear, however. We know that he was fussy about some aspects of performances of his works and relaxed about others, so we cannot reliably infer his stance from general principles. His fussiness is evident in his emphasis on perfection of tone, his insistence on allowing sounds time to 'breathe', his documented interventions in rehearsals, and his associated contempt for performances that exhibit an 'art of improvisation'. Contrast his apparently blasé attitude to 'serious' errors in performances of his graph music in a conversation with Cage recorded in 1967, in which he suggested – admittedly under some pressure from Cage – that he would regard them as 'interesting',[64] and his willingness to allow the Kronos

---

[62] For comparable attitudes of Arturo Toscanini and Wilhelm Furtwängler to aspects of Johannes Brahms' Symphony No. 4 in E minor, Op. 98 (1885), see Aaron Ridley, 'Brilliant performances', *Royal Institute of Philosophy Supplement*, vol. 71 (October 2012), 216–20.

[63] 'The far-out pianist', 52–3.   [64] Cage and Feldman, *Radio Happenings*, 143–5.

Quartet to perform a substantially abridged version of his mammoth *String Quartet II* at its premiere in 1983.[65]

That said, various factors point to a degree of flexibility on Feldman's part. In particular, the surviving record indicates a softening of his early stance on spontaneous decision-making during performances, as noted in Chapter 8. Perhaps he came to accept that *Intersection 3* resisted being performed in the way he had envisaged and that Tudor's approach was the only practical alternative method of performing this particular work, and, later on, his general mistrust of improvisers may have made him more comfortable with performers making their selections in advance, even though he retained a long-standing preference for spontaneous decision-making.[66]

There is also reason to think Feldman was prepared to be flexible about Cage and Tudor's chord-based approach to *Ixion*. His decision not to include the set of written notes reproduced in Figure 9.2 in the published edition certainly suggests that he decided to accommodate their reading. If Cage was unable to play the work in its original form, we can imagine that Feldman may have felt under considerable pressure to do so, given the practical circumstances that had led him to undertake a transcription.

Most probably, Feldman was not aware of Tudor's practice of blurring divisions between registers. In 1961, he explained to Cardew that he had previously presented his only copies of the scores of *Intersections 2–3* to Tudor as a 'personal' gesture,[67] so it is doubtful whether he ever followed the latter's performances in the score, and there is no evidence to suggest that he studied the pianist's performance materials. If he had been made aware of Tudor's approach, then it is difficult to gauge what his attitude might have been. Unlike the cases discussed above, this one appears to have involved a calculated disregard for his notation not warranted by practical concerns. Perhaps he would have reacted as indicated in his 1967 comments to Cage, seeing Tudor's errors as merely 'interesting'. Alternatively, he may have regarded them as more like the 'Yankee Doodle' case, as involving a somewhat less evident, but nonetheless equally objectionable, act of deliberate 'murder'.

---

[65] Feldman alluded to the shortening of *String Quartet II* in 'Morton Feldman: conversation without Cage (Michael Whiticker), July 1984' [1989], in Villars (ed.), *Morton Feldman Says*, 185.

[66] This section has focused on cases in which the performer writes out parts or all of a performance, but similar comments apply to those in which specific selections are memorised in advance.

[67] Morton Feldman to Cornelius Cardew, 25 April 1961.

10 Connections with works in other notations

Feldman's practice of switching between different varieties of musical notation was a conspicuous aspect of his approach during the 1950s and 1960s, but it is one that resists tidy analysis. Feldman himself explained that he had viewed each notation as a different 'idiom' associated with its own 'style' of music and compared his modus operandi with that of an artist moving back and forth between painting and sculpture.[1] These comments flatly contradict the accusation that his approach was attributable to vacillation,[2] as do remarks he made elsewhere, which suggest that he always worked with whatever notation he felt 'the work called for'.[3] All the same, they seem to represent an oversimplified account of his working practices. Certainly there were periods in which he moved back and forth between notations, but it is equally certain that this was not always so, and even when he worked this way, he was not always happy with the results. Previous chapters highlighted a rejection of the graph format in the mid-1950s and persistent dissatisfaction with his efforts in conventional notation in the late 1950s and early 1960s that are unaccounted for by his analogy, as is his practice of juxtaposing different types of notation within the same score, which emerged in . . .*Out of 'Last Pieces'* and preoccupied him in non-graph works in the mid- and late 1960s.

An inventory of Feldman's published output (Example 10.1) and a review of his surviving comments suggest that two different types of alternation operated during the 1950s. On the one hand, there were fluctuating patterns in his general preferences over longer periods of time that advanced or precluded the use of a particular type of notation or which caused him to suppress his efforts in a specific format. On the other hand, his work-to-work choices between notations that he deemed concurrently viable altered more frequently. This more frequent variation is evident from a review of his published output by year. For example, in 1951 he composed seven graphs and three conventionally notated works that he deemed worthy of

---

[1] '*Soundpieces* interview', 91.
[2] Noble, *Composing Ambiguity*, 146, which suggests that this was attributable to a persistent dissatisfaction with his graphs.
[3] 'Morton Feldman talks to Paul Griffiths', 47.

Example 10.1 Feldman's output of works composed in 1947–72 and published in his lifetime, by notation

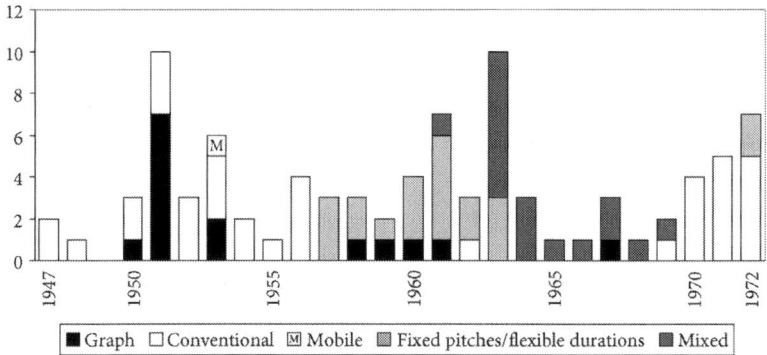

publication,[4] followed by two graphs, three conventionally notated works and one mobile in 1953.[5] Similarly, in 1958 he composed one graph and two works with fixed pitches and indeterminate durations,[6] whereas in 1959 he produced one of each of these types.[7] Evidently, Feldman's analogy with an artist switching between different mediums seems better suited to these more frequent variations between concurrently viable formats. His characterisation of his various notations as stylistically distinct idioms and his practice of utilising only one in each work both point to a focus on stylistically unified works in this period.

Feldman's analogy with a painter-cum-sculptor highlights a point of comparison between his working methods and those of several artists in his immediate circle, including Pollock and Rauschenberg.[8] Arguably, however, there were other, deeper affinities between this aspect of his approach and the contemporary art scene in New York City. For example, his movement between conventional staff and graph notation in the early 1950s represented a to-ing and fro-ing between greater and lesser degrees of control that can be seen as reflecting opposing elements of Abstract Expressionist painting,[9] which is often portrayed as combining surrealism's preoccupation with the

[4] The graphs: *Projections 2–5*; *Intersections 1–2*; and *Marginal Intersection*. The conventionally notated works: *Four Songs to e. e. cummings*; *Structures* for string quartet; and *Extensions 1*.

[5] The graphs: *Intersections 3–4*. The conventionally notated works: *Extensions 4–5*; and *Eleven Instruments*. The mobile: *Intermission 6*.

[6] *Ixion* for chamber ensemble, *Piano Four Hands* and *Two Instruments*.

[7] *Atlantis* and *Last Pieces*.

[8] For Pollock's sculptures, see O'Connor and Thaw (eds.), *Jackson Pollock*, 119–30. For Rauschenberg's, see Tomkins, *The Bride and the Bachelors*, 208.

[9] Noble, *Composing Ambiguity*, 9.

unconscious, and therefore uncontrol, with a deep concern for formal attributes of the resulting work, and therefore control, without the use of a single-point perspective. Pollock's method of dripping, flicking and pouring paint exemplifies both elements. The uncontrolled aspects of this method are obvious, but Pollock was at pains to stress that he regulated the outcome – 'I *can* control the flow of the paint'[10] and, more emphatically, 'No chaos damn it'[11] – and most critics, following Greenberg's lead, have concurred.[12]

At first sight, Feldman's course in the 1960s points to a significant change in stance. Many of the works composed in this period, including . . .*Out of 'Last Pieces'* and *The King of Denmark*, utilise more than one notation.[13] In some cases, though not these two, different notations are used in a single work to similar extents, meaning that it is no longer possible to discern a single primary format.[14] Even so, this mixing of styles is not inconsistent with the idea that Feldman continued to see his various notations as of fundamentally different types provided the combinations are seen as forms of collage – a process that often combines radically different kinds of material in a single work. As discussed in Chapter 7, collage was a pervasive theme in the art scene in New York City in the early 1960s, and it is reasonable to assume that it was one that Feldman's practice of combining notations was meant to echo, if only at the syntactic level.

This chapter assesses the extent to which Feldman's works in graph notation should be seen as a genuinely distinct idiom with a characteristic musical style within his broader output. This question has attracted conflicting views over the years. Cage, for one, perceived a seamless fit between Feldman's early graphs and his conventionally notated output, suggesting that 'Feldman's conventionally notated music is himself playing his graph music',[15] a view not clearly consistent with Feldman's own assessment. Cardew, by contrast, took a view closer to Feldman's own position when he suggested that the early graphs 'spring from some other place in his character' and are 'executed by some other faculty'.[16] This issue is addressed in the opening section, whereas those that follow discuss other

---

[10] '"My home is in Springs. . ." (ca. 1951)' [1978], in Nancy Jachec, *Jackson Pollock: Works, Writings and Interviews* (Barcelona: Ediciones Polígrafa, 2011), 128. Pollock's emphasis.

[11] 'Letter to the editor, *Time*, 1950' [1950], in Karmel (ed.), *Jackson Pollock*, 71.

[12] See, for example, Michael Leja, *Reframing Abstract Expressionism: Subjectivity and Painting in the 1940s* (New Haven: Yale University Press, 1993), 276–83.

[13] In Example 10.1, the notations of . . .*Out of 'Last Pieces'* and *The King of Denmark* are classified as mixed.

[14] *Piano Piece 1964* (1964) is one of several examples.

[15] This formulation of Cage's remark was first reported in O'Hara, 'New directions in music', 216.

[16] 'The American School of John Cage', in Prévost (ed.), *Cornelius Cardew: A Reader*, 46.

aspects of the relationships that hold between the graphs and his works in other notational formats. These include his occasional use of graph-like intermediaries in the production of conventionally notated works and his alleged use of conventionally notated intermediaries in the production of graphs. A final section considers why the grid of boxes used in the graphs eventually surfaced in the presentation of his non-graph scores from 1960 and assesses its impact on them.

Difference in idiom

One way of trying to flesh out Feldman's idea of a difference in idiom between his graphs and conventionally notated works is in terms of discrepancies between their audible properties. This approach quickly encounters difficulties. These stem from the considerable variety that exists within his graph music and also within his conventionally notated output, which makes it hard to identify common characteristics within either group for use in a benchmarking exercise. The distinction between contrasting types of pointillism apparent in the graph series, highlighted in Chapter 4, is only one aspect of this issue. There are other differences. For example, the marked contrast between the relatively homogeneous sound world of the *Projections*, which is uniformly quiet, tenuous and slow, and the more varied, but typically more agitated and robust sound world of the *Intersections*, in which dynamics are free. Moreover, Claren has observed a corresponding variety in the conventionally notated works composed in the same period.[17]

The difficulty this creates can be illustrated by a review of comments made by David Nicholls, who suggested that the graphs are distinct from the conventionally notated works because '[t]he graph pieces – especially the earlier ones – tend toward a pulsed rhythmic stasis. The notated pieces, meanwhile, are rhythmically precise, often introducing subdivisions of the basic pulse'.[18] The implied homogeneity of the conventionally notated works from the early 1950s is misleading, however. It is certainly true that most of these works involve subdivisions of the underlying pulse, and we might add that many make extensive use of grace notes, but there are exceptions. The first movement of *Nature Pieces* utilises notes and rests with simple values – each equivalent to an integer number of crotchets – that are always aligned with beats, and although the other movements are rhythmically more complex, all include passages in which

---

[17] *Neither*, 59.   [18] 'Getting rid of the glue', 30.

a regular pulse is audible. Then there is *Piano Piece 1952*, which consists of two offset, but rhythmically uniform, successions of equal notes without rests – one in each hand – which creates what one commentator has described as 'a surface of implacably straight-jacketed rhythm and kinetic motion'.[19]

Moreover, it is simply not true that all the graph music is 'pulsed'. Even if we ignore the far-fetched insinuation that this might be true of the graphs from *Ixion* onwards and restrict our attention to the early graphs only, the thesis remains unconvincing. Some passages in the *Projections* and *Intersections* do produce this effect, as noted elsewhere in this volume, but many others do not. Indeed, entrances in the *Intersections* are never fixed, meaning that rhythm is partly determined by the choices of performers. No doubt these are constrained by the sheer difficulty of rendering the scores in some places, but this is certainly not always the case and it is rarely true in *Intersection 1* or *Marginal Intersection*. Although the locations of sound endings remain tied to the underlying beat, these are not nearly as prominent in the listening experience as their onsets, for reasons outlined in Chapter 1.

To characterise the difference in terms of 'stasis' is equally unhelpful, especially in view of the widespread tendency to apply this epithet to so much modern classical music. Pulsed works are sometimes described this way, the idea being that the regularity of a pulse is insufficiently varied and too predictable to be engaging,[20] and perhaps this was all that Nicholls had in mind. However, there are other senses in which a musical work can be said to be 'static', but none of these seem especially helpful in this context. For example, although it is true that in the early (but not the later) graph music the apparent motion attributable to perceptual grouping over time is slow, it is considerably slower in the conventionally notated *Variations* – admittedly a work that remained unpublished in Feldman's lifetime – which has a tempo of only 64 ictuses per minute, a lower average density of activity per ictus and longer silences than are found in any of the graph music from any period. Also, the presence of passages of persistent repetition of individual notes and short phrases in several of the conventionally notated works from the early 1950s – notably *Structures* for string quartet, *Intermission 5* and *Extensions 3* – and many of the long, late works, which are organised around the repetition of single-bar constructions, which Feldman sometimes referred to as 'patterns' or 'modules', disrupts the audible momentum, creating a sense of imprisonment in time that has no counterpart in the

[19] Noble, *Composing Ambiguity*, 73.   [20] Boutwell, 'Marvelous Accidents', 67.

graph music, in which the only compulsory repetition – in *The Straits of Magellan* – is on a much more modest scale. Although there are many places in which individual notes or sequences of notes may be repeated, performers are under no obligation to do so.

The crux of the problem is that the early graphs and the conventionally notated works from the same period both exhibit a wide variety of audible properties. These overlap only in specific cases, making it impossible to ground a meaningful difference in idiom between the two types in these terms. Such an approach is better suited to the task of demarcating the later graphs, which are audibly distinct, not only from the early graphs but also from the contemporary works in other formats. Feldman himself alluded to this disparity in a 1976 interview, in which he described *Ixion* as 'not a characteristic score of mine',[21] but he had clearly forgotten having persisted with the same style in the immediately ensuing graphs and with a more diluted form of the same in all those that he composed thereafter. This observation is of little use for current purposes, however, given the fact that it applies only to a subset of his graph music, and it will prove advantageous to consider alternative approaches.

The first of two to be considered appeals to a difference in speed of composition. The close proximity of the dates appended to *Projections 2–4* and *Intersection 1* testify to a rapid mode of composition, as do Feldman's comments about composing *The King of Denmark* in a single afternoon, and it is safe to assume that his allover method of working and his decision to refrain from specifying pitches, which reduced the number of possible permutations within an ictus once the instrumentation was decided, both assisted in this regard by facilitating a more spontaneous way of working.[22] No doubt rapidity of progress was of some importance to Feldman until the mid-1960s, given that until then he composed on a part-time basis while employed in his family business, and it is suggestive that the only graph composed after that time – *In Search of an Orchestration* – appears to have emerged at a considerably slower pace. We know that by 1980 he regarded his slower rate of working in conventional notation as a distinct advantage because it encouraged a more reflective approach that was 'involved more with thought than ideas',[23] but this was from a later perspective of full-time employment in music. The fact that in the early 1950s he restricted his efforts in

---

[21] 'Studio International interview', 65.
[22] Feldman alluded to the increase in spontaneity facilitated by the graph format in 'Soundpieces interview', 90.
[23] Ibid.

conventional notation to works for solo instruments or small ensembles, whereas his graph music included orchestral works from very early on, is also consistent with the hypothesis that he worked more quickly with graph notation, at least initially.[24]

If Feldman was thinking along these lines, then the comparison that he made with a painter-cum-sculptor would obviously have been bettered by a closely related analogy with an artist switching between painting in oil and sketching in pencil, and this is a small but vexing weakness of this interpretation of his view. The following alternative is therefore to be preferred, even though it may seem trivial at first sight. The suggestion made here is that Feldman's graphs and his conventionally notated works represent different idioms just because the former are unlike the latter in being indeterminate.

The ramifications of this difference have been a central theme in this monograph, but the stylistic impact of the lack of specificity about pitch and, in some cases, other parameters in the graph music remains to be discussed. Thus far, this lack of specificity has been portrayed simply in terms of reduced or absent guidance about which notes to play, when to enter and so on, but it is so much more than this from a stylistic viewpoint. This is because the style of the conventionally notated music is determined, at least in part, by the specific choices about these matters that Feldman made. For example, a pervasive trait of Feldman's conventionally notated music is his use of semitones and their octave displacements. Although the graph notation can replicate many aspects of his conventionally notated music, such as orchestration, density, pacing etc., it simply cannot reproduce a preference for specific intervals, and this is therefore an important stylistic difference between the two types of work. Much the same can be said of repetition or near-repetition, which Feldman used to great effect in conventionally notated works throughout his career, because generally speaking repetition is not specified in the graphs, although the possibility of repetition is frequently left open. This is not a weakness of the graph music; the graph notation could very easily have been modified to allow the specification of repeated elements, indeed it was modified in this manner in *The Straits of Magellan*, as previously noted. That said, it is a significant difference between the two types of work, and it is differences such as these that I believe should be seen as underpinning the difference in idiom and style that Feldman highlighted.

---

[24] His first work in conventional notation for a larger ensemble was *Eleven Instruments*, dated December 1953.

The use of graphs in composing conventionally notated works

In a liner note issued with a recording of *Structures* for string quartet in 1973, Lejaren Hiller – at that time a colleague of Feldman's at the State University of New York at Buffalo – wrote:

> [I]t has been remarked that it [i.e. *Structures*] could well serve as an example of how the composer himself might realize one of his graphical scores. This is precisely what Feldman actually did. He sketched out a plot of what one might call musical events (versus elapsed performance time), filling in this graph until it satisfied him. It should be understood that this was not a literal plot of, say, frequency versus time but a general guide to laying out event successions. Once this was done, Feldman then transcribed the material into a precisely notated conventional score so that performances of this piece [. . .] are relatively fixed. This particular compositional technique he has only used twice, once in the present instance and once in composing, also in 1951, a piano piece for Merce Cunningham, who then choreographed it as 'Variations' [*sic*] for solo dancer.[25]

Working towards a conventionally notated finish through an intermediate graph stage, from less precise indications in the graph to more precise specifications in the finished work, would have been a natural strategy for Feldman to try out, and he might also have been attracted to the idea because it would have enabled him to apply the 'allover' technique he was developing in his graph music at this time in composing conventionally notated music. Indeed, on one occasion, he suggested that this is precisely what he did in *Structures* and in *Variations*, the other work referred to by Hiller, which Feldman composed for Cunningham's dance with the same name.[26] This corroborates Hiller's report, which is independently credible in view of its detailed character, which strongly suggests that it was based on information obtained directly from Feldman himself. Consequently, we are justified in taking it at face value, even though no graph-like intermediaries used in composing either work appear to have survived.[27]

---

[25] 'Morton Feldman: Structures for string quartet (1951)' [1973], in liner notes with *American String Quartets 1950–1970*, Vox Music Group, CDX 5143, 24.

[26] 'The future of local music', unpublished transcript, 23. The passage in question is quoted in Chapter 5.

[27] Cage stated that Feldman's *Two Pieces for Two Pianos* 'are conventionally notated: i.e., he has himself interpreted his graph' ('Program notes (1959)', 81). This wording suggests that Cage meant to highlight a generic equivalence between Feldman's graphs and his conventionally notated music, and not a specific characteristic of *Two Pieces for Two Pianos*. For Cage, this was grounded in an avoidance of compositional systems and a reliance on unfettered intuition in both cases: hence his comment elsewhere that Feldman's 'works on music paper are not essentially different from those on graph for when he writes the notes and note values he does so directly and unhesitatingly, not involved with the idea of making a construction of a logical nature' ('Juilliard lecture', 100).

Nevertheless, Hiller's comments leave an unresolved puzzle if we go on to assume – what is by no means certain – that the intermediary stages were tantamount to finished graphs and not just graph-like working materials that he may have felt free to interpret in any way. This is because *Structures* and *Variations*, which were completed in the period between finishing *Intersection 1* and *Marginal Intersection*, both have properties that differ from those one might have expected to find in conventionally notated works derived from finished graphs in that period. The focus of interest is the occasional use of grace notes in *Structures* and their ubiquitous presence in *Variations*, which appear inconsistent with Feldman's official explanations of his notation in these graphs. These suggest that a designated event must extend to the end of the bracket in which it occurs, whereas grace notes are usually understood as floating free of the underlying pulse. It is true that every grace note in *Structures* and many that appear in *Variations* are placed at the very end of the bar in which they occur, which may have been meant to suggest that they be played just before the next beat.[28] Even so, there are many examples in *Variations* that appear in other locations within bars, and their presence is not strictly consistent with the use of an intermediary graph stage whose notation was understood by Feldman as above.

The use of conventionally notated works in composing graphs

An undated sketch, in Feldman's handwriting, located in the Morton Feldman Collection of the Paul Sacher Foundation, is an early version of the opening of *Intersection 1*. Like the published edition of the score, the sketch includes four instrumental parts that are placed above one another on the page, and the labelling of the parts in the sketch and the published edition are also very similar. There is a substantial difference in presentation, however. This is because the sketch, shown in Figure 10.1, is presented with notes on staves and not on graph paper.

This is not the only case of this type. For example, one of Feldman's surviving notebooks, which is also located in the same collection (where it is catalogued as 'Sketchbook 3') contains an incomplete set of sketches of instrumental parts for *Marginal Intersection* in his handwriting, and these sketches are also presented with notes on staves. Parts for woodwinds (labelled 'ww'), brass and strings are laid out individually, whereas others are presented in groups of three: wood, glass and metal; and piano, electric guitar and record ('elect'). Figure 10.2 shows a page that includes the end of the part for

---

[28] Unattached grace notes occur in two bars (43 and 296) in *Structures*, but each is located at the end of its bar.

Figure 10.1 *Intersection 1*, sketch in more conventional notation

Figure 10.2 *Marginal Intersection*, sketch in more conventional notation, end of part for woodwind instruments followed by start of part for brass instruments

woodwinds and the start of the part for brass. Each extant part is complete (189 bars), but no materials for the high and low oscillators are included. These items are not dated, but some other items in the same sketchbook do bear dates, which suggest that they stem from the period 1951 to 1953.

Boutwell has described the sketch materials for *Intersection 1* and *Marginal Intersection* as follows:

> Feldman initiated sketches for both of the orchestral *Intersections* in conventional notation before altering their conception and turning to the graph. Unusually, in the case of *Marginal Intersection*, he also appears to have begun by composing the work's parts independently of one another.[29]

Boutwell made these remarks as an aside, but if he was right, his conclusion is significant, and not just for the light it throws on Feldman's early methods. His suggestion was, in effect, that Feldman abstracted these graphs from more conventionally notated intermediate materials, which could suggest that conventionally notated music still enjoyed a degree of pre-eminence in his thinking.

However, a more robust interpretation of these materials is possible, and a convenient place to begin is with the observation that the notations used in the sketches only appear conventional, for they were certainly not intended to be read in a conventional manner. Note heads only ever occur in three vertical locations on the stave: on the bottom, middle and top lines. In the sketch of *Intersection 1* and most of the parts included in Sketchbook 3, note heads appear in all three positions, but in the parts for wood, glass and metal only one position is used, and when this is the case, note heads always appear on the middle line.

Evidently, the staves were being used in an unconventional manner, as an alternative presentation of the graph format. In cases in which activity is not limited to the middle line of the stave, the top, middle and bottom lines signal high, middle and low registers, as in the standard tri-partite division of the early graphs. In those Sketchbook 3 materials in which activity is restricted to the middle line only, this was being used, inconsistently with its employment in the three-row format, to signal any register. This notation corresponds with the single-row format used in the published edition of *Marginal Intersection* to indicate brackets in which sounds in any register are to occur. Read this way, the pitch-related content of the more conventionally notated materials for *Marginal Intersection* is close to that specified in the published edition of the graph score, and the same is also true of the opening bars of the more conventionally notated fragment of *Intersection 1*. Clearly,

---

[29] A Static Sublime, 73.

the more conventionally notated format and the graph notation were intended to provide exactly the same information about register.

Similarly, most of the differences between their rhythmic aspects are only apparent, except in the closing stages of the sketch of *Intersection 1*, in which the musical contents of the sketch and published edition are quite different. Where the musical contents of sketches and published editions are closely aligned, the numbers of units of pulse indicated by minims and semibreves, which are sometimes dotted and often tied in the sketches, are generally equal to the lengths of the corresponding brackets in the graphs. Although the notation of the sketch materials is more naturally read as indicating the intended durations of sounds, we can reasonably suppose that Feldman meant it to be read as specifying brackets. This is not indicated in the Sketchbook 3 materials for *Marginal Intersection*, but he went to considerable lengths to explain that this is how it should be understood in the similarly notated excerpt from the score of *Intersection 1*, to which he added the following note:

1. Any rhythmic entrance within given time. In the case of a sustained sound any entrance within the length of that sound holding to the end of notated duration.
2. Any dynamic[.]

The only significant rhythmic difference between the more conventionally notated sketches and the published editions, in places where their register-related contents are similar, is that some, but not all, of the parts for *Marginal Intersection* in Sketchbook 3 begin with the time signature 4/4.[30] This implies a pattern of emphasis within each bar that there is little other reason to believe Feldman meant to apply. The assumption here is that his occasional use of time signatures in these parts was a mistake.

What was the intended purpose of these sketch materials? Beginning with the more conventionally notated parts for *Marginal Intersection*, one possibility is that they were indeed sketches used in 1951 in the compositional process, not as more determinate versions from which the graphs were subsequently abstracted, but as early versions of the same material that were subsequently recopied into the graph format. The existence of two complete sketches on graph paper argues against this, however.[31] This is because both these drafts are amended, whereas the more conventionally notated materials are not. Feldman's use of a truncated presentation of groups of silent bars in the parts on staves, with a number above a diagonal

---

[30] Only the parts for woodwinds, wood, glass and metal bear this time signature.
[31] Morton Feldman Collection, Paul Sacher Foundation.

line used to indicate the number of silent bars to be inserted, also argues against the idea that the material on staves pre-dated the sketches on graph paper. This device disrupts any alignment between the evolution of the various parts on the page and their evolution in time because the locations and lengths of truncated bars differ between parts. If Feldman had begun composing the parts on staves, it would have been difficult for him to obtain a sense of how the various parts would line up using this presentation.

More likely, the sketches of *Marginal Intersection* with notes on staves were produced after the graph and are, perhaps, Feldman's first attempts at producing a set of instrumental part-books for performers unwilling, or unable, to play from the graph notation itself, and this reading gains support from a comparison with the performance materials for several orchestral graphs that are available for hire from Peters. The presentation of the part-books for *Ixion* for chamber ensemble (Example 10.2), *Atlantis* (Example 10.3) and ...*Out of 'Last Pieces'* has many similarities with the layout of the Sketchbook 3 materials, and this points to a similarity in intent. Like the Sketchbook 3 materials, the part-books also use a modified staff notation. Each is presented on staves divided by bar lines, with no clef, and unlike those in the sketch materials, these are equally spaced. The number '5' is printed inside the stave at the start of each part-book, indicating the number of beats per bar.[32] In the Sketchbook 3 materials, notes are drawn in the normal way, but in the rental materials the presence of sounds is shown by a solid note head with an associated number but no stem, with the number matching the one in the corresponding cell in the published edition. In the part-books for *Ixion* and ...*Out of 'Last Pieces'*, groups of empty bars are written out, but those for *Atlantis* use the truncated presentation of groups of empty bars found in Sketchbook 3.[33]

In the rental materials, the register of the sound is shown by the vertical position of the note head in the stave. High sounds, which dominate *Ixion*, *Atlantis* and ...*Out of 'Last Pieces'*, are indicated by note heads placed on the top line, while sounds in the low register intermissions all appear on the bottom line. The transition from high to low register sounds, which occurs at the beginning of each low register intermission, is emphasised by the addition of a corresponding label, as is the subsequent transition back to high register (see Examples 10.2–10.3).[34]

Feldman's decision to resuscitate his early experiments in notating part-books was probably underpinned by a desire to placate musicians who

---

[32] The part-books from Peters lack time signatures.

[33] Part-books are not available for any early graphs.

[34] There are no middle register sounds in *Ixion* for chamber ensemble. Those in *Atlantis* and ...*Out of 'Last Pieces'* are played by the piano, for which part-books in the 'easier-to-read' notation are not provided.

Example 10.2 *Ixion* for chamber ensemble, part-book for clarinet, page 1

were uncomfortable reading his graph notation. The timing of his decision is not documented, but it is possible that it was triggered by his experiences in the rehearsals for the premiere of *Ixion* for chamber ensemble on 17 August 1958. Years later, Cage explained:

[T]here've been so many problems [with using new notations]. Remember that interesting one with [. . .] 'Ixion', where it was written on graph and used numbers and that was the piece, of course, and that was the way to read it. But

Example 10.3 *Atlantis*, part-book for trumpet, page 1

through the exigencies of rehearsals and so forth, I translated it into something conventional – with quarter notes, you remember? – which was not what the piece was, but which permitted the musicians to quickly play it. Where the numbers meant that they would have had to devote themselves in a way that they actually didn't have the time or inclination to do.[35]

[35] Cage and Feldman, *Radio Happenings*, 181.

As noted in Chapter 7, two part-books in Cage's handwriting have survived. These differ from the rental materials only in that they include a 5/4 time signature, utilise a one-line stave and include the John Cage tempo changes, described in the same chapter.

Anything that can be expressed in the graph notation can also be expressed in the more conventional notation of the rental materials, but even so there are several reasons why the former is preferable. The use of aspects of more conventional notation was not only less elegant, because of the redundant presence of unused lines, but it was also more likely to mislead because its conventional use is ingrained. For example, the common situation of note heads that designate high sounds on the top line of the stave and of note heads designating low sounds on the bottom line may create the incorrect impression that all sounds in the same register are of the given pitch, while the use of a solid note head, which is part of a familiar symbol with an established use in indicating durations, may create the incorrect impression that the duration of each sound or group of sounds is equal to the duration of its associated bracket. Closely connected criticisms can be made of the similar presentation of the part-books for the chamber ensemble version of *Ixion* in Cage's handwriting and those for *Intersection 1* and *Marginal Intersection* that Feldman experimented with in the early 1950s.

The part-books for *In Search of an Orchestration*, available for hire from Universal Edition, are unlike those mentioned above in being presented in graph format (see Example 10.4), and are therefore superior. Some of Feldman's working materials still survive,[36] and it is evident that he constructed them using a cut-and-paste method, initially dissecting a copy of the finished graph score into its component rows and then pasting these onto separate sheets, with each sheet containing rows for two, three or four instruments.[37] No doubt performers wishing to play earlier graphs from part-books presented in graph notation could consider trying something similar.

Interpreting the more conventionally notated fragment from *Intersection 1* is complicated by the significant differences between the musical content of the fragment and the opening stages of the published score. Although there are strong similarities between their pitch-related contents, as noted above, the agreement is far from exact, especially in the second half of the fragment, and whereas the lowest stave is labelled 'Cellos', the corresponding area in the graph is marked 'Cellos and basses'.

---

[36] Morton Feldman Collection, Paul Sacher Foundation.
[37] The notation of the percussion parts in the published edition of the score occasionally straddles several rows of the grid, and this necessitated a revised presentation in some places in the corresponding part-books.

Example 10.4   *In Search of an Orchestration*, part-book for piccolo etc., page 6

These differences suggest that the fragment was produced before the compositional process was completed. Moreover, in this case, groups of adjacent, empty bars are not truncated; vertical bar lines straddle all four staves in the system, meaning that corresponding horizontal locations in each part are synchronised.

A clue to the provenance of the fragment appears to the right of the written note quoted above, where Feldman wrote out six different examples of how the first bar for woodwinds could be played. In each example, he varied dynamics ('p', 'mf', 'ff', 'ppp', 'f' and 'mp') and the rhythmic placement of the indicated high register sound. Curiously, only two of his suggestions about placement relative to the pulse are strictly consistent with the notation in the first bar, if the notation is read as in the published edition. Although it is just possible that this was a sketch of materials intended for use in communicating the musical content of the graph to performers who were unwilling or unable to tackle it in graph format, these errors suggest that this was an early attempt to think through a revised interpretation of the notation of the *Projections* for use in *Intersection 1*.

This completes the review of the sketches on staves described above, but an apparently similar item, located elsewhere, remains to be discussed. This is an undated fragment in Feldman's handwriting, shown in Figure 10.3, which is

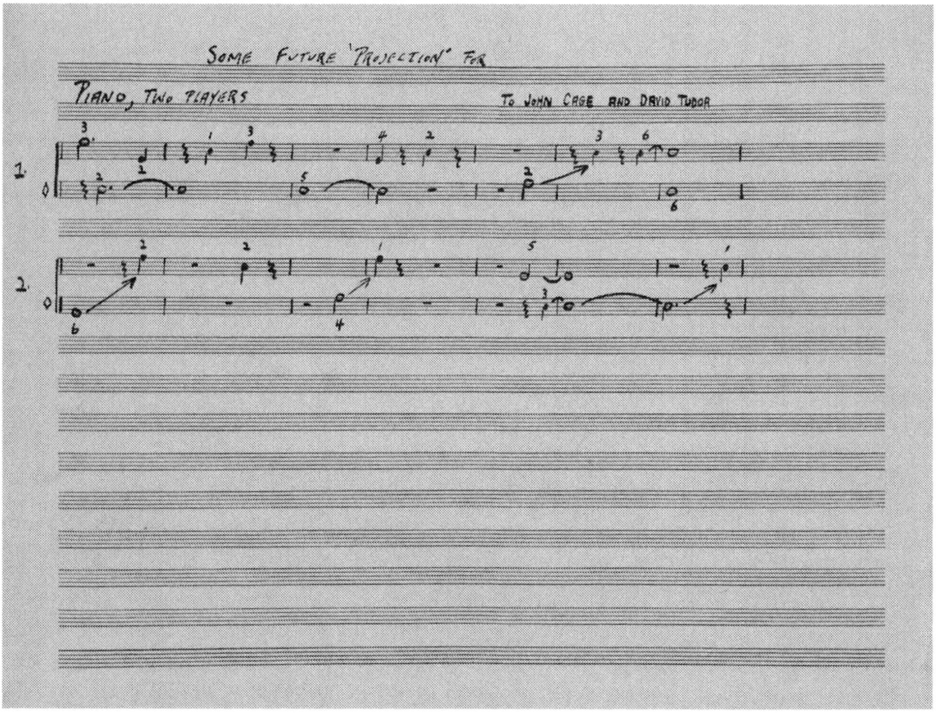

Figure 10.3 'Some Future "Projection" for Piano, Two Players', sketch

dedicated to Cage and Tudor.[38] Even though its title indicates that it is a plan for a 'Projection', it consists of notes on staves on music manuscript paper. The one-page fragment includes the first seven bars of the new *Projection*, with each piano part presented on two staves. The upper stave specifies notes to be struck while the lower stave (labelled '◊') marks keys to be depressed silently. There are notable similarities between the content of the fragment and the opening of *Projection 3*, especially in the part for the second piano, which suggest that it was a preliminary plan for the published graph. The implication appears to be that Feldman sketched the beginning of *Projection 3* using more conventional notation before presenting it in the graph format.

The use of note heads with associated numbers in the rental materials from Peters links them to 'Some Future "Projection" for Piano, Two Players', which also uses numbers, but with more conventionally structured symbols (with stems). As in the Sketchbook 3 materials, Feldman used only three positions on his staves, and it is now obvious that this is

---

[38] John Cage Collection, Northwestern University Music Library.

another example of him reinterpreting staff notation, with the three positions representing the high, middle and low registers.

Having said that, we cannot interpret this particular fragment as a restatement of material previously composed in the graph format because the title indicates that it was a plan for a forthcoming work. The use of the term 'Projection' and the restricted use of the staves both suggest that a graph was intended, unless the fragment pre-dated the graph format altogether. Yet this is unlikely, not only because it would contravene Feldman's testimony presented in Chapter 1, but also because the use of the term 'Projection' as a stand-alone title was not established until *Projection 2*: the only complete sketch of its published predecessor is headed 'Composition for Cello (Projection 1)', as previously noted. If, however, the fragment postdated Cage's wild rice dinner party, Feldman must have worked out the initial idea for *Projection 3* in more conventional notation, even though he had already conceived of the graph format. That being so, the compositional process would not have involved abstracting the graph from the more conventionally notated material, because the pitches notated in the fragment are already indefinite, and to the same degree as in the early graph music.

If this is what happened and if it was representative of the way in which Feldman composed the earliest graphs, there cannot have been an 'allover' aspect to his method of working of the sort previously described. However, it is surely unlikely that Feldman typically worked this way, even in the early days. His own testimony is at odds with the idea: in a passage quoted in full in Chapter 4, he explained how, in 1951, he had 'put sheets of graph paper on the wall' to work on,[39] and Wolff remembered seeing him proceed in this way.[40] Also, sketches of several early graphs in graph format that bear traces of having been worked on by Feldman still survive,[41] including those for *Marginal Intersection* mentioned above and elsewhere in this study. In these, the presence of significant amendments makes it much less likely that the graphs were simply transcribed from a more conventionally notated source. Given that no other materials of this type survive, it is highly unlikely that this was Feldman's usual method of composing, even in the early days, and its use in this case is, instead, probably attributable to mundane factors, such as his not having had any graph paper to hand.

Using graphs as tools in producing conventionally notated works involves working from less precise indications of register in the graph to more precise specifications in the finished composition, and this makes evident sense,

---

[39] 'Crippled symmetry' [1981], 147.
[40] 'Taking chances', 68.
[41] An example from *Projection 5* is shown in Figure 6.1 (Chapter 6).

but working in the opposite direction, towards a graph through a conventionally notated intermediate stage, seems a somewhat unnatural approach, involving unnecessary specificity, and the surviving record, properly construed, gives no indication that Feldman ever utilised this method.[42]

The legacy of the graphs in Feldman's other music

The completed manuscripts of almost all Feldman's conventionally notated works are presented in unusual fashion,[43] with bar lines drawn at regular intervals so that every stave contains the same number of bars and every page is arranged in the same, regimented fashion.[44] This mode of presentation implies a rectilinear organisation that invites comparison with the grid frames of his graphs. Feldman himself drew attention to this similarity in a 1983 interview, in which he stated that 'I still use a grid. But now the grid encompasses conventional notation'.[45]

The origins of this practice remain obscure; in particular, it is unclear which of Feldman's conventionally notated works from the 1950s were conceived in this regimented fashion from the outset and which were simply re-copied by him into this format soon after completion or in the early 1960s as he prepared final versions for publication by the C. F. Peters Corporation. Claren has noted that pre-publication copies of several of the conventionally notated scores from this period exist in multiple formats, some of which exhibit a grid-like homogeneity whereas others do not, and that it is usually a matter of debate which came first.[46]

Feldman also used a comparable grid-like organisation in most of his works with fixed pitches and indeterminate durations, even though these often lack bar lines. In many of the published editions of these works,[47] each stave contains the same number of evenly spaced beats or notes, meaning that those in one stave are vertically aligned with those in others. Once again, this produces a rectilinear organisation that is replicated on

---

[42] Boutwell and Noble both mention a sketch of *Projection 4* in conventional notation (A Static Sublime, 69, and *Composing Ambiguity*, 144), which this section has ignored. The materials in question (Morton Feldman Collection, Paul Sacher Foundation), which are not in Feldman's handwriting, are, in fact, a transcription of the opening of a recorded performance of *Projection 4* by David Tudor and Mathew Raimondi. The first ten bars are included in David Behrman, 'What indeterminate notation determines', *Perspectives of New Music*, vol. 3, no. 2 (Spring–Summer 1965), 65.

[43] The early *Journey to the End of the Night* (1947) and *Illusions* are notable exceptions.

[44] Typically, this aspect of their presentation has been altered or lost in typeset editions. For a discussion, see Tom Hall, 'Notational image, transformation and the grid in the late music of Morton Feldman', *Current Issues in Music*, vol. 1 (2007), 19, 21.

[45] 'An interview with Morton Feldman, Jan Williams', 153.   [46] *Neither*, 136–7.

[47] Very few have been engraved or typeset.

each page. Claren has argued that, very probably, the works of this type that preceded the contract with the C. F. Peters Corporation were not presented in a similarly organised manner originally, but were instead re-copied into a more organised format at this time.[48] One of the lessons that Feldman learned from Cage – who had helped him fine tune the presentation of his graph music in 1951 and whose scores had by 1960 been exhibited and sold as visual art – was the value in presenting musical works in an attractive and distinctive manner.

From the early 1960s onwards, it is likely that Feldman often worked with similar grids from the outset, initially in works with fixed pitches and indeterminate durations. This is evident from the fact that the published layout can sometimes be seen to have shaped the resulting work. For example, the architectural significance of individual page lengths in *Two Pieces for Clarinet and String Quartet* (1961) is revealed by the fact that activity regularly dissipates towards the end of a page before beginning anew on the very first beat of the next page,[49] and is equally clear in part II of *Rabi Akiba* (1963), in which a slightly altered version of the material that appears in the first system – there are two systems per page – is presented in every subsequent system except the last. This mirrors Feldman's similar preoccupation with individual pages in *...Out of 'Last Pieces', The Straits of Magellan* and *In Search of an Orchestration*. A closely related tendency is evident in his propensity to scale many of the works from this period so that they extend across the entire width of a whole number of score pages.[50] *Two Pieces for Clarinet and String Quartet, Durations 5* (1961) and *For Franz Kline* all include a regular arrangement of seventeen columns of evenly spaced beats or notes per page, with a last system that spans the exact width of the final page, whereas all four movements of *Intervals* (1961) end in exactly this manner.

Other effects of the pre-established layout are evident in several conventionally notated works, most notably those – like *On Time and the Instrumental Factor* – that include elements of superimposition. This process, which involved superimposing whole pages and parts of pages in order to produce closely related, but denser material, would have been greatly assisted by the use of the same geometric arrangement of material on source and destination pages.

There is, however, no evidence to suggest that Feldman used the grid-like organisation of his pages to facilitate a fully fledged allover method of

---

[48] *Neither*, 138–9.

[49] See the transitions between the following systems: system 2, page 3 and system 1, page 4; system 2, page 4 and system 1, page 5; and system 2, page 5 and system 1, page 6.

[50] Claren, *Neither*, 139.

working like the one used in his graphs. That said, he does seem to have made use of a closely related but somewhat less extreme procedure, comparable with the cut-up techniques of Brion Gysin and William S. Burroughs, in at least some of the long, late conventionally notated works, including *Crippled Symmetry* and *For Philip Guston* (1984).[51] As Feldman himself recalled, 'I began to not tie things over the bar line so that the measures themselves would be flexible when, and if, I want to juxtapose them around',[52] and elsewhere he was clear that to 'juxtapose them around' involved physically removing these single-bar constructions from one location in the score and pasting them into another location.[53] Evidently, the grid-like organisation of his pages, which standardised the size of each bar, greatly assisted in this process.

No doubt Feldman valued these and other specific outputs of his decision to transplant the grid-based organisation of his graph notation, but he also highlighted a more general benefit:

> The grid is very very important. And by the grid I mean that I decide [. . .] how big the measures are gonna be. [. . .] and usually it's decided by the amount of material [. . .] what I like about a grid is that [. . .] it's a time structure [. . .] I'm placing this in time. [. . .] I'm on an interesting ruler [. . .] and I got this idea ten years ago from my rugs [. . .] I was always going from mm, cm, inches and I decided I was going to do the same thing in music. In other words most music starts, it's consistent [. . . the composer] thinks in feet, yards [. . .] the grid is not the same. The grid to me is a substitute for pulse, it helped me get rid of the pulse.[54]

His idea, it seems, was that the grid functioned as a succession of points of reference and a predetermined compartmentalisation, by page and cell, which facilitated an organised approach to placing sounds during the compositional process. Unlike a uniform pulse, which could also perform a similar role, this framework remained largely inaudible in the listening experience. The unusual aspect of this idea stems from the fact that his conventionally notated works from the 1970s and 1980s typically make use of regularly mutating time signatures, which sometimes vary in consecutive bars, and which often differ between parts; hence his reference to different units of measurement. In some cases, but not in others, the differences between bars cancel each other out eventually or, more often, at regular intervals and the parts temporarily realign.

---

[51] Feldman compared his method with that of Burroughs in *Naked Lunch* in 'The future of local music', unpublished transcript, 232.

[52] 'Between Disney and Mondrian. Lecture, 2 July 1987', in Mörchen (ed.), *Morton Feldman in Middelburg*, 592.

[53] '"I'm reassembling all the time"', 58.

[54] 'The future of local music', unpublished transcript, 8–10.

Herein lies the principal difference from the grid of the graphs, in which there is a proportional relationship between space on the page and elapsed time in performance. In the conventionally notated works from the 1970s and 1980s, by contrast, this simple relationship is lost and replaced by one that is not only mutable, but also multidimensional because each performer proceeds through the given material at a different rate. Whereas the graph notation provides a more literal picture of the associated music than standard uses of conventional notation, it is clear that these in their turn provide a more literal picture than Feldman's non-standard use of the same notation in his later works. Much the same can be said of his employment of a grid-like underpinning in his works with fixed pitches and indeterminate durations, but these differ in that the dislocation between page and sound is not explicitly notated. Here individual instruments or groups of instruments are to proceed at their own pace, which may or may not be steady and which may or may not be the same as the pace assumed by other performers. In both cases, the literal aspect of the picture presented by the graph notation is compromised.

Speaking of *Crippled Symmetry*, Feldman wrote:

> [T]he patterns that interest me are both concrete and ephemeral, making notation difficult. [. . .] Though these patterns exist in rhythmic shapes articulated by instrumental sounds, they are also in part *notational images* that do not make a direct impact on the ear as we listen. A tumbling of sorts happens in midair between their translation from the page and their execution. To a great degree, this tumbling occurs in all music – but becomes more compounded in mine, since there is no rhythmic 'style,' a quality often crucial to the performer's understanding of how and what to do. I found this just as true in my music of the fifties – where rhythm was not notated, but left to the performer.[55]

A comparison between this passage, written long after he had ceased composing in graph notation, and his earliest published statements, written in the thick of composing his first graphs, gives us a glimpse of subtle changes in his outlook that had taken place over the years. All refer to images, which we can assume were, for Feldman, the mental modes of presentation of the auditory and visual properties of his works or, perhaps, their most essential elements, experienced by him during the creative act, but also in recollection.[56] However, in the early passages, the image associated with a work is unitary and an apparently seamless synthesis of visual and aural aspects, whereas in the passage quoted above he claims a plurality

---

[55] 'Crippled symmetry' [1981], 143. Feldman's emphasis.
[56] 'Image is something you remember' ('Interview, Saturday, June 29, 1985').

of images, each associated with a particular 'pattern', which is usually contained within a single bar, and although each has visual and aural aspects, the connection between them is now enigmatic.

The impact of the graphs on his other music was therefore significant, but rather indirect. Through the mechanism of the grid, they shaped a great deal of his output, but only through a distorting lens that reconfigured its meaning and necessitated a reorientation in conceptual foundations. The literalness of the picture presented by the graph notation, which ensured a seamless link between the visual and the aural, was a vital element in Feldman's philosophy in the heyday of his graph music because it was this that squared his apparently incompatible interests in visual aspects of his notation, on the one hand, and sound itself, on the other. With the perspicuity of his notation compromised in his later music, necessitating what he referred to in the passage quoted above as a 'tumbling of sorts [that] happens in midair between their translation from the page and their execution', this reconciliation and therefore the idea of giving sole emphasis to sound were no longer available.

11 Moving on

The spontaneous creative act that resulted in Feldman's invention of graph notation at Cage's wild rice dinner party in 1950 was a seminal event in the history of post-war classical music. This is because there are compelling grounds for seeing it, and the early graphs that it spawned, as originating the widespread interest in graphic notations and less precise specifications of outcomes that began to emerge in the mid-1950s and which was prevalent in the United States and Europe throughout the 1960s.

This is not a claim about the historical precedence of Feldman's graphs. Although they may have been the first series of finished musical works to be presented in a workable proportional notation and the first to be presented on graph paper, for example, they were certainly not the first compositions from the modern era to include indeterminate elements, as noted in the introduction to this monograph. They may not even have been the first indeterminate works from a New York School composer; as previously noted, it is possible that this accolade belongs to Wolff, although this is by no means certain.

All the same, Feldman's graphs have a historical pedigree not shared by any prior works, which stems from the fact that it was they that triggered the causal chains that culminated in the outcomes mentioned above. In saying this, my intention is neither to suggest that Feldman's graphs were *ex nihilo* nor to belittle the historical significance of many other vitally important, subsequent links in these same chains, some of which are mentioned in what follows.

Despite the seminal character of his formative contribution to the history of indeterminacy and graphic notations, Feldman's subsequent input to this history appears to have been modest, both in terms of works composed and by dint of his physical presence. As previously noted, his innovations were quickly taken up and developed by others in ways that clearly demonstrated their immense potential in facilitating new forms of musical expression. No doubt this was part of their appeal, as was the fact that they offered an innovative response to the alleged weaknesses of total serialism, including its self-defeating excess of control over sounds in performance and closely connected tendency to depreciate the creative input of the performer.[1] It is true that Feldman experimented with equally radical ideas, detailed in Appendix 1, but he did not pursue them, and eventually settled on a programme of modifying and perfecting his graph notation and his later notations for fixed pitches and indeterminate durations, thereby relinquishing the vanguard to a succession of others. Given his insistence on the importance of sonority, this is perhaps unsurprising, and by the early 1960s he was openly critical of innovation for its own sake: as he put it: '[i]nnovations be damned – it's a boring century'.[2]

Brown was one of several important agents in the subsequent dissemination of ideas about new notations and indeterminacy to an international audience through his regular presence in Europe from 1956 onwards.[3] However, it seems to have been the brilliant marketing efforts of Cage and Tudor that had the greatest impact. It is true that their influence on specific individuals, such as Stockhausen and Boulez, who would become avid supporters of some forms of indeterminacy – initially open form – in the mid-1950s, is disputed.[4] Even so, the general success of Tudor's ambassadorial work in promoting new music from the United States in Europe (and new music from abroad in the United States) in 1954–64 is now generally agreed,[5] as is the importance of Cage's presence at the Darmstadt International Summer Course for New Music in September 1958.[6] A recent study has argued that the 'shock' produced by Cage's activities at Darmstadt destroyed the apparent collegiality of the Darmstadt composers by nurturing and exposing previously existing differences of ideology and approach,[7] resulting in 'open warfare',[8] but on a more prosaic level Cage's polemical lecture on indeterminacy,[9] which was the second of three he presented at the festival that year, certainly gave the concept centre stage. Although *Intersection 3* was a mainstay of Tudor's repertoire in concerts in Europe in the mid-1950s and one of Cage's exemplars of indeterminacy in

---

[1] Behrman, 'What indeterminate notation determines', 58–9.

[2] 'Mr. Schuller's history lesson' [1963], in Friedman (ed.), *Give My Regards*, 9.

[3] For Brown's contacts with Berio, Boulez and Maderna, see his comments in 'An interview with Earle Brown', 341–2.

[4] Stockhausen and Boulez began working with indeterminacy after encountering the work of the Americans, but both attributed their inspiration primarily to other sources. Boulez emphasised literary influences, including James Joyce and Stéphane Mallarmé ('Sonate, que me veux-tu?', *Perspectives of New Music*, vol. 1, no. 2 (Spring 1963), 32–7), but agreed that 'the current state of musical thought' also had an impact on his thinking (*ibid.*, 32). More recently, he stated that he 'learned much from the spirit of the time and from Earle [Brown] too' ('..."ouvert", encore...', 340). Stockhausen emphasised the influence of his study of information theory under Werner Meyer-Eppler ('Interview with Karlheinz Stockhausen held August 11, 1976', by Ekbert Faas, *Interface: Journal of New Music Research*, vol. 6 (1977), 191).

[5] Beal, *New Music, New Allies*, 82–6.

[6] See, for example, Peyser, *Boulez*, 140, and Iddon, *New Music at Darmstadt*, 196–299.

[7] *Ibid.*, 286.   [8] *Ibid.*, 295.   [9] 'Composition as process: II. Indeterminacy', 35–40.

his Darmstadt lecture, Feldman would remain in the United States until 1966, when he travelled to the UK. He does not seem to have visited Continental Europe until 1971,[10] by which time international enthusiasm for indeterminacy and graphic notations was already waning.

There can be little doubt that the complex chain of events triggered by Feldman's efforts subsequently affected the development of his own music, and previous chapters outlined some of the ways in which the escalating repercussions of his original innovation resounded in his subsequent output. The following sections complete the chronological survey begun in Chapters 1–2 by arguing that later elements in the causal chain formed part of a complex web of influences that led him away from graph music.

Rapprochement with conventional notation

After completing *In Search of an Orchestration* during the first half of 1967, Feldman resumed working with fixed pitches and indeterminate durations in a series of compositions in which activity within individual sections of the ensemble is loosely coordinated with vertical and diagonal lines between note heads or strictly coordinated using conventional notation, but in which the individual sections proceed independently of one another after a coordinated first entrance.[11] Even so, he retained an active interest in graph music. For example, in July 1968, he replied to Gerd Zacher's request for a new work for organ by suggesting that it might be possible to make a 'brilliant realization' of *Intersection 3*.[12] He also suggested to Bertram Turetzky performing *Intersection 4* on contrabass.[13] As noted in Chapter 8, these events are odd in view of the great importance he claimed to place on instrumentation;[14] they strongly suggest that he was actively courting interest in his graph music at this time.

Feldman's comments reported in a magazine article published in December 1968 establish that he was still comfortable with the idea of composing new graphs around this time, more than a year after completing *In Search of an Orchestration*.[15] The author, John Gruen, explained that

[10] Claren, 'A Feldman chronology', 266–8.
[11] *First Principles* (1967) for chamber ensemble, *False Relationships and the Extended Ending* (1968) for trombone, three pianos, chimes, violin and cello and *Between Categories* (1969) for two pianos, two chimes, two violins and two cellos.
[12] Morton Feldman to Gerd Zacher, July 1968. Zacher's first performance of *Intersection 3* on organ took place on 26 June 1969.
[13] Programme, University of Michigan School of Music, 8 April 1969, and Programme, USCD Music Department, 8 December 1969.
[14] 'Unpublished writings: III', 205–7.
[15] John Gruen, '"This modesty of sound"', *VOGUE*, December 1968, 283.

Feldman planned to write a new work for 'inaudible frequencies' for the Experiments in Art and Technology (EAT) group. Feldman outlined his EAT project as follows:

> I will be composing a music that exists at the threshold of sound – and at varying degrees below it [. . .] Audibility will go into an inward state. I will be able to discover whether inaudible frequencies of sound can be transmitted – if they can be communicated . . . I want to create a music that is the closest to the initial impetus of composition – that is, before it becomes audible language.[16]

Gruen explained that Rauschenberg and Billy Kluver, central figures in the EAT group, would perform Feldman's work on specially created electronic instruments in January 1969 'from Feldman's graph-like score'.[17] It is unclear whether this or the planned performance ever materialised, but the article demonstrates that Feldman retained an interest in producing new graphs. There is no evidence to suggest that he contemplated doing so subsequently, however. Given that he regarded *In Search of an Orchestration* as his most important graph work, his apparent loss of interest in the graph format at this time is initially puzzling.

Despite Feldman's previous reservations about conventionally notated music, a rekindled confidence in it had emerged in 1960, when he began composing *Structures* for orchestra, a work presented only in this format, which he completed in 1962. The following year, he produced *De Kooning*, which was the first of a group of works in which passages with fixed pitches and indeterminate durations appear alongside passages in staff notation, as noted in Chapter 2. This revival of interest in a more conventional format culminated in *On Time and the Instrumental Factor* (1969) for orchestra, the first work written entirely in conventional staff notation since *Structures*. From then on, conventional notation would be his preferred choice, although an interest in indeterminate durations did resurface, temporarily, in *Five Pianos* (1972) and *Pianos and Voices* (1972).[18]

---

[16] *Ibid.* Feldman's idea of getting close 'to the initial impetus of composition' was surely connected with Rainer Maria Rilke's speculations about whether the needle of a gramophone drawn across the coronal suture of a skull might produce a 'primal sound' that articulates the 'feelings' of its owner ('Primal sound', in *Selected works: Volume 1: Prose*, trans. G. Craig Houston (London: Hogarth Press, 1954), 53). Feldman was devoted to Rilke's works and had used a text by him in the very early composition *Only* (1947) for female voice.

[17] "'This modesty of sound'", 283.

[18] *Five Pianos* was originally titled 'Pianos and Voices'. *Pianos and Voices* was originally titled 'Pianos and Voices 2'.

The timing of his change of heart is striking because it coincided with a radical shift in emphasis in Western classical music, away from indeterminacy and serialism towards conventional notation and in some cases tonality, and it seems likely that this nurtured Feldman's altered stance. Several other composers who have featured prominently in this monograph also underwent important stylistic changes at this time. For example, in 1969, after years of designing processes for use in constructing performable works, Cage composed *Cheap Imitation* for piano by imitating the rhythms and phrase structures of Erik Satie's *Socrate* (1918), and he would go on to compose several comparable pieces using similar imitative methods.[19] Unlike most of his works of the 1960s, this was a performable composition in its own right,[20] and it was more traditional than its immediate predecessors in other ways also. For example, Cage relied on his own preferences, as well as the algorithms and chance that he had long favoured, in making note-to-note choices.[21] Moreover, he presented the finished work in conventional notation rather than one of the more bespoke symbol systems that he had been working with, meaning that it leaves no scope for increased performer choice.[22] Meanwhile, Wolff included an 'actual real tune' of his own in *Burdocks*,[23] which he began composing in 1970, and in subsequent works 'included pre-existing melodic material (from folk music mostly, and politically related), [...] notated conventionally pulsed rhythms, specified the pitches [...] and used recognizable counterpoint'.[24] After several years of producing graphic and verbal scores in which much is left to the discretion of the performers, Stockhausen tired of hearing what he regarded as their familiar choices and reverted to specifying events more precisely using conventional notation in *Mantra* (1970).[25]

No doubt this dramatic shift in the musical climate had multiple causes, which included political, social and economic factors and also the equally remarkable changes that these same forces engendered in other arts. Within music, the emergence of minimalism, which was seen by some as marking a return to a more consonant and accessible form of music

---

[19] Pritchett, *The Music of John Cage*, 165.   [20] *Ibid.*, 164.

[21] Marc Jensen, 'The role of choice in John Cage's "Cheap Imitation"', *Tempo*, vol. 63, no. 247 (January 2009), 25–6.

[22] William Brooks, 'Choice and change in Cage's recent music', in Peter Gena and Jonathan Brent (eds.), *A John Cage Reader: In Celebration of his 70th Birthday* (New York: Peters, 1982), 86–7.

[23] Christian Wolff to David Cline, 29 February 2012 (email).

[24] 'Wolff', interview, in James Saunders (ed.), *The Ashgate Research Companion to Experimental Music* (Farnham: Ashgate, 2009), 362.

[25] 'Stockhausen: is he the way and the light?', interview by Peter Heyworth, *New York Times*, 21 February 1971, Section 2, 13.

making, and a marked increase in political activism, which encouraged the use of less esoteric modes of expression, are often cited as influential, but it is likely that there were many other factors also in play. One of these is the inherently performer-centric aspect of the more extreme forms of indeterminate music from the 1960s, which actively sought to engage the performer's creative input. Inevitably, this generated tensions between composers and performers in some cases,[26] and it may have alienated audiences, who were not always the primary focus of the composer's attention. As one observer commented, '[t]he listener/spectator is liable to find himself in the position of someone on the edge of a party where some people know each other but the strangers are never introduced. How nice it would be to join in that intriguing conversation *Stimmung* [. . .] or even take part in that complicated game *Prozession*'.[27]

In a letter dated 16 December 1975, in which Feldman responded to a question posed by William Colleran of Universal Edition – by then his publisher – about the reasons why he no longer composed graphs, he explained that it was his graph music and his 'free durational music of the 60's' that had 'abandoned its composer', and not vice versa.[28] The implication was that he ceased producing graph music without rejecting it, and there is no evidence to suggest that he ever held a different view, although he did refer to what he regarded as the chief weaknesses of the graph format – namely, the associated risk of performers making inappropriate choices and its grounding in a regular tempo – on subsequent occasions.[29] In his letter, Feldman went on to express misgivings about being able to 'give a blow by blow description of what took place'. Although this is frustrating for us, it is not without significance, for it clearly insinuates that there were several factors involved in his change of stance. Consequently, justice demands a narrative account of his metamorphosis with more than one strand.

Feldman's letter to Colleran includes the following postscript: '[a]ctually, the divorce between my graph music and myself ended amicably. It received untold alimony: my past'.[30] This strongly suggests that

---

[26] Stockhausen's relations with some performers of his indeterminate works became strained in the late 1960s, and this seems to have precipitated his changed approach. For his disagreement with Vinko Globokar over authorship of improvised performances of *Aus den sieben Tagen* (1968), see Kurtz, *Stockhausen*, 174. For his suppression of elements of improvised performances that he disliked from the mixing desk at Darmstadt in 1970, see Peter Heyworth, 'Composer-prophet', *The Observer*, 25 April 1971, 9.

[27] Christopher Shaw, 'Stockhausen: *Mantra* by Alfons and Aloys Kontarsky, Karlheinz Stockhausen', *Tempo*, New Series, no. 102 (1972), 41.

[28] Morton Feldman to William Colleran, 16 December 1975, Morton Feldman Collection, Paul Sacher Foundation. Feldman terminated his contract with the C. F. Peters Corporation in 1969.

[29] *'Soundpieces* interview', 91.   [30] Morton Feldman to William Colleran, 16 December 1975.

Feldman associated the final break with graph music with a schism in his life. Although he wrote that he could not remember what had taken place, it is clear that the late 1960s and early 1970s were years of tumultuous change for him. These changes, which included the break-up of his second marriage,[31] were, I suggest, parts of a complex web of influences that stimulated a desire for a new direction in his music.

Rosenberg's attack

Feldman's family business 'went kaput' in the mid-1960s and his financial situation became tenuous:[32] as he put it, in a letter to Cage, 'now I'm blessed with total insecurity'.[33] Continuing to produce overtly 'far-out' music must have seemed a risky way of establishing a professional career as a composer, which became his aim. In the early 1950s, his graphs had given him notoriety, but by the mid-1960s the use of indeterminacy and unusual notations was commonplace. Moreover, his graphs had already been exposed to a wider audience through the New York Philharmonic's performances of . . .*Out of 'Last Pieces'* and had failed to achieve the kind of positive response he needed. Even so, he persisted with the graph format, composing *In Search of an Orchestration*, but he was evidently concerned about its reception. In an interview recorded in early 1967, while working on it, he admitted that his music 'was not very successful with the general public',[34] and a newspaper article printed the following month reported him as saying that 'there are few that really like and understand it'.[35] His fears appear to have been well founded: as noted in Chapter 2, *In Search of an Orchestration* seems to have encountered little interest from potential performers.

A Guggenheim Fellowship, awarded in 1966, alleviated Feldman's financial concerns temporarily and facilitated a number of lecture tours in the UK,[36] but any doubts he had about continuing to compose as previously would certainly have been heightened by an article published in 1969 that included a vigorous attack on the conceptual foundations of his graph music. The article, by Harold Rosenberg – Greenberg's main rival in interpreting Abstract Expressionism – began by arguing that the

---

[31] Claren suggests that they separated in 1970 ('A Feldman chronology', 268).
[32] Morton Feldman to John Cage, 29 March 1966, John Cage Collection, Northwestern University Music Library.
[33] *Ibid.*   [34] 'Traffic light music', 25.
[35] David D. Dolin, 'Brush blade, pen: harbinger of spring – on stage', *Texas Catholic Herald*, 17 March 1967, 10.
[36] Claren, 'A Feldman chronology', 266.

words and concepts connected with a contemporary work of art are essential to its status as an artwork. This is because they create a 'mist of interpretation' between the physical object and the senses that transform the object into something more.[37] Rosenberg contrasted his position with two competing views: the first, exemplified by earthworks sculpture, attempted to compensate for the physical inaccessibility of an alleged work by overemphasising the associated concepts; the second underemphasised concepts in what he described as a vain attempt to let the materials '"speak for themselves"'.[38]

Rosenberg took Feldman's remarks in his programme note for the New York Philharmonic's performances of ...*Out of 'Last Pieces'* as a prime example of this second error. In these, Feldman had stated that 'sound *in itself* can be a totally plastic phenomenon, suggesting its own shape, design and poetic metaphor',[39] a position that Rosenberg compared, unfavourably, with the paintings of Willem de Kooning and Pollock, both artists whose works Feldman admired. According to Rosenberg, neither painter merely allowed the paint to be itself; both achieve 'a synthesis of will and chance' because 'the animated paint takes its form from the artist's personality'.[40] By way of contrast, Rosenberg presented Feldman's stance as a musical equivalent of Helen Frankenthaler's soak-stain painting technique, which Rosenberg rejected: 'since she is content to let the pigment do most of the acting, her compositions fail to develop resistances against which a creative act can take place'.[41] The implication was that Feldman also failed to develop the 'resistances' that are a prerequisite of producing an artwork, and the unstated conclusion was that Feldman's graphs, like Frankenthaler's paintings, could not be regarded as works of art. For Rosenberg, Feldman's error was compounded by a fundamental incoherence in the aesthetic viewpoint that underpinned it: not only were his methods incapable of producing art, but they were also based on a near-contradiction, 'because no material can in fact be "left to its own devices."'[42] Evidently, Rosenberg's position was that a minimum of intervention was necessary, if only in the selection process.

As arguments against Feldman's position, these points are hardly compelling. Rosenberg's jibe that Feldman's music and Frankenthaler's paintings were not art was not supported by a credible ontology; he did not say why 'resistances' were necessary and, more importantly, how many 'resistances', of which types and of what degree needed to be present. If his

---

[37] 'Art and words' [1969], in *The De-Definition of Art* (University of Chicago Press, 1983), 55.
[38] *Ibid.*, 60. The scare quotes are Rosenberg's.   [39] '...Out of "Last Pieces"', G.
[40] 'Art and words', 61.   [41] *Ibid.*, 64.   [42] *Ibid.*, 68.

allegation was simply that Feldman and Frankenthaler had expended insufficient effort, then the importance of this aspect of the creative process had been called into question earlier in the twentieth century by Marcel Duchamp's readymades, and in the 1960s was being tested again by Minimalist and Conceptual Art. Furthermore, Feldman's remark that 'sound *in itself* can suggest 'its own shape, design and poetic metaphor', which Rosenberg objected to, was doubtless an overstatement.[43] As noted in Chapter 4, he had expressed his view more carefully in a 1966 interview, in which he explained that his idea was to create 'a precarious balance between the material and its manipulation',[44] a position indistinguishable from the one that Rosenberg attributed – approvingly – to de Kooning and Pollock.

Nonetheless, it is likely that Feldman was embarrassed and unsettled by this public rebuke, especially in view of Rosenberg's close connections with the painters that he felt closest to: Guston depended upon him for encouragement and support, for example.[45] Feldman's consequential hostility was evident in his next major essay, in which he described the term 'action painting', Rosenberg's best-known contribution to the art scene of the early 1950s, as one he had 'never understood'.[46]

Problems in performances

Feldman had first-hand experience of controversial performances of indeterminate works in the early 1970s, which may have taken an additional toll. Two documented cases stem from his year-long stay in Berlin on a DAAD scholarship in 1971–2, which followed a two-year stint as Dean at the New York Studio School. One was the premiere of *Five Pianos*, performed by Cage, Cardew, Frederic Rzewski, Tudor and Feldman himself, in Berlin on 16 July 1972. In this particular work, starting points are staggered and not coordinated, but durations are constrained by a more involved description of the intended degree of flexibility than found in earlier works with fixed

---

[43] He also overstated his position in 'Morton Feldman – waiting', 40.

[44] 'Morton Feldman talking to Wilfrid Mellers'.

[45] For Rosenberg's friendship with Guston, see Dore Ashton, *A Critical Study of Philip Guston* (Berkeley: University of California Press, 1990), 131.

[46] 'Give my regards to Eighth Street', 99. Anecdotal evidence suggests that Feldman was unusually sensitive to criticism; hence his refusal to speak to Brown for years after a disagreement over the use of mathematics in composing. For other examples, see Morton Feldman, 'Johannesburg lecture 1: current trends in America, August 1983', in Villars (ed.), *Morton Feldman Says*, 164, and Christopher Fox, 'Imperfection and colour', *The Musical Times*, vol. 147, no. 1896 (Autumn 2006), 103. Brown recalled Cage describing Feldman as 'very, very, very, very sensitive' ('An interview with Earle Brown', 350).

pitches and indeterminate durations. The performance did not go well, with Cage's contribution lasting much longer than those of the other pianists. Some reports suggested that Feldman was angry with Cage,[47] whereas others suggested that he regarded Cage's performance as the only accurate one – his own rushed efforts having misled the other pianists.[48]

A different issue emerged in a performance of Wolff's *Burdocks* by the Scratch Orchestra in Munich later that year. Feldman, who attended the concert, stood up and denounced the performance before it was finished, apparently incensed by the inclusion of folk songs in one of the indeterminate parts.[49] Wolff was not present, but later explained that he was not uncomfortable with the Scratch Orchestra's approach.[50] Even so, Feldman's reaction demonstrates his sensitivity to what he perceived as inappropriate interpretations of indeterminate music.

More generally, attitudes to indeterminacy had shifted in the 1960s in ways Feldman must have found unsettling, with some musicians questioning the authority of graphic scores as specifications of actions or sounds, and using them instead as they saw fit; this shift in attitudes is reflected in Cardew's evolving stance towards his *Treatise* (1967), with later entries in his 'Treatise Handbook' portraying the intended use of his score in increasingly flexible terms.[51] Feldman was bound to lack sympathy with this shift given his professed disinterest in inviting creative input from performers and outright disdain for free improvisation.

Tudor's declining interest in the piano can only have heightened his awareness of performance-related risks. Although Tudor played in the premiere of *Five Pianos*, his enthusiasm for the instrument had dwindled during the 1960s as he focused increasingly on composing and performing electroacoustic works of his own.[52] This meant that Feldman could no longer rely on the services of the performer who had been most closely associated with his graph music since its inception.

---

[47] According to Cage, the slowness of his own performance 'stopped Morty from ever writing that way again!' ('John Cage and the Glaswegian circus: an interview around Musica Nova 1990', by Steve Sweeney Turner, *Tempo*, New Series, no. 177 (June 1991), 4).

[48] Amy Beal, Patronage and Reception History of American Experimental Music in West Germany, 1945–1986, unpublished PhD thesis, University of Michigan (1999), 289. The performance received unfavourable reviews (*ibid.*, 289–90, and Beal, *New Music, New Allies*, 236).

[49] The performance and reactions to it are discussed in John Tilbury, *Cornelius Cardew (1936–1981): A Life Unfinished* (Essex: Copula, 2008), 605–9.

[50] 'In a kind of no-man's land', 256.

[51] 'Treatise handbook' [1971], in Prévost (ed.), *Cornelius Cardew: A Reader*, 95–134. For a discussion of the shift in Cardew's stance, see Tilbury, *Cornelius Cardew (1936–1981)*, 234–42.

[52] Tudor's first electroacoustic works were *Fluorescent Sound* (1964) and *Bandoneon !* (1966). In 1966, Cage remarked that Tudor practised playing the piano only rarely (Cage and Feldman, *Radio Happenings*, 21).

Farewell to Abstract Expressionism

Feldman was appointed Slee Professor at the State University of New York at Buffalo in 1972, and in this new role he taught composition. Whether this was instrumental in his change in stance is not documented, but it is surely possible that his interest in securing a university appointment or the reality of university life initially engendered a desire for academic respectability, which drew him towards a more conventional mode of expression. Be that as it may, this section focuses on a different element in the causal chain that led him away from graph music. This was the gradual displacement of Abstract Expressionism, which had dominated art in the United States throughout the 1950s, from its previous position at the forefront of modern painting.

This process was a lengthy one, but by 1960 the rot had set in,[53] and by the mid-1960s the movement was increasingly seen as having been superseded by others, including Pop Art and Minimalism.[54] Several of its leading figures were already dead,[55] and the expressive brushstrokes associated with more gestural examples of the style, which were formerly seen as traces of aesthetic freedom and heroic individualism, had come to be viewed by many as a mannerism to be avoided or even parodied.[56] For reasons that will become clear, Guston's response to the changing status of the movement merits special attention.

Initially, Guston, who had painted in an Abstract Expressionist mode since the late 1940s, resisted the changing times, unveiling a new monochrome look in 1966, which included no fewer than eighty-one recent abstractions in which irregularly shaped black forms, which typically resist any more precise classification, float in a sea of grey brushstrokes,[57] but notices were poor, and in some cases scathing.[58] In an interview recorded shortly after the show, Guston admitted that 'the New York School' – he disliked the title 'Abstract Expressionism' – 'was a powerful revolutionary

---

[53] John Canaday, 'In the gloaming: twilight seems to be settling rapidly for Abstract Expressionism', *New York Times*, 11 September 1960, Section 2, X21.

[54] Hilton Kramer, 'Art: abstractions of Guston still further refined', *New York Times*, 15 January 1966, 22.

[55] Pollock, Franz Kline and David Smith died in 1956, 1962 and 1965, respectively.

[56] Lawrence Alloway, 'Systemic painting' [1966], in *Topics in American Art Since 1945* (New York: W. W. Norton, 1975), 82, and Robert Slifkin, *Out of Time: Philip Guston and the Refiguration of Postwar American Art* (Berkeley: University of California Press, 2013), 20.

[57] Guston had been grappling with the return of a representational imagery of sorts – one loosely suggestive of solid objects that resist tidy classification – into his previously pure abstractions since the mid-1950s. A striking example (*Head – Double View*) appeared on the cover of Feldman's 1959 Columbia LP record.

[58] For a particularly vicious example, see Kramer, 'Art', 22.

instinct which may have lost its power, which may have lost its efficacy in our current emotional climate. That's possible, but that can change',[59] but by the following year he seems to have given up any hope that the situation would reverse, writing dejectedly to Rosenberg that 'It's all over for the likes of us – I see the HANDWRITING ON The WALL [...] I feel like a sliding of values'.[60]

In 1967, Guston moved from New York City to Woodstock and, working in isolation, began drawing and then painting recognisable images of everyday objects. 'I can't seem to prevent doing what I am doing – It may be all a vast detour', he wrote to Feldman,[61] but it was not a detour, for these figurative works would be the basis of a new style that he would explore until his death in 1980. This combined the gestural brushstrokes and palette of reds, pinks, greens, greys and blacks of his earlier Abstract Expressionist paintings with disturbing cartoon-like imagery. Ku Klux Klansmen populate many of the new canvases, and this was one of several elements blatantly appropriated from his works that pre-dated his conversion to Abstract Expressionism.

These new figurative paintings were shown publicly for the first time in October 1970 in New York. Feldman recalled:

> It was a big show and a glamorous gallery – the Marlborough Gallery – and the place was jammed. I was looking at a picture, he comes over and says, 'What do you think?' And I said, 'Well, let me just look at it for another minute.' And with that, our friendship was over.[62]

Feldman was not alone in being underwhelmed by the dramatic shift in Guston's style; reviews were generally unfavourable and only a single drawing sold.[63] The difficulty was not simply his use of recognisable images – Pollock and de Kooning had previously achieved that feat without creating a similar backlash. It was the nature of the imagery, which was deliberately crude and darkly humorous and seen as a renunciation and even a betrayal not only of the vaunted 'purity' of Abstract Expressionist

---

[59] 'Conversation with Joseph Ablow', 58.

[60] Philip Guston to Harold Rosenberg, undated [ca. 1967], Harold Rosenberg Papers, Getty Research Institute. Dated ca. 1967 in Slifkin, *Out of Time*, 95. Guston was not the only artist struggling with the changing times. In a letter written while he was teaching at the University of California, Berkeley, Rothko complained: 'For my students here I am an old man with values belonging to a past' ('Letter to Elsie Asher and Stanley Kunitz, 1967', in López-Remiro (ed.), *Mark Rothko*, 156).

[61] Philip Guston to Morton Feldman, 24 February 1969, Morton Feldman Collection, Paul Sacher Foundation.

[62] 'For Philip Guston' [1988], in Friedman (ed.), *Give My Regards*, 198. See also Brian O'Doherty, 'Morton Feldman: the Burgacue years', in Kissane (ed.), *Vertical Thoughts*, 65.

[63] For only one drawing being sold, see Slifkin, *Out of Time*, 176.

art – 'I got sick and tired of all that Purity! wanted to tell Stories!'[64] – but also the deep seriousness of the associated ideal of existential angst. Worse still, it invited a political reading as a response to prevailing civil unrest that was seen as naïve:[65] hence, the title of the review in the *New York Times*: 'A mandarin pretending to be a stumblebum'.[66]

Although the negative response of the first reviewers has given way in recent years to a deeply appreciative reassessment of the Marlborough paintings and those that followed, there can be little doubt that the show marked Guston's 'farewell to the New York School', as the *New York Times* noted.[67] Indeed, a recent study has argued that the 'fading' of Abstract Expressionism, exemplified in the 'ghostliness' of the KKK hoods, which in these new works appear to symbolise painters, was one several key themes of the paintings,[68] which 'seep and seethe' and sometimes mock the lofty ideals of the movement.[69]

George Rochberg noticed a parallel between the trajectory of Guston's career – from representational imagery to abstraction and back to representational imagery – and his own musical development, which he described as 'from the intuitively naive tonal preoccupation of my early years and a publicly declared return to tonality after an intense period of immersion in total chromaticism via the 12-tone method'.[70] Rochberg's return to tonality, which culminated in his *String Quartet No. 3* (1971), a work which juxtaposes serial elements with material written in a nostalgic tonal idiom, is usually seen as emblematic of the shift from modernism to postmodernism in classical music, and this is how Rochberg presented it and Guston's reversion to figuration, as indicative of a changing *Zeitgeist* that 'clamored for and demanded concreteness'.[71] For Rochberg, the notable similarity between the trajectories of his career and Guston's around 1970 was simply a product of the changing times, but the suggestion made here is that there was a considerably more intimate link between

---

[64] Guston quoted in Bill Berkson, 'The new Gustons', *ARTnews*, vol. 69, no. 6 (October 1970), 44.

[65] Slifkin, *Out of Time*, 31–2.

[66] Hilton Kramer, 'A mandarin pretending to be a stumblebum', *New York Times*, 25 October 1970, Section 2, D27.

[67] *Ibid*. For a similar view, see John Gruen, 'Demons and daisies', *New York Magazine*, 9 November 1970, 62.

[68] Silfkin, *Out of Time*, 110

[69] *Ibid*., 104, 113–19. Slifkin has also argued that the Marlborough works include many allusions to the 1930s – not only to Guston's own biography and his figurative works from that time, but also to many less personal motifs – and should be seen as part of a larger 1930s renaissance during the late 1960s (*ibid*., 76–99). Note that Slifkin's analysis has benefited the discussion of Guston's change in style presented in this chapter in several places.

[70] 'Guston and me: digression and return', *Contemporary Music Review*, vol. 6, no. 2 (1992), 5.

[71] *Ibid*., 7.

the changes in Feldman's music around this time, which led him back to an exclusive focus on conventional notation, and Guston's concurrent metamorphosis.

As noted at many points in this monograph, Feldman's graphs, and to a lesser extent his works with fixed pitches and indeterminate durations, were closely associated in his mind with Abstract Expressionist painting. In the case of the graphs, the alleged directness of his engagement with the inherent properties and propensities of sound, conceived of as material substance, through the proportionality of his notation, his allover method of working, the 'flatness' of the resulting works and the spontaneity he expected in performances were all elements that linked them in his mind with the movement. With his long-standing friendship with Guston now in tatters, and other leading lights of the New York School, including Barnett Newman and Mark Rothko, who had also been friends, recently deceased,[72] Feldman's personal links with a style of painting that many had come to regard as outmoded, were now diminished. His response paralleled Guston's: he accepted the facts, bid farewell to Abstract Expressionism and moved on.

---

[72] Hans Hofmann died in 1966, Reinhardt in 1967. Rothko died on 25 February 1970, followed by Newman a few months later, on 4 July.

Epilogue

When Feldman conceived of his graphs in 1950, the expressive power of his notation was genuinely new, and this was one of its strengths. His tripartite division of pitches into high, middle and low created a new resource that enriched prevailing musical vocabulary by facilitating the expression of deliberately less precise thought about pitch. Boulez ('[m]uch too imprecise')[1] was not alone in failing to understand that less can be more. For example, Wolpe criticised Feldman's recourse to high, middle and low registers in a lecture given in 1952 on the grounds that finer-grained distinctions are audible.[2] Plainly, a parallel argument could be brought against his own preference for using the twelve tones of the scale of equal temperament, but his argument and its parallel are both misplaced because finer-grained distinctions were surplus-to-requirements in both cases.

Despite its groundbreaking status, Feldman's graph music should be seen as an outgrowth of musical tradition. Unlike many who would follow him in producing indeterminate works, Feldman was not interested in inviting new forms of creative input from performers. His aim, like those of generations of composers before him, was to record on paper musical works for subsequent live performance.[3] This traditional aspect of his outlook may be part of the reason why he found it natural to segue between graph notation and other formats and why he seems to have found it easy to discontinue working with graph notation (and other non-standard means of expression) in order to focus exclusively on producing fully conventionally notated music.

This monograph has argued that the course of the graph series was influenced by several factors, including the pool of performers initially available to Feldman, Abstract Expressionist painting and ideology, his efforts to develop an allover method of working, the costumes for *Summerspace*, collage, and concurrent developments elsewhere in music. It was also influenced by his attempts to address what he perceived as its weaknesses, and it is fitting to weigh the significance of his own critique in this final section.

---

[1] Nattiez (ed.), *The Boulez-Cage Correspondence*, 103, with Boulez's underlining.
[2] 'Thoughts on pitch and some considerations connected with it', *Perspectives of New Music*, vol. 17, no. 2 (Spring–Summer 1979), 47.
[3] Exceptions include *Intersection for Magnetic Tape* and his film music.

Feldman was uncomfortable with the close alignment between his sounds and the beats of a uniform pulse, and it was this that drove the transition from the notation of durations in the *Projections* to the less precise specification of entrances in the *Intersections* and the subsequent decision to allow performers to terminate some sounds before the ends of the brackets in which they occur. Despite these changes, he seems to have retained a residual discomfort with this aspect of his graph music, which nevertheless underpinned the proportional character of the notation – a key advantage.

Evidently, his graphs need not have been any more reliant on the use of a regular pulse than conventionally notated music, as there are no syntactic barriers to introducing variations in tempo like those that Feldman experimented with in *Intersection 2*. True, doing so would have interfered with the proportionality of the notation, reducing the extent to which it presented a transparent visual impression of the designated sounds. An alternative course, avoiding this outcome, would have been to interpret the horizontal axis in analogue fashion; this would have permitted him to specify locations for sound entrances and endings that did not coincide with beats. Sadly, none of those who interviewed Feldman asked him why he resisted this option. As previously noted, his conception of notated rhythm may have been too firmly rooted in the idea of counting beats to allow him to take this additional step, and he may have had concerns about the legibility of an analogue reading and the associated risk of encouraging the preparation of more precisely notated versions in advance of performances.

A second reservation concerned the lingering presence of cause and effect continuity. The allover method – perfected by the time that he produced the *Intersections* for solo performers – was designed to address this issue, and his 'vertical' orientation in later graphs would also have helped. Even so, traces of teleology are discernible in the presence of number strings until late in the series. His attraction to 'wonderful designs' was certainly at odds with his philosophy of emphasising sounds, but this was an issue that he did address eventually. The significant expansion in the pool of symbols on which he drew in the graphs from *The Straits of Magellan* onwards may have been intended to mitigate this risk by inhibiting his ability to include numerical patterns, or so this study has argued.

Finally, there was the mismatch between Feldman's intentions and the sounds produced in some performances, which triggered the temporary break with graph music in the mid-1950s. Clearly, Feldman's conception of his early graph music was less indeterminate than the musical works delineated by his scores, meaning that there is a case for maintaining that the notation was unfit for its intended purpose of specifying the music he had in mind. Once it became apparent that certain ways of playing were undesirable, he needed to sharpen his guidance and make clearer what was to be avoided, but none of the explanatory notes provided by him discuss unwanted approaches. In theory, he could have enumerated the combinations to be excluded using more conventional notation, but in practice this would have involved formidable effort, even for the simplest graphs. This solution would also have had the unattractive consequence of making the graph notation dependent on supplementary material in a fundamentally different notational format.

The project of specifying an indeterminate result with certain particular outcomes excluded is, of course, a challenging one to undertake using a formal or quasi-formal notation when the number of acceptable and unacceptable outcomes is large. Supplying informal explanations of what he wanted or what he did not want would have been a solution; however, he seems to have resisted the use of copious notes, believing instead that the intended meaning 'should be implicit in the score'.[4] Evidently, he was mistaken. More explanations were needed and could have been provided by him, but they were not. Arguably, this was a blind spot.

In the later graphs, the need for supplementary instructions was less pressing. By this time, he had started to present an outline of his position in published writings. Moreover, he had built into many of these later works a degree of protection. His strategy was not an especially elegant one: compositional flexibility was certainly curtailed by his methods of discouraging undesirable inputs and any that breached his defences were to be merely muffled as a last resort. For all that, it seems to have mitigated his concerns, despite the fact that he continued to encounter inappropriate choices in rehearsals.

Consequently, the principal deficiencies of his graph notation that he recognised were either resolved by him or resolvable by means that he chose not to employ. My concluding thought, therefore, is that the notation itself, like the graph music that Feldman composed and presented in it, was an innovative and viable, but currently underrated, contribution to the music of the second half of the twentieth century.

---

[4] Cage and Feldman, *Radio Happenings*, 179.

Appendix 1 Two unpublished graphs

Intersection for Magnetic Tape

Intersection for Magnetic Tape occupies a special place in Feldman's output, not only because of its idiosyncratic notation but also because, as its title suggests, it was for use in producing magnetic tape recordings; as such, it is Feldman's only known tape work.[1] Two sketches survive.[2] One of these, which is undated, is presented on graph paper. The other, later sketch, shown in Figure A1.1, which is dated and altogether more polished, is presented on onionskin paper, which strongly suggests that Feldman prepared it for publication. Although its presentation is similar to those of *Intersections 2–4*, the intended meanings of the symbols clearly differ. The score consists of six systems, each comprising three rows of cells. Each cell contains a number, apart from a few blanks in the middle row of each system.[3] A plus or minus sign precedes some numbers in the upper and middle rows.

The sketch reproduced in Figure A1.1 lacks explanatory notes, but a set headed 'Imaginary Lan[d]scape After A Title By John Cage', included on the back of the less polished version, gives guidance as follows.[4] Numbers in the first row of each system specify lengths of magnetic tape in inches, with the tape to be read at fifteen inches per second – hence, the given lengths of tape imply durations in seconds. Those in the second row, by contrast, indicate quantities of sounds to be spliced into the given lengths; evidently, blanks mean zero sounds. Finally, those in the third row specify the number of loudspeakers, up to a maximum of eight, with Feldman noting that this is equal to the number of monaural tape tracks across which the given quantity of sounds is to be distributed. His idea was that the eight monaural tapes would play back simultaneously, one through each of eight speakers.

The notes also specify that the sounds to be used for assembling the eight tapes are from 'any catag.': this is a reference to the library of 500–600

---

[1] A very preliminary, undated sketch of the opening bars of another magnetic tape work, titled 'Marginal Intersection #2 for magnetic tape', has also survived (Morton Feldman Collection, Paul Sacher Foundation), as noted in Chapter 1.

[2] Morton Feldman Collection, Paul Sacher Foundation.

[3] In the less polished sketch, the corresponding cells contain zeros.

[4] Morton Feldman Collection, Paul Sacher Foundation.

INTERSECTION FOR MAGNETIC TAPE (1953)

Morton Feldman

+1/16	1/4	1/2	5	33	2	7	-1	35	-33	1/8	-16	+1	39	3	-1/2	+16	+16	21	4	+1	-1/16	1/4	1/16	+1	17	1/2	1/2	1/4	+1/2	-3/4	11	11	1/15	1/9	1/4	1/17	1/8	1/16	2
19	1	3	-600	1	1400	3	+70	16	700	1		+63	4000	1		25	53	-901	93	80	93		3	-500	1	+30	-30	+10	-200		5011	5011		1	-50	+50	+60	1	
4	7	1	5	1	6	2	1	3	2	5	8	8	7	6	8	4	7	8	7	5	7	8	1	8	1	1	7	1	7	8	8	5	8	4	3	8	6	2	8

7	5	9	13	1	1/3	-1/2	1/16	2/8	12	1/10	83	3 1/2	5	1/15	6 1/4	11	1/2	9	4	12/3	10	1 2/3	2/3	3	3/15	+1	-17	-1	3 3/4	92	17	+3	8	1 1/2	23	16	-1/3	9	67
2013	1400	1900	1900	1		+50	35	366	-73	900	-674		-22		356	-67	1		-2018	-456	83	-94	+60	-27		3028	-77		7	14	-91		-150	11	1031	1		25
7	8	5	3	8	1	8	8	1	1	8	7	8	8	8	8	7	8	1	8	8	7	8	8	2	8	8	8	8	8	8	2	3	8	8	8	7	2	8	2

5 1/3	4	+1/3	-15	72	16	3	11	1/4	+2	1/8	-7	+1/3	4	72	18 1/2	+10	94	80	19	63	76	1/2	15	1 1/4	33	29	22	5	2	13	45	16	1/4	31	2 1/5	4	1	15	1/10
591	3		-600	51	5	4	9	-49		3		5		19	603	83	7063	4000	1		3500	80		1		-2400	14	5	12	4		511	7	311	263	447	29		+35
8	1	8	3	8	8	3	5	6	8	2	8	6	8	7	4	3	8	8	6	8	7	8	8	1	8	6	3	6	1	1	8	4	3	5	7	5	5	8	8

23 1/2	8 1/3	13	3/4	7	15	23	6	4	3	1 1/2	3/14	7	3	1	16	2	33	21	2 1/2	13	9	3/4	16	5	31	17	6	25	8	1/2	1/3	11	29	18	47	7	6 1/4	23	9
	1	7300		2000		19	870	700	733	12	+15	400	-900	103	1923	200	8300	12		6	33	97	82	620	14	3011	39	8	411	6	1	3086	740	31	15	-300	908	211	940
8	1	5	8	3	8	2	7	1	8	8	2	3	7	5	6	5	7	6	8	4	7	8	2	8	5	7	3	3	4	1	1	8	4	7	3	8	4	2	7

5 1/2	11	13	1/3	1 1/4	1/2	3/4	1	93	18	3	2	1 1/2	3	10	1 1/2	1/3	5	7	34	6	23	1/2	2	13	9	3	16	1 1/4	39	43	5 1/4	23	1/2	3	17	34	1/3	15	2
19	333	7	80	80		+5		65	2500	98		17	114	23	739		983		515	2317	11000	180	6	39	3000	5		800		1900	3		90	45	19	8900	23		1
3	6	5	7	7	8	1	8	6	5	2	8	1	5	7	8	8	3	8	4	5	8	8	4	8	7	2	8	8	8	5	4	8	7	3	2	3	6	8	1

16	21	13	4	17	1/2	25	1	57	14	6	1	3	16	2 1/8	5	7	1/2	1/4	18	11	3	43	15	8	3 1/4	1/16	81	12	14	1/3	4	2	9	16	21	13	7	3	11
9	2	8	80		+70		63		175		4	2		5	800	19		15	1400		95		83	97	357	80	19		6		81		9	970		1750		9	
7	3	6	5	8	4	8	2	8	8	1	8	3	4	7	8	2	6	8	4	8	5	4	3	6	5	8	7	8	5	8	8	7	8	5	8	8	8

1953

Figure A1.1 *Intersection for Magnetic Tape*, sketch

Table A1.1. Intersection for Magnetic Tape, *range of numbers used in score*

Grid row	Minimum	Maximum
Upper	1/17	94
Middle	1	19,800
Lower	1	8

recorded sounds that were collected and organised into six categories for cutting and splicing in the venture known variously as 'Project: Sound' and 'Project for Music for Magnetic Tape'.[5] This venture, which was instigated and led by Cage, ran from 1952 to 1954, producing recordings of several magnetic tape works, including Wolff's *For Magnetic Tape I* (1952), Cage's *Williams Mix* and Brown's *Octet I* (1953).[6] The six categories of sound were: 'city sounds'; 'country sounds'; 'electronic sounds'; 'manually produced sounds, including the literature of music'; 'wind produced sounds, including songs'; and 'small sounds requiring amplification to be heard with the others'.[7]

Brown remembered that he and Cage invited Feldman to compose a magnetic tape work for the project after they finished work on *Williams Mix* and *Octet I*,[8] and it is clear that they expended a great deal of time and effort assembling tapes from Feldman's score in late 1953 or early 1954.[9] How they selected sounds is not documented. In producing tapes for *Williams Mix*, Cage had tossed coins to determine the appropriate category,[10] and it is possible that he and Brown used a similar method with *Intersection for Magnetic Tape*.

The most striking aspect of Feldman's score is the unusually wide range of numbers present, which includes small fractions and large integers. Ignoring the plus and minus signs, which cannot have been intended in their ordinary arithmetic sense, the range of numbers used in each row is shown in Table A1.1. A similarly diverse mix of

---

[5] For 'Project: Sound', see John Cage, 'Music for magnetic tape: history', undated, unpublished typescript with annotations, John Cage Papers, Special Collections and Archives, Wesleyan University, 2. For 'Project for Music for Magnetic Tape', see Christian Wolff, 'Program notes: For Magnetic Tape I (1952)', in Gronemeyer and Oehlschlägel (eds.), *Christian Wolff*, 484.

[6] For a description of Project for Music for Magnetic Tape, see Larry Austin, 'John Cage's *Williams Mix* (1951–3): the restoration and new realisations of and variations on the first octophonic, surround-sound tape composition', in Patricia Hall and Friedemann Sallis (eds.), *A Handbook to Twentieth-Century Musical Sketches* (Cambridge University Press, 2004), 191–4.

[7] See the explanatory notes with the score of Cage's *Williams Mix*.

[8] 'Earle Brown interview with Volker Straebel', August 1995, unpublished transcript, Earle Brown Music Foundation.

[9] Brown commented that they 'worked so hard on it!' ('An interview with composer Earle Brown', 295).

[10] John Cage, '[Williams Mix]' [1960], in Kostelanetz (ed.), *John Cage*, 109–10.

numbers appears in Cage's *Imaginary Landscape No. 4*, composed in 1951.[11] The fact that the less polished sketch is headed 'Imaginary Lan [d]scape After A Title By John Cage' suggests the possibility of a formal connection between the numbers used in the two works. Promising as this line of thought appears to be, any linkage between them is not readily apparent. Certainly, those that appear in *Intersection for Magnetic Tape* were not simply extracted from Cage's score. The range included in *Imaginary Landscape No. 4*, which extends from 1/12 to 172, is narrower than Feldman's, and even within this narrower range there is limited overlap between the numbers present. Furthermore, many groups of adjacent numbers in Feldman's score stand in simple arithmetic relationships to one another, such as those shown in Example A1.1. This suggests that Feldman generated some numbers by adding others already present, not by excising them from an independent source.

The task of unpicking Feldman's calculations is complicated by the fact that some numbers present can be generated in multiple ways; also, it is not known if Feldman restricted the scope of his calculations to adjacent entries and those separated only by empty cells, as in the cases highlighted in the example. If he restricted their scope, it is highly likely that his method was accretive, with newly generated numbers being placed between those he summed, thereby obscuring their previous proximity. That said, numerical patterns that are present in some areas – most notably in the middle row of the fourth system (e.g. 11,000 = 1,700 + 100 + 103 + 3,011 + 3,086 + 3,000) – point to him having added entries in more dispersed groups.

It is not clear how Feldman would have portrayed his use of this arithmetical procedure. One possibility is that he would have charac-terised it as a simple heuristic device for selecting a set of larger numbers for inclusion; this would imply a degree of disinterest in the specific values chosen, making his method tantamount to the use of chance. Alternatively, he may have portrayed it as giving the work a degree of unity, but if so, his view lacked credibility. Example A1.1 attests to the fact that he added entries that appear in different rows in the same system. Although this creates a modest degree of syntactic unity within the score, it is hard to see why it would generate unity within the

---

[11] In this case, fractions indicate divisions of a whole note, integers between 3 and 15 specify loudness and higher numbers give tuning in kilocycles or tempo in beats per minute.

Example A1.1 *Intersection for Magnetic Tape*, arithmetical patterns evident in the final system

$$16 = 9 + 7$$

$$21 = 13 + 8 \qquad 25 + 1 + 63 + 37 + 19 + 6 + 1 + 4 + 3 + 16 = 175 \qquad 83 = 43 + 15 + 8 + 8 + 5 + 4$$

$$13 + 4 = 17 \qquad 25 + 1 + 37 = 63 \qquad\qquad 31 = 12 + 19$$

$$2 + 8 + 70 = 80 \qquad 19 = 4 + 7 + 8 \qquad 19 = 6 + 5 + 8$$

16	21	13	4	17	⅔	25	1	37	19	6	1	3	16	2¾	5	7	½	¾	18	11	3	43	15	8	3½	1¼	31	12	⅕	4	2	9	16	21	13	7	3	11
9	2	8	80	+70		63		175			2		5	800	19		15	1400		95		83	97	357	80	19		6		81		9	970		1750				
7	3	6	5	8	4	8	2	8	3	8	1	8	3	4	7	8	2	6	8	4	8	5	3	6	5	8	7	8	5	8	8	7	8	5	8	8	8	8

Example A1.2 *Intersection for Magnetic Tape*, first column in first system

$+\frac{1}{16}$
29
4

associated work given that the meanings of numbers in different rows are quite different.

Another striking aspect of the score is that the notation is not proportional. Numbers in the first row of each system specify lengths of magnetic tape that range from 1/17 to 94 inches. This implies that columns correspond to periods of between 0.004 and 6.3 seconds. In this case, the visual correspondence between score and music is minimal.

The notes with the less polished sketch do not explain the meanings of the plus and minus signs, but Feldman alluded to them in a conversation recorded in 1987:

> I was never precise about the amount of information I wanted. I felt that it was ethically unfair to say, 'two thousand sounds on six tracks,' so I would write 'minus six thousand' or 'plus six thousand.' Cage and David Tudor were very methodical people, and they knew how to quickly count off six hundred and then one would apply it with the . . . oh, I forgot the apparatus to use . . . so it didn't negate itself. [12]

This suggests that the plus and minus signs were present to make splicing easier, but how they helped is not entirely clear. The thought that they mean 'greater than' and 'less than' is not credible, as this would imply that actual values might diverge to any extent from the given figures. Another thought is that they mean 'equal to or slightly above' and 'equal to or slightly below'. If so, then the first column in the first system, shown in Example A1.2, means that the splicer should cut twenty-nine sounds of suitable length from the materials in the sound bank and splice them into tiny sections at the beginning of four of the eight monaural tapes. Each of these sections is to have a length of one-sixteenth of an inch or a little longer.

[12] 'Do we really need electronics? Conversation with Kaija Saariaho, 3 July 1987', in Mörchen (ed.), *Morton Feldman in Middelburg*, 754. The extent of Tudor's involvement in preparing the tapes from Feldman's score is unclear. However, Brown remembered that his own arrival from Denver allowed Tudor to take a back seat in Project for Music for Magnetic Tape, permitting him to focus instead on practising at the piano ('Earle Brown interview with John Holzaepfel').

Example A1.3   *Intersection for Magnetic Tape*, sixth column in first system

2
1400
6

Example A1.4   *Intersection for Magnetic Tape*, twenty-second column in first system

$-\frac{1}{16}$
93
7

This interpretation is credible, but it remains unclear why some of the columns that are likely to prove most troublesome include numbers that lack plus or minus signs. For example, the sixth column in the first system (Example A1.3) requires splicing 1,400 sounds into six sections of tape, each two inches in length. The implied density of sounds is 128 per inch, even higher than the implied density of 116 per inch in Example A1.2.

It is also unclear why Feldman included a minus sign, rather than a plus, in the column shown in Example A1.4, which specifies the highest density of sounds per inch to be found anywhere in the score. If the minus sign means 'equal to or slightly below', then its presence does not seem to assist the splicers. On this reading, the column specifies 93 sounds in seven tiny sections of tape, each one-sixteenth of an inch in length *or a little shorter* (not *or a little longer*, as one might have expected). This implies 213 sounds per inch or more.[13]

With today's technology, it would be a simple matter to produce any number of realizations of *Intersection for Magnetic Tape* on digital media, but the high degree of difficulty it originally presented is readily apparent in these examples.[14] In this respect, the work fits seamlessly with the

---

[13] Some columns specify the use of very large quantities of sounds, but the density of sounds per inch is generally not highest in these cases.

[14] Cage described the degree of difficulty involved as 'crazy' ('John Cage and Richard Kostelanetz: a conversation about radio', *The Musical Quarterly*, vol. 72, no. 2 (1986), 223).

other graphs that Feldman composed in the same period (*Intersections 2–4*), all of which are for virtuoso performers.

That said, Cage and Brown seem to have met – or come reasonably close to meeting – Feldman's specifications using only the primitive means then available by cutting and splicing slivers of tape, and although the master tapes appear lost, a recording on reel-to-reel tapes survives.[15] In view of their apparent success, it seems reasonable to assume that Feldman consulted with them about what they were capable of achieving with the primitive technology then available.

In the conversation from 1987 referred to above, Feldman hinted at a connection between his interest in high densities of sounds per inch of magnetic tape and information theory, which generated a great deal of interdisciplinary research and commentary throughout the 1950s:

> Remember that it was in the period of information theory [...] I was interested in all the information you get on fifteen inches. That fascinated me. And I was also interested in the fact that we had eight tracks. So the score was just the distribution of all this material on the eight tracks [...] I was interested in degrees of white noise and whether one could hear it or not, this differentiation.[16]

The implication is that Feldman intended the use of high densities to test the limits of the communication channel between composer and listener. Presumably, the attraction of the magnetic tape medium was that the information presented in a relatively short space of time on replay was stored on a relatively long, and easily manipulated, length of tape.[17] This telescoping of time in space meant that it was possible, through splicing, to introduce temporal detail that was much finer-grained than achievable with other methods; hence, Feldman's question about the amount of temporal detail it was possible to communicate.

Listening to the tapes made by Cage and Brown, it is immediately apparent that a great deal of detail specified by the score is not discernible to the naked ear.[18] Although Feldman's specifications do not appear to have exceeded the capacity of the communication channel between composer and tape, they assuredly did exceed the capacity of the channel

[15] Brian Brandt and Philipp Vandré, 'About the recordings', liner notes with *Morton Feldman – First Recordings: 1950s*, Mode Records, mode 66.

[16] 'Do we really need electronics?', 752, 754. Enthusiasm for information theory followed the publication of Claude E. Shannon and Warren Weaver, *The Mathematical Theory of Communication* (Urbana: University of Illinois Press, 1949).

[17] As Cage explained in 'John Cage and Richard Kostelanetz', 223.

[18] The recording is included on *Morton Feldman – First Recordings: 1950s*, Mode Records, mode 66.

between tape and listener. For example, the recording begins with a very short burst of activity that corresponds to Feldman's indications in the first four columns, comprising 633 sounds all presented in a span of approximately 0.4 seconds. The ear cannot discern these components and the entire episode is heard as a short burst of white noise that ends with a sound that may be the trace of a human voice. From this perspective, *Intersection for Magnetic Tape* was a failed experiment, and it is tempting to connect this verdict with Feldman's apparent antipathy towards it. In a letter quoted from in Chapter 1, he only grudgingly gave permission for the tapes prepared by Cage and Brown to be played in public.[19]

By the time that Feldman signed a publishing agreement with the C. F. Peters Corporation in 1962, his stance must have softened. His publisher certainly knew of its existence; Peters even allocated it a publication code (EP6947) and subsequently included it in a listing of his works that appeared on covers of some of his scores. However, it was not forthcoming. A royalty report for 1966 listed the score as 'not yet delivered by composer',[20] and a letter from Peters in early 1971 reveals that he had only very recently agreed to supply them with a 'magnetic tape'.[21] As late as 1978, it was still listed as 'not yet delivered',[22] and whether it was Feldman who eventually supplied the tape that is now in their possession is not documented.

Brown remembered that Feldman rejected the 'piece',[23] but Feldman's only surviving comments suggest that he rejected the work undertaken by the splicers, not his own efforts, as noted in Chapter 2. In 1980, he explained that he did not want it 'realized by others' because they would make it 'sound more interesting than the piece should sound'.[24] This is a thinly veiled criticism of the tapes assembled in 1954; evidently, he regarded the sound bank that Cage and Brown had used as too garish.

A review of the extant recording lends weight to this view. Although it includes much white noise, there are a variety of recognisable sound bites, including sine waves, speech, a car horn, babies crying, an episode of heavy breathing and at least one unidentified musical excerpt. There is no precedent for this type of material elsewhere in Feldman's output and,

---

[19] Morton Feldman to John Cage, 18 March 1954. The tape was played publicly for the first time in 1955 (Programme, Marine's Memorial Theatre, San Francisco, 15 November 1955).

[20] C. F. Peters Corporation royalty report for Morton Feldman for the period 1 January 1966–9 December 1966, C. F. Peters Corporation.

[21] Gertrud Mathys to Morton Feldman, 11 January 1971, C. F. Peters Corporation.

[22] C. F. Peters Corporation royalty report for Morton Feldman for the period 1 January 1978–31 December 1978, C. F. Peters Corporation.

[23] 'An interview with composer Earle Brown', 295.   [24] '*Soundpieces* interview', 87.

arguably, its gaudiness sits uncomfortably with the subtlety that characterises most of his music.

A final observation is that the tapes prepared by Cage and Brown sound superficially similar to those that had been prepared previously with *Williams Mix* and *Octet I*.[25] All three recordings could be mistaken for one another on a first hearing, and one wonders whether Feldman regarded the absence of discernible individuality on playback as another argument against their efforts. No doubt the resemblances are attributable to several factors, including their similar lengths and the regular use in all three of very short sounds, but it must also reflect the use of the same, restricted sound bank of material. As noted above, this included only 500–600 sounds. The modest scale of this resource is evident in comparison with the fact that *Intersection for Magnetic Tape* alone specifies the use of 168,035 fragments.

Intersection+

The Paul Sacher Foundation has two sketches of *Intersection+*.[26] This section focuses initially on the more polished of the two, shown in Figure A1.2, which is dated spring 1953. This is presented on two pages of graph paper that are joined by transparent, sticky tape; another strip of sticky tape – brown in this case – is evident on the upper edge and it seems safe to assume that this was used to hang the sketch in an upright position.

The organisation of the score is unique, with symbols placed in, and around, rectangular boxes that are arranged in a geometric pattern. There are eighty-four rectangular boxes in all, each two cells wide and five cells tall; these boxes are arranged in two concentric rectangular annuli. It is immediately apparent that the horizontal axis is not being used to refer to units of regular pulse.

Ten boxes are empty, but the others contain up to five numbers. These are stacked from the top downwards within boxes, meaning that boxes containing fewer than five numbers have their lowest positions empty. Numbers in boxes range from 1–1,013. Each box is associated with an adjacent numerical label. This consists of a number from 1 to 91, preceded in some, but not all, cases by a plus or minus sign.

In an interview published in 1972, Tudor remarked that 'there was one [*Intersection*] in which you could go from any box to any other, which was the furthest he [i.e. Feldman] ever went with the idea of freedom', and he

[25] See *The 25-Year Retrospective Concert of the Music of John Cage*, WERGO, WER 6247-2, and *Earle Brown: Selected Works 1952-1965*, New World Records, 80650-2.
[26] Morton Feldman Collection.

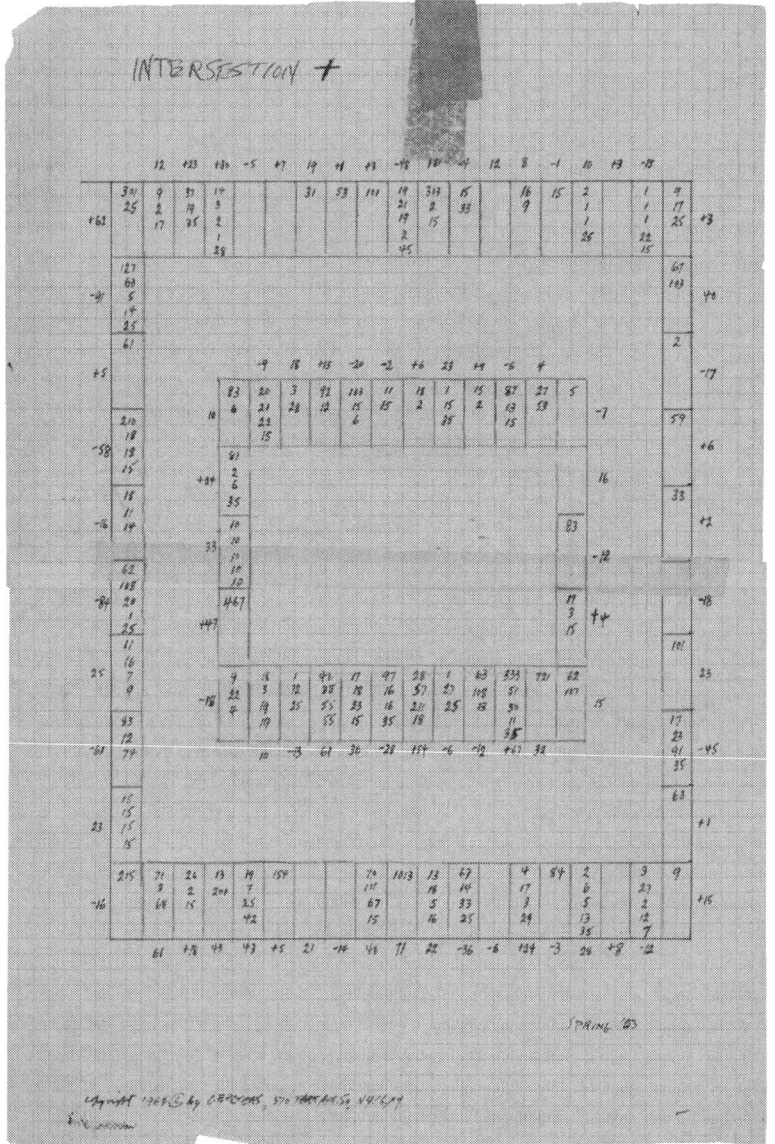

Figure A1.2 *Intersection+*, sketch

remembered discussing this particular work with Stockhausen during the period in which Stockhausen conceived of *Klavierstück XI*.[27] One commentator has taken these comments to refer to Feldman's *Intermission 6*,[28] which specifies fifteen sounds using discrete staves that are distributed around the one-page score in haphazard fashion, and instructs the performer to begin with any sound and then to proceed to any other. However, in a 1987 interview, Tudor commented that the work in question had never been performed.[29] Given that Cage and Tudor are known to have performed *Intermission 6* in 1958,[30] it is highly likely that he was referring to another composition.

Various factors point to its being *Intersection+*, aside from Tudor's mention of boxes. To begin with, his comments quoted above do not seem applicable to any other work in Feldman's catalogue, and they certainly do not apply to any other surviving *Intersection*. Also, Tudor is known to have begun preparing a performance of this particular work; his papers contain a copy of the score and written-out versions of some boxes in conventional notation.[31]

No explanatory notes have survived in this case, which is a considerable obstacle to understanding given the atypical notation. Not even the instrumentation is stated, although we know that Tudor intended a version for solo piano. That said, the flexibility afforded to the performer is certainly greater than that granted by *Intermission 6* because this particular work gives far fewer details of the musical content to be played. For example, it is likely that the box shown in Example A1.5 specifies eighty-three notes of the performer's choosing. This was also Tudor's interpretation; his papers include two near-identical written-out versions of this box, both involving eighty-three notes grouped in seventeen chords. Similarly, his written-out version of the box shown in Example A1.6, which contains four occurrences of the number 15, involves four bracketed groups of sounds each containing fifteen notes (plus a number of keys depressed silently). His written-out version of the box shown in Example A1.7, which contains the number 1,013, comprises three pages (twelve systems) of densely packed notes, mostly demisemiquavers. These examples are drawn from pages on which Tudor noted the numerical label associated with a box at the beginning of his version ('-12', '23' and '71' in the instances just cited). However,

[27] 'From piano to electronics', 25. This meeting took place in Europe in 1956.
[28] Boutwell, A Static Sublime, 147, but see his more circumspect comments in "'The breathing of sound itself'", 567. Feldman was also under the impression that the work that Tudor had shown to Stockhausen was *Intermission 6* ("'I'm reassembling all the time'", 98–100).
[29] 'David Tudor: interview with Peter Dickinson', 86.   [30] Claren, *Neither*, 554.
[31] David Tudor Papers, Getty Research Institute.

Example A1.5   *Intersection+*, box-with-label from right side of inner annulus

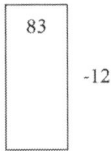

```
┌─────────┐
│   83    │
│         │
│         │ -12
│         │
│         │
└─────────┘
```

Example A1.6   *Intersection+*, box-with-label from left side of outer annulus

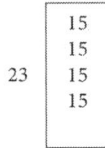

```
      ┌─────────┐
      │   15    │
      │   15    │
  23  │   15    │
      │   15    │
      │         │
      └─────────┘
```

Example A1.7   *Intersection+*, box-with-label from lower side of outer annulus

```
┌─────────┐
│  1013   │
│         │
│         │
│         │
│         │
└─────────┘
    71
```

labels are not included on several pages of his sketch materials, making it more difficult to correlate his indications with boxes in these cases.

It is not clear how Tudor interpreted the numerical labels. There can be little doubt that they should be understood as composite, with each including two elements: one of them a number, the other a plus or minus sign or, in some cases, a null entry. One possibility is that the number indicates the duration of the bracket in which the sounds specified in the box are to be played in beats or seconds; the fact that boxes containing high numbers typically have high number labels is consistent with this supposition. Evidently, the second element of the label gives guidance about some other parameter, such as pitch or dynamics or the direction of movement of the performer's eye around the score. Perhaps Tudor interpreted it in the last of these ways, as the other alternatives just mentioned are not consistent with his selections. Reading it thus, a number of different interpretations are easily envisaged. For example, the plus and minus signs could mean 'move clockwise within an annulus' and 'move anticlockwise within an annulus', respectively, with a null entry meaning 'move anticlockwise, clockwise or between annuli'.

An outstanding question is whether Feldman told Tudor how he meant his notation to be interpreted or simply left him to his own devices. If he left him to his own devices, he may have expected him to decipher the intended meaning – that is, to treat it as a puzzle to be solved. Alternatively, he may have meant him to use the score in any way he felt fit, although this is less likely, not only because there are no other documented examples of this type in Feldman's output, but also because some elements of the notation seem replete with intended meaning.

A "copy" of the graph score in Tudor's handwriting, which is among his papers at the Getty Research Institute, complicates any assessment. In most, but not all, cases in which Feldman included a number ending in 5 (e.g. '25') as the last entry in a box, this entry is replaced in Tudor's copy by a composite symbol comprising the immediately preceding digit ('2') and the letter 'S' (yielding '2S' in this case).[32] Whether this change was sanctioned by Feldman and why it was deemed to be desirable are not clear. An initial thought is that the new symbols indicate periods of silence, and that the introduction of these pauses was intended to give the performer more time to select the next box to be played, but this makes it unclear why the last entries in other boxes were not also reinterpreted. Other unknowns include the circumstances in which a performance should cease and, closely connected with this, whether Tudor regarded his conventionally notated materials as constituting a complete performance.

The physical condition of the other surviving sketch at the Paul Sacher Foundation also warrants commentary. This is presented on a single page of plain paper that is attached to a thick sheet of cardboard of the same size with vertical strips of transparent sticky tape (now browned) that cover the entire face of the graph. No doubt this more robust version of the score was for use in performance, which strongly suggests that Feldman envisaged the performer making selections spontaneously while playing.

Plainly, in this particular case, we can distinguish between performances in which the musician selects the boxes to play and the notes to play in connection with them during the course of a performance and those in which he or she decides only upon the boxes to play, the specific notes associated with each box having been selected in advance. Both scenarios appear to present considerable difficulties. Choosing which notes to play during the course of a performance is bound to involve a great deal of very laborious counting. Even if this proves possible to undertake, the indicated freedoms are sometimes so drawn-out that

---

[32] The box shown in Example A1.6 is one of several exceptions.

they are bound to be indistinguishable from free improvisation, and we know that this was an outcome that Feldman came to dislike. By the same token, choosing which preselected material to play by recourse to the score seems certain to engender hair-raising logistical issues, with the performer attempting to shuffle reams of paper at breakneck speed while playing.

Perhaps these are among the reasons why Feldman decided not to publish *Intersection+*, but they are not the only issues that may have given him cause for concern. He once remarked that '[t]he question continually on my mind all these years is: to what degree does one give up control, and still keep that last vestige where one can call the work one's own?'[33] Perhaps he was thinking of *Intersection+* and *Intersection for Magnetic Tape*, for it is easy to imagine him worrying about the extent of his own contribution in a performance of either work. As noted above, Tudor wrote out three pages of densely packed musical material in connection with just two numbers in the score of *Intersection+* and one group of three numbers in *Intersection for Magnetic Tape* instructs the splicers to cut and paste 19,800 sounds into 43″ sections on five tapes. In both cases, the efforts required by those using the scores would surely have belittled the extent of Feldman's own input.

[33] 'The anxiety of art', 30.

Appendix 2 Other perspectives on compositional methods

Projection 1

John Welsh has suggested a partitioning of *Projection 1*, which he has posited as an aspect of its 'formal design'.[1] Based on the supposition that silences of four or more ictuses mark section ends, his analysis begins by dividing the work into six sections.[2] He proceeds to argue that the work has a two-part design, with the first part containing the first three sections and the second part containing the remaining three,[3] with the boundary between the third and fourth sections and therefore the first and second parts being marked by 'an exchange of timbral and registral roles'.[4] This is a reference to the fact that the most frequently sounding register and timbre in section four are absent in section three, whereas the most frequently sounding timbre and one of the two most frequently sounding resisters in section three are absent from section four.[5]

The suggested partitioning is questionable because silences lasting four ictuses are neither emphasised in the score nor naturally heard as special. The work also contains eleven silences that are three ictuses in length, each with an implied duration of around 2.5 seconds at the given tempo. Arguably, these are as important in the listening experience, given that sounds separated by 2.0 seconds or more cannot be grouped by the human auditory system, as previously noted. Moreover, silences lasting four ictuses are not the longest present; one close to the end of the work lasts eleven ictuses and is significantly more prominent on the page and in the listening experience.

Evidently, Welsh chose his method of locating section endings because it resulted in a partitioning into a comfortable number of elements. Taking silences of three ictuses or more as marking divisions would have revealed seventeen sections, an initially unlikely amount of horizontal structure in a work that includes only seventy-five sounds. The long silence, spanning eleven ictuses, is prominent in the score and also the listening experience because it is so much longer than all the others. This could suggest a division of the work into two parts, with the first part including almost everything and the second part containing only two

---

[1] 'Projection 1 (1950)', 21, 31, 35.   [2] *Ibid.*, 22.   [3] *Ibid.*, 31.   [4] *Ibid.*, 30.   [5] *Ibid.*, 30–1.

short sounds at the end. This is barely a partitioning at all, and seems unlikely to be the source of any great insight into Feldman's creative process.

Welsh's choice might have been vindicated if it had disclosed compelling evidence of organisation around the implied partitioning, but it does not. One issue is that the 'exchange of timbral and registral roles' that his analysis highlights does not coincide with boundaries between his sections, as is evident in Example A2.1.[6] He points out that the middle register is entirely absent in section three (ictuses 130–44) and highlighted in section four (ictuses 145–66),[7] but in reality the absence of the middle register precedes the start of his third section and extends back to ictus 122. Similarly, he points out that pizzicato is the most frequently sounded timbre in section three but entirely absent in section four,[8] but in reality the emphasis on pizzicato precedes the start of his third section, extending back to ictus 125, whereas the subsequent absence of pizzicato extends four ictuses beyond the end of his fourth section to ictus 170.

More importantly, none of the other boundaries between sections are shown to mark points of significant change. To take just one example, Welsh notes that his fifth and sixth sections (ictuses 167–99 and ictuses 200–4, respectively) both highlight pizzicato and the high and low registers. What differentiates them, in his view, is that his fifth section includes sounds in every register and timbre whereas harmonic, arco and middle register sounds are absent in section six. In reality, section six is tiny (five ictuses) and only contains two sounds; consequently, it is inevitable that absences are a feature. Moreover, the two sounds it contains (ictuses 200–1) replicate two that appear just before the middle of section 5 (ictuses 180–1). Plainly, the sections are not reasonably regarded as strikingly different.

Intersection 3

Welsh's view is that *Projection 1* and *The King of Denmark*, to which he subsequently applied similar ideas with equally unconvincing results,[9] were deliberately partitioned with silences placed at irregular intervals, but Alistair Noble has suggested that *Intersection 3* was deliberately

---

[6] As in Example 1.1 (Chapter 1) and Figure 3.1 (Chapter 3), the upper, middle and lower rows of boxes refer to harmonic, pizzicatio and arco, respectively.

[7] *Ibid.*   [8] *Ibid.*

[9] 'The secret structure in Morton Feldman's "The King of Denmark" (1964) part one', *Percussive Notes*, April 2008, 34–41, and 'The secret structure in Morton Feldman's "The King of Denmark" (1964) part two', 32–9.

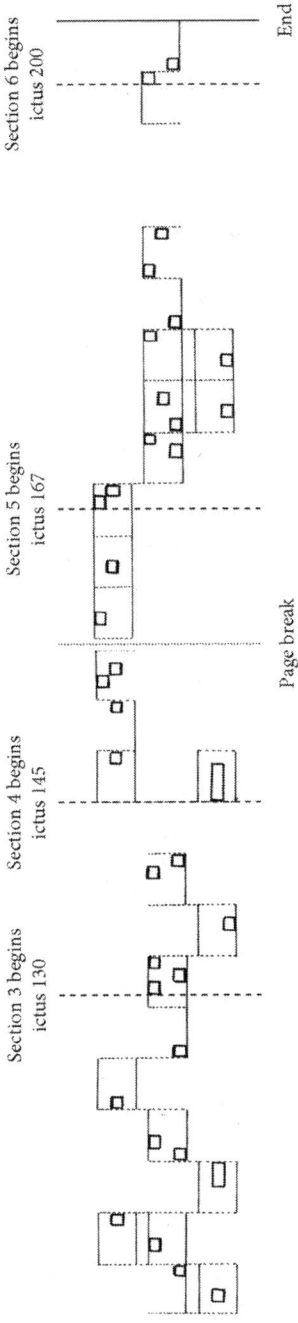

Example A2.1 *Projection 1*, ictuses 105–204, Welsh's sections partitioned using arithmetic divisions of the time axis into halves, thirds, quarters and so on.[10] This suggestion emerges from his analysis of three of Feldman's non-graph works from 1952 to 1953;[11] these, he argues, are underpinned by analogous structures.

Noble's analysis begins with the observation that there are eleven numbers explicitly present in the score (1–11) plus one number implicitly present in empty cells (0), giving 12 numbers in total.[12] His view is that Feldman delineated proportional subdivisions of the work with completions of this 'chromatic' field,[13] where a chromatic field is completed every time all its members have been presented as one scrolls left to right through the score. There are fifteen completions in total plus one field that is incomplete in the last few ictuses. Noble argues that the placement of the completions articulates 'a complex network of intersecting spaces' based on proportional divisions into two, three and four equal parts.[14] These are applied to the work as a whole and, iteratively, to the resulting subdivisions, creating 'a sophisticated and elegant origami-like construction'.[15]

The credibility of Noble's thesis rests on its ability to explain surface features of Feldman's works, but this appears to be very limited. The presence of an incomplete field in the last few ictuses is an initial cause for concern. Noble dismisses the missing number 10 as a deliberate omission, but in reality its absence marks a significant mismatch between his thesis and the data. Certainly, the thesis would have been more credible if the last field had been complete. This is because that outcome would be much less likely to have occurred by chance. Consequently, the presence of a complete final field would have been prima facie evidence that Feldman worked in the suggested way, and the case would have been strengthened further if completions were found to coincide with end points of scores elsewhere in his output. Instead, we learn from Noble that 'incomplete closing fields are not uncommon in Feldman's other works'.[16]

Another weakness is that the placement of chromatic field completions relative to points of proportional subdivision is insufficiently exact to provide evidence that Feldman was consciously highlighting them (Table A2.1). Even though Noble contemplated iterative operations that

---

[10] *Composing Ambiguity*, 150–61.   [11] *Intermission 5, Piano Piece 1952* and *Intermission 6*.
[12] *Ibid.*, 153.
[13] *Ibid.* For the use of aggregate completions in twentieth-century music, see Miloš Zatkalik, 'Reconsidering teleological aspects of nontonal music', in Denis Collins (ed.), *Music Theory and its Methods: Structures, Challenges, Directions* (Frankfurt am Main: PL Academic Research, 2013), 265–300.
[14] *Composing Ambiguity*, 158.   [15] *Ibid.*   [16] *Ibid.*, 153.

Table A2.1. Intersection 3, *location of completions versus location of proportional divisions highlighted by Noble*

Completion	Location (ictus)	Highlighted division	Location (ictus)	Deviation (ictuses)
1	135	1/3	140	5
2	144	1/3	140	4
3	203	1/2	209.5	6
4	209	1/2	209.5	0
5	215	1/2	209.5	5
6	231	5/9	233	2
7	286	2/3	279	7
8	297	17/24	297	0
9	310	3/4	314	4
10	331	19/24	332	1
11	351	5/6	349	2
12	369	7/8	367	2
13	375	8/9	372	3
14	387	11/12	384	3
15	415	1	419	4

Note: *Noble does not associate the completion at ictus 331 with a specific division of the whole. In this case, the table includes the nearest division that is consistent with the partitioning into twenty-four equal parts assumed elsewhere in his analysis.*

divide *Intersection 3* into as many as twenty-four equal parts,[17] only two of the fifteen completions (at ictuses 209 and 297) are precisely aligned with points of proportional subdivision. In all other cases, the alignment is inexact, with relevant locations differing by up to seven ictuses. If we are prepared to divide the whole into a sufficiently large number of parts or accept a sufficiently high degree of mismatch in locations as evidence of an association, then inevitably any entry in any score will appear to be associated with a point of proportional subdivision.

Noble clearly believes that similar structures may be discerned elsewhere in the graph series but here he encounters the difficulty that no other graph includes the same chromatic field (Table A2.2). He invites us to consider alternatives, suggesting that the field of *Projection 1* may consist of the nine possible combinations of register (high, middle and low) and timbre (harmonic, pizzicato and arco). Using these, he observes that there are two completions, the second of which 'marks the exact mid-point of the work's duration'.[18] This is incorrect because the second field is completed

---

[17] *Ibid.,* 157.   [18] *Ibid.,* 160.

Table A2.2. *Number symbols by graph*

Graph	Range
Projection 1	Nos. not used
Projection 2	1–5, 7, 9–12
Projection 3	1–10
Projection 4	1–5, 9
Projection 5	1–6, 8–11
Intersection 1	Nos. not used
Marginal Intersection	1–3, 5, 7, 9, 11
Intersection 2	1–12
Intersection 3	1–11
Intersection 4	1–5, 7, 9–10
Ixion for chamber ensemble	1–19, 24
Atlantis	1–18
Ixion for two pianos	1–18
...Out of 'Last Pieces'	1–13, 15
The Straits of Magellan	1–13, 15–17
The King of Denmark	1–7
In Search of an Orchestration	2–11, 13

in ictus 106, whereas the mid-point of the work's duration is situated midway between ictuses 102 and 103. He fails to mention the fact that the first completion is located at an arithmetically insignificant point (ictus 61). Moreover, the incompleteness of the final field, which extends through most of the second half of the work in this case, and which sits so uncomfortably with his suggested analysis, is once again in evidence.

Intersection 2 provides a useful test of Noble's view because the numbers 1–12 – and they alone – are explicitly present in its case, as highlighted in Table A2.2, meaning that we can assume a chromatic field consisting of them without recourse to implicitly present zeros. However, this chromatic field is completed only once, at ictus 1,121, with the second field remaining incomplete. The completion is approximately 13/17 of the way through the score – hardly compelling evidence of a proportional subdivision.

Bibliography

All interviews are listed under the name of the interviewee.

Alloway, Lawrence, 'Systemic painting' [1966], in *Topics in American Art Since 1945* (New York: W. W. Norton, 1975), 76–91.

Ames, Paula, Kopstick '*Piano* (1977)', in Thomas DeLio (ed.), *The Music of Morton Feldman* (New York: Excelsior Music Publishing Company, 1996), 99–143.

Antheil, George, 'Abstraction and time in music, n.d.' [1925], in Mary Ann Caws (ed.), *Manifesto: A Century of Isms* (Lincoln: University of Nebraska Press, 2001), 650–2.

George Antheil to Morton Feldman, 1 February 1951, Morton Feldman Collection, Paul Sacher Foundation.

George Antheil to Nicolas Slonimsky, 21 July 1936, Nicolas Slonimsky Collection, Music Division, Library of Congress.

George Antheil to Virgil Thomson, 29 January 1951, The Virgil Thomson Papers, Yale University Music Library.

'My Ballet Mecanique: what it means', *Der Querschnitt*, vol. 5, no. 9 (September 1925), 789–91.

Ashton, Dore, *A Critical Study of Philip Guston* (Berkeley: University of California Press, 1990).

Austin, Larry, 'John Cage's *Williams Mix* (1951–3): the restoration and new realisations of and variations on the first octophonic, surround-sound tape composition', in Patricia Hall and Friedemann Sallis (eds.), *A Handbook to Twentieth-Century Musical Sketches* (Cambridge University Press, 2004), 189–213.

Beal, Amy C., *New Music, New Allies: American Experimental Music in West Germany from the Zero Hour to Reunification* (Berkeley: University of California Press, 2006).

Patronage and Reception Histroy of American Experimental Music in West Germany, 1945–1986, unpublished PhD thesis, University of Michigan (1999).

'"Time Canvases": Morton Feldman and the painters of the New York School', in James Leggio (ed.), *Music and Modern Art* (New York: Routledge, 2002), 227–45.

Behrman, David, 'What indeterminate notation determines', *Perspectives of New Music*, vol. 3, no. 2 (Spring–Summer 1965), 58–73.

Belgrad, Daniel, *The Culture of Spontaneity: Improvisation and the Arts in Postwar America* (University of Chicago Press, 1998).

Berger, Arthur, 'Music news: Jeritza back, "Dybbuk" off; chance games', *New York Herald Tribune*, 28 January 1951, Section 4, 8.

Berkson, Bill, 'The new Gustons', *ARTnews*, vol. 69, no. 6 (October 1970), 44–8, 85.

Bernard, Jonathan W., 'Feldman's painters', in Steven Johnson (ed.), *The New York Schools of Music and Visual Arts: John Cage, Morton Feldman, Edgard Varèse, Willem de Kooning, Jasper Johns, Robert Rauschenberg* (New York: Routledge, 2002), 173–215.

Bernstein, Leonard, 'Aleatory composers', unpublished typescript dated 4 February 1964 with handwritten amendments, Leonard Bernstein Collection, Music Division, Library of Congress.

Bjorkman, Richard, 'Coming face to face with Feldman', www.cnvill.net/mfbjrkmn.htm (accessed 24 June 2015).

Blatter, Alfred, *Instrumentation and Orchestration*, 2nd edn (New York: Schirmer Books, 1997).

Blum, Eberhard, 'Notes on Morton Feldman's "The King of Denmark"', www.cnvill.net/mfblumking_eng.pdf (accessed 24 June 2015).

Bonime, Joan [New York Philharmonic], Joan Bonime to Morton Feldman, 28 January 1964, Morton Feldman Papers, Music Library, State University of New York at Buffalo.

Borio, Gianmario, 'Morton Feldman e l'espressionismo astratto', in Gianmario Borio and Gabrio Taglietti (eds.), *Itinerari della musica Americana* (Lucca: Una Cosa rara, 1996), 119–34.

Boulez, Pierre, 'Anton Webern', in *Stocktakings from an Apprenticeship*, trans. Stephen Walsh (Oxford University Press, 1991), 293–303.

'. . ."ouvert", encore. . .', *Contemporary Music Review*, vol. 26, nos. 3/4 (June/August 2007), 339–40.

'Sonate, que me veux-tu?', *Perspectives of New Music*, vol. 1, no. 2 (Spring 1963), 32–44.

Boutwell, Brett, '"The breathing of sound itself": notation and temporality in Feldman's music to 1970', *Contemporary Music Review*, vol. 32, no. 6 (December 2013), 531–70.

'Marvelous Accidents': The *Concerto for Prepared Piano and Chamber Orchestra* of John Cage, unpublished M. Mus thesis, University of North Texas (1999).

'Morton Feldman's graphic notation: *Projections* and trajectories', *Journal of the Society for American Music*, vol. 6, no. 4 (2012), 457–82.

A Static Sublime: Morton Feldman and the Visual, 1950–1970, unpublished PhD thesis, University of Illinois at Urbana-Champaign (2006).

Brandt, Brian and Philipp Vandré, 'About the recordings', liner notes with *Morton Feldman – First Recordings: 1950s*, Mode Records, mode 66.

Bregman, Albert S., *Auditory Scene Analysis: The Perceptual Organisation of Sound* (Cambridge, MA: MIT Press, 1990).

Broekman, David, 'Music in the making: may make jobs for musicians', *International Musician*, February 1953, 10–11.

Brooks, William, 'Choice and change in Cage's recent music', in Peter Gena and Jonathan Brent (eds.), *A John Cage Reader: In Celebration of his 70th Birthday* (New York: Peters, 1982), 82–100.

Brown, Carolyn, *Chance and Circumstance: Twenty Years with Cage and Cunningham* (New York: Alfred A. Knopf, 2007).

'Summerspace: three revivals', *Dance Research Journal*, vol. 34, no. 1 (Summer 2002), 74–82.

Brown, Earle, 'Earle Brown and Frans von Rossum', April 1990, unpublished transcript, Earle Brown Music Foundation.

'Earle Brown interview with Douglas Cohen', 24 May 1983, unpublished transcript, Earle Brown Music Foundation.

'Earle Brown interview with John Holzaepfel', 23 March 1992, unpublished transcript, Earle Brown Music Foundation.

'Earle Brown interview with Volker Straebel', August 1995, unpublished transcript, Earle Brown Music Foundation.

Earle Brown to David Tudor, 9 February 1977, David Tudor Papers, Getty Research Institute.

Earle Brown to Morton Feldman, 4 October 1961, Morton Feldman Collection, Paul Sacher Foundation.

'An interview with composer Earle Brown', by John Yaffé, *Contemporary Music Review*, vol. 26, nos. 3/4 (June/August 2007), 289–310.

'An interview with Earle Brown', by Amy C. Beal, *Contemporary Music Review*, vol. 26, nos. 3/4 (June/August 2007), 341–56.

'The notation and performance of new music', *The Musical Quarterly*, vol. 72, no. 2 (1964), 180–201.

'Notes on some works: 1952–1971', *Contemporary Music Newsletter*, vol. 6, no. 1 (January/February 1972), 1–3.

'On December 1952', *American Music*, vol. 26, no. 1 (Spring 2008), 1–12.

'"Selbsportrait" for Donaueschingen, 1965', unpublished typescript circa 1965, Earle Brown Music Foundation.

'Some notes on composing', in Gilbert Chase (ed.), *The American Composer Speaks: A Historical Anthology, 1770–1965* (Baton Rouge: Louisiana State University Press, 1966), 299–305.

'Transformations and developments of a radical aesthetic', *Current Musicology*, nos. 67–8 (Autumn 1999), 39–57.

[Untitled, on notational problems], in Carlton Gamer and Barney Childs (eds.), *American Society of University Composers: Proceedings of the Fifth Annual Conference, April 1970* (New York: American Society of University Composers, 1972), 8–14.

Brown, Richard H., 'The spirit inside each object: John Cage, Oskar Fischinger, and "the future of music"', *Journal of the Society for American Music*, vol. 6, no. 1 (2012), 83–113.

Burkholder, J. Peter, 'Collage', Grove Music Online, Oxford University Press.

Burris-Meyer, Harold, Harold Burris-Meyer to John S. Boyers, Magnecord, Inc., 7 May 1951, Edgard Varèse Collection, Paul Sacher Foundation.

'The place of acoustics in the future of music', *The Journal of the Acoustical Society of America*, vol. 19, no. 4, part 1 (July 1947), 532–4.

'Theatrical uses of the remade voice, subsonics and reverberation control', *The Journal of the Acoustical Society of America*, vol. 13, no. 1 (July 1941), 16–19.

Burton, Humphrey, *Leonard Bernstein* (London: Faber and Faber, 1994).

Busoni, Ferruccio, *Sketch of a New Esthetic of Music*, trans. Theodore Baker (New York: Schirmer, 1911).

Cage, John, *I–VI* (Cambridge, MA: Harvard University Press, 1990).

    'Anything I say will be misunderstood: an interview with John Cage', by William Duckworth, *Bucknell Review*, vol. 33, no. 2 (1989), 15–33.

    'An autobiographical statement (1989)' [1991], in Richard Kostelanetz (ed.), *John Cage: Writer – Previously Uncollected Pieces* (New York: Limelight Editions, 1993), 237–47.

    'A composer's confessions' [1992], in Richard Kostelanetz (ed.), *John Cage: Writer – Previously Uncollected Pieces* (New York: Limelight Editions, 1993), 27–44.

    'Composition as process: I. Changes' [1961], in *Silence: Lectures and Writings*, 5th edn (London: Marion Boyars, 1999), 18–34.

    'Composition as process: II. Indeterminacy' [1961], in *Silence: Lectures and Writings*, 5th edn (London: Marion Boyars, 1999), 35–40.

    'Composition: to describe the process of composition used in *Music of Changes* and *Imaginary Landscape No. 4*' [1952], in *Silence: Lectures and Writings*, 5th edn (London: Marion Boyars, 1999), 57–9.

    'Experimental music: doctrine' [1955], in *Silence: Lectures and Writings*, 5th edn (London: Marion Boyars, 1999), 13–17.

    'Four statements on the dance: grace and clarity' [1944], in *Silence: Lectures and Writings*, 5th edn (London: Marion Boyars, 1999), 89–93.

    'Four statements on the dance: in this day. . .' [1957], in *Silence: Lectures and Writings*, 5th edn (London: Marion Boyars, 1999), 94–5.

    'History of experimental music in the United States' [1959], in *Silence: Lectures and Writings*, 5th edn (London: Marion Boyars, 1999), 67–75.

    'An interview with John Cage', by Anthony Brown, *Asterisk: A Journal of New Music*, vol. 1, no. 1 (December 1974), 26–32.

    'John Cage', in Bálint András Varga, *Three Questions for Sixty-Five Composers* (University of Rochester Press, 2011), 40–1.

    'John Cage and Richard Kostelanetz: a conversation about radio', *The Musical Quarterly*, vol. 72, no. 2 (1986), 216–27.

    'John Cage and the Glaswegian circus: an interview around Musica Nova 1990', by Steve Sweeney Turner, *Tempo*, New Series, no. 177 (June 1991), 2–6, 8.

    'John Cage (b. Los Angeles, 1912; d. New York, 1992)', in William Duckworth, *Talking Music: Conversations with John Cage, Philip Glass, Laurie Anderson, and Five Generations of American Experimental Composers* (New York: Schirmer Books, 1995), 3–28.

John Cage to Morton Feldman, 15 March 1954, Morton Feldman Collection, Paul Sacher Foundation.

John Cage to Peter Yates, 6 June 1960, Peter Yates Papers, Mandeville Special Collections Library, UC San Diego.

'Juilliard lecture' [1967], in *A Year from Monday: New Lectures and Writings by John Cage* (London: Marion Boyars, 1968), 95–112.

'Lecture on nothing' [1959], in *Silence: Lectures and Writings*, 5th edn (London: Marion Boyars, 1999), 109–27.

'Lecture on something' [1959], in *Silence: Lectures and Writings*, 5th edn (London: Marion Boyars, 1999), 128–45.

'Music for magnetic tape: history', undated, unpublished typescript with annotations, John Cage Papers, Special Collections and Archives, Wesleyan University.

'On Robert Rauschenberg, artist, and his work' [1961], in *Silence: Lectures and Writings*, 5th edn (London: Marion Boyars, 1999), 98–108.

'Program notes (1959)' [1959], in Richard Kostelanetz (ed.), *John Cage: Writer – Previously Uncollected Pieces* (New York: Limelight Editions, 1993), 81–2.

'Remarks before a David Tudor recital (1959)' [1959], in Richard Kostelanetz (ed.), *John Cage: Writer – Previously Uncollected Pieces* (New York: Limelight Editions, 1993), 71–3.

'Tokyo lecture and three mesostics', *Perspectives of New Music*, vol. 26, no. 1 (Winter 1988), 6–25.

[Untitled, typescript, headed 'Dartmouth Spring '55'], John Cage Papers, Special Collections and Archives, Wesleyan University.

'[*Williams Mix*]' [1960], in Richard Kostelanetz (ed.), *John Cage: An Anthology* (New York: Da Capo Press, 1991), 109–11.

Cage, John and Alison Knowles (eds.), *Notations* (New York: Something Else Press, 1969).

Cage, John and Morton Feldman, *Radio Happenings I–V: Recorded at WBAI New York City, July 1966–January 1967* (Cologne: MusikTexte, 1993).

Canaday, John, 'In the gloaming: twilight seems to be settling rapidly for Abstract Expressionism', *New York Times*, 11 September 1960, Section 2, X21.

Cannam, Chris, Christian Landone and Mark Sandler, 'Sonic Visualiser: an open source application for viewing, analysing, and annotating music audio files', *Proceedings of the ACM Multimedia 2010 International Conference* (New York: Association for Computing Machinery, 2010), 1467–8.

Cardew, Cornelius, 'The American School of John Cage', in Edwin Prévost (ed.), *Cornelius Cardew: A Reader* (Matching Tye: Copula, 2006), 39–48.

Cornelius Cardew to Morton Feldman, 18 May [1961], Morton Feldman Collection, Paul Sacher Foundation.

'Treatise handbook' [1971], in Edwin Prévost (ed.), *Cornelius Cardew: A Reader* (Matching Tye: Copula, 2006), 95–134.

Carr, Ian, *Miles Davis: The Definitive Biography* (London: HarperCollins, 1998).

Chase, Stephen and Philip Thomas (eds.), *Changing the System: The Music of Christian Wolff* (Farnham: Ashgate, 2010).

Chou, Wen-Chung, 'A Varèse chronology', *Perspectives of New Music*, vol. 5, no. 1 (Autumn–Winter 1966), 7–10.

Claren, Sebastian, 'A Feldman chronology', in Chris Villars (ed.), *Morton Feldman Says: Selected Interviews and Lectures 1964–1987* (London: Hyphen Press, 2006), 255–75.

Neither: Die Musik Morton Feldmans (Hofheim: Wolke Verlag, 2000).

Cline, David, 'Allover method and holism in Morton Feldman's graphs', *Perspectives of New Music*, vol. 51, no. 1 (Winter 2013), 56–98.

Morton Feldman: Dimensions of Graph Music, unpublished PhD thesis, University of London (2011).

'Straightening the record: Morton Feldman's return to graph music', *Twentieth-Century Music*, vol. 10, no. 1 (March 2013), 59–90.

Copland, Aaron, 'Musical imagination in the Americas (1952)' [1952], in Richard Kostelanetz (ed.), *Aaron Copland: A Reader – Selected Writings 1923–1972* (New York: Routledge, 2004), 70–82.

What to Listen for in Music, revised edn (New York: McGraw-Hill, 1957).

Cowell, Henry, 'Current chronicle', *The Musical Quarterly*, vol. 38, no. 1 (January 1952), 123–36.

'Relating music and concert dance' [1937], in Dick Higgins (ed.), *Essential Cowell: Selected Writings on Music* (New York: McPherson, 2001), 223–31.

Cunningham, Merce, *The Dancer and the Dance: Merce Cunningham in Conversation with Jacqueline Lesschaeve* (New York: Marion Boyars, 1985).

Merce Cunningham to Morton Feldman, postmarked 25 August 1958, Morton Feldman Papers, Music Library, State University of New York at Buffalo.

Merce Cunningham to Robert Rauschenberg, 12 July 1958, in *Changes: Notes on Choreography*, ed. Frances Starr (New York: Something Else Press, 1968).

'Space, time and dance (1952)' [1952], in Richard Kostelanetz (ed.), *Merce Cunningham: Dancing in Space and Time* (London: Dance Books, 1992), 37–9.

Davies, Stephen, *Musical Works and Performances* (Oxford: Clarendon Press, 2001).

de Kooning, Elaine, 'Hofmann paints a picture', *ARTnews*, vol. 48, no. 10 (February 1950), 38–41, 58–9.

DeLio, Thomas, '*Last Pieces* #3', in Thomas DeLio (ed.), *The Music of Morton Feldman* (New York: Excelsior Music Publishing Company, 1996), 39–68.

Denyer, Frank, 'Feldman's search for the ecstasy of the moment', liner notes with *Morton Feldman: The Ecstasy of the Moment*, Etcetera Record Company, KTC 3003.

Dickinson, Peter, 'Feldman explains himself during his first visit to Europe in 1966, Peter Dickinson, April/May 1966' [1966], in Chris Villars (ed.), *Morton Feldman Says: Selected Interviews and Lectures 1964–1987* (London: Hyphen Press, 2006), 19–22.

Dolin, David D., 'Brush blade, pen: harbinger of spring – on stage', *Texas Catholic Herald*, 17 March 1967, 10.

Dummett, Michael, 'The philosophical basis of intuitionistic logic' [1973], in *Truth and Other Enigmas* (London: Duckworth, 1978), 215–47.

Dunning, William V., *Changing Images of Pictorial Space: A History of Spatial Illusion in Painting* (Syracuse University Press, 1991).

Edgar, Natalie (ed.), *Club Without Walls: Selections from the Journals of Philip Pavia* (New York: Midmarch Arts Press, 2007).

Eitan, Zohar and Roni Y. Granot, 'How music moves: musical parameters and listeners' images of motion', *Music Perception: An Interdisciplinary Journal*, vol. 23, no. 3 (February 2006), 221–47.

Emmerik, Paul van, 'An imaginary grid: rhythmic structure in Cage's music up to circa 1950', in David W. Patterson (ed.), *John Cage: Music, Philosophy, and Intention, 1933–1950* (New York: Routledge, 2002), 217–38.

'A John Cage compendium', www.xs4all.nl/~cagecomp/1912-1971.htm (accessed 24 June 2015).

Erickson, Robert, *Sound Structure in Music* (Berkeley: University of California Press, 1975).

Ericson, Raymond, 'Music-in-Making ends its season', *New York Times*, 18 March 1961, 17.

Feisst, Sabine M., 'John Cage and improvisation: an unresolved relationship', in Gabriel Solis and Bruno Nettl (eds.), *Musical Improvisation: Art, Education, and Society* (Urbana: University of Illinois Press, 2009), 38–51.

'Morton Feldman's indeterminate music', liner notes with *Morton Feldman: Indeterminate Music*, Mode Records, mode 103.

Feldman, Morton, 'The anxiety of art' [1965], in B. H. Friedman (ed.), *Give My Regards to Eighth Street: Collected Writings of Morton Feldman* (Cambridge, MA: Exact Change, 2000), 21–32.

'Around Morton Feldman: interview by Robert Ashley, New York City, March 1963', unpublished transcript, Morton Feldman Collection, Paul Sacher Foundation.

'The avant-garde: progress or stalemate?', *New York Times*, 5 March 1967, D27.

'The barrier of style. Conversation with Iannis Xenakis, 4 July 1986', in Raoul Mörchen (ed.), *Morton Feldman in Middelburg: Words on Music* (Cologne: MusikTexte, 2008), 308–35.

'Between categories' [1969], in B. H. Friedman (ed.), *Give My Regards to Eighth Street: Collected Writings of Morton Feldman* (Cambridge, MA: Exact Change, 2000), 83–9.

'Between Disney and Mondrian. Lecture, 2 July 1987', in Raoul Mörchen (ed.), *Morton Feldman in Middelburg: Words on Music* (Cologne: MusikTexte, 2008), 593–633.

'Captain Cook's first voyage: an interview with Morton Feldman, Richard Wood Massi, 3 March 1987' [1989], in Chris Villars (ed.), *Morton Feldman Says:*

Selected Interviews and Lectures 1964–1987 (London: Hyphen Press, 2006), 217–27.

'A compositional problem' [1972], in B. H. Friedman (ed.), *Give My Regards to Eighth Street: Collected Writings of Morton Feldman* (Cambridge, MA: Exact Change, 2000), 109–11.

'Conversation about Stefan Wolpe, Austin Clarkson, 13 November 1980', in Chris Villars (ed.), *Morton Feldman Says: Selected Interviews and Lectures 1964–1987* (London: Hyphen Press, 2006), 97–113.

'Conversation between Morton Feldman and Walter Zimmermann, November 1975' [1976], in Chris Villars (ed.), *Morton Feldman Says: Selected Interviews and Lectures 1964–1987* (London: Hyphen Press, 2006), 51–60.

'Conversations with a young composer', unpublished typescript circa 1956, David Tudor Papers, Getty Research Institute.

'Crippled symmetry', *Res*, vol. 2 (Autumn 1981), 91–103.

'Crippled symmetry' [1981], in B. H. Friedman (ed.), *Give My Regards to Eighth Street: Collected Writings of Morton Feldman* (Cambridge, MA: Exact Change, 2000), 134–49.

'Darmstadt lecture, 26 July 1984' [1985], in Chris Villars (ed.), *Morton Feldman Says: Selected Interviews and Lectures 1964–1987* (London: Hyphen Press, 2006), 191–209.

'Do we really need electronics? Conversation with Kaija Saariaho, 3 July 1987', in Raoul Mörchen (ed.), *Morton Feldman in Middelburg: Words on Music* (Cologne: MusikTexte, 2008), 752–85.

'Earle Brown' [1966], in B. H. Friedman (ed.), *Give My Regards to Eighth Street: Collected Writings of Morton Feldman* (Cambridge, MA: Exact Change, 2000), 42–4.

'Far-out composer Feldman says: "think of it as an environment"', interview by Ann Holmes, *Houston Chronicle*, 13 March 1967, Section 2, 4.

'Feldman throws a switch between sight and sound', interview by Brian O'Doherty, *New York Times*, 2 February 1964, XII.

'For Frank O'Hara' [1976], in B. H. Friedman (ed.), *Give My Regards to Eighth Street: Collected Writings of Morton Feldman* (Cambridge, MA: Exact Change, 2000), 127.

'For Philip Guston' [1988], in B. H. Friedman (ed.), *Give My Regards to Eighth Street: Collected Writings of Morton Feldman* (Cambridge, MA: Exact Change, 2000), 197–200.

'Four Instruments' [1965], in B. H. Friedman (ed.), *Give My Regards to Eighth Street: Collected Writings of Morton Feldman* (Cambridge, MA: Exact Change, 2000), 20.

'Frank O'Hara: lost times and future hopes' [1972], in B. H. Friedman (ed.), *Give My Regards to Eighth Street: Collected Writings of Morton Feldman* (Cambridge, MA: Exact Change, 2000), 103–8.

'The future of local music' [1985], in B. H. Friedman (ed.), *Give My Regards to Eighth Street: Collected Writings of Morton Feldman* (Cambridge, MA: Exact Change, 2000), 157–95.

'The future of local music', unpublished transcript of Feldman's week-long seminar at Theater am Turm, Frankfurt, February 1984.

'Give my regards to Eighth Street' [1971], in B. H. Friedman (ed.), *Give My Regards to Eighth Street: Collected Writings of Morton Feldman* (Cambridge, MA: Exact Change, 2000), 93–101.

'H. C. E. (here comes everybody), Morton Feldman in conversation with Peter Gena, January 1982' [1982], in Chris Villars (ed.), *Morton Feldman Says: Selected Interviews and Lectures 1964–1987* (London: Hyphen Press, 2006), 115–32.

'"I am interested in the commitment". Conversation with Frits Lagerwefff, 4 July 1987', in Raoul Mörchen (ed.), *Morton Feldman in Middelburg: Words on Music* (Cologne: MusikTexte, 2008), 786–833.

'I met Heine on the Rue Fürstemberg' [1973], in B. H. Friedman (ed.), *Give My Regards to Eighth Street: Collected Writings of Morton Feldman* (Cambridge, MA: Exact Change, 2000), 112–21.

'"I'm not negative, I'm critical". Lecture, 4 July 1987', in Raoul Mörchen (ed.), *Morton Feldman in Middelburg: Words on Music* (Cologne: MusikTexte, 2008), 834–71.

'"I'm reassembling all the time". Lecture, 2 July 1985', in Raoul Mörchen (ed.), *Morton Feldman in Middelburg: Words on Music* (Cologne: MusikTexte, 2008), 46–155.

'*International Times* interview, Alan Beckett, November 1966' [1966], in Chris Villars (ed.), *Morton Feldman Says: Selected Interviews and Lectures 1964–1987* (London: Hyphen Press, 2006), 30–3.

'Interview, Saturday, June 29, 1985, Middelburg', by Paul van Emmerik, unpublished transcript.

'An interview with Morton Feldman, David Charlton and Jolyon Laycock, May 1966' [1967], in Chris Villars (ed.), *Morton Feldman Says: Selected Interviews and Lectures 1964–1987* (London: Hyphen Press, 2006), 25–8.

'An interview with Morton Feldman, Jan Williams, 22 April 1983' [1983], in Chris Villars (ed.), *Morton Feldman Says: Selected Interviews and Lectures 1964–1987* (London: Hyphen Press, 2006), 151–9.

'Introduction by Roger Smalley to "The anxiety of art" – Morton Feldman talks to Andrew Forge', BBC broadcast on 21 April 1967, unpublished transcript, BBC.

'Johannesburg lecture 1: current trends in America, August 1983', in Chris Villars (ed.), *Morton Feldman Says: Selected Interviews and Lectures 1964–1987* (London: Hyphen Press, 2006), 161–72.

'Johannesburg lecture 2: Feldman on Feldman, August 1983', in Chris Villars (ed.), *Morton Feldman Says: Selected Interviews and Lectures 1964–1987* (London: Hyphen Press, 2006), 175–9.

'The Johannesburg Masterclasses, July 1983: Session 9', www.cnvill.net/mfmas
terclasses09.pdf (accessed 24 June 2015).

'Lecture in USC Composition Forum, April 4th, 1986', unpublished transcript.

'A life without Bach and Beethoven' [1964], in B. H. Friedman (ed.), *Give My Regards to Eighth Street: Collected Writings of Morton Feldman* (Cambridge, MA: Exact Change, 2000), 15–18.

'Liner notes' [1962], in B. H. Friedman (ed.), *Give My Regards to Eighth Street: Collected Writings of Morton Feldman* (Cambridge, MA: Exact Change, 2000), 3–7.

'Marginal Intersection, Intersection II, Intermission VI' [1963], in B. H. Friedman (ed.), *Give My Regards to Eighth Street: Collected Writings of Morton Feldman* (Cambridge, MA: Exact Change, 2000), 11.

'Marginal Intersection (1951), Intersection 2 (1951), Intermission 6 (for one or two pianos)', *Kulchur*, vol. 3, no. 11 (Autumn 1963), 33–6.

'Morton Feldman: conversation without Cage (Michael Whiticker), July 1984' [1989], in Chris Villars (ed.), *Morton Feldman Says: Selected Interviews and Lectures 1964–1987* (London: Hyphen Press, 2006), 185–9.

'Morton Feldman', in Bálint András Varga, *Three Questions for Sixty-Five Composers* (University of Rochester Press, 2011), 76–89.

'Morton Feldman', interview, in Brian O'Doherty, *Object and Idea: An Art Critic's Journal 1961–1967* (New York: Simon and Schuster, 1967), 99–101.

'Morton Feldman Slee Lecture, November 20, 1972: Baird Hall, University at Buffalo, The State University of New York', http://library.buffalo.edu/music/special-materials/morton-feldman/mfslee315.html (accessed 24 June 2015).

'Morton Feldman talking to Wilfrid Mellers about his work and the problem of new music', audio recording of BBC broadcast on 28 August 1966, British Library.

'Morton Feldman talks to Paul Griffiths, August 1972' [1972], in Chris Villars (ed.), *Morton Feldman Says: Selected Interviews and Lectures 1964–1987* (London: Hyphen Press, 2006), 46–9.

Morton Feldman to Cornelius Cardew, 25 April 1961, Cornelius Cardew Papers, British Library.

Morton Feldman to David Tudor, 15 June 1953, David Tudor Papers, Getty Research Institute.

Morton Feldman to Earle Brown, 12 October 1961, Earle Brown Music Foundation.

Morton Feldman to Earle Brown, 16 June 1967, Earle Brown Music Foundation.

Morton Feldman to Gerd Zacher, July 1968, Gerd Zacher.

Morton Feldman to John Cage, 18 March 1954, John Cage Collection, Northwestern University Music Library.

Morton Feldman to John Cage, 29 March 1966, John Cage Collection, Northwestern University Music Library.

Morton Feldman to Leonard Bernstein, 19 June 1963, Leonard Bernstein Collection, Music Division, Library of Congress.

Morton Feldman to Peter Dickinson, 27 June 1966, in Chris Villars (ed.), *Morton Feldman Says: Selected Interviews and Lectures 1964–1987* (London: Hyphen Press, 2006), 22–3.

Morton Feldman to William Colleran, 16 December 1975, Morton Feldman Collection, Paul Sacher Foundation.

'Morton Feldman: touch', interview, 20 May 1985, in Michael Auping, *30 Years: Interviews and Outtakes* (Fort Worth, TX: Modern Art Museum of Fort Worth in association with Prestel, 2007), 139–44.

'Morton Feldman – waiting, Martine Cadieu, May 1971' [1992], in Chris Villars (ed.), *Morton Feldman Says: Selected Interviews and Lectures 1964–1987* (London: Hyphen Press, 2006), 38–40.

'Morton Feldman with Dore Ashton – place, date not given', unpublished transcript, Oral History of American Music, Yale University Library.

'Mr. Schuller's history lesson' [1963], in B. H. Friedman (ed.), *Give My Regards to Eighth Street: Collected Writings of Morton Feldman* (Cambridge, MA: Exact Change, 2000), 9–10.

'Neither European nor American. Conversation with Konrad Boehmer, 2 July 1987', in Raoul Mörchen (ed.), *Morton Feldman in Middelburg: Words on Music* (Cologne: MusikTexte, 2008), 634–705.

'Neither/nor' [1969], in B. H. Friedman (ed.), *Give My Regards to Eighth Street: Collected Writings of Morton Feldman* (Cambridge, MA: Exact Change, 2000), 80–2.

'...Out of "Last Pieces"', in Edward Downes (ed.), *New York Philharmonic, One Hundred Twenty-Second Season 1963–64, The Avant-Garde – Program V, 6–9 February 1964* (programme booklet, Philharmonic Hall, Lincoln Center, New York, 6–9 February 1964), G.

'Philip Guston: 1980/the last works' [1981], in B. H. Friedman (ed.), *Give My Regards to Eighth Street: Collected Writings of Morton Feldman* (Cambridge, MA: Exact Change, 2000), 128–32.

'Pie-slicing and small moves, Stuart Morgan, Autumn 1977' [1978], in Chris Villars (ed.), *Morton Feldman Says: Selected Interviews and Lectures 1964–1987* (London: Hyphen Press, 2006), 79–84.

'Predeterminate/indeterminate' [1966], in B. H. Friedman (ed.), *Give My Regards to Eighth Street: Collected Writings of Morton Feldman* (Cambridge, MA: Exact Change, 2000), 33–6.

'Some elementary questions' [1967], in B. H. Friedman (ed.), *Give My Regards to Eighth Street: Collected Writings of Morton Feldman* (Cambridge, MA: Exact Change, 2000), 63–6.

'Sound, noise, Varèse, Boulez' [1958], in B. H. Friedman (ed.), *Give My Regards to Eighth Street: Collected Writings of Morton Feldman* (Cambridge, MA: Exact Change, 2000), 1–2.

'*Soundpieces* interview, Cole Gagne and Tracy Caras, 17 August 1980' [1982], in Chris Villars (ed.), *Morton Feldman Says: Selected Interviews and Lectures 1964–1987* (London: Hyphen Press, 2006), 87–94.

'String Quartet II' [1984], in B. H. Friedman (ed.), *Give My Regards to Eighth Street: Collected Writings of Morton Feldman* (Cambridge, MA: Exact Change, 2000), 196.

'*Studio International* interview, Fred Orton and Gavin Bryars, 27 May 1976' [1976], in Chris Villars (ed.), *Morton Feldman Says: Selected Interviews and Lectures 1964–1987* (London: Hyphen Press, 2006), 63–73.

'"Sublimation is the word". Lecture, 2 July 1986', in Raoul Mörchen (ed.), *Morton Feldman in Middelburg: Words on Music* (Cologne: MusikTexte, 2008), 162–203.

'To have known Stefan Wolpe', www.cnvill.net/mfwolpe.htm (accessed 24 June 2015).

'Toronto lecture, 17 April 1982', in Chris Villars (ed.), *Morton Feldman Says: Selected Interviews and Lectures 1964–1987* (London: Hyphen Press, 2006), 135–49.

'Traffic light music', interview by Charlotte Phelan, *Houston Post*, 26 February 1967, 24–5.

'Twelve tone technique in Varèse's *Déserts*, lecture given at California Institute of the Arts (CalArts) in February 1981', www.cnvill.net/mfdeserts.pdf (accessed 24 June 2015).

'Unpublished writings: III', in B. H. Friedman (ed.), *Give My Regards to Eighth Street: Collected Writings of Morton Feldman* (Cambridge, MA: Exact Change, 2000), 205–8.

'Vertical thoughts' [1963], in B. H. Friedman (ed.), *Give My Regards to Eighth Street: Collected Writings of Morton Feldman* (Cambridge, MA: Exact Change, 2000), 12–14.

Feldman, Morton and La Monte Young, 'A conversation on composition and improvisation (Bunita Marcus, Francesco Pellizzi, Marian Zazeela)', *Res*, vol. 13 (Spring 1987), 152–73.

Feldman, Morton, Pierre Boulez, John Cage and Christian Wolff, '4 musicians at work', *trans/formation*, vol. 1, no. 3 (1952), 168–72.

Fénéon, Félix, 'From "The Impressionists in 1886" (1886)' [1966], in Norma Broude (ed.), *Seurat in Perspective* (Englewood Cliffs, NJ: Prentice-Hall, 1978), 36–8.

Fetterman, William, *John Cage's Theatre Pieces: Notations and Performances* (New York: Routledge, 2010).

Fox, Christopher, 'Imperfection and colour', *The Musical Times*, vol. 147, no. 1896 (Autumn 2006), 102–8.

Fraisse, Paul, 'Rhythm and tempo', in Diana Deutsch (ed.), *The Psychology of Music* (New York: Academic Press, 1982), 149–80.

'Time and rhythm perception', in Edward C. Carterette and Morton P. Friedman (eds.), *Handbook of Perception, Volume VIII – Perceptual Coding* (New York: Academic Press, 1978), 203–54.

Friedman, B. H. (ed.), *Give My Regards to Eighth Street* (Cambridge, MA: Exact Change, 2000).

Gage, John, 'The technique of Seurat: a reappraisal', *The Art Bulletin*, vol. 69, no. 3 (September 1987), 448–54.

Gann, Kyle, *No Such Thing as Silence: John Cage's 4'33"* (New Haven: Yale University Press, 2010).

Glanville-Hicks, Peggy, 'Music in the Making at Cooper Union', *International Musician*, (March 1953), 13, 35.

Goldwater, Robert, 'Reflections on the New York School' [1960], in David Shapiro and Cecile Shapiro (eds.), *Abstract Expressionism: A Critical Record* (Cambridge University Press, 1990), 126–38.

Goodnough, Robert (ed.), 'Artists' session at Studio 35, 1950' [1952], in Clifford Ross (ed.), *Abstract Expressionism: Creators and Critics: An Anthology* (New York: H. N. Abrams, 1990), 212–25.

Gore, Frederick, *Abstract Art* (London: Methuen, 1956).

Grainger, Percy Aldridge, 'Free Music' [1972], in Teresa Balough (ed.), *A Musical Genius from Australia: Selected Writings by and about Percy Grainger* (Nedlands, WA: University of Western Australia, Dept of Music, 1982), 143–4.

Greenberg, Clement, '"American type" painting' [1955], in *Art and Culture: Critical Essays* (Boston: Beacon Press, 1989), 208–29.

'The crisis of the easel picture' [1948], in *Art and Culture: Critical Essays* (Boston: Beacon Press, 1989), 154–7.

'Towards a newer Laocoon' [1940], in David Shapiro and Cecile Shapiro (eds.), *Abstract Expressionism: A Critical Record* (Cambridge University Press, 1990), 61–74.

Gresser, Clemens, (Re-)Defining the Relationships Between Composer, Performer and Listener: Earle Brown, John Cage, Morton Feldman and Christian Wolff, unpublished PhD thesis, University of Southampton (2004).

Griffiths, Paul, *Modern Music and After*, 3rd edn (Oxford University Press, 2010).

Gruen, John, 'Demons and daisies', *New York Magazine*, 9 November 1970, 62.

'"This modesty of sound"', *VOGUE*, December 1968, 283.

Grunfeld, Fred, 'Cage without bars', *Saturday Review*, vol. 20, no. 3 (4 February 1960), 35, 37.

Guston, Philip, 'Conversation with Joseph Ablow (1966)' [1994], in Clark Coolidge (ed.), *Philip Guston: Collected Writings, Lectures and Conversations* (Berkeley: University of California Press, 2011), 56–71.

'Conversation with Morton Feldman (1968)', in Clark Coolidge (ed.), *Philip Guston: Collected Writings, Lectures, and Conversations* (Berkeley: University of California Press, 2011), 80–108.

Philip Guston to Harold Rosenberg, undated [ca. 1967], Harold Rosenberg Papers, Getty Research Institute.

Philip Guston to Morton Feldman, 24 February 1969, Morton Feldman Collection, Paul Sacher Foundation.

'Statement in *Twelve Americans* (1956)' [1956], in Clark Coolidge (ed.), *Philip Guston: Collected Writings, Lectures, and Conversations* (Berkeley: University of California Press, 2011), 10.

Hall, Tom, 'Notational image, transformation and the grid in the late music of Morton Feldman', *Current Issues in Music*, vol. 1 (2007), 7–24.

Hering, Doris, 'The season in review', *Dance Magazine*, vol. 25, no. 3 (March 1951), 16, 41, 42.

Heyworth, Peter, 'Composer-prophet', *The Observer*, 25 April 1971, 9.

Hicks, Michael, 'The imprisonment of Henry Cowell', *Journal of the American Musicological Society*, vol. 44, no. 1 (Spring 1991), 92–119.

Hicks, Michael and Christian Asplund, *Christian Wolff* (Urbana: University of Illinois Press, 2012).

Hiller, Lejaren, 'Morton Feldman: Structures for string quartet (1951)' [1973], in liner notes with *American String Quartets 1950–1970*, Vox Music Group, CDX 5143, 24–5.

Hinrichsen, Walter, Walter Hinrichsen to Morton Feldman, 7 June 1962, C. F. Peters Corporation.

Walter Hinrichsen to Morton Feldman, 17 June 1963, C. F. Peters Corporation.

Hitchcock, H. Wiley, 'Current chronicle: United States, New York', *The Musical Quarterly*, vol. 50, no. 1 (January 1964), 91–8.

'Last Pieces for piano; A Joyous Procession and a Solemn Procession. For high and low voices, trombones, and percussion; Ittrospezione No. 2 per orchestra', *Notes*, 2nd Ser., vol. 21, no. 4 (Autumn 1964), 609–10.

Holzaepfel, John, 'Cage and Tudor', in David Nicholls (ed.), *The Cambridge Companion to John Cage* (Cambridge University Press, 2002), 169–85.

David Tudor and the Performance of American Experimental Music, 1950–1959, unpublished PhD thesis, City University of New York (1994).

'Painting by numbers: the *Intersections* of Morton Feldman and David Tudor', in Steven Johnson (ed.), *The New York Schools of Music and Visual Arts: John Cage, Morton Feldman, Edgard Varèse, Willem de Kooning, Jasper Johns, Robert Rauschenberg* (New York: Routledge, 2002), 159–72.

Homer, William Innes, *Seurat and the Science of Painting* (Cambridge, MA: MIT Press, 1964).

Hughes, Allen, 'Dance: at Lincoln Center', *New York Times*, 8 March 1965, 34.

Iddon, Martin, *John Cage and David Tudor: Correspondence on Interpretation and Performance* (Cambridge University Press, 2013).

New Music at Darmstadt (Cambridge University Press, 2013).

Jeans, James, *Science & Music* (Cambridge University Press, 1937).

Jensen, Marc, 'The role of choice in John Cage's "Cheap Imitation"', *Tempo*, vol. 63, no. 247 (January 2009), 25–37.

Johnson, Steven, 'Jasper Johns and Morton Feldman: what patterns?', in Steven Johnson (ed.), *The New York Schools of Music and Visual Arts: John Cage, Morton Feldman, Edgard Varèse, Willem de Kooning, Jasper Johns, Robert Rauschenberg* (New York: Routledge, 2002), 217–47.

Jones, David [American Recorded Music Society], David Jones to Morton Feldman, 25 June 1966, Morton Feldman Collection, Paul Sacher Foundation.

Jordan, Stephanie, 'Freedom from the music: Cage, Cunningham and collaborators', *Contact*, no. 20 (Autumn 1979), 16–19.

Joseph, Branden W., *Random Order: Robert Rauschenberg and the Neo-Avant-Garde* (Cambridge, MA: MIT Press, 2003).

Kagel, Mauricio, Mauricio Kagel to Morton Feldman, 23 June 1962, Morton Feldman Collection, Paul Sacher Foundation.

Kane, Angela, 'A catalogue of works choreographed by Paul Taylor', *Dance Research: The Journal of the Society for Dance Research*, vol. 14, no. 2 (Winter 1996), 7–75.

Kastendieck, Miles, 'Electric music wired for boos', *New York Journal – American*, 7 February 1964, 18.

Kershaw, David, Tape Music with Absolute Animated Film: Prehistory and Development, unpublished PhD thesis, University of York (1982).

Kim, Rebecca Y., In No Uncertain Musical Terms: The Cultural Politics of John Cage's Indeterminacy, unpublished PhD thesis, Columbia University (2008).

'John Cage in separate togetherness with jazz', *Contemporary Music Review*, vol. 31, no. 1 (February 2012), 63–89.

Kissane, Seán (ed.), *Vertical Thoughts: Morton Feldman and the Visual Arts* (Dublin: Irish Museum of Modern Art, 2010).

Klein, Howard, 'The avant garde advances', *New York Times*, 19 December 1965, X26.

'Music: avant-garde festival closes', *New York Times*, 4 September 1964, 18.

Kramer, Hilton, 'Art: abstractions of Guston still further refined', *New York Times*, 15 January 1966, 22.

'A mandarin pretending to be a stumblebum', *New York Times*, 25 October 1970, Section 2, D27.

Krasner, Lee, '"Jackson Pollock at work: an interview with Lee Krasner," *Partisan Review*, 1980' [1980], by Barbara Rose, in Pepe Karmel (ed.), *Jackson Pollock: Interviews, Articles, and Reviews* (New York: Museum of Modern Art, 1999), 39–47.

Krauss, Rosalind, 'Grids', *October*, vol. 9 (Summer 1979), 50–64.

Kurka, Martin J., A Study of the Acoustical Effects of Mutes on Wind Instruments, unpublished M. Mus. thesis, University of South Dakota (1950).

Kurtz, Michael, *Stockhausen: A Biography*, trans. Richard Toop (London: Faber and Faber, 1992).

Landau, Ellen G., 'Channeling desire: Lee Krasner's collages of the early 1950s', *Woman's Art Journal*, vol. 18, no. 2 (Autumn 1997–Winter 1998), 27–30.

Larson, Steve, *Musical Forces: Motion, Metaphor, and Meaning in Music* (Bloomington: Indiana University Press, 2012).

Lee, Alan, 'Seurat and science', *Art History*, vol. 10, no. 2 (June 1987), 203–24.

Leja, Michael, *Reframing Abstract Expressionism: Subjectivity and Painting in the 1940s* (New Haven: Yale University Press, 1993).

Levine Packer, Renée, *This Life of Sounds: Evenings for New Music in Buffalo* (New York: Oxford University Press, 2010).

London, Justin, *Hearing in Time: Psychological Aspects of Musical Meter* (New York: Oxford University Press, 2004).

MacDonald, Malcolm, *Varèse: Astronomer in Sound* (London: Kahn & Averill, 2003).

Maconie, Robin, *The Works of Karlheinz Stockhausen* (London: Oxford University Press, 1976).

Magnes, Frances, Interview by John Holzaepfel, White Plains, New York, 22 July 1999, unpublished transcript.

Malina, Judith, *The Diaries of Judith Malina, 1947–1957* (New York: Grove Press, 1984).

Manchester, P. W., 'Dance in review', *Dance News*, vol. 33, no. 1 (September 1958), 16.

Mathys, Gertrud [C. F. Peters Corporation], Gertrud Mathys to Morton Feldman, 11 January 1971, C. F. Peters Corporation.

Mattis, Olivia, 'From bebop to poo-wip: jazz influences in Varèse's *Poème électronique*', in Felix Meyer and Heidy Zimmermann (eds.), *Edgard Varèse: Composer, Sound Sculptor, Visionary* (Woodbridge: Boydell Press, 2006), 309–17.

'Morton Feldman: music for the film *Jackson Pollock* (1951)', in Felix Meyer and Heidy Zimmermann (eds.), *Settling New Scores: Music Manuscripts from the Paul Sacher Foundation* (Mainz: Schott, 1998), 165–7.

'The physical and the abstract: Varèse and the New York School', in Steven Johnson (ed.), *The New York Schools of Music and Visual Arts: John Cage, Morton Feldman, Edgard Varèse, Willem de Kooning, Jasper Johns, Robert Rauschenberg* (New York: Routledge, 2002), 57–74.

Meyer, Leonard B., *Music, The Arts, and Ideas: Patterns and Predictions in Twentieth-Century Culture* (University of Chicago Press, 1994).

Miller, Leta E., 'Henry Cowell and John Cage: intersections and influences, 1933–1941', *Journal of the American Musicological Society*, vol. 59, no. 1 (2006), 47–112.

'Henry Cowell and modern dance: the genesis of elastic form', *American Music*, vol. 20, no. 1 (Spring 2002), 1–24.

Mörchen, Raoul (ed.), *Morton Feldman in Middelburg: Words on Music* (Cologne: MusikTexte, 2008).

Morris, Desmond, *The Naked Ape: A Zoologist's Study of the Human Animal* (London: Jonathan Cape, 1967).

Morris, Robert, 'Aspects of performance practice in Morton Feldman's *Last Pieces*', presented at the Third Biennial International Conference on Twentieth-Century Music, University of Nottingham, 29 June 2003.

Mumma, Gordon, 'Cage as performer', in David W. Bernstein and Christopher Hatch (eds.), *Writings through John Cage's Music, Poetry, and Art* (University of Chicago Press, 2001), 113–19.

Nattiez, Jean-Jacques (ed.), *The Boulez-Cage Correspondence* (Cambridge University Press, 1993).

Neuhaus, Max, Max Neuhaus to Morton Feldman, postmarked 10 February 1966, Morton Feldman Collection, Paul Sacher Foundation.

'Morton Feldman, *The King of Denmark* (realization date, 1964)', liner notes with *The New York School: Nine Realizations of Cage, Feldman, Brown*, Alga Marghen, plana-P 22NMN.052.

Nicholls, David, 'Getting rid of the glue: the music of the New York School', in Steven Johnson (ed.), *The New York Schools of Music and Visual Arts: John Cage, Morton Feldman, Edgard Varèse, Willem de Kooning, Jasper Johns, Robert Rauschenberg* (New York: Routledge, 2002), 17–56.

John Cage (Urbana: University of Illinois Press, 2007).

Noble, Alistair, *Composing Ambiguity: The Early Music of Morton Feldman* (Farnham: Ashgate, 2013).

Noorden, L. van, *Temporal Coherence in the Perception of Tone Sequences* (Eindhoven: Druk vam Voorschoten, 1975).

O'Connor, Francis Valentine and Eugene Victor Thaw (eds.), *Jackson Pollock: A Catalogue Raisonné of Paintings, Drawings and Other Works, Volume 4: Other Works, 1930–1956* (New Haven: Yale University Press, 1978).

O'Doherty, Brian, 'Morton Feldman: the Burgacue years', in Seán Kissane (ed.), *Vertical Thoughts: Morton Feldman and the Visual Arts* (Dublin: Irish Museum of Modern Art, 2010), 62–75.

O'Hagan, Peter, '"Trope" by Pierre Boulez', *Mitteilungen der Paul Sacher Stiftung*, no. 11 (April 1998), 29–35.

O'Hara, Frank, 'New directions in music: Morton Feldman' [1959], in B. H. Friedman (ed.), *Give My Regards to Eighth Street: Collected Writings of Morton Feldman* (Cambridge, MA: Exact Change, 2000), 211–17.

Oja, Carol J., *Making Music Modern: New York in the 1920s* (New York: Oxford University Press, 2000).

Osmond-Smith, David, *Playing on Words: A Guide to Luciano Berio's* Sinfonia (London: Royal Musical Association, 1985).

Perkins, Francis D., 'New School recital', *New York Herald Tribune*, 3 May 1952, 8.

Peyser, Joan, *Boulez: Composer, Conductor, Enigma* (London: Cassell, 1977).

Piekut, Benjamin, *Experimentalism Otherwise: The New York Avant-garde and its Limits* (Berkeley: University of California Press, 2011).

Pollock, Jackson, 'Interview with William Wright, The Springs, Long Island, New York, late 1950, broadcast on radio station WERI, Westerly, Rhode Island, 1951', in Pepe Karmel (ed.), *Jackson Pollock: Interviews, Articles, and Reviews* (New York: Museum of Modern Art, 1999), 20–3.

   'Letter to the editor, *Time*, 1950' [1950], in Pepe Karmel (ed.), *Jackson Pollock: Interviews, Articles, and Reviews* (New York: Museum of Modern Art, 1999), 71.

   '"My home is in Springs..." (ca. 1951)' [1978], in Nancy Jachec, *Jackson Pollock: Works, Writings and Interviews* (Barcelona: Ediciones Polígrafa, 2011), 128.

   '"My painting," *Possibilities*, Winter 1947–48' [1947–48], in Pepe Karmel (ed.), *Jackson Pollock: Interviews, Articles, and Reviews* (New York: Museum of Modern Art, 1999), 17–18.

Potter, Keith, An Introduction to the Music of Morton Feldman, unpublished MA thesis, University of Wales (1973).

Potter, Michelle, '"A license to do anything": Robert Rauschenberg and the Merce Cunningham Dance Company', *Dance Chronicle*, vol. 16, no. 1 (1993), 1–43.

Pound, Ezra, *Antheil and the Treatise on Harmony, with Supplementary Notes* (Chicago: Pascal Covici, 1927).

Pratt, Daryl, 'Performance analysis: Morton Feldman, *The King of Denmark*', *Percussive Notes Research Edition*, vol. 25, no. 3 (March 1987), 70–83.

Pritchett, James, 'David Tudor as composer/performer in Cage's "Variations II"', *Leonardo Music Journal*, vol. 14 (2004), 11–16.

   The Development of Chance Techniques in the Music of John Cage, 1950–1956, unpublished PhD thesis, New York University (1988).

   'From choice to chance: John Cage's *Concerto for Prepared Piano*', *Perspectives of New Music*, vol. 26, no. 1 (Winter 1988), 50–81.

   The Music of John Cage (Cambridge University Press, 1993).

Rastall, Richard, *The Notation of Western Music: An Introduction* (London: Dent, 1983).

Revill, David, *The Roaring Silence – John Cage: A Life* (New York: Arcade Publishing, 1992).

Ridley, Aaron, 'Brilliant performances', *Royal Institute of Philosophy Supplement*, vol. 71 (October 2012), 209–27.

Rilke, Rainer Maria, 'Primal sound', in *Selected works: Volume 1: Prose*, trans. G. Craig Houston (London: Hogarth Press, 1954), 51–6.

Rochberg, George, 'Guston and me: digression and return', *Contemporary Music Review*, vol. 6, no. 2 (1992), 5–8.

Rosenberg, Harold, 'Art and words' [1969], in *The De-Definition of Art* (University of Chicago Press, 1983), 55–68.

Rothko, Mark, 'Letter to Elsie Asher and Stanley Kunitz, 1967', in Miguel López-Remiro (ed.), *Mark Rothko: Writings on Art* (New Haven: Yale University Press, 2006), 156.

Rothko, Mark and Adolph Gottlieb, 'Rothko and Gottlieb's letter to the editor, 1943' [1943], in Miguel López-Remiro (ed.), *Mark Rothko: Writings on Art* (New Haven: Yale University Press, 2006), 35–6.

Roueché, Berton, '"Unframed space," *The New Yorker*, August 1950' [1950], in Pepe Karmel (ed.), *Jackson Pollock: Interviews, Articles, and Reviews* (New York: Museum of Modern Art, 1999), 18–19.

Rubin, William, '"Jackson Pollock and the modern tradition," *Artforum*, February–May 1967' [1967], in Pepe Karmel (ed.), *Jackson Pollock: Interviews, Articles, and Reviews* (New York: Museum of Modern Art, 1999), 118–75.

Sachs, Joel, *Henry Cowell: A Man Made of Music* (New York: Oxford University Press, 2012).

Salzman, Eric, 'Mittler recalls quartet's debut', *New York Times*, 8 February 1960, 36.

Sargeant, Winthrop, 'Musical events: first causes', *New Yorker*, 15 February 1964, 124–6.

Schapiro, Meyer, '"The liberating quality of avant-garde art", 1957' [1957], in Clifford Ross (ed.), *Abstract Expressionism: Creators and Critics: An Anthology* (New York: H. N. Abrams, 1990), 258–69.

'Seurat' [1958], in *Modern Art: 19th & 20th Centuries* (New York: George Braziller, 1994), 101–9.

Schick, Steven, *The Percussionist's Art: Same Bed, Different Dreams* (University of Rochester Press, 2006).

Schillinger, Joseph, *The Schillinger System of Musical Composition* (New York: Carl Fischer, 1946).

Schonberg, Harold C., 'The far-out pianist', *Harper's Magazine*, June 1960, 49–54.

Seckler, Dorothy Gees, 'Gallery notes: start of the season – New York', *Art in America*, vol. 49, no. 3 (1961), 84–6, 128, 130, 132, 134.

Seiberling, Dorothy, '"Jackson Pollock: is he the greatest living painter in the United States?" *Life*, August 1949' [1949], in Pepe Karmel (ed.), *Jackson Pollock: Interviews, Articles, and Reviews* (New York: Museum of Modern Art, 1999), 63–4.

Seitz, William C., *The Art of Assemblage* (New York: Museum of Modern Art, 1961).

Shanet, Howard, Howard Shanet to Morton Feldman, 9 March 1961, Morton Feldman Collection, Paul Sacher Foundation.

Shannon, Claude E. and Warren Weaver, *The Mathematical Theory of Communication* (Urbana: University of Illinois Press, 1949).

Shattuck, Roger, *The Banquet Years: The Origins of the Avant Garde in France, 1885 to World War I: Alfred Jarry, Henri Rousseau, Erik Satie, Guillaume Apollinaire*, revised edn (New York: Vintage Books, 1968).

Shaw, Christopher, 'Stockhausen: *Mantra* by Alfons and Aloys Kontarsky, Karlheinz Stockhausen', *Tempo*, New Series, no. 102 (1972), 41–2.

Sheffer, Jonathan, 'The music', liner notes with *Music for Merce*, BMG Music, 09026-68751-2.

Shively, David P., Indeterminacy and Interpretation: Three Realizations, unpublished DMA thesis, University of California, San Diego (2001).

Silverman, Kenneth, *Begin Again: A Biography of John Cage* (New York: Alfred A. Knopf, 2010).

Slifkin, Robert, *Out of Time: Philip Guston and the Refiguration of Postwar American Art* (Berkeley: University of California Press, 2013).

Sloboda, John A., *The Musical Mind: The Cognitive Psychology of Music* (Oxford: Clarendon Press, 1985).

Slonimsky, Nicolas, 'Chamber music in America (1963)' [1963] in Electra Slonimsky Yourke (ed.), *Nicolas Slonimsky: Writings on Music, Volume 4* (New York: Routledge, 2005), 3–55.

Smigel, Eric, 'Recital hall of cruelty: Antonin Artaud, David Tudor, and the 1950s avant-garde', *Perspectives of New Music*, vol. 45, no. 2 (Summer 2007), 171–202.

Smith, Arnold Jay, 'Reaching for the cosmos: a composers' colloquium', *Down Beat*, 20 October 1977, 19–20.

Steinbrink, Mark, 'Why artists design for Paul Taylor', *New York Times*, 3 April 1983, section 2, 1, 24.

Stern, Daniel, 'Morton Feldman's glass sequence', in Helen A. Harrison (ed.), *Such Desperate Joy: Imagining Jackson Pollock* (New York: Thunder's Mouth Press, 2000), 305–8.

Stockhausen, Karlheinz, 'Interview with Karlheinz Stockhausen held August 11, 1976', by Ekbert Faas, *Interface: Journal of New Music Research*, vol. 6 (1977), 187–204.

    'Stockhausen: is he the way and the light?', interview by Peter Heyworth, *New York Times*, 21 February 1971, Section 2, 13, 26.

    'Weberns Konzert für 9 Instrumente op. 24: Analyse des ersten Satzes' [1953], in *Texte zur Musik – Band 1: Texte zur elektronischen und instrumentalen Musik* (Cologne: M. DuMont Schauberg, 1963), 24–31.

Storr, Robert, 'Guston's trace', in Harriet S. Bee (ed.), *Philip Guston in the Collection of the Museum of Modern Art* (New York: Museum of Modern Art, 1992), 7–27.

Straebel, Volker, 'Morton Feldman: early piano pieces (1950–1964): notes on the edition', in Volker Straebel (ed.), *Morton Feldman: Solo Piano Works 1950–64*, EP67976 (New York: C. F. Peters, 1998), 57–62.

Strongin, Theodore, 'The music of Morton Feldman and Earle Brown is presented: works that leave decisions to performers are heard in Town Hall concert', *New York Times*, 12 October 1963, 21.

Taylor, Paul, *Private Domain: An Autobiography* (New York: Alfred A. Knopf, 1987).

Thomas, Philip, 'Determining the indeterminate', *Contemporary Music Review*, vol. 26, no. 2 (April 2007), 129–40.

Thomson, Virgil, 'Rockwell, John: a conversation with Virgil Thomson' [1977], in *A Virgil Thomson Reader* (Boston: Houghton Mifflin, 1981), 525–41.

Tilbury, John, *Cornelius Cardew (1936–1981): A Life Unfinished* (Essex: Copula, 2008).

Tomkins, Calvin, *The Bride and the Bachelors: The Heretical Courtship in Modern Art* (New York: Viking Press, 1965).

Tracy, Robert, 'a Summerspace for Merce', *Dance Magazine*, July 1999, 54–8.

Trimble, Lester, 'Music', *The Nation*, 20 February 1960, 175–6.

Tudor, David, 'Composing the performer: David Tudor remembers Stefan Wolpe', interview by Austin Clarkson, *Musicworks*, no. 73 (Spring 1999), 26–32.

'David Tudor: interview with Peter Dickinson, Ibis Hotel, London, July 26, 1987', in Peter Dickinson, *CageTalk: Dialogues with and about John Cage* (University of Rochester Press, 2006), 81–92.

David Tudor to John Simon Guggenheim Memorial Foundation, 1 October 1979, David Tudor Papers, Getty Research Institute.

'From piano to electronics', interview by Victor Schonfield, *Music and Musicians*, vol. 20, no. 12 (August 1972), 24–6.

'Reminiscences of a twentieth-century pianist: an interview with David Tudor', by John Holzaepfel, *The Musical Quarterly*, vol. 78, no. 3 (Autumn 1994), 626–36.

Varèse, Edgard, 'The Art-Science of music today', amended typescript, Edgard Varèse Collection, Paul Sacher Foundation.

'The liberation of sound', in Elliott Schwartz and Barney Childs (eds.) with Jim Fox, *Contemporary Composers on Contemporary Music*, expanded edition (New York: Da Capo Press, 1998), 195–208.

Varèse, Edgard and Alexei Haieff, 'Edgard Varèse and Alexei Haieff questioned by 8 composers', *possibilities*, vol. 1, no. 4 (Winter 1947/8), 96–100.

Varnedoe, Kirk, 'Comet: Jackson Pollock's life and work', in Kirk Varnedoe with Pepe Karmel, *Jackson Pollock* (London: Tate Gallery Publishing, 1999), 15–85.

Vaughan, David, *Merce Cunningham: Fifty Years* (New York: Aperture, 1997).

Vigil, Ryan, 'Compositional parameters: *Projection 4* and an analytical methodology for Morton Feldman's graphic works', *Perspectives of New Music*, vol. 47, no. 1 (Winter 2009), 233–67.

Vilhjálmsson, Vilhjálmur Örn, 'The King and the Star: myths created during the occupation of Denmark', in Mette Bastholm Jensen and Steven L. B. Jensen (eds.), *Denmark and the Holocaust* (Copenhagen: Institute for International Studies, Department for Holocaust and Genocide Studies, 2003), 102–17.

Villars, Chris (ed.), *Morton Feldman Says: Selected Interviews and Lectures 1964–1987* (London: Hyphen Press, 2006).

Volans, Kevin, 'What is Feldman?', *Tempo*, vol. 68, no. 270 (October 2014), 7–14.

Webster, J. Carson, 'The technique of Impressionism: a reappraisal (1944)' [1944], in Norma Broude (ed.), *Seurat in Perspective* (Englewood Cliffs, NJ: Prentice-Hall, 1978), 93–102.

Welsh, John, '*Projection 1* (1950)', in Thomas DeLio (ed.), *The Music of Morton Feldman* (New York: Excelsior Music Publishing Company, 1996), 21–35.

'The secret structure in Morton Feldman's "The King of Denmark" (1964) part one', *Percussive Notes*, April 2008, 34–41.

'The secret structure in Morton Feldman's "The King of Denmark" (1964) part two', *Percussive Notes*, June 2008, 32–9.

Williamson, Timothy, *Vagueness* (Oxford: Routledge, 1994).

Winckel, Fritz, *Music, Sound and Sensation: A Modern Exposition* (New York: Dover, 1967).

Wolff, Christian, 'Cage and beyond: an annotated interview with Christian Wolff', by David Patterson, *Perspectives of New Music*, vol. 32, no. 2 (Summer 1994), 54–87.

'A chance encounter with Christian Wolff', interview by Frank J. Oteri, www.newmusicbox.org/articles/a-chance-encounter-with-christian-wolff/ (accessed 24 June 2015).

'Christian Wolff', interview, in Geoff Smith and Nicola Walker Smith (eds.), *American Originals* (London: Faber and Faber, 1994), 251–9.

'Christian Wolff', interview, in James Saunders (ed.), *The Ashgate Research Companion to Experimental Music* (Farnham: Ashgate, 2009).

'Experimental music around 1950 and some consequences and causes (social-political and musical)', *American Music*, vol. 27, no. 4 (Winter 2009), 424–40.

'Immobility in motion: new and electronic music' [1958], in Gisela Gronemeyer and Reinhard Oehlschlägel (eds.), *Christian Wolff: Cues: Writings and Conversations* (Cologne: MusikTexte, 1998), 24–37.

'In a kind of no-man's land. Conversation with Cole Gagne' [1993], in Gisela Gronemeyer and Reinhard Oehlschlägel (eds.), *Christian Wolff: Cues: Writings and Conversations* (Cologne: MusikTexte, 1998), 234–77.

'Program notes: For Magnetic Tape I (1952)', in Gisela Gronemeyer and Reinhard Oehlschlägel (eds.), *Christian Wolff: Cues: Writings and Conversations* (Cologne: MusikTexte, 1998), 484.

'"...something hazardous with which we may try ourselves". Questions' [1964], in Gisela Gronemeyer and Reinhard Oehlschlägel (eds.), *Christian Wolff: Cues: Writings and Conversations* (Cologne: MusikTexte, 1998), 52–5.

'Taking chances. From a conversation with Victor Schonfield' [1969], in Gisela Gronemeyer and Reinhard Oehlschlägel (eds.), *Christian Wolff: Cues: Writings and Conversations* (Cologne: MusikTexte, 1998), 66–77.

[Untitled, liner notes], *Music for Merce 1952-2009*, New World Records, 80712-2, 99–102.

Wolfram, Eddie, *History of Collage: An Anthology of Collage, Assemblage and Event Structures* (London: Studio Vista, 1975).

Wolpe, Stefan, 'Thoughts on pitch and some considerations connected with it', *Perspectives of New Music*, vol. 17, no. 2 (Spring–Summer 1979), 28–55.

York, Wes, 'For John Cage (1982)', in Thomas DeLio (ed.), *The Music of Morton Feldman* (New York: Excelsior Music Publishing Company, 1996), 147–95.

Zatkalik, Miloš, 'Reconsidering teleological aspects of nontonal music', in Denis Collins (ed.), *Music Theory and its Methods: Structures, Challenges, Directions* (Frankfurt am Main: PL Academic Research, 2013), 265–300.

Zimmermann, Heidy, 'Recycling, collage, work in progress: Varèse's thought in speech and writing', in Felix Meyer and Heidy Zimmermann (eds.), *Edgard Varèse: Composer, Sound Sculptor, Visionary* (Woodbridge: Boydell Press, 2006), 264–71.

Zimmermann, Walter, 'Morton Feldman – der ikonolast', in Walter Zimmermann (ed.), *Morton Feldman Essays* (Cologne: Beginner Press, 1985), 10–23.

(ed.), *Morton Feldman Essays* (Cologne: Beginner Press, 1985).

Zuckerkandl, Victor, *Sound and Symbol*, trans. Willard R. Trask (London: Routledge & Kegan Paul, 1956).

Unsigned items

[A] 'Brushed off for years, avant garde music finally gaining recognition', *Variety*, 21 February 1962, 53.

[B] 'Composers: far-out at the Philharmonic', *Time*, 14 February 1964, 80.

[C] 'Composing by knucklebone', *Time*, 13 April 1962, 55–6.

[D] 'Is it music?', *Newsweek*, 2 September 1963, 53.

[E] 'Music here this week', *New York Herald Tribune*, 9 November 1952, Section 4, 8.

[F] 'Music in the Making', *New York Herald Tribune*, 10 November 1952, 13.

[G] *Selections from the Private Collection of Robert Rauschenberg* (New York: Gagosian Gallery, distributed by Rizzoli International Publications, 2012).

[H] 'Sound of cybernetics', *Newsweek*, 17 February 1964, 88.

Index

Page numbers in italics refer to examples, figures or tables.

Printed in Great Britain
by Amazon